Old Church Slavonic Grammar

Old Church Slavonic Grammar

Seventh Revised Edition

by
Horace G. Lunt

Mouton de Gruyter
Berlin · New York 2001

Mouton de Gruyter (formerly Mouton, The Hague)
is a Division of Walter de Gruyter GmbH & Co. KG, Berlin

♾ Printed on acid-free paper which falls within the guidelines
of the ANSI to ensure permanence and durability.

Library of Congress Cataloging-in-Publication Data

Lunt, Horace Gray, 1918–
Old Church Slavonic grammar / by Horace G. Lunt. – 7th rev. ed.
p. cm.
Includes bibliographical references and index.
ISBN 3110162849 (cloth : alk. paper)
1. Church Slavic language–Grammar. I. Title.
PG619.L8 2001
491.8′17015–dc21 2001030588

Die Deutsche Bibliothek – CIP-Einheitsaufnahme

Lunt, Horace Gray:
Old church Slavonic grammar / by Horace G. Lunt. – 7., rev. ed. – Berlin ; New York : Mouton de Gruyter, 2001
ISBN 3-11-016284-9

Printing: WB-Druck, Rieden/Allgäu.
Binding: Lüderitz & Bauer, Berlin.
Printed in Germany.

PREFACE

This description of the structure of Old Church Slavonic is intended to present fully the important data about the language, without citing all the minutiae of attested variant spellings. The facts have been treated from the point of view of structural linguistics, but pedagogical clarity has taken precedence over the conciseness required for elegant formal description.

Old Church Slavonic was used over a period of some two hundred years and in various geographical parts of the Slavic world precisely at the time when the Slavic languages were undergoing rapid, fundamental, divergent changes. Some of these changes are doubtless reflected in the variant spellings in the few texts which have survived from this period, so that while most variations in grammar and vocabulary are the sorts of stylistic and idiosyncratic differences that are found in the standard or literary language of any single epoch, some important variant details result from different regional dialectal history. It has thus been necessary to include occasional references to historical and comparative linguistics in the first half of this book, although in principle these problems do not fall within the scope of a strictly descriptive, synchronic grammar.

It is necessary to normalize forms to present the grammatical structure as a consistent whole, and the normalization inevitably obscures the differences in the language of the various manuscripts. A clear picture of the different combinations of linguistic elements making up each of the texts is not to be achieved by lists of spelling variants or tables of percentages, but it is worth while to point out some of the striking variations. First-hand acquaintance with the texts and constant comparison of variant readings is the only way to arrive at an understanding both of the underlying unity of the texts as a whole and of the major and minor differences between them.

Little mention is made here of another type of comparison—the relationship of the OCS translated texts to the Greek originals. And yet it is in the Greek and in the translation technique that the explanations of hundreds of tiny problems (expecially of syntax) are to be found, and certain major structural problems need to be posed in terms of the influence of Greek on OCS. However, so few students have enough Greek to profit by such comparisons that it did not seem worth the considerable space that would be required. Excellent work in this field is available, though some scholars tend to forget that even a poor translator is governed by the structure of the language into which he is translating. The "Notes on Syntax" in Chapter Six are offered on the premise that something is better than nothing. It is particularly in this area that translation techniques need to be analyzed.

After forty years of teaching OCS and related topics in the history and structure of modern Slavic languages, my views on the nature of language and the models for describing language have evolved away from the Bloomfieldian structuralism of my training. The data of OCS have not changed importantly from the material described by scholars a century ago, although some details from imprecise editions have been discarded and a few new details must be accounted for. I continue to believe that every language is a coherent structure, and that each language can be described in terms of static and dynamic elements and learned by novices who do not have the slightest knowledge of its history.

Departures from tradition in classifying the data in no way change the facts themselves. The OCS verb, for example, is complicated, and classification will not make it less so. *Xvaliti, velěti,* and *želěti* do belong to different paradigms, whether one labels them IV A, IV B, and III 2 with Leskien, or IV, III 1 and III 2 with Diels, or II.8k, II.8e,1k, and I.4a,2b with Koch. I believe that it is most efficient simply to encourage students to learn the form from which the rest of the paradigm can be generated according to rules (*xvali-ti, velě-ti,* but *želěj-ǫtъ*) and leave them to study the tables on pp. 114-117 and 136-137 for similarities and differences between paradigms. The present form of description is based on my belief that it is the morpheme that is the basic unit of communication.

A comparison of Old Church Slavonic—a language I believe to be a partially standardized written form of Late Common Slavic—with either its hypothetical ancestors or the descendants or collateral descendants of other forms of LCoS—is not the task of the synchronic description that takes up the first five chapters of this book. In the 1974 edition, I presented an epilogue ("Toward a generative phonology of OCS") that was based on a generative theory that proved to be too ambitious. Chapter Six in this book is an entirely new and relatively traditional sketch of the genesis of OCS (as a representative of Late Common Slavic).

This work was influenced by my teachers of long ago and by the students and colleagues I encountered during my years of teaching. I will not attempt to list them here. I can only express general thanks to the students who asked challenging questions and to their fellow-students and the colleagues throughout the scholarly world who helped me (in direct or indirect ways) find some of the answers. Special gratitude is due to Thomas J. Butler for his help in reading proof.

This edition too I dedicate to the memory of Professor S. H. Cross of Harvard, who introduced me to the study of Slavic, and to Professor G. R. Noyes of the University of California, who gave me my first lessons in Old Church Slavonic.

Horace G. Lunt

TABLE OF CONTENTS

ABBREVIATIONS

A = accusative
a., act. = active
AslP = Archiv für slavische Philologie
As = Assemanianus
Bg = Bulgarian
ByzSl = Byzantinoslavica
C = any consonant
Cl, Cloz = Clozianus
Cz = Czech
comp. = comparative
D, dat. = dative
ECoS = Early Common Slavic
Eu, Euch = Euchologium Sinaiticum
Ev. = Gospel(s)
f., fem. = feminine
G, gen. = genitive
Gk = Greek
Gmc = Germanic
Go = Gothic
I, impfv. = imperfective
I, instr. = instrumental
IJSLP = International Journal of Slavic Linguistics and Poetics
imv. = imperative
impf. = imperfect
inf. = infinitive
J = St. John
JF = Južnoslovenski Filolog
KF = Kiev Folia
L = St. Luke
L, loc. = locative
LCoS = Late Common Slavic
m, masc. = masculine
Mar = Marianus

MCoS = Middle Common Slavic
Mk = St. Mark
Mt = St. Matthew
ms = manuscript
mss = manuscripts
n = note
n, neut. = neuter
N, nom. = nominative
O = Old
OCS = Old Church Slavonic
P = perfective
P, Pol = Polish
Ps. = Psalterium Sinaiticum
part. = participle
pass. = passive
pl., plur. = plural
RÉSl = Revue des Études slaves
Sa = Sanscrit
Sav = Savvina kniga
SC = Serbo-Croatian
sg., sing. = singular
Slk = Slovak
Sln = Slovene
SPb = Sanktpeterburg
Su, Supr = Suprasliensis
Vat = Vatican Cyrillic Palimpsest
Zo, Zogr = Zographensis
ZoF = Zograph Folia
/ = or
~ = alternates with; is opposed to

Numeration of the paragraphs is decimal; every number to the right of the decimal point is to be read as a separate unit. Thus 15.642 = 15.6.4.2, i.e. the second subdivision of 15.64, which is the fourth subdivision of 15.6. For personal names in references (Diels, Vaillant, etc.) see the bibliography, §0.341 (pp. 12-14). For details about the codices, see §0.321 ff. (pp. 7-10). Citations are made by page and line for Cloz, Euch, Supr, and KF; by chapter and verse for Zo, Mar, As, Sav, and Vat; and by psalm and verse (Eastern numeration, as in the Septuagint) for Ps.

INTRODUCTION

EXTERNAL HISTORY AND SOURCES

0.0 Old Church Slavonic is the name given to the language of the oldest Slavic manuscripts, which date from the tenth or eleventh century. Since it is a literary language, used by the Slavs of many different regions, it represents not one regional dialect, but a generalized form of early Eastern Balkan Slavic (or Bulgaro-Macedonian) which cannot be specifically localized. It is important to cultural historians as the medium of Slavic culture in the Middle Ages and to linguists as the earliest form of Slavic known, a form very close to the language called Proto-Slavic or Common Slavic which was presumably spoken by all Slavs before they became differentiated into separate nations.

0.1 The Slavs are mentioned by historians with increasing frequence from the fifth century CE, but there is no reason to believe that they wrote their language down before the ninth century. In 862, Prince Rastislav, ruler of Morava (located somewhere in the Danube Basin), appealed to the Byzantine Emperor Michael III for a teacher who would give instruction in Christian law "in our own language." Michael appointed a priest, the experienced diplomat and able scholar Constantine, called the Philosopher, to the difficult and important mission. Constantine was a native of Salonika, and the Emperor pointed out that all the people of Salonika spoke Slavic well (**Солоунѣне вьси чисто словѣньскы бесѣдоуѭтъ**). Constantine went to Morava accompanied by his brother Methodius, a former civil administrator who had become a monk.

The brothers elaborated an alphabet for the Slavic language, translated the most important liturgical books, and started to train Moravans for the clergy. They travelled to Rome to visit the Pope and have some of their pupils ordained into the priesthood. On the way, the "Slavic apostles" stopped at the court of the Slavic prince Kocel (**Коцьлъ**) of Pannonia (in what is now western Hungary), where they were welcomed enthusiastically and acquired more pupils.

The Pope received them favorably and approved of their work, condemning the "three-tongue" heresy of those who claimed that only Greek, Latin, and Hebrew had the right to serve as written and liturgical languages. Constantine, however, fell sick in Rome, and on his death-bed he took monastic vows and assumed the name of Cyril (869). Later he was sainted.

Methodius was now appointed Archbishop of Pannonia (including Morava), and he set out for Morava with his newly consecrated pupils. Rastislav had been deposed and blinded in 870, and the new ruler Sventopulk (Свѧтопълкъ) was surrounded by Frankish priests who bitterly opposed the Slavic liturgy and the eastern, Greek influences it represented. The Franks had Methodius imprisoned in Bavaria, and only after two years did the Pope come to his aid. The Slavic rite was established in Morava, but on Methodius's death in 885 the Frankish clergy did their best to stamp it out. Driven from Sventopulk's realm, some of the Slavic priests apparently found asylum in Bohemia, and for some time they were able to maintain the Slavic liturgy and the writing that went with it. However, in the eleventh century Slavic culture steadily lost ground in the area and in 1097 the last Slavic monastery was abolished and the Slavic liturgy was formally prohibited.

Meanwhile, the Bulgar ruler Boris had been baptized in 864 and established Christianity as the official religion of his extensive realm. The meager historical sources offer no information about the language used in the new churches, but since Methodius apparently visited Constantinople and left two of his disciples and books in care of the Emperor and Patriarch, it is plausible that some knowledge of OCS existed in the eastern Bulgarian lands. In any case, the main body of Methodius's followers found refuge in Bulgarian territory, and OCS was nourished in two cultural centers, one in the east at the court of the Bulgarian Tsar Simeon (893–927) and one in the west, in Macedonia. Political conditions were favorable, and Slavic culture prospered, but not for long. After the destruction of the Bulgarian state in the east by the Byzantine armies at the beginning of the 970s, a state in Macedonia arose and flourished briefly. The might of Byzantium finally, after a dozen years of warring, crushed the last vestiges of independence by annihilating the armies of King Samuil in 1014. Even after this catastrophe, some degree of learning was maintained in the Bulgarian, Macedonian and Serbian monasteries, and in distant Croatia. When Christianity was accepted by the Rus' prince Volodimer in 988, Slavic books may have found a modest place among East Slavs. In the 1030s Prince Jaroslav "the Wise" apparently adopted the Slavonic rite, and books and perhaps teachers from the Bulgarian lands made it possible for the East Slavs to adapt Old Church Slavonic for their own use. By the 1050s Kiev and Novgorod were creative cultural centers.

0.2 The few early manuscripts which have come down to us do not go back to the days of Cyril and Methodius, but date at the earliest from the end of the tenth century and more probably from closer to the 1050s. Being thus the products of the period of turmoil attendant upon the destruction of the Macedonian state, they do not represent a thriving, developing culture, but only remnants. The scribes, it seems, were not well trained, and the manuscripts contain blunders which not even the most ingenious theory can bring into accord with a plausible linguistic system.

It is assumed that most of these manuscripts contain translations made by Cyril and Methodius, and the rest are translations made by their disciples, probably during the first decades after the death of the saints. However, since we lack contemporary manuscripts, or even the immediate copies which were doubtless made in the heyday of the states of Simeon and Samuil, we cannot know in precise detail the language actually written by the Slavic Apostles. Their own works, taken to Bohemia, Bulgaria, and Macedonia, were copied and recopied, edited and modified by generations of workers, and we possess only a few random examples of the copies.

The native dialect of Cyril and Methodius, who were born in Salonika, was presumably southeastern Macedonian. Perhaps Methodius adopted some features of the dialect of the Slavic-speaking province (possibly in the mountains northeast of Salonika) where he was an administrator for a time. In Constantinople the brothers may have become acquainted with the speech of Slavs from other areas. It is not impossible that the local dialects of Morava and Pannonia may have influenced the language of the translations. But in any case all evidence indicates that in the ninth century the difference between Slavic dialects from the Baltic to the Adriatic and Aegean Seas, from the Elbe to the steppes of Kievan Rus', were minimal, and it is probable that the dialect of Salonika was readily understandable to the Moravans and Pannonians of the Danube Basin.

0.21 Whatever the spoken dialects were, the *church language* appears to have been essentially the same in different areas. Because this language was used in the west and south and then served for centuries in Rus', in the Grand Duchy of Lithuania, and in Muscovy as a literary language (which naturally became modified progressively with the course of time), it is known as **Church Slavonic**. Since the majority of the early manuscripts which have survived were copied in the Bulgaro-Macedonian area and since there are certain specifically eastern Balkan Slavic features, many scholars have preferred to call the language **Old Bulgarian**, although **Old Macedonian** could also be justified. Early nineteenth-century scholars conjectured that this language was based on the dialect of Pannonia, and accordingly called it **Old Slovenian**. In the earliest sources, the language and letters are referred to by the adjectives **словѣньскъ**, Greek σκλαβικός, σθλοβενικός, or σκλαβινικός, Latin *sclavinica, sclavinisca* or *sclavina,* all of which mean simply *Slavic* (or *Slavonic*).

0.3 The tenth and eleventh centuries witnessed far-reaching changes in the several Slavic macrodialects. Reflections of the changes in the spoken languages appear in the spelling and the grammatical forms in the manuscripts and enable us to identify them as Serbian, Macedonian, Bulgarian, or Rusian (early East Slavic). As a convenient (but arbitrary) date, it is generally reckoned that non-East Slavic manuscripts written (or believed to have been written) before 1100 are Old Church Slavonic, as opposed to the Macedonian-Church Slavonic,[1] Bulgarian-Church Slavonic, or Serbian-Church Slavonic written after that time.[2] Most grammars of Old Church Slavonic exclude the considerable body of manuscripts produced in Rus' before 1100, because they have unmistakeably East Slavic traits. In fact, some Rus' manuscripts come about as close to the theoretical ideal described in grammars as the "classical" manuscripts do.

None of the OCS manuscripts is dated. None can be much older than the year 1000, and some may be considerably younger. It is not easy to establish even the relative age of the manuscript, since a text with archaic phonetic features may present younger morphological forms and vice versa, and the chronologies established on grounds of paleography are not reliable for this earliest period.

---

1 The line between OCS and post-OCS manuscripts is arbitrary and terminology is varied. The common term "Middle Bulgarian" is usually contrasted to "Old Bulgarian" (= OCS), and loosely used for manuscripts whose language demonstrates a broad spectrum of regional and temporal dialect features, often clearly the result of generations of copying by scribes with different habits.

2 These later forms of Church Slavonic are also known as the Serbian, Russian, etc. *recensions* of Church Slavonic. There is also a Croatian recension, attested in glagolitic mss throughout the Middle Ages and still used in some Croatian parishes. There is evidence (beside KF, cf. §0.311) for a Bohemian or "Moravian" recension, although only isolated fragments from this area have survived.

It must therefore be emphasized that Old Church Slavonic, as we deal with it in describing the grammatical patterns, is a theoretical, reconstructed language. The manuscripts written over a period of many decades, in different parts of the Balkan peninsula, present numerous variations in spelling, grammar, and vocabulary. It is assumed that the variations are later modifications affecting the originally unified type of language used by Cyril and Methodius and their immediate associates. On this assumption, all grammars of OCS have dealt with the "original" language, with some concessions to the usage of the several manuscripts. Indeed, the myriad attested variants constitute long and essentially uninformative lists. Therefore this grammar too describes a norm, a generalized type of dialect which does not correspond exactly to the facts of any one manuscript. Definable classes of variants are mentioned, and important individual deviations in detail are noted.

0.301 For the purposes of a grammatical description of the oldest attainable stage of OCS, it is imperative to restrict the data to the oldest manuscripts. I prefer a narrower "canon" than many linguists have defined in recent years (see below). The study of broader cultural problems is quite a different matter. There is no doubt that the scribes who produced the surviving OCS manuscripts were familiar with many texts that are available to us only in copies that were written down decades or centuries later. The language of some of these copies no doubt reflects OCS in many details—but precisely what is old and what is new constitutes a long series of controversial questions. In particular, just what words can be called *Old* Church Slavonic? Lexicographers have admitted a series of texts into the domain of OCS; many more could be justified. But for historical study of the language and related dialects, investigators should be alert to the antiquity of the manuscripts from which each item is cited as evidence.

0.31 There is no clear-cut set of features which differentiate the language of the manuscripts called Old Church Slavonic from the oldest of the texts termed simply Church Slavonic, but the relatively "correct" usage of certain letters and the relatively high occurrence of certain morphological forms which comparative evidence shows to be old give us some criteria. In the spelling, the use of the letters for the nasal vowels (*ǫ*, *ę* and perhaps *ję*) are of great importance. It is the "misuse" of these letters which is the clearest sign of an East Slavic scribe and the reason why such manuscripts as the *Ostromirovo Evangelie* (dated 1056-57, the oldest *dated* Slavic ms) are excluded from a description of OCS. Further, the writing of the symbols ъ and ь more or less where we expect them, and the consistent usage of the letter *ě* (ѣ) help to identify the language. Chief among the morphological characteristics are the use of the root-aorists (an archaism which was irregular from the point of view of the over-all system of OCS) and the uncontracted forms of the long adjectives. All of these features together, in conjunction with paleographical evidence (the details of the shape of the letters and the style of writing them), and the *absence* of specifically dialect features, serve to mark a manuscript as OCS.[3]

0.311 Three groups of manuscripts can be distinguished on the grounds of variant phonetic and morphological features. The Kiev Folia, with at least one pervasive Czech trait (see below §0.326), are the only representative of a variant of OCS which was presumably used in Bohemia or perhaps Moravia. (The location of the "Morava" where Constantine and Methodius worked in the 860s is unknown.) It is to be regarded as a "literary dialect", following local norms worked out in a specific area and opposed to the other OCS texts. Two of the cyrillic texts (Sav and Supr, see below) show in general some fairly specific eastern Bulgarian features, but the differences are neither great enough nor consistent enough to make it necessary to oppose a Macedonian "dialect" to a "Bulgarian" dialect of OCS.[4]

0.32 The "classical" or "canonical" texts of OCS include eight fairly extensive manuscripts (one a palimpsest), two sizeable fragments, and a number of single folia and parts of pages. Best represented is the *Gospel* text, with five manuscripts. The *psalms* are nearly complete, and there is

---

3 Citations from post-OCS mss that are believed to be reasonably faithful copies of originally OCS texts will be marked **OCS* in this book (e.g. *OCS *snъxa* 'daughter-in-law'): the label is marked, not the word.

4 Elaborate schemes of "OCS dialects" have been set up by some scholars on the basis of minute orthographic and morphological details, cf., e.g., Kul'bakin, Vieux Slave 354ff., Margulіés, Codex Supr., 227ff. The chief objection to this method is that it regards each scribe as a careful, trained phonetician who was trying to reproduce his own pronunciation. In reality the scribes were chiefly concerned with writing "correctly"—which sometimes meant copying exactly, and sometimes meant applying slightly different orthographical rules to the text being copied. We can determine literary norms (i.e. the spellings and grammatical forms given scribes or groups of scribes thought were proper), but to determine the phonetic details of pronunciation and from them the local origin of a scribe is impossible from the type of manuscript which we have in OCS. Cf. N. Durnovo, 'Slavjanskoe pravopisanie X-XII vv.', *Slavia* 12.45-84.

a *prayer-book,* a fragment of a *missal,* parts of a few *hymns,* *sermons* and *saints' lives*. To these manuscripts must be added dated Slavic text, a short gravestone inscription set up by the M king Samuil in 993.

The amount is actually quite modest: if the entire body of material were set up and format of this book, it would make a volume well under a thousand pages, including perhaps 350 which represent variants and not separate texts. The individual mss would occupy roughly the following number of pages (for abbreviations see below): Supr 300, Mar 175, Zo 150, Sav, Ps and Euch each 75, Vat 60, Cloz 20, and the fragments another 20.

0.321 Perhaps the oldest manuscripts are the two full versions of the Gospels, the so-called *tetraevangelia,* both written in glagolitic (see the next chapter, particularly §1.01). The **Codex Zographensis** (Zo) has 271 folia in OCS, plus 17 in an old Macedonian ChSl glagolitic version (Zo^2), and some later addenda in cyrillic. The OCS text contains Matthew 3:11 through the end of John (but Mt 16:20-24:20 is later, Zo^2). Phonetically it is nearest to the theoretical norms posited for the language of Cyril and Methodius, but certain morphological forms (especially aorists) and some textual readings seem to be rather younger. The **Codex Marianus** (Mar) has 174 folia, containing the Gospel text from Mt 5:23 to John 21:7. Certain deviations from the theoretical norms indicate Macedonian influences, others possibly Serbian (if not northern Macedonian). In the nineteenth century both were still on Mt. Athos, Zo in the Zograph Monastery, and Mar in the *skete* of the Virgin Mary. Zo is now in the Russian State Library in St. Petersburg, Mar in the Russian National Library in Moscow. Zo may be presumed to have been written in the 1020s, Mar in the 1030s; any dating is guesswork.

0.322 Quite different arrangements of gospel materials are found in the three *gospel lectionaries,* where the excerpts from the four gospels are presented as lessons to be read on specific days of the year.[5] The Greek term for such a book is εὐαγγέλιον, borrowed into OCS as **евангелие**. In the Greek Orthodox tradition the lectionary, as the primary source for the Word of God, is itself a sacred object that requires special care; it is for this reason that some 25% of all surviving Slavic medieval manuscripts are gospel lectionaries. Yet the individual manuscripts ordinarily vary in content, because—unlike the *tetraevangelion,* which contains the full gospels of Matthew, Mark, Luke, John—the lectionary is a general plan

[5] In Rus' a lectionary could be called **апракосъ**—apparently an adaptation of a Greek designation.

that provides well over 350 slots that designate a particular gospel pericope (reading, lection) that may or should be read. The usual selection provides lections (1) for all Saturdays and Sundays, the weekdays for the six weeks of the Great Fast (Lent) and the seven weeks from Easter to Ascension, and (2) selected Feast Days defined by day of the month. The first part is relatively standard, while the second part varies considerably because each manuscript was written with the needs of a particular region or individual church in mind. The glagolitic **Codex Assemanianus** (As), with 158 folia, has a chaotic innovating orthography, but retains numerous archaisms; it was written after 1038, and perhaps well after 1050, almost certainly in Macedonia. The newly discovered **Vatican palimpsest cyrillic lectionary** (Vat) is only partially legible, for the OCS text was washed off sometime near 1200 and a Greek lectionary text was written over the cyrillic lines. Although 96 folia had cyrillic writing, only about half of them contain reasonably legible connected text. Vat seems to be generally conservative, but with enough innovations to place it perhaps in the 1040s, possibly in Macedonia. **Sava's Book**, or **Savvina Kniga** (Sav) retains only 129 out of the original 200 or so folia. It is written in cyrillic, and while it retains some old textual readings, the language is definitely innovative, and seems to reflect central or eastern Bulgarian dialects. It probably was written in the 1030s. The Assemanianus was found in Jerusalem in the eighteenth century and taken to Rome, where it is kept in the Vatican Library. Vat is housed in the same library. Sav was in Rus' by the fourteenth century, to judge from the fact that lost folia were replaced by pages written in an East Slavic hand of that time. It was found in a Pskov monastery in the nineteenth century and is now in the Rossijskij Gosudarstvennyj Arxiv Drevnix Aktov in Moscow.

0.323 The Psalter and Prayer-Book are both still in the Monastery of St. Catherine on Mount Sinai, and are named accordingly. The glagolitic **Psalterium Sinaiticum** contains the 151 psalms plus ten canticles and some common prayers. The text is riddled with faults, but preserves archaisms along with innovating spelling reflecting Macedonian phonetics; it was produced by several scribes who worked together, very likely in the 1040s.[6] From the glagolitic **Euchologium Sinaiticum** (Euch), 137 folia have survived of what must have been a much larger book. Euch

---

6 A second glagolitic psalter, apparently from the same workshop, was found at St. Catherine's in 1975, but it has not yet been adequately described and is known to the scholarly world from a single photograph.

contains also three damaged folia from an eastern missal (or liturgiarium). The language of the two manuscripts is in many respect similar, and both appear to be from Macedonia.

0.324 The largest Old Church Slavonic manuscript is the **Codex Suprasliensis** (Supr), with 285 folia. It is a menaeum (четья минея in Russian terminology) for the month of March, that is, a collection of saints' lives for daily reading, and contains also a series of sermons for Holy Week and Easter. The writing is cyrillic, and the language is in every particular younger than that of the other texts, excepting Sav. It seems to have been written in central or eastern Bulgaria. Found in 1823 in a monastery in what is now Poland, it was later broken up: part (1-236, numbering each side) is now in the National Library in Ljubljana (Slovenia), while a second part (237-268) somehow (stolen?) found its way to Russia, where it is now in the Russian State Library in St. Petersburg. The largest section (269-570) remained in Warsaw. Removed from the Zamojski Library during World War II, it reappeared in the US in 1968, was acquired by an American and returned to Poland.

0.325 Another book which must have contained a large number of homilies (some of which are also in Supr) has survived only in fragments, fourteen folia in glagolitic called the **Glagolita Clozianus** (Cloz). One part of this ms has been demonstrated to be a sermon composed by Methodius. Like Mar, the language of Cloz shows both Macedonian and Serbian influences. Formerly the property of Count Cloz, two of the folia are now in the Ferdinandeum in Innsbruck (Austria), the other twelve in the Museo Civico in Trento, Italy.

0.326 The remnants of a missal (more precisely, sacramentary) of the western rite is possibly the oldest of our texts. The seven glagolitic folia known as the **Kiev Folia** (KF) are generally considered as most archaic from both the paleographic and the linguistic points of view, but at the same time this text replaces the most characteristically Bulgarian phonetic traits of the other mss with unmistakably Czech features.[7] By this simple modification of the most striking foreign features, the literary language was adapted for local use. Unfortunately the small amount of text of the

---

[7] The Bg *št* and *žd* which stem historically from **tj* (and **kt*), **dj* are kept, as a rule, in Rusian and Serbian ChSl, although they stand out as specifically foreign elements. But in KF they are regularly replaced by the Czech *c*/*z*, e.g. *prosęce* VIb6 'begging,' *pomocь* 'help,' *podazь* 'give' for Bg *prosęšte*, *pomoštь*, *podaždь*.

KF does not permit far-reading conclusions as to the place of the Czech type of language in the development of the early Slavic literary languages. The ms was taken from Jerusalem (perhaps originally from Sinai) to Kiev in 1870, and is now in the Vernadskyi Central Library.

0.327 A few isolated pages or fragments which are generally considered OCS are of importance chiefly to confirm the linguistic evidence offered by the larger texts and to demonstrate the early date of some of the literature. The **Słuck Psalter** (Sl), now lost, was five leaves of a cyrillic ms, containing part of the 118th psalm. Two leaves from a glagolitic gospel lectionary are known as the **Ochrid Folia** (Ochr).[8] The Church Fathers are represented by the two cyrillic **Hilandar Folia** (Hil) containing a text of Cyril of Jerusalem and the glagolitic **Rila Folia** (Ril, formerly called *Macedonian Frag.*), with parts of sermons by Ephraim the Syrian. The two cyrillic **Zograph Folia** (ZogrF) are from a monastic code of St. Basil.[9] Eight partially legible pages of liturgical hymns survive in the glagolitic **St. Petersburg Octoich**.

0.33 The mass of later manuscripts that have survived, mostly now in libraries, offer irrefutable evidence that the literature of the Slavs before 1100 must have been far more extensive than this small list. Doubtless Cyril and Methodius themselves translated the Acts and Epistles (*Apostolъ*, in Slavic terminology), and Methodius may well have finished translating the Old Testament. A code of church law (*nomokanon*) and a *patericon* (didactic tales about famous monks and hermits) are also attributed to the Slavic Apostles. It is probable that a number of liturgical works were translated from Latin as well as from Greek in the earliest period: the Kiev Folia are an example. Some of the prayers in Euch reflect Old High German versions. The hagiographic *Lives* (Žitija) of Ss. Cyril and Methodius are early; Methodius may well have written about his brother. At least two poems (*Proglasъ* and the *Alphabet Acrostic*) must be attributed to the immediate pupils of the Slavic Apostles if not to Cyril himself, and another poem (*Poxvala Simeonu*) is from the early tenth century. Some original hymns surely go back to tenth-century Bulgaria. However, all

---

8 *Undol'skij's Fragments,* two folia of a cyrillic gospel lectionary usually called OCS, are rather to be classed with the *Enina Apostol* (discovered in 1960) as representing a slightly more recent kind of language.

9 The badly damaged *Cyrillic Macedonian Folium* is usually called OCS, but it has some later features and in any case supplies no crucial data for grammar. The text appears to be from St. Cyril's preface to his translation of the Gospel.

these works have come down to us in a language which has been modified to suit the tastes of later scribes and which we therefore do not consider in the linguistic study of Old Church Slavonic.

0.34 The study of Church Slavonic, the literary language of all the Orthodox East and South Slavs (and some Catholic Croats), was begun early by native writers, but their grammars were unoriginal adaptations of Greek and Latin works, wholly inadequate to describe a Slavic language. The best and most famous grammar was published by the Rutherian Meletij Smotryc'kyj in 1619. Modern study of ChSl begins with the great Czech scholar Josef Dobrovský's *Institutiones linguae slavicae dialecti veteris,* 1822. The exploration and description of old manuscripts was continued by the Slovenes Jernej Kopitar and Franjo Miklošič (Miklosich) and the Russian Aleksandr Vostokov (among others), but it was the exemplary editions of the codices Zographensis (1879) and Marianus (1883) by the Croat Vatroslav Jagić that finally made it possible to separate Old Slavonic from later accretions.

The classical description was made by the great leader of the "Young Grammarians", August Leskien, in his *Handbuch der altbulgarischen (altkirchenslavischen) Sprache*. This manual appeared first in 1871, was revised four times, translated into Russian (1890), and has never gone out of use as a textbook. Moreover, its principle of including historical and comparative data beside the synchronic description set the style for nearly all later grammars and textbooks. The reference grammar by Václav Vondrák (1912) is an example. Unquestionably the most important book of this type is the encyclopedic *Altkirchenslavische Grammatik* by Paul Diels (1932), still an indispensable tool for anyone doing detailed work with OCS, although newer editions of some of the manuscripts show that some of his evidence needs to be modified. The Dutch scholar Nikolaas van Wijk lays an even greater emphasis on the historical factors in his *Geschichte der altkirchenslavischen Sprache* (1931).

The fundamental discussion of Common Slavic (or Proto-Slavic), with reference to its relations with other Indo-European languages and to the modern Slavic languages, is Antoine Meillet's *Le Slave Commun* (2nd ed., with A. Vaillant, 1934), which is of course based largely on the material of OCS.

An excellent non-historical description of OCS is André Vaillant's *Manuel du Vieux Slave*[2] (1964). It is rich in detail and frequently cites data from later texts to clarify some of the obscure points in OCS, but the treatment of sounds is somewhat old-fashioned for the time. Nikolaj

Trubetzkoy's uneven *Altkirchenslavische Grammatik* (written before 1938, published 1954) offered stimulating new views on the writing system and the organization of morphological description.

Syntax is given some attention by Vondrák and Vaillant, and more problems are discussed in the 1963 volume edited by Kurz. More comprehensive treatment of many questions is available in Večerka.

The lexicon of the short list of canonical texts, along with a broad selection of words from post-OCS manuscripts whose text is believed to go back to the OCS period, is treated in the *Slovník jazyka staroslověnského,* published by the Czech Academy, 1958–97. A single-volume distillation of SJS is *Словарь старославянского языка*, 1994, edited by Raisa Cejtlin and others [reprinted in 1999].

0.341 Bibliography. The number of books and articles that deal wholly or in part with OCS is enormous. Here I list only the editions of the OCS texts, some analyses, and some of my own works that provide the background for my decisions. Further titles will appear in footnotes.

A. TEXTS. [The editions are listed first (a) and then studies (b).]

1. Glagolitic

KF: (a) Jos **Schaeken**, *Die Kiever Blätter*. (= *Studies in Slavic and General Linguistics,* 9) Amsterdam. (b) H. G. **Lunt**, 'Once Again the Kiev Folia,' *SEEJ* 32 (1988): 341-83.

Zo: (a) V. Jagić (ed.), *Quattuor evangeliorum Codex Glagoliticus olim zographensis*. Berlin, 1879. (b) L. **Moszyński**, 'Ze studiów nad rękopisem kodeksu zografskiego,' Wrocıaw-Warszawa-Kraków; idem, *Język Kodeksu Zografskiego, I* (1975), *II* (1990).

Mar: (a) V. **Jagić** (ed.), *Quattuor evangeliorum ... Codex Marianus glagoliticus*. St. Petersburg, 1883 [contains study and lexicon].

As: (a) Josef **Kurz**, *Evangeliarium Assemani II* Prague, 1955 [Cyrillic transcription]; I. **Dujčev** (ed.), *Асеманиево евангелие*. Sofia, 1981 [photo-reproduction of ms, in color]. (b) H. G. **Lunt**, 'On the Old Church Slavonic codex Assemanianus,' *Makedonski jazik* 31-32 (1981-82): 405-16. Christoph **Koch**, *Kommentiertes Wort- und Formenverzeichnis des altkirchenslavischen Codex Assemanianus* (= Monumenta Linguae Slavicae Dialekti Veteris, XLIII), Freiburg i. Br., 2000.[10]

[10] The extensive comments provide meticulous data that elucidate scores of major and minor details (of spelling, morphology, syntax, meaning, translation technique).

Ps: (a) S. **Severjanov**, *Синайская псалтырь*. Petrograd, 1922 [Cyrillic transcription, with lexicon]; Moshé Altbauer, *Psalterium Sinaiticum*. Skopje, 1971 [photoreproduction]; F. V. **Mareš**, *Psalterii Sinaitici pars nova (monasterii s. Catharinae codex slav. 2/N)* (= Österreichische Akademie der Wissenschaften Phil.-hist. Kl., Schriften der Balkan-Kommission, Philol. Abt., 38), Vienna, 1997 [Cyrillic transcription with lexicon].
Euch: (a) Rajko **Nahtigal**, *Euchologium Sinaiticum I* [photo-reproduction], *II* [Cyrillic transcription, copious notes]. (= *Dela* 1, 2, of *Akad. znanosti in umetnosti, filoz.-filol.-histor. razred*), Ljubljana, 1941–42; Ján **Frček**, *Euchologium Sinaiticum, Texte slave avec sources greques et traduction française* (= *Patrologia Orientalis,* XXIV, 5, XXV, 3), Paris, 1933, 1939 [important for Greek sources].
Cloz: Antonín **Dostál**, *Clozianus, codex palaeoslovenicus glagoliticus*. Prague, 1959 [Cyrillic and Roman transcriptions, Greek texts, translations, lexicon].
Ril: Ivan **Gošev**, *Рилски глаголически листове*, Sofia, 1956 [Cyrillic transcription, lexicon]. (b) H. G. **Lunt**, *IJSLP* 1/2 (1959): 16-37.
SPbO: fragmentary, unpublished; preliminary report by **Lunt**, 'On Slavonic Palimpsests,' *American Contributions to the Fourth Internat'l Cong. of Slavicists, Moscow, September 1958* (= Slavistic Printings and Reprintings, XXI), The Hague, 1958, pp. 191-200.

2. Cyrillic

Sav: (a) Vjač. **Ščepkin**, *Саввина Книга*. StPbg, 1903 [with lexicon]; ed. O. A. **Knjaževskaja**, L. A. **Korobenko**, E. P. **Dogramadžieva**, *Саввина книга*. Moscow, 1999
Vat: (a) T. **Krъstanov**, A-M **Totomanova**, I. **Dobrev** (eds.), *Vatikansko Evangelie*. Sofia, 1996. (b) H. G. **Lunt**, 'On Defining OCS; the Case of the Vatican Cyrillic Palimpsest,' *IJSLP* 43 (2001).
Supr: (a) S. **Severjanov**, *Супрасльская рукопись*. SPb, 1904; J. **Zaimov** and Mario **Capaldo**, *Супрасьлски или Ретков сборник*. 2 vol. [photoreproduction, Severjanov's text; Greek texts], Sofia, 1982-83. (b) H. G. **Lunt**, 'On Editing Early Slavic Manuscripts: the Cases of the Codex Suprasliensis ...,' *IJSLP* 30 (1984): 7-34, 74-6.
Sl: (a) V. **Jagić**, *Specimina linguae palaeoslovenicae* (SPb, 1882)

---

[11] This edition arrived after the present grammar was already complete; all references to Sav are based on Ščepkin's edition.

Hil: (a) Angelina **Minčeva**, *Старобългарски кирилски откъслеци* (Sofia, 1978) 24-39.
ZogrFol: (a) **Minčeva**, pp. 39-45.
[Note: *Zo, Mar, Ps, Sav, Supr* were reprinted under the auspices of the Seminar für slavische Philologie of the University of Graz, Austria.]

B. GRAMMARS

Paul **Diels**, *Altkirchenslavische Grammatik*[2], I-II, Heidelberg, 1963. André **Vaillant**, *Manuel du vieux slave*[2] I-II, Paris, 1964. *Граматика на старобългарския език* (ed. Ivan Duridanov), Sofia, 1991.

C. DICTIONARIES

Slovník jazyka staroslověnského, Prague, 1958-1997. *Старославянский словарь,* ed. R. **Cejtlin**, Moscow, 1994.

D. STUDIES

On aspect: Antonín **Dostál**, *Studie o vidovém systému v staroslověnštině*, Prague, 1954.
On verbal forms: Christoph **Koch**, *Das morphologische System des altkirchenslavischen Verbums,* Munich, 1990.
On syntax: *Исследования по синтаксису старославянского языка,* ed. Josef **Kurz**, Prague. 1963. Rudolf **Večerka**, *Altkirchenslavische (altbulgarische) Syntax,* I-III, Freiburg i. Br., 1989, 1993, 1996.
On the prehistory of Slavic: Antoine **Meillet** (with André Vaillant), *Le slave commun*[2]*,* Paris, 1934. H. G. **Lunt**, *The Progressive Palatalization of Common Slavic,* Skopje, 1981; 'Common Slavic, Proto-Slavic, Pan-Slavic: What Are We Talking About? I. About Phonology,' *IJSLP* 41 (1997) 7-67; 'On Common Slavic Phonology: Palatalizations, Diphthongs, and Morphophonemes,' *IJSLP* 42 (1998) 7-14; 'Thoughts, Suggestions, and Questions about the Earliest Slavic Writing Systems', *Wiener slavistisches Jahrbuch* 46 (2000); 'Cyril and Methodius with Rastislav Prince of Morava: Where *Were* They?' *Thessaloniki Magna Moravia*, Thessaloniki, 1999. pp. 87-112.

CHAPTER ONE

THE OLD CHURCH SLAVONIC WRITING SYSTEMS

1.0 Old Church Slavonic manuscripts are written in two alphabets, *glagolitic* and *cyrillic,* which are functionally equivalent but visually quite different.

1.01 The *glagolitic* (named from *glagolъ* 'word') was probably invented by Constantine-Cyril, perhaps with the aid of his brother Methodius, in or about 863 CE. It is a unique and homogeneous graphic system, despite reminiscences from various styles of Greek, Coptic, and other alphabets. Doubtless the "Slavic Apostles" made the letter-shapes different because they wanted to create a unique system for the new language which was to be used for the praise and glory of God. This is in accordance with the Byzantine tradition allowing autonomy and equality for all of the languages of eastern Christianity, such as Georgian, Armenian, Syriac, and Coptic. Since glagolitic is the work of one man, or one man and his immediate associates, it is pointless to try to trace the gradual *development* of various letters from other symbols in other alphabets.

1.02 The *cyrillic,* a less esoteric alphabet that medieval Slavs attributed to St. Cyril, consists of the Greek uncial letters supplemented by symbols for typically Slavic sounds. It surely developed in the border zones where Greek teachers were proselytizing their pagan Slavic neighbors, and possibly represents authoritative decisions made by an "inventor" whose work was to adapt, systematize, and popularize suggestions made by a number of missionaries. It is not impossible that Constantine and his helpers worked out the number and value of symbols first on the basis of the Greek graphic model, and then devised a sharply contrasting set of letters that would proclaim the non-Greek individuality of the language. The earliest cyrillic manuscripts look remarkably like ninth or tenth-century Greek manuscripts. Glagolitic pages look nothing like either Greek or Latin. Perhaps the exotic shapes of glagolitic letters were intended to produce a visual image that might help persuade hostile Frankish or Italian missionaries in Morava that Constantine's mission was not Greek. In any case, the Greek-based alphabet is the ancestor of the cyrillic alphabets used today in the Balkans and among the East Slavs.

1.03 Glagolitic manuscripts were written in Macedonia well into the thirteenth century, and they were read and copied (in transliteration) in Rus' and the Balkans for some centuries, but the glagolitic alphabet was productive only in Croatia. There it was widely used as late as the seventeenth century, and a few priests in northern Dalmatia still use glagolitic missals to this day.

It is normal for scholars now to publish glagolitic texts in cyrillic or roman transliteration.

The two Slavic alphabets are admirably suited to the language for which they were devised. The dominant principle *one letter for one significant sound* is supplemented by arbitrary spelling conventions, some of which rely on the phonotactic structure of the language.

Like Greek and other eastern alphabets, OCS makes its letters serve as numerals as well as phonetic symbols. The numerical value of the glagolitic letters runs according to the alphabetical order, while the cyrillic numerals are patently borrowed from Greek. Letters representing Slavic phonemes that have no Greek analogue generally have no numerical value in cyrillic.[1]

1.04 Neither Greek nor Latin contained certain consonants and vowels which were common in Slavonic, and the classical alphabets were unsuitable for Slavic without extensive modification. Their inadequacy is demonstrated by the oldest datable Slavic written on parchment, the Freising texts—three short confessional formulae written in Latin letters and included in a manuscript which can be dated between 998 and 1027. For instance the letter *z* may stand for any of five different phonemes, *z s c č* or *ž*, while the phoneme *s* may be spelled with s, ʃ, z, zz, or ʃz (e.g. zeʃztoco = **ž**e**s**toko, ocima = o**č**ima, zinzi = **s**in**c**i or **s**yn**c**i, zla = **z**la; zloueza = **s**love**s**a, sodni =- **s**ǫdni, ʃunt = **s**ǫt, bozza = bo**s**a, goʃzpodi = go**s**podi).

The inconsistencies and obscurities of the spelling of these brief texts, plus certain marked Slovene dialect features, set them apart from the language of the other old texts, and they will not be treated in this work in spite of their age.

1 Greek has two numerals (i.e. letters with only numerical value): *stigma* (ϛ) '6', and *koppa* (ϙ) '90'. See § 1.5.

Glagolitic	numerical value	Cyrillic	numerical value	transcrip-tion	approximate phonetic value: notes
Ⰰ	1	а	1	a	a
Ⰱ	2	б	–	b	b
Ⰲ	3	в	2	v	v
Ⰳ	4	г	3	g	go as in *go*
Ⰴ	5	д	4	d	d
Ⰵ	6	є	5	e	e
Ⰶ	7	ж	–	ž	a**z**ure
Ⰷ	8	ꙃ (ѕ)	6	ʒ	a**dz**e
Ⰸ	9	ꙁ	7	z	z
Ⰹ, Ⰺ	10	і (ї)	10	i	i
Ⰻ	20	и	8	i	i
Ⰼ	30	(ћ)	–	-ǵ	see below, §1.213
Ⰽ	40	к	20	k	k
Ⰾ, Ⰾ	50	л	30	l	l
Ⰿ	60	м	40	m	m
Ⱀ	70	н	50	n	n
Ⱁ	80	о	60	o	o
Ⱂ	90	п	70	p	p
Ⱃ	–	р	100	r	r
Ⱄ	200	с	200	s	s
Ⱅ, Ⱅ	300	т	300	t	t
Ⱆ	400	оу	400	u	u
Ⱇ	500	ф	500	f	f (p?) cf. §1.216
Ⱚ	–	ѳ	9	th	**th**in? t? cf. §1.2161
Ⱈ	600	х	600	x	Ger. a**ch**, R **х**орошо
Ⱉ	700	ѡ	800	v	o
Ⱋ	800?	щ	–	št	Eng. sht
Ⱌ	900	ц	900	c	ts
Ⱍ	1000	ч	(§1.34)	č	*ch*eese

Glagolitic	numerical value	Cyrillic	numerical value	transcrip-tion	approximate phonetic value: notes
Ⱎ	2000?	ш	–	š	sh
Ⱏ	–	ъ	–	ъ	**pu**t, cf. §1.237
ⰟⰊ ⰟⰋ	–	ъı	–	y	Russian ы
Ⱐ	–	ь	–	ь	**pi**t, cf. §1.237
Ⱑ	800?	ѣ ꙓ	–	ě	**pa**d, cf. §1.238
Ⱓ	–	ю	–	ju	Eng. you
–	–	ꙗ	–	ja	ya
–	–	ѥ	–	je	ye
Ⱔ, Ⱔ	–	ѧ ѧ ѧ ѧ	900	ę	nasalized e
Ⱘ	–	ѫ	–	ǫ	nasalized o
Ⱗ	–	(ѩ)	–	ję	y + nasalized e
Ⱙ	–	ѭ	–	jǫ	y + nasalized o
–	–	ѯ	60	ks	a**x**
–	–	ѱ	700	ps	a**ps**e
Ⱛ	400?	ѵ ѵ	400	ü	**you** cf. §1.233
–	–	ҁ	90	–	see §1.5

1.1 The preceding table lists the two sets of symbols found in the oldest texts. It does not attempt to indicate the exact make-up of the original alphabets, since unambiguous evidence is lacking. It is probable that some of the letters listed here are relatively recent.

1.10 The theoretical ideal that *one symbol* = *one phoneme* (with the implication that one significant sound will always be represented by its own symbol) is violated because the number of phonemes is different from the number of symbols. Some sounds are not unambiguously represented. OCS spelling includes *rules of combination*: the precise significance of certain letters depends on the preceding letter. In particular, certain letters symbolize vowels if they immediately follow a consonant-letter but otherwise (that is, if they are word-initial or follow a vowel-letter) they indicate a syllable that consists of the consonant iod (*j*) plus a vowel (e.g. *eę* = /jeję/). The position after a consonant-letter may be called *blocked*; otherwise a vowel-letter is *unblocked*. Details are given below.

The actual spellings of the manuscripts vary widely in detail, because they were written at different times in different places, and the traditions and schooling of the scribes doubtless prescribed different norms. Thus quotations from the manuscripts will not always agree with the "same" forms which are cited in the grammatical discussion. The conventions observed in transliterating from glagolitic into cyrillic, and for rendering both in roman letters, must also be kept in mind. As a rule, cyrillic will be used here in citing cyrillic manuscripts and in sample paradigms. Roman will be used for normalized OCS words, for hypothetical reconstructed forms, and for transliteration from glagolitic manuscripts.

1.101 *Normalized* forms mean the spellings which are in accord with the theoretical standard we posit for OCS, although sometimes the "normal" form may occur only rarely in the actual texts. Thus the nominative and accusative singular of 'day' are spelled variously: dьnь, denь, denъ, dnь and dnъ. The sum of the evidence available tells us that in the language of Cyril the form must have been *dьnь*, so that is the normalized form.

1.102 *Reconstructed* forms are those which are never found in the manuscripts, but which we have deduced from all available evidence, including that of modern Slavic dialects and other languages, ancient and modern. Thus the reconstructed gen. pl. of 'day' is *dьnьjь*, although neither OCS alphabet has any means of spelling the combination *jь*. Reconstructed forms are always marked with the asterisk (*).

It may be pointed out here that the asterisk ought to be placed before many forms which are usually not so marked. There is no inventory of all attested forms, and often grammatical discussions adduce words that in fact are not to be found in the manuscripts. For instance, one confidently gives the full declension of *kostь* 'bone' in all 16 forms. Yet in all of OCS only two cases in the singular and five in the plural are attested. Inasmuch as the other forms are found in slightly younger manuscripts, and the grammatical endings are easily established by analogy with other words of the same category, it is not deemed necessary to label these forms as hypothetical. Thus in the paradigms in this book only really hypothetical forms in the less regular categories will be marked with the *, e.g. certain forms of the irregular verbs 'to be' and 'to give'.

1.20 The chief evidence for the phonology is the writing, but since the writing is a complex system (with glagolitic and cyrillic variants), the individual symbols are most readily defined in terms of the phonological units we deem pertinent. The following discussion takes for granted the

11 vowels and 24 consonants listed in the tables on pp. 30-31 in the next chapter.

1.21 Seventeen consonants are represented by unambiguous letters:

п	б	ф	в	м	т	д	с	ꙁ	ц	ѕ	ч	ш	ж	к	г	х
p	b	f	v	m	t	d	s	z	c	ʒ	č	š	ž	k	g	x

The dental sonorants /n l r/ are written with “n l r”, but the same letters may stand for the palatals /nj lj rj/, see §1.22 below.

The front glide /j/ is noted or implied in several ways, see §1.24 below.

1.211 The voiced affricate ʒ was symbolized by a special glagolitic letter called *ʒělo*. In many dialects the sound had lenited to *ź* or *z* and scribes used “z” (named *zemlja*). The chief OCS cyrillic mss, Su and Sav, have no /ʒ/, but ѕ occurs in Hil, ZoF, and Vat. In transliterating from glagolitic to cyrillic it is customary to use the symbol ѕ (which in OCS cyrillic mss functions only as a numeral, ‘6’).

1.212 The letter щ (Ⱋ in glagolitic) alternates with two-letter spellings, e.g. свѣшта = свѣща ‘candle’. The pronunciation probably varied from region to region, but functionally we may posit *št,* two phonetic units that together serve as a special morphophonological item (see §2.121).[2]

1.213 Glagolitic Ⰼ “ǵ” (called *djerv*) represents a Greek *gamma* (nearly always before front vowel): *iǵemonъ* = ‘(Roman) governor’. Its pronunciation in Slavic is unknown. It is conventionally transliterated into cyrillic by ћ, borrowed from later Serbian mss, though SJS normalizes ѓ, with the diacritic that will be treated below in §1.31.[3]

1.214 The first glagolitic letter of the word хлъмъ ‘hill’ has a special “spider shape” four times in Ps Sin and once in As (but the normal “x” is used in Zogr, Mar, Euch and once in Ps Sin). No plausible phonetic or other reason for this exceptional letter has been found.

1.215 Cyrillic occasionally writes *ks* and *ps* (consonant clusters not permitted in Slavic words) with ѯ and ѱ, taken from Greek ξ (*ksi*) and ψ (*psi*).

---

2 Neither the cyrillic nor the glagolitic shape can be plausibly explained as a compound symbol, ш over т.

3 Evidence is too sparse and contradictory to prove or refute any hypothesis about “щ” and “*djerv*”, but as an act of faith I believe that Durnovo and Trubetzkoy were essentially correct in speculating that they were originally devised as separate symbols for the regional reflexes of earlier **tj* and **dj* (probably palatal stops). See §26.4. Surviving mss reflect many decades of evolution in orthography and different regional and generational attitudes toward the texts and their pronunciation.

1.216 The letter "f" (cyr. ф) occurs in borrowed stems spelled in Greek with φ (*phi*) or in Latin with "f" or "ph". There is no [f] in native Slavic words, but OCS use of the phi-letter is quite consistent in common names (e.g. филипъ 'Phillip', иосифъ 'Joseph'), and we may assume it was pronounced *f* by many Slavs.[4]

1.2161 The letter "th" (cyr. ѳ) may correspond to Greek spellings with *theta* (θ), but it is usually replaced by "t" in the oldest texts, e.g. тома for ѳома 'Thomas'. The phone [θ] probably was not part of normal OCS pronunciation.[5]

1.22 The three palatal sonorants /nj lj rj/[6] may be represented (1) by a diacritic on the letters "n l r" and/or (2) by the use of certain vowel-letters, but often they are not marked; readers are expected to choose the appropriate pronunciation from spellings that are ambiguous; see §1.31. The ubiquitous glide /j/ (iod) has no uniform spelling, but is usually indicated by contextual signals; see below.

1.230 The nine oral and two nasal vowels are written by means of 12 glagolitic graphs and their combinations or 17 cyrillic graphs and their combinations. These graphs also serve to imply the glide /j/.

1.2301 The structure of Slavic words is (C)VCVCV—a sequence of open syllables.[7] The symbol C in this formula stands for a limited number

---

4 Latin had a native *f* but spelled borrowed Greek stems with "ph".

5 Neither Latin nor the Romance dialects that might have been in contact with Constantine and his mission had phonetic θ, but Latin orthography distinguished "th" in borrowings. It is probable that /f/ was permissible in stem-morphemes in many Slavic 9th-c dialects, but that /θ/ was not. The scribes who wrote the OCS mss surely were familiar with several sets of spelling conventions, but we can only guess what they may have been. Facts such as that Gk φοίνιξ 'palm-tree' appears as *pinikъsъ* in PsSin but *finikъ* in J 12:13 when we might expect фүникъ(ъс)ъ (or фүниѯъ) merely underline types of variation that may or may not conceal different types of pronunciation. The Gk phrase *is ta paθi* (εἰς τὰ πάθη) 'for the passions' (= special lections on Good Friday) comes out *na ta fati* (see SJS sub паѳи).

6 Throughout this book these three units will be spelled with digraphs, to avoid the visual disparity between Croatian *ń* and *ļ*, and the inappropriate phonetic associations implied by the symbol *ŕ*.

7 Ninth-century Greek had six vowels: *i* (spelled H, I, EI), *ü* (sp. Y, OI), *u* (sp. OY), *e* (sp. E, AI), *o* (sp. O, Ω), *a* (sp. A). Sequences of vowels within a word were common. Word-initial vowels were marked with a diacritic (placed on the second letter of a digraph), e.g. ἀ-, ἁ-, ἰ-, ἱ-, αἰ-, οὐ-, οὑ-. These "breathings" were merely a visual signal of the beginning of a word. Other diacritics could appear on any vowel to mark the stressed vowel. To write "accents" (*circumflex* ˆ, *acute* ´, *grave* \`),

of possible consonant clusters (cf. §2.43 below), while the V means only a single vowel. The circumstance that a vowel sound may not be immediately followed by another vowel in the same word underlies a fundamental orthographical convention that distinguishes two possible readings of certain vowel-letters. "VV"—a sequence of two vowel-letters—ordinarily means /VjV/; the glide /j/ is indicated. The syllables /ju, je, jǫ, ję, ja/ are distinguished fairly clearly, but the important difference between /ji/ and /jь/ is not written; it must be deduced by readers from the context, see §1.24 below.

1.2302 A vowel-letter is *blocked* if it follows a consonant-letter, *unblocked* otherwise. Unblocked position thus means syllable-initial, either within a word or at the beginning of a word.

1.231 The letters "o" (cyrillic "о") and "ω" (called *omega,* cyr. "ѡ") stand for the vowel *o*. Omega is rare; its principal uses are in the exclamation 'oh', as a decorative capital letter interchangeable with "o", and in the preposition or prefix *ot(ъ)*—often ѿ. It may be written in names to imitate Greek spelling.

1.232 The cyrillic "ѵ" or "ѵ"(called *ižica*) functions chiefly as the second element of a digraph оѵ for the tense high back rounded vowel *u*. A space-saving variant ȣ, with the second element above the first, is used sparingly.

In glagolitic, the complex shape of *ižica* is maintained when it stands alone, but in the digraph "oü" (cyr. оѵ, phonetic *u*) it is usually simplified and fused with the first element; the result looks like a single letter.

Ižica appears independently in a few Greek words and names which were spelled with upsilon, representing a high front rounded *ü*. Whether the Slavic scribes indeed pronounced this foreign sound, they endeavored to keep the traditional spelling. Thus *sümeonъ* сѵмеонъ συμεών 'Symeon', *sürię* сѵриꙗ σύρια 'Syria'. Substitution of *i* or *u* is not uncommon, симеонъ соѵмеонъ, сириꙗ соѵриꙗ.

1.233 The unit letter "ju" (cyr. ю) denotes the sequence /ju/. See also §1.24.

1.234 The glagolitic "e" denotes *e* if in blocked position, *je* if unblocked. Cyrillic "є" functions the same way in Sav, but the shape ѥ is usual in Su for unblocked position.

---

scribes had to memorize general rules and long lists of specific words. A dieresis may be used to show that a vowel-letter is not part of a digraph (e.g. αϊ = *ai* [two syllables], not *e*).

1.2341 In cyrillic, the letter "ѫ" unambiguously means *ǫ*, while "ѭ" means *jǫ*. That is, one unit stands for the back nasal vowel, and another (albeit visually related) unit stands for *iod* plus the vowel. The unit "ѧ" (or variants ѧ, ѧ, ѧ) is *ę* in blocked position (i.e. after a consonant-letter) but *ję* otherwise.[8]

1.2342 In glagolitic, a letter Ⱔ (transliterated *N*) generally serves to indicate nasal quality associated with the preceding vowel-letter: "oN" and "eN" are digraphs usually transliterated "ǫ" and "ę" and taken to be equivalent of the cyrillic letters "ѫ" and "ѧ". A third digraph has a letter that occurs only before "N" and may be represented in roman as "öN" or "ǫ̈". Its cyrillic equivalent is the unitary "ѭ" and it surely stands for the sequence *jǫ*. (See also §1.241.)

The digraph "eN" is universal in unblocked position, but some scribes used the "N" by itself in blocked position for *ę*. Thus "tN" = /tę/ 'thee [Acc sg]' ~ "toN" = /tǫ/ 'that [Acc sg fem]' (but "toeN" = /toję/ "that [Gen fem sg]"); cyr. тѧ ~ тѫ (тоѧ). Blocked "eN" is consistent in the Kiev Folia and the Sinai Psalter, and usual in the Rila Folia; there are frequent examples in As and occasional instances elsewhere.

1.2343 Scholarly tradition dictates that "eN" should be spelled ѩ when transliterating from glagolitic, and also when writing normalized OCS in cyrillic. The shape ѩ is not found in early South Slavic, but is regular in unblocked position in the East Slavic Ostromir Gospel.[9] The widespread use of ѩ in the authoritative editions of OCS glagolitic manuscripts obscures the nature of the orthographic relationships; cyrillic transliterations like тѩ look strange to Slavists, while тоѩ—a type of spelling unknown in canonical cyrillic OCS manuscripts—appears normal. In this book є and ѧ will be used in normalized cyrillic.

1.235 Glagolitic texts make no clear distinction between the three letters for *i* (Ⰺ Ⰹ Ⰻ), and cyrillic texts use their two letters (и, і) almost interchangeably. Readers have to take the orthographic and semantic context into account as they decide the value of each individual spelling. In

---

8 In Russian, ѫ is called юс большой, ѧ is юс малый, while ѭ and ѩ (§1.2343) are described as йотирóванные, *iotized*. Thus *jus* and *jusy* are used as cover terms in discussing these letters and their variants.

9 Here are typical usages of spellings for *e* and *ję* in OCS manuscripts:

	Su	Sav	Hil	Ost	KF	Zo, etc.
blocked	є ѧ	є ѧ	є ѧ	є ѧ	e eN	e N
unblocked	ѥ ѧ	є ѧ	ѥ ѧ	ѥ ѩ	e eN	e eN

blocked position, the value is always *i*. In unblocked position the value is *i* if it stands for the conjunction or emphatic particle 'and; even' and either *ji* or *jь* otherwise (unless the preceding symbol is ъ or ь, see next paragraph). It is tempting to speculate that the different shapes had specific contrasting values (perhaps *i, jь*) in Cyril's language, but attested usage is unsystematic.

In transliterating glagolitic into cyrillic, it is conventional to maintain the threefold usage of the original by means of a third letter, either ι, which is not found in any real cyrillic manuscript, or the ї of Supr (и = Ⰹ, ı = Ⰺ, ι or ї = Ⰻ). In normalized texts only cyrillic и and roman *i* are written. (In historical reconstructions and grammatical discussions, the combinations *ji* and *jь* may be used when pertinent, but this has no support in OCS spelling.)

1.236 The tense high back unrounded vowel *y* is written with a combination of two letters, ъ + any of the three symbols for *i* in glagolitic, and ъ + either of the *i*-symbols in cyrillic. In cyrillic, ъı is by far the commonest form.[10] A rare shape ьı (with ь as first element) occurs in Su. Occasionally the two elements are joined by a line, ꙑ or ꙑ. In some contexts it is difficult to decide whether the ъ + i sequences represent one syllable or two, *y* or *yi* (with an independent unblocked *i*-letter signifying *yji* **or** *yjь*; cf. §4.30121). This sort of ambiguity is rarely an impediment to understanding the words.

1.237 The letters ъ and ь stood for high lax vowels in most ninth-century dialects, comparable to the vowels in Eng. *put* and *pit,* respectively. These letters are called *jers*: *ъ* is the back or hard jer (Russian ëp), *ь* is the front or soft jer (R ëpь). The two high lax vowels might appropriately be written *ŭ* and *ĭ* in roman. Yet because their complex development within the OCS period was striking and puzzling to early modern scholars, the jers were put in a special classification as "reduced" or "irrational" vowels symbolized conventionally by the cyrillic letters. Instead of *sŭnŭ* 'sleep' and *dĭnĭ* 'day', Slavists usually write *sъnъ, dьnь*. The two jer-vowels were ubiquitous in the language of Cyril and Methodius; they occurred in all sorts of morphemes. By the time the OCS manuscripts

[10] The use of the *i*-letters in KF differs from that of most other scribes. The words *slyšati, byti,* and **moji/*mojь,* for example, vary as follows:

Supr/Sav	слъıшати	бъıти	мои
ZoMarEuch	слъıшати	бъıти	мои
KF	слъишати	бъити	моі

were written, however, these sounds had disappeared in some instances and changed quality in others. We assume that 9th-century OCS spelling used the jer-letters consistently in accordance with pronunciation. The scribes whose work constitutes our evidence attempted to spell words according to the old pronunciation, but they often erred. One of the major tasks facing students of OCS is to learn the hypothetical shape of morphemes and to recognize the orthographic variables in order to identify the jers that are posited for ideal or normalized words. See §2.51–2.53, below.

1.238 The letter *ě* (cyrillic ѣ, called "ять" in Russian) probably represented a tense low front vowel (similar to that in English *pat*) in the dialects of the Bulgarian lands. The *ě* of Western South Slavic regions apparently had a higher, more closed pronunciation. In glagolitic texts the letter stands where historically we expect the vowel *ě* after a non-palatal consonant, the sequence *ja* otherwise: thus m*ě*sto 'place', b*ě*la*ja* 'white [nom. sg. fem.]', *ja*ko 'as' are spelled "m*ě*sto, b*ě*la*ě*, *ě*ko" (мѣсто, бѣлаѣ, ѣко in cyrillic transliteration). In blocked position, then, the glagolitic letter "*ě*" represents the front vowel; in unblocked position it unambiguously represents *j* plus the tense low back vowel *a*. Cyrillic uses ѣ only in blocked position; the symbols ꙗ or ѧ (surely based on Greek uncial IA) are reserved for unblocked positions.

1.24 The glagolitic alphabet has no hint of a letter for the front glide *j* (called *iod*). This gap is filled (1) by two letters that stand for *j* plus back vowel, and (2) a convention that interprets a front-vowel letter in unblocked position as *j* plus the appropriate vowel (with a rule that assigns the value *ja* to unblocked "ě", see §1.238 above).[11]

Cyrillic lacks a specific symbol for *j* but has three letters with an initial element suggesting Gk *iota*:

phonemic	ju	je	jǫ	ję	ja	ji	jь	
glagolitic	ü	e	öN	eN	ě	i_1 i_2 i_3		unblocked
cyrillic	ю	ѥ (ѥ)	ѭ	ѩ ѧ ѧ ѩ	ꙗ	и і ї		

The lack of a device to differentiate *jь* from *ji* is the most serious defect in the writing systems. It was not remedied for centuries.

---

11 A sequence of vowel letters ordinarily implies an intervening word boundary. However, in foreign stems and sometime within native words, an unblocked *a, u,* or *ǫ* may indicate /j/: *farisea* фарисеа /fariseja/, *bělaa* бѣлаа /bělaja/.

1.241 The letters *ü* and *ǫ̈* (cyr. ю and ѭ) may be used after "č š ž c ʒ" and the groups "št žd" (cyr. ч ш ж ц ѕ, шт [щ] жд) instead of "u" and "ǫ" (cyr. оу and ѫ). Usage is extremely varied: шю and чю are particularly common; жю, щю (штю), ждю less so, and цю and ѕю are rare. щѭ (штѭ) is favored. These alternants surely result from scribal rules that varied with place and time. It is unlikely that the spellings give any real help in determining the pronunciation or phonetic nuances of either vowel or consonant.[12]

1.30 The writing in the manuscripts contains various superscript marks. Most of them are over vowel-letters, usually in unblocked position. No spaces are provided between words; unblocked vowels are usually word-initial. A superscript mark thus may be a reader-friendly visual signal of a word beginning with a vowel, but it is linguistically redundant. It may be a reminiscence of the Greek use of "breathings" that were obligatory on word-initial vowel-letters.[13]

1.31 One diacritic is used in normalized OCS over or next to the three letters "n l r", to stand for the palatal sonorants *nj, lj, rj*: thus *n̂ l̂ r̂* or н̂ л̂ р̂. This usage is borrowed from the cyrillic Suprasliensis and the glagolitic Zographensis, where the presence of these palatals is usually (if not fully consistently) noted. In Supr, for instance, the theoretical forms **jeleni* '2 deer [nom. dual]' and **jelenji* 'deer's [poss. adj. loc. sg.]' are spelled ѐлени ~ ѐлен̂и. The nominative singular (masculine) forms, which do not

---

12 Meticulous collections were assembled by scholars before the concept of the phoneme was explicit, but they interpreted the letters as scientific phonetic symbols, carefully chosen by trained linguists; the careful statistics concerning *letter* combinations have little to do with *phonemic* distinctions. Even if one grants a phonemic /ü/ and /ǫ̈/ opposed to /u/ and /ǫ/, it is clear that the opposition was neutralized after /š ž št žd/, so that the choice of vowel-letter in these cases was immaterial. The variation in choice of *jers* after palatal consonants (e.g. чь vs. чъ) is similarly insignificant.

13 There are supralinear markings in the Kiev Folia that suggest a significant system. Yet the marks are sparse and their distribution so inconsistent that scholars have been unable to agree whether the diacritics signify length, pitch, accent, musical notation for chanting, or perhaps more than one of these. (See Schaeken, Lunt).

Early East Slavic hymnological manuscripts with full Byzantine musical notation surely reflect a lost heritage of OCS mss of this type. It is highly probable that the Slavs chanted scriptural lections in accord with Eastern Orthodox custom. Some of the linear punctuation marks in Vat and the Ostromir Gospel hint at the system of *ekphonetic* notation known from Byzantine lectionaries; no indubitable sample of this type for any period has survived (though the Rusian *Novgorod Folia* are a likely candidate).

happen to be attested, would be similarly distinct: ѐлєнь ~ ѐлєн҄ь for *-nь* ~ *-njь*. In other mss, the palatal sonorants may be noted by "ju" (ю) and "jǫ" (ѭ): *ljubljǫ* любл҄ѭ 'I love'. For the most part, readers must deduce these three sonorants from the context.

1.32 Normalized texts often use both the diacritic and the "iotized" letters ꙗ ѥ ѩ ю ѭ: such spelling includes combinations that are not found in any OCS manuscript.

1. ѥ has no counterpart in glagolitic and does not occur in Sav (one exception) and certain fragments. In Supr it is usual in unblocked position, but є is not infrequent.

2. Zo is fairly consistent in marking **lj *nj* with the diacritic. Supr scarcely ever marks *l* before *ju* (лю, not л҄ю), and normally writes simply "ǫ" for "jǫ" after a marked consonant (л҄ѫ, н҄ѫ, less often лѭ, нѭ, rarely л҄ѭ, н҄ѭ). **rj* is less well attested because the palatal quality was lost early in South Slavic dialects. It is rarely marked in Supr, somewhat more often in Zo. Other manuscripts do not have this softness-diacritic except for a handful of examples in Mar, plus a couple of doubtful instances in Ps Sin.

In Sav, лꙗ is regular for *lja,* but нѣ for *nja* (Sav never uses the diacritics). Supr writes *lja* and *nja* inconsistently, e.g. л҄ꙗ/л҄ѣ/лꙗ/лѣ. ꙗ never occurs after a consonant-letter other than л or н.

3. Vat does not use the diacritic. The scribes apparently pronounced sequences **pj *bj *vj *mj* that are foreign to the standard language (see §2.420, below); they write these sequences: пѥ, бѥ, вѥ, мѥ, пꙗ, бꙗ, вꙗ, мꙗ, пѭ, бѭ, вѭ, мѭ.

1.331 The Hilandar Fragment has a special letter ꙉ which looks like a combination of *l* and the diacritic. Its usage even within the short text is not consistent, and it occurs where no historical **j* is posited. East Slavic mss of the 11th-12th centuries have besides ꙉ a parallel symbol ҥ (n +ˆ) and in some texts (e.g. the Čudov Psalter) the two letters are used with great accuracy for **lj* and **nj*. The Hil Fr would suggest that the Rus' borrowed this usage from the Balkan Slavs, though it is not impossible that it was a Rusian innovation.

1.332 Zogr and Supr often write ˆ over *k g x* followed by a front vowel, a combination of phonemes that is non-Slavic and therefore occurs only in newly borrowed words, mostly names: к҄єсар҄ь 'caesar', к҄инъсъ Gk κῆνσος 'poll-tax', єванг҄єлиє 'Gospel'. However, in this feature, as in many others, the spelling of foreign words shows wide variation.

1.34 In all of the texts there are words which are not spelled out in full. There are abbreviations of two types. The first writes the first and last letter of the stem plus the grammatical ending, and a line is placed over the word: b̄gъ, b̄gu = bogъ, bogu. In Greek this was originally a means of emphasis rather than a space-saving device, and it was restricted to the *nomina sacra,* the names of Divinity, such as 'God', 'Jesus', 'Spirit'. OCS early extended it to certain other words; it is particularly common with the forms of the verb *glagolati* 'speak, say': гл҃етъ, гл҃ѧ = glagoljetъ, glagolję, etc. The second type is more clearly to save space. A letter of those omitted on the line is written above the others, under a little roof: гⷶлв glava, еⷡѵ evvangelie, бⷭ҇ꙑ bystъ, мⷭ҇ѧпоⷭ҇ꙋ męsopustъ, etc. Such abbreviations are increasingly frequent in later manuscripts.

Some of the commonest abbreviations: ап҃лъ = апостолъ; аћ҃лъ, анг҃лъ = анћелъ; б҃жии = божии; б҃лна, б҃лгна = благословена; в҃лка = владꙑка; г҃ь = господь; г҃нь = господьнь; дв҃дъ = давꙑдъ; д҃ша = доуша; иꙁ҃ль, и҃ль = издраилⷭ҇ь; им҃ъ, ил҃мъ = иероусалимъ; ис҃ъ, і҃с = исоусъ; кр҃стъ = крьстъ; нб҃скъ = небесьскъ; оц҃а = отьца; сп҃си - съпаси; х҃ъ = христъ, христосъ; цр҃ь = цѣсарь; чк҃ъ, чл҃къ = чловѣкъ.

1.4 The punctuation in OCS mss is primitive. No space is left between words. Large-size letters may occur in headings, but there is no capitalization in the modern sense. A dot on the line (.) or raised (·), or two dots (:), may be written to divide the text into phrases, but they are not systematically used, and occasionally they occur within words. Larger divisions are sometimes marked with more complex symbols (such as ·: or ·:·). No OCS manuscript uses any of these devices consistently.

1.5 Numerals are indicated by putting a line above the letter, often also by setting off the letter or letters by a dot on either side: ·л҃· = 30, ·л҃ѳ· = 39, ·т҃иі· = 318. The unit ordinarily precedes the ten in the teens: ·в҃і· (= ·і҃в·) = 12 (corresponding to *dъva na desęte*, see §20).

The symbol ѕ (or ꙁ) has the numeral value of 6 (cf. Gk stigma, ς), even in manuscripts where it is not used as a letter. The letter ꙁ (= ʒ, *dz*) is not used as a numeral.

The symbol ҁ (cf. Gk koppa, ϙ) means 90. (After about 1300 ч replaced it.)

The thousands do not happen to be attested in the OCS glagolitic mss. Later evidence hints that separate letters (š, etc.) had these functions. In cyrillic, however, the thousands are denoted by the units with a preceding special symbol: ҂в҃ = 2000, ҂ѕтѯ҃г = 6363.

CHAPTER TWO

THE SOUND SYSTEM
PHONEMICS AND MORPHOPHONEMICS

2.0 The two alphabets, interpreted in the light of information from modern Slavic dialects and ancient and modern related languages, represent the phonemes of OCS very well. There are both too many and too few symbols, but in practice the individual words are clearly delineated; real ambiguities are rare, and readers easily recognize the correct word from the context in which it occurs. While the Greek alphabet and orthography—how the letters are combined to represent Greek words—clearly influenced the selection of OCS symbols and their conventional combinations, Cyril and Methodius created a new system admirably adapted to the phonology of OCS.[1]

2.01 It is probable that in the frontier zones where Slavs and Greeks were in close contact many Greek words had been adopted into Slavic speech. Such words, along with foreign names, inevitably were used in translating the basic Christian texts. The consonant *f* appears to have been accepted, surely as a markedly foreign item, in enough words and names so that the letters representing Greek φ (*phi*) are generally correctly used by OCS scribes. This sound was not part of the native phonological inven-

---

[1] Nikolaj Trubetzkoy assumed that glagolitic represented an ideal phonemic alphabet: each letter stands for one phoneme, each phoneme has its own letter. Previous editions of this book adhered to this thesis, and apportioned considerable space to deviations from the expected effects. It is more realistic to speculate that Greek missionaries who undertook to write Slavic did so by attempting to adapt their ingrained Greek habits to the new language. It is plausible that an intelligent experimenter endowed with authority to impose new rules on a group indeed created the system actually recorded in the surviving manuscripts. I assume that Constantine was the decisive figure in the process of inventing the OCS alphabets. For most people writing is a complex process governed by rules that have been learned with great labor; to write "correctly" is a matter of remembering what is learned. Devising a new writing system is an extraordinary feat; it is no wonder that it was seen as a miraculous accomplishment granted by God to Constantine.

tory, however, and *p* may appear as a substitute. Thus the name 'Phillip' usually is written *Filipъ* **Филипъ**, although occasionally *Pilipъ* **Пилипъ** is found. The continuant θ is often spelled with its own letter, but much more often the stop *t* is substituted: **Тома** rather than **Θома** for 'Thomas'. The θ-sound is negligible among borrowed stems. The voiced velar continuant γ may possibly have been used by some Slavic speakers in Greek stems; it is more plausible to assume that the "g" of glagolitic and the "г" of cyrillic were pronounced as a voiced stop, even in names and foreign words. We assume that /f/ was a separate unit for most users of OCS, but it plays no role in the morphology. /θ/ was probably unknown to most; it is a problem not of phonology but of orthography.

2.02 It is plausible that some scribes pronounced [ü] in words with Greek οι or υ, e.g. glagolitic "üsopъ" (cyr. **ѵсопъ**) 'hyssop, ὕσσωπος', **сѵкамина** 'mulberry tree, συκάμινος', cf. §1.232 and fn. 7, p. 21. This too concerns spelling more than pronunciation.

2.03 OCS spelling, as we have seen, is deficient in four particulars:
(1) the lack of a specific symbol for the glide *j* (§1.24);
(2) no unambiguous way to write the vowel /y/ (§1.236);
(3) no device for distinguishing the sequence /jь/ from /ji/ (§1.235); and
(4) the lack of a systematic indicator to distinguish dental /n, l, r/ from the corresponding palatals /nj lj rj/. See §1.3–.331.

2.04 On the whole, however, the OCS alphabets can be regarded as essentially phonemic. Thus *damъ* 'we (will) give' differs from *damь* 'I (will) give' in that in one the phoneme /m/ is followed by the vowel /ъ/ and in the other the same phoneme /m/ is followed by /ь/, any phonetic variation in the *m* being non-significant. There is no reason to assume that there were phonemically palatalized consonants in OCS.[2]

2.11 OCS had nine oral and two nasal vowels, defined by the distinctive features back/front, high/low, tense/lax, and rounded/unrounded:

	i	**y**	**u**	**ь**	**ъ**	**e**	**o**	**ě**	**a**	**ę**	**ǫ**
back	–	+	+	–	+	–	+	–	+	–	+
high	+	+	+	+	+	–	–	–	–	(–)	(+)
tense	+	+	+	–	–	–	–	+	+	(+)	(+)
rounded	–	–	+	–	(±)	–	+	-	(–)	–	(±)
nasal	–	–	–	–	–	–	–	–	-	+	+

[2] NB: palatal*ized* consonants are those characterized by a double articulation, palatal + something else (labial, dental, etc.). *Palatal* consonants have only a single – palatal – articulation.

Rounding is distinctive only in the high tense vowels; the ъ was probably rounded only in central Macedonia and in Rus'. The back nasal *ǫ* was non-distinctively rounded in central Late Common Slavic (including Rus' and the southwest [pre-Serbo-Croatian and Slovenian dialects]), but unrounded in the northwest (pre-Polish) and southeast (Macedono-Bulgarian) regions. This is implied by spellings in OCS where "o" is written instead of "ъ", "u" and "ju" (cyr. оу, ю) instead of "ǫ" and "jǫ" (cyr. ѫ, ѭ).

2.12 The basic consonantal inventory (without the borrowed *f*) is this:

	labial	dental	palatal	velar
obstruents	**p b**	**t d s z c ʒ**	**č** [ǯ] **š ž**	**k g x**
sonorants	**m**	**n l r**	**nj lj rj**	
glides	**w**		**j**	

The obstruents may further be subdivided into continuants (*s z š ž* [sibilants], *x*) and stops (*p b t d k g* vs. affricate [or delayed-release] *c ʒ č ǯ*).

The labial continuant is classed here as a glide /w/, though we use the traditional letter *v*. Like other sonorants it may be preceded by either voiced or voiceless obstruents, e.g. *tv, dv*. It is the only sonorant that may be followed by another sonorant, in *vl* and *vr*. The sequence {ov} in some morpheme-defined positions alternates with *u*, while in others the {v} behaves like {p b m}. Cf. §3.7, §6.21.

2.121 The two-phoneme sequences *št* and *žd* function morphophonemically as palatal units.

The underlying shapes may be posited as *šč* and *žǯ*; a late generative rule converts the affricates (*č* and *ǯ*) to stops (*t* and *d*). Cf. §2.413.

2.122 The dental affricates *c ʒ* may be termed "soft" (and written *ć ʒ́*) because they have different restrictions of combination from either the "hard" dentals *t d* or the "soft" palatal *č* (§2.51). In many dialects, *ʒ́* had become a continuant *ź*. The diacritic marks are not needed for *c ʒ*, but *ź* will be written to distinguish it from the more common hard dental *z*.

2.123 An exceptional phoneme *ś* is to be posited for the anomalous pronouns *ś-ь* 'this' and *vьś-ь* 'all'; see §4.201.

2.2 Throughout this book, the letter *j* will be used for initial and intervocalic /j/ in accord with usual manuscript spellings: *jaže, juže, jǫže, tvoja, tvoju, tvojǫ* ~ *eže, ęže, tvoe, tvoę*—whereby the "front-vowel letters" *e* and *ę* in unblocked position are to be understood as representing /je/ and /ję/. Further, the ambiguous manuscript spellings will be followed in words like *iže* and *tvoi,* to be interpreted according to the context as /jiže/ or /jъže/, /tvoji/ or /tvojь/; see §1.24.

2.21 The texts show fluctuation between *a* and *ja* at the beginning of certain words (*aviti* ~ *javiti* 'show', a*gnьcь* ~ *jagnьcь* 'lamb'). This surely reflects dialect variations rather than alternate forms in a single dialect.

2.22 In some dialects, a *j* between two vowels was lost: *dě*ja*ti* 'do', *raska*ja*ti* 'repent' > d*ě*a*t*i, *rask*aa*ti*. The two vowels could contract (*dě*t*i, rask*a*ti*).

Other spellings reflect contractions *ъjь/yjь* > y, *ьjь/ijь* and *ьji/iji* > i. The consequences are significant for certain present tenses (see §6.5) and the compound declension (see §4.301).

2.3 It is probable that there were prosodic features of length and stress which gave an even greater diversity to the OCS vowel system (and greater contrasts among dialects), but since the manuscripts give no information about prosody, we cannot reconstruct the particulars.

2.31 There are, however, certain spelling variations that help to identify some auxiliary morphemes as enclitics or proclitics that are prosodically bound to a major word. Prepositions surely formed an accentual unit together with the following noun; they were doubtless proclitic, as they are in nearly all modern Slavic dialects. The two demonstrative pronominal forms *tъ* 'that' and *sь* 'this' (nom. acc. sg. masc.) and **jь* 'him' (acc. sg. masc.) seem in certain cases to have functioned as enclitics, forming an accentual unit with the noun or verb they followed. Thus *vъ tъmě* 'in the dark', *sъ mъnojǫ* 'with me', *rabъ tъ* 'that slave', *viditъ i* 'sees him' were accentual units.

2.4 The following general restrictions on the occurrence and combinations of phonemes obtain.

2.411 The vowels *y, ъ, ь, e* and *ę* do not occur in word-initial position. The vowel *ě* in the root *ěd-* 'eat' may have been allowed word-initially in some dialects; glagolitic spelling with "ěd-" is perhaps ambiguous. Cyrillic manuscripts usually write ꙗд- (but prefixed обѣд-, сънѣд-, cf. §3.3101).

2.4111 It is possible that some loan-words may have had initial /e/, but adaptation to the native pattern with /je/ is probable for many. The use of cyrillic є vs. ѥ is not systematic (§1.234) and therefore provides no sure evidence.

2.412 After *k g x* only *y u ъ o ǫ a* may stand; that is, a front vowel (*i ь e ę ě*) may not follow a velar consonant.

2.4121 This rule is frequently violated by words of demonstrably recent foreign origin, e.g. *kitъ* 'κῆτος, whale', *kesarjь* 'καῖσαρ, Roman emperor', *arxierei* ἀρχιερεύς 'archpriest', *xeruvimъ* χερουβίμ 'cherub'. In Greek, these consonants were non-distinctively palatal [ḱ x́]; some Slavs possibly imitated this pronunciation. Words with a Greek gamma before front vowel are spelled sometimes with *g*, sometimes *ǵ* (cf. §2.4121): *angelъ* ~ *anǵelъ* 'angel'. Doubtless the pronunciation of such words varied in different areas and traditions. What is important is that foreign stems were ordinarily provided with derivational suffixes and inflectional desinences that fitted them into the overall-system of OCS.

2.413 After palatals (*š ž č št žd nj lj rj* and *j*) only *i e ę u a ǫ* may stand (NOT *o y ь ě*). Note that the groups *št* and *žd* are treated as units whose behavior differs from that of *t* and *d*, §2.121. (And keep in mind that the digraphs *nj lj rj* represent unit phonemes, §1.22) Note also that the sequence /jъ/ is written *i* (so **tvojь* is spelled *tvoi*, cf. §1.24). The consonants listed here are traditionally called "soft".

2.414 After *c* and *ʒ*, *y o* and *ъ* cannot stand (but *i u e ę ǫ ě a ь* may).

2.415 Any vowel may follow the other consonants (labials, *p b v m*; and dentals, *t d s z n l r*).

2.51 These phonotactic restrictions define four groups of consonants: the velars, the "soft consonants", the pair *c ʒ*, and what may be termed "neutral consonants". Here is a summary in tabular form (*plus* [+] means that a vowel may occur in the position indicated, *minus* [–] that it may not):

	ě	y	ъ	ь	o	e	i	ę	u	a	ǫ
1. initial	(-)	-	-	-	+	-	+	-	+	+	+
2. after *k g x*	-	+	+	-	+	-	-	-	+	+	+
3. after *š ž č št žd nj lj rj j*	-	-	-	+	-	+	+	+	+	+	+
4. after *c ʒ*	+	-	-	+	-	+	+	+	+	+	+
5. after *p b t d s z v m n l r*	+	+	+	+	+	+	+	+	+	+	+

This table shows that three vowels (*u a ǫ*) have no restrictions. The contrasts in the first four positions show that *y ъ o* are in complementary distribution with *i ь e*. The front nasal vowel *ę* is not so directly opposed to the back nasal *ǫ*, and the low front tense *ě* differs even more from the low back tense *a*.

2.52 The syllabic structure is simple: there is a single vowel which may be preceded by a maximum of four consonants (CCCC)V. All syllables are thus open, and any succession of vowels is automatically to be interpreted as a succession of syllables. This occurs when a vowel-final prefix joins a stem-initial vowel (e.g. *naučiti, vъorǫžiti*), and apparently in the imperfect tense suffix *ěa/aa* (cf. §9.1). It seems to be a relatively new development in some desinences of the compound adjectives (*aa* < *aje, uu* < *uje*).

2.521 Often the expected two-unit groups *plj, blj, vlj, mlj* are spelled without any l-letter, implying a Bulgaro-Macedonian substitution of /j/ in place of the palatal sonorant /lj/, and therefore groups *pj, bj, vj, mj*. Thus, e.g., *ka*plj*a*, *lju*bljǫ, *a*vlj*ati*, *ze*mlj*a* changed to *ka*pj*a*, *lju*bjǫ, *a*vj*ati*, *ze*mj*a*. Most usually this is shown by ь in place of the l-letter, but before front-vowel letters the ь may be omitted: e.g. **ѕемьꙗ, ѕемьи, ѕеми, любьѭ, приставение**. See also §1.32 (3).

Other dialectal developments affecting the validity of the rules stated here are isolated and unimportant.

2.522 Consonant clusters are limited to sequences that can be described in a general formula: sibilant + (non-continuant or *x*) + (*v*) + (sonorant). *Moreover*: No doubled consonants occur.
And: An initial sibilant must be voiced or voiceless according to the voicing of the following obstruent and palatal before a palatal consonant.

	obstruent					sonorant				
s	**p**	**t**	**k**	**c**	**x**	**v**	**r**	**l**	**m**	**n**
z	**b**	**d**	**g**	**ʒ**						
š		**č**	**(št)**				**rj**	**lj**		**nj**
ž		**ž**	**(žd)**							

Not all possible combinations occur (see §3.311). Many clusters (printed in italics in the following list) are attested only within a word.

sp	**st**	**sk**	*sc*	*sx*	**sv**	**sr**	**sl**	**sm**	**sn**	**pr**	**pl**	**plj**	*pn*	**tv**	**tr**	*tn*		**kr**	**kl**	**klj**	*kn*		**cv**
zb	*zd*	*zg*		*zʒ*	**zv**	**zr**	**zl**	*zm*	**zn**	**br**	**bl**	**blj**	*bn*	**dv**	**dr**	*dn*	*dm*	**gv**	**gr**	**gl**	**gn**	*gnj*	**ʒv**
					xv	**xr**	**xl**		*xn*	**vr**	**vl**												
spr	*spl*	*splj*	*stv*	**str**	**skr**	*skv*	*skl*	*sklj*	**skvr**		*scv*	*sxv*	**čr**	**čl**		**št**	*šv*	*šlj*	*šnj*	*štvlj*		*štr*	
zbr	*zbl*	*zblj*	*zdv*	*zdr*	*zgr*	*zgv*	*zgl*						**žr**	**žl**	*žlj*	*žd*			*žnj*				*ždrj*

2.5221 The glide /j/ occurs only as the initial consonant in its syllable. In underlying structure, however, *j* may follow a consonant or cluster; it may also appear in an intermediate stage of generation. See §3.6.

2.523 Only one exception to the formula exists: adjacent stops appear in the adverbial suffix *-gda* (e.g. *kogda* 'when', *togda* 'then', cf. §4.812).

2.53 Borrowed stems with deviant consonant clusters probably inserted jers (ъ, ь) to break the clusters, e.g. *pъsalъmъ* 'psalm', *Avъgustъ* 'Augustus, Αὐγούστος' (pron. [avγústos]), *Pavьlъ* 'Paul, Παύλος' (pron. [pávlos]). The spelling is chaotic and many details are difficult to interpret. See also §2.65.

2.6 The two high lax vowels—the *jers*—ъ and ь (cf. §1.237), are subject to special processes.

2.61 Before /j/, the tense/lax opposition is neutralized in the high non-rounded vowels: /ь/ is in free alternation with /i/, and /ъ/ with /y/. Thus *ljud**ь**je and *ljud**i**je, *nov**ъ**jь and *nov**y**jь are equivalent; scribes employ alternate spellings like **лю**дье and людие, **новъи** and **новъıи**. The vowels in this position will be called *tense jers* (although some scholars prefer the term *reduced y/i*).

The ь-letter is used frequently but inconsistently, while the ъ-letter is rare. This is partly due to the fact that tense /ь/ occurs in many more words and categories than tense /ъ/.

This neutralization applies within a phonological word (or accentual unit, cf. §2.31), so that the jer of a preposition is affected by the /j/ of the following word, and a final jer is affected by an enclitic **jь*; e.g. *vъ istinǫ - vy istinǫ* 'in truth', *osǫdetъ i - osǫdety i* 'they will condemn him', *prědamь i - prědami i* 'I will betray him'.

2.620 The invention of the jer-letters and their use in the oldest manuscripts guarantee that the two high lax vowels were distinct phonemes in the language of the 9th century. They were surely characteristic of all Slavic dialects at the time. Yet they soon began to change; in certain positions (called *weak*) within a phonological word they simply disappeared, while in other positions (called *strong*) they were pronounced with lower articulation, creating new and regionally varied vowel systems. The early stages of this complex process, dubbed the *jer-shift,* followed the same rules in all of Slavdom, but the details and the eventual results and phonemic accommodations differ from dialect to dialect. OCS attests a generalized type of southeastern Late Common Slavic, but the actual use of the jer-letters in the surviving manuscripts shows that the jer-shift was far advanced or complete at the time the scribes wrote those mss.[3]

Phonologically, the high lax vowels were lost; at a more abstract level, however, they survived as vowel/zero morphophonemes: under specific phonotactic conditions they are vowel phonemes, while under other conditions they are not pronounced—they are phonetic nulls.

2.621 A jer may be either *strong* or *weak*. A jer is weak in a syllable followed directly by a syllable with a non-jer vowel (i.e. at the end of a

---

[3] The change seems to have started in the southwest (perhaps in Slovene, Czech, or Croatian regions) during the tenth century, spread throughout the Slavic world, reaching Kiev Rus' not earlier than the beginning of the twelfth century, and Novgorod and the northeast somewhat later. Many of the 11th and 12th-century mss of Rus' origin use the jer-letters far more "correctly" than do the OCS texts.

word not followed by an enclitic). A jer is strong only in a syllable directly before a syllable with a weak jer. For example, with weak jers in *italics* and strong jers in **bold-face**: d**ь**n*ь* 'day', d*ь*ne (gen. sg.), t*ь*m**ь**n*ъ* 'dark (nom. sg. masc)', t**ь**m*ь*no (nom. sg. neut.), s**ъ**n*ъ* 'sleep', s*ъ*n**ь**n*ъ* 'of sleep (adj. nom. sg. masc.)', s**ъ**n*ь*na (nom. sg. fem.), *moj*ь* (written moi), *ljud**ь**j*ь* (written ljudьi); v**ъ** t*ь*mě 'in the dark', rab**ъ** t*ъ* 'that slave', s**ъ** m*ъ*nojǫ 'with me' (cf. §2.31) (Detailed examples are given in §2.65, below.)

In the groups spelled *consonant* + *l* or *r* + *consonant,* the jer, in the great majority of cases, is neither strong nor weak, but *neutral*. See §2.63.

2.622 As the jer-shift progressed, the weak jers ceased to be pronounced. A strong jer was replaced by a non-high vowel. In central Macedonia, **ь** > *e*, **ъ** > *o*: *den,* (**tmen*), *temno, son,* (**snen, *sonna*), *moj, ljudej (written* ljudei*), vo tmě, rabo t, so mnojǫ*. In most Bulgarian dialects ъ became an independent vowel /ə/, still written with the jer-letter, while ь also became /ə/ in roots, but /e/ in suffixes. In some central and eastern Bulgarian dialects ь > *ə* in all positions. In all of Serbo-Croatian and Slovene, the two jers fell together in a single vowel *ə*.[4]

2.623 In the manuscripts these changes are not clearly shown, largely because of the force of written tradition, combined with habits of special—and, surely, often artificial—church pronunciation of sacred texts.[5] The influence of different regional and historical dialects on the texts as they were copied time after time introduced all sorts of modifications, and scribes continually made mistakes. Writing weak jers became a matter of arbitrary rule or random choice. Spellings that deviate fairly systematically from etymological expectations seem to hint at local phonetic usage during stages when weak jers could be pronounced or omitted. In Zogr, for example, ъ usually is written before a syllable with a back vowel, ь before a syllable with a front vowel. Detailed studies of the work of all the major OCS scribes have failed to prove that orthographical usage reflects the pronunciation, but some general principles can be detected. Jers that

---

[4] In Serbian mss it was written ь (changing to *a* in the 14th century).

[5] The maintenance of a vowel even in weak position was supported in some communities by the habit of singing or chanting many liturgical texts to old tunes which were composed to match the musical structure to the vowels (including jers) of archaic texts. See for example the 16th-17th century Russian hymns in E. Koschmieder in *Die ältesten Novgoroder Hirmologien Fragmente* (Abhandlungen d. Bayerisch. Akad., Phil. hist. Kl., NF 53), Munich, 1952, where e/o consistently appears for old jers, e.g. весе миро for vъsь mirъ.

were always in weak position, especially in an initial syllable, are almost regularly omitted by some scribes (e.g. čto, kto, mnogo for čьto, kъto, mъnogo). Many scribes consistently write ъ instead of ь after *š* and *ž*. Word-final jers were retained for centuries as a visual signal of the end of the word (since space was not ordinarily left between words).

2.624 In spelling strong jers, the manuscripts also differ: KF writes them correctly—viz. where we expect them on the basis of comparative evidence. They are generally correct in Supr and Sav, perhaps because both jer-letters could be pronounced as /ə/. The other mss all have some examples of *e* for strong ь; in As *e* occurs in nearly 85% of all possible cases, while in Euch it is almost without exception. All the mss have a few instances of *o* for strong ъ; Euch has it in about 30% of the possible cases. It is possible that such spellings in some words reflect conventions from an authoritative tradition. Yet "errors" also occur: thus s**ъ**tьnikъ 'centurion' appears as s**ь**tьnikъ as well as s**o**tьnikъ. Sav consistently omits the strong jer in **днь** 'day' and **всь** 'all (NA masc. sg.)'.

All in all, the use of the jer-letters demonstrates only that scribes felt that these symbols were part of correct spelling.

2.6241 The phonological calculation of strong jers originally started with the end of a word: tьm**ь**nъ but t**ь**mьna. Examples of the type **tmen temna* demonstrate the expected development of vowel versus zero in different morphological forms of a single stem. By the end of the OCS period, however the calculation started from the beginning of a word: the recursive rule was *a jer is strong if a jer is in the next syllable*. Therefore underlying

{tьmьnъ} > t**ь**mьnъ > t**ь**m**ь**nъ > t**ь**m**ь**nъ > /temen/
{tьmьno} > t**ь**mьno > t**ь**mьno > /temno/

Though the principles of such developments are clearly illustrated in OCS mss, the conservative and inconsistent spellings not only of OCS but of most immediately post-OCS texts obscure the details.

2.625 The sequence **jь* cannot be expressed in either OCS alphabet, but is written with an i-letter (§1.24). Nonetheless, the presence of the strong or weak jer is sometimes apparent. The adjective /dostoj**ь**nъ/ 'worthy' is spelled dostoinъ or (after the strong jer has lowered) dostoenъ (/dostojen/).

The sequences **ьjь* and **ъjь* contain tense jers (§2.61) that are strong. The gen. pl. *ljud**ь**jь may be spelled ljudьi or ljudii or (with lowered strong jer) ljudei (for /ljudej/). A tense jer that is weak serves to define a jer in the preceding syllable as strong: tr**ь**stьjǫ (written also trъstijǫ) > trestijǫ. See §2.65 for some other examples.

2.626 A great deal has been written about these variant spellings and innumerable and ingenious theories built up, but the fact remains that we are dealing with *spellings* and can only guess at the sounds they represented and speculate about the phonological system or systems. It must be emphasized that NOT ONE SINGLE OLD CHURCH SLAVONIC MANUSCRIPT has the jers written in all cases where the grammars (including this one) posit them. Our chief guide for reconstruction is the East Slavic usage of some of the oldest mss (11th and early 12th century), where the jers seem to have been written according to the older Slavonic tradition. It is even probable that many Rusian scribes, guided by their native speech, corrected the "errors" they found in the South Slavic manuscripts they were copying.

2.63 Spellings in the groups involving *r* or *l* + jer between consonants (traditionally expressed by the formulas trьt/trъt/tlьt/tlъt, where *t* represents any consonant) pose certain problems of interpretation. OCS scribes preferred ъ in these words, but Sav has only ь. We follow etymology in normalizing such words: hence, *sъmrъtь* 'death', *krъvь* 'blood', *slьza* 'tear', *slъnьce* 'sun'.

2.631 Spellings of such words vary in ways that, with the help of evidence from later dialects and related languages, suggest two groups: in one the jer represents a vowel that originally followed the liquid (krъvь, slьza), while in the other the jer-vowel originally preceded the *r*/*l* (*sъmьrtь, *sъlnьce). In spelling the first type, some mss (esp. Zo) distinguish the two jer-letters well. Moreover, the jers in these words may when weak serve to make a preceding jer strong (v**ъ** > v**o** in v**o** krъvi as in v**o** vьsěxъ), or if themselves strong may be replaced by *o*/*e*: kr**o**vь, sl**e**zъ [gen. pl.]). In short, these are normal /ь ъ/.

Words whose ь or ъ preceded the liquid are conventionally written with ъ (but always with ь in Sav). We may term this kind of written jer *neutral*.[6] There are no cases indicating the development of such a jer into

[6] Early Rus' mss regularly write neutral jers before the liquid: **съмьрть, сълньце**, but **кръвь, сльза**. Modern Russian equivalents normally indicate the order of phonemes for the etymology: R *er*/*or* indicates **ьr*/*ъr* and R *re*/*ro* shows **rь*/*lъ*; e.g. sm**e**rt' < *sъmьrtь*, kr**e**st < *krьstъ*. That is, if the vowel precedes the *r* in Russian, the jer preceded it in (the early Rusian dialect of) Late ComSl. R/U *le*/*lo* reflect LCoS *lь*/*lъ* (sleza < *slьza*, pl**o**t' < *plъtь*), but **ьl* became *ъl* in early Rus, and both yielded R *ol* (polnyj - OCS *plьnь*).

another vowel according to the rules for strong jers, nor does a jer preceding such a syllable act as if in strong position. It is highly possible that the 9th-century dialect of the original translations still distinguished two separate types of syllable, while the OCS evidence reflects a substantially modified later system. South Slavic developed syllabic liquids in both types. Forms like *smrt* and *slnce* may have appeared slightly earlier, while alternations such as *krov* ~ *krvi* (< kr**ъ**vь krъvi) and *krest* ~ *krsta* (< kr**ь**stъ 'cross' krьsta) developed and were eliminated in favor of uniform stems with a syllabic sonorant (*krv krvi, krst krsta*). In any case, arbitrary spellings that position jer-letters after the liquid-letters persisted for centuries.

2.64 The loss of the weak jers meant that the scribes pronounced consonant groups in many places where the older mss had a jer-letter. The ideal visual image included many "silent" letters that separated consonants, and scribes occasionally wrote a jer where it did not belong. For example, when *bьrati* 'take' lost its jer, it became identical with *brati* 'fight'; both are subsequently written *brati* or *bьrati* or *bъrati*. A scribe who pronounced *umreši* 'you will die' but knew it should be spelled *umьreši,* could easily add a spurious jer to the infinitive, writing *umьrěti* or *umъrěti* instead of etymological *umrěti*.

In foreign words and names jers are often added between consonant-letters; we cannot be sure just when this is meaningful and when not.

2.65 Here are some examples of typical spellings of words containing jers. The normalized form (whether actually attested or not) is given first, in roman letters, then the attested variants in cyrillic. Keep in mind these basic general rules—For strong position: a jer-letter is expected (though it may be the "wrong" one; or, ь is replaced by є (often), while ъ is replaced by о (rarely). For weak position: non-final letters may be omitted, with or without a supralinear mark; the choice between jer-letters is essentially random. In the work of individual scribes spelling rules (or at least tendencies) may be detected (see §2.523 above):

čьto: чьто, чъто, ч̇то. *dьnь* (nom. sg.): дьнь, дьнъ, дєнь, днь. *dьnъ* (gen. pl.): дьнъ, дєнъ. **dьnьjь* (gen. pl.): дьньи, дьнии, днєи. *dьnьe* (nom. pl.): дьньє, дєньє, дєниє. *otьcь*: отьць, отьцъ, отєць, отєцъ. *pravьdьnъ*: правьдьнъ, правьдєнъ, правьдєн̇ (правєдєнъ §2.5241). *pravьdьna*: правьдьна, правєдьна, правєдъна. *tьmьno*: тьмьно, тьмно, тємьно. *podobьstvьju*: подобєствью. **jьmъ*: имъ, ємъ. *vьzьmъ*: въꙁьмъ, въꙁємъ, вьꙁємъ. **božьjь*: божьи, божии, божєи. *cěsarьstvьe*: цр҃єствьє. *prišьstvьe*: пришєствиє. *črьnьcь*: чрьньць, чрънєць, чрънєцъ. *skrьžьtъ*: скрьжьтъ, скръжєтъ. *skrьžьtanьe*: скрьжътаниє. *skrьžьšetъ*: скрьжьштєтъ,

скрежьштетъ. *отъ skvrьnьnъ pomyšljenьі*: **отъ скврънень помышленеи**. *kъto*: **къто, к҇то, кто**. *vъ njь* **вън҄ь, во нь**. *umьrъši*: **оумеръши**. *umьrъšь*: **оумьрьшъ, оумерошъ** (§2.6241). *mъnožьstvo*: **мъножъство, мьножъство, множство**. *ljubъvь*: **любовь**. *ljubъvi*: **любьви**. *sъtьnikъ*: **сътьникъ, сотьникъ, сьтьникъ**. *sъzьdanьe*: **съзъданье, создание**. **svętъjь*: **свѧтъи, свѧтыи, свѧтои**. *prědamь *jь* 'I will betray him': **прѣдамъ и, предамеи, прѣдамі і**.

Certain borrowings were adjusted to the native pattern; thus in Ps Sin the word 'psalm' is usually *psalomъ* or *pъsalomъ* (but loc. pl. *pъsalъměxъ*), implying older pъsal**ъ**mъ. On the whole, the presence or absence of a jer-letter within a consonant cluster in foreign words—particularly names—is of no linguistic significance.

2.70 Occasionally the symbols for the nasal vowels are replaced in the mss by some other vowel-letters, or they stand instead of some other letter. The invention of *jusy*—the letters for nasal vowels—and their generally correct use by OCS scribes (despite the variation in graphs) implies that the two nasal vowels were distinct phonemes in the language of the 9th century. The deviant spellings suggest both regional and historical dialect differences during the OCS period.[7]

2.701 Most modern Slavic dialects lack nasal vowels, except for Polish. In a small northwestern marginal zone of Slovenian (largely in Austria), and the southern periphery of Macedonian and Bulgarian (in Albania and northern Greece) systematic traces of OCS nasality remain. Though much is unclear about the course of divergent developments, it is certain that the old distribution of **ę* and **ǫ* was being modified during the 11th and 12th centuries. In Serbo-Croatian well before 1200 **ę* was replaced by *e,* and **ǫ* by *u*; northern Macedonian dialects shared these shifts.

2.71 Certain morphemes had nasal and non-nasal variants:
a. the roots **mud/*mǫd* (muditi/mǫditi 'be late', mudьnъ/mǫdьnъ 'tardy'),**nud/*nǫd* (nuditi/nǫditi 'to force', nužda/nǫžda 'force'), and **gnus/*gnǫs* (gnusiti/gnǫsiti 'be disgusted', gnusьnъ/gnǫsьnъ 'disgusting').
b. the stem **su-mьn/*sǫ-mьn* (sumьněti/sǫmьněti 'to doubt, suspect').
c. the verb *poměnǫti/pomęnǫti* 'remember'.

7 The two glagolitic symbols "eN" and "oN" for *ę* and *ǫ* may mistakenly be written without the second element "N". It is not easy to distinguish this kind of scribal error from a more purposeful scribal choice based on a copyist's own pronunciation: the historical change **ę* > *e* took place in many South Slavic dialects; *o* ultimately from **ǫ* is found in certain localities in Macedonia and Bulgaria, but it is improbable that it was present as early as the 12th century.

These surely represent individual adjustments in contexts with nasal consonants.

d. Variation in the borrowed stem *sǫbota*/*sobota* 'Sabbath, Saturday' is probably based on different Greek pronunciations. *Sǫbota* is usual; *sobota* is the only form in Mar, while both forms are in PsSin (3 *ǫ*, 4 *o*) and As (88+% *ǫ*). Vat has one **сѫботы** to perhaps 10 legible examples of **соб-**. This distribution probably reflects traditional spelling with "ǫ" versus a local authorization of "o" that was attenuated in later copies.

2.72 Variant spellings that point to individual dialects provide conflicting information. Thus Mar has some confusion between *ǫ* and *u* or *jǫ* and *ju* (e.g. Mar ljublj*u*, for ljublj*ǫ* 'I love', dat. sg. nem*ǫ*, for nem*u* 'to him') that imply a scribe from northern Macedonia or Serbia, regions where *u* < **ǫ*. But it also has instances of *ě* (gr*ě*di, for gr*ę*di 'come [imv. sg.]!'), suggesting the pronunciation of southern Macedonia. Perhaps the scribe of one of the copies of the model used for Mar introduced these southern deviations, while the scribe of Mar itself had the more northerly type of dialect. In Ps, *o* and *ǫ* are confused: p*o*tь, for p*ǫ*tь 'road'; s*ǫ*bojo, for soboj*ǫ* 'self (inst. sg.)'. For *ę* there are several cases where *e* is written (e.g. *ezyci*, for *ę*zyci 'tongues'); the opposite is extremely rare: im*ę*ni. The number of examples is small, however, and "correct" usage of these letters is one of the criteria for the antiquity of a manuscript.

The Ostromir Gospel of 1056–57 is excluded from the canon of OCS (§0.32) chiefly because the scribes clearly used ѫ and ѭ as equivalents of ѹ and ю, ѧ = а in certain positions, and ѩ = ꙗ, although in fact the number of "errors" is minimal. In phonological terms, **ǫ* merged with **u*, while **ę* remained a separate unit, redefined as a low front vowel /ä/ that was distinct from both /e/ (< ComSl **e*) and /ě/ (< ComSl **ě*).

2.73 In most Macedonian and Bulgarian regions the front/back distinction between /ę/ and /ǫ/ was preserved when the vowel followed a labial or dental consonant (the neutral consonants, §2.51), but was blurred or lost after palatals and /c ʒ/. In spelling, the letter "jǫ" (ѭ) may be replaced by "ję" (ѧ ѧ ѧ ѧ), while after spelled "č š ž št žd" or the "n l r" that represent /lj nj rj/ "ǫ" may be written "ę" (ѧ ѧ ѧ ѧ). The glagolitic manuscripts all have examples, but they are notable only in the glagolitic Assemanianus. Thus As *pomažętъ* (for *-ǫtъ*, 'they annoint' Mk 16:2), *lъžęšte* (for *-ǫšte* 'lying' Mt 5:11); *oblěšǫ* (for -aor. *-šę* 'they dressed' J 19:2). In J 8:44, *lъžę* (for *lъžǫ* acc. sg. 'lie') is potentially serious, since it involves meaning, but perhaps the scribe intended a plural; this sort of minor textual alteration is not uncommon.[8]

---

8 Mar J 21:6 has acc. sg. mrěžǫ 'net', while Zo As have pl. mrěžę; at the end of the verse, all three have ne možaaxǫ privlěšti *eę* 'they were not able to draw *it* in' (with gen. sg. of negation, §23.22)—this fits the singular of Mar (and the Greek) and marks Zo and As as "incorrect". More serious is Mt 19:9 in Vat, **творитъ ѩ прѣлюбы творити**, 'makes *them* commit adultery' instead of 'her' (see table on p. 63). This sort of confusion becomes more and more frequent in post-OCS manuscripts.

2.8 The letters for *ʒ* are absent from some manuscripts and written inconsistently in others. It is apparent that very early *ʒ* was replaced by *ź* in most of Slavdom (although *ʒ* has survived in Macedonian and Bulgarian dialects). The "soft" *ź* (§1.211) is not distinguished orthographically from a *z* of other origins.

MORPHOPHONEMICS

3.0 The smallest meaningful unit is a *morpheme*. Morphemes are thus the semantic building-blocks of words and sentences. A basic morpheme-shape is posited as a linguistic item in the lexicon. It consists of one or more phonemes, including zero (represented by Ø).

OCS words belong to two types; simple and complex. *Simple* words are at the same time morphemes and are invariable: most prepositions and conjunctions and some adverbs are of this type. *Complex* words have a stem and an inflectional suffix. A stem must contain a *root* morpheme and it may include one or more *affix*-morphemes—prefixes and suffixes.

Thus the word *bezmilostivъ* 'merciless (nom. sg. masc.)' consists of a prefix, a root, a noun-formant suffix, an adjective-formant suffix (which together constitute a meaningful lexical stem) and a case-gender-number inflectional suffix: bez-*mil*-ost-iv-ъ. In this book curly brackets will be used to signify underlying morphemes or morpheme-shapes: e.g. {bez-mil-ost-iv-ъ}. In this case, the theoretical underlying sequence is unchanged in the surface structure, though the syllable division in the pronounced word differs: *be.zmi.lo.sti.vъ*.[9] The word *istekǫtъ* '(they) will run out' consists of a prefix, a root, a zero verb-forming suffix, a present tense-marker that is coordinated with a person-marker to indicate plural: {iz-tek-Ø+ǫ-tъ}. Here the underlying structure has been modified: the surface phonology has [s] for {z} and of course nothing at all for {Ø}; five morphemes combine in four syllables, *i.ste.kǫ.tъ*.

3.1 Many surface morphemes have more than one shape, depending on the phonological environment. The environment differs chiefly because of different derivational or inflectional affixes that are used to create words.

Root-morphemes normally keep the underlying vowel in all inflected forms; different vowels usually indicate different lexical entries. The final

[9] Complex stems with two roots are called compounds, e.g. {mъnog-o+mil-ost-iv-ъ} 'greatly merciful'.

consonant(s) of a root may change to adapt to various suffixes. The root **rek**, for example, appears also as *reč, rьc-*, and *rě-* in different conjugational forms of the somewhat anomalous verb {rek-Ø+} 'to say' (where *zero* is a verb-forming suffix with null phonological content): ***rek**ǫtъ* 'they will say', ***reč**e* 'he said', ***rьc**i* 'say!', ***rě**xъ* 'I said' (whereby the last two shapes are somewhat irregular and need to be noted in the lexical entry for this verb). The variants *rok, roc-, roč-, ric-, rič-* and *rěk-* belong in derived words, such as pro***rok***ъ 'prophet' pl. pro***roc***i, voc. pro***roč***e!, prě***rěk***ati 'contradict', na***ric***ati 'to name', 3 sg. na***rič***etъ.

Prefix-morphemes, however, appear in different shapes as a morpheme-final consonant adapts to the root-initial consonant to which it is attached to make a new lexical word. Thus, for example, the prefix **iz** has alternate forms *izd-, is-* and *i-* (***iz***idǫtъ 'they will go out', ***izd***rekǫtъ 'they will express', ***is***pьjǫtъ 'they will drink', ***i***sъxnǫtъ 'they will dry up').

Suffix-morphemes often have alternating shapes used with different stem-final consonants. The alternating vowels are given in the lexicon. Thus, for example, the neuter nominative singular suffix for the twofold nominal declension is {o/e}, that is, *-o* in měst***o*** 'place' but *-e* in lic***e*** 'face'.

3.2 The permitted structure of OCS words in terms of syllables, consonant groups, and consonant+vowel sequences has been described above.

The underlying morphemic structure may violate some of the surface prescriptions; the differences are eliminated by generative rules.

3.21 Root-morphemes fit a formula ((((C)V)C)V)C. Thus all roots must end in a consonant. Only the pronominal roots *t-* 'that', **ś-* 'this' (see §4.201), *k-* 'who (interrogative)', and **j-* (§4.25) 'who, which (relative)' consist of a single consonant. Monosyllabic roots without initial consonant are few but include pronouns (*ov-* 'that yonder'), nouns (*ux-* 'ear', *ǫgl-* 'coal'), and verbs (*or-* 'plow'). The great majority of common roots have the shape CVC—where C may be a cluster—and many have two syllables, CVCVC.

3.22 Borrowed stems admit more varied structures, but behave like roots. If the stem in Greek ended in a vowel, the Slavic stem usually has *j*: marij-a Μαρία [mar'ia], *isajij-a Ἠσαΐας [isa'ias], *ijudej-ь or *ijuděj-ь Ἰουδαῖος [iud'eos]. See §4.12.

3.23 Except for borrowed stems, the consonant+vowel sequences within roots conform to §2.51.

3.24 The underlying morpheme {ьm} 'take' becomes {jьm} unless preceded by a consonant: vъzьmъ, but *jьmъ, *pojьmъ 'having taken (nom. sg. masc.)'. This contrast is obscured by the spelling, *imъ, poimъ*.

3.25 The morpheme {vъp} 'cry out' lacks the initial {v} when {vъz} is prefixed: imperfective vъpiti, but perfective vъzъpiti.

3.31 Changes in consonants take place at morpheme boundaries; they serve to adjust underlying sequences to the cluster-formula in §2.522. As a rule, if two adjacent elements are incompatible, the first adjusts to the second.

Adjustments at the prefix + stem boundary sometimes differ from those at the stem + desinence boundary.

3.3101 A few verbal roots prefix an *n* (the "epenthetic n") when combined with the prefixes *sъ* and *vъ*: **ьm-/ę-/emlj-* 'take'; *id-* 'go'; *ěd-* 'eat'. Thus sъ*n*ьmǫtъ, sъ*n*ęti, sъ*n*emljǫtъ, sъ*n*idǫtъ, sъ*n*ědętъ, vъ*n*ьmǫtъ, vъ*n*ęti, vъ*n*emljǫtъ, vъ*n*idǫtъ.

3.3102 Epenthetic n occurs after *vъ* with two nouns: (1) optionally with *uši* (dual) 'ears': vъ uši ~ vъ *n*uši 'into the ears'; and (2) if in direct contact with *ědra* (pl.) 'bosom': vъ *n*ědra moja ~ vъ svoja ědra.

3.3103 The stem of the third-person pronoun is *j-*, nom. sg. masc. {j-ь} spelled *i* (§1.24): gen. sg. masc. {jego}, spelled *ego*. In forms governed by a preposition, *j* is replaced by *nj*: otъ *nj*ego 'from him'.

3.311 The prepositions/prefixes *bez, vъz,* and *iz,* and the prefix *raz* adapt to the voicing and palatal specifications of the cluster:

z is lost before *s, z,* or *š*: e.g. raz+slabiti > raslabiti 'weaken'; vъz+zъvati > vъzъvati 'call'; iz+šьdъ > išьdъ 'having gone out'.

z + *ž* > *žd*: e.g. iz+ženǫtъ > iždenǫ ' I'll drive out'.

z > *s* before *p t k x*: e.g. i*z*iti 'to exit' but i*s*padati 'to fall out', i*s*točiti 'pour out', i*s*kopati 'dig out', i*s*xoditi 'go out'.

z before *č* either is lost, or else *zč* > *št*: e.g. {iz-čist-i+} > ičistiti or ištistiti 'purify, cleanse'; (bez-čisl-ьn-ъ} bečislьnъ or beštislьnъ 'innumerable'.

z before *c* either is lost, or else *zc* > *sc* or *st*: e.g. {iz-cěl-i+} > icěliti or iscěliti or istěliti 'heal'.[10]

z + *r* > *zdr*: e.g. {raz-rěš-i+} raz*d*rěšiti 'untie, free'.[11]

---

[10] Historically, the clusters *sč*, *ǯʒ*, and *sc* are to be expected. Shift of the affricate to stop would be normal. Loss of the initial sibilant is hard to explain. In stem-final position (where *sk* is followed by marked *i* or *ě*) the cluster *sc* may alternate with *st*, but the initial sibiliant always remains. All this variation surely reflects, in haphazard fashion, different regional and temporal dialects.

[11] The cluster *zr* is permitted in root-initial position, but not, apparently, across the morpheme boundary.

3.3111 OCS spelling suggests that these phonetic rules applied to prepositions and prefixes alike. For example: be*s* tebe 'without you', i*s* kraja 'from the end', vъ*s* krai 'on the edge', be*št*ęda 'without a child' (čęda), i*št*rěva/i-crěva 'from the bowels', i*s* crъkъve 'from church', i-crъkъvъ 'from churches', bez-*d*-razuma 'without understanding', iz-*d*-rěky 'from the river'; be-zъla 'without evil', be-srama 'without shame', i-syna 'from the tower', i-svoego domu 'from his house'. Modern editors must choose whether to leave the usual space after the preposition or to use hyphens or a combination of devices.

The scribes of the younger OCS manuscripts (chiefly the Suprasliensis) are inclined to preserve the visual aspect of the prefix/preposition morpheme, and frequently the *s* or *z* is written, sometimes followed by a non-etymological jer: e.g. be*z*ъ tъštety, be*z*ъ čisla, i*z*čazati, i*z*ъčeze, i*s* črěva, i*z*šedъ, i*s*šedъ, i*s*ъšedъ, i*z*ъ crъkъve, be*z*ъ razlǫky, i*z*ъrasti, ra*z*rušenie. Such spellings in part reflect a shift in orthographical rules, but they also imply that the complex changes of some forms had been abolished by reforming the word.

Spelled assimilation of the type i*ž* njego, be*ž* njego, and vъ*ž*ljubiti is extremely rare; the normal spellings are i*z* njego, be*z* njego, vъ*z*ljubiti.[12]

3.312 The prefix *ob* + *v*- > *ob*-: {ob-vlač-i+} > oblačiti 'wrap around', {ob-vьj-Ø+ti} > obiti 'wrap, wind around'. The cluster *bv* does not occur.

3.3121 The verb *ostǫpiti* means 'retreat, move back' but also 'besiege, surround', implying {ot-st-} vs. {ob-st-} with loss of the prefix-final consonant before obstruent. Further *okryti* 'open' and *oxoditi* 'surround' have doublets, *otъkryti* and *otъxoditi*. Apparently the obscurity of such forms led to a reformation of the prefixes to {obъ, obь} and {otъ}. As a general rule, *o*- before a consonantal root represents *ob*, but there are often doublets with a spelled consonant.

3.313 A root-final consonant comes to stand before a consonantal-initial suffix in stem-derivation (with the classifier {-nǫ+}), and in conjugation (l-participle, infinitive and supine). If the C is a sonorant, it may include the preceding vowel in the alternation: *ov* > *u*; *ьj*/*ij* > *i*; *ъj*/*yj* > *y*; ь + *nasal* > ę (see §11.212, §13.2).

---

12 Spelling which keeps a single visual image of a morpheme and ignores automatic phonemic changes is called morphophonemic (or, somewhat misleadingly, etymological). Russian is of this type, but treats some prefixes less consistently than did the pre-1917 rules, e.g. бесконечный, бессмертный vs. old безк-, безсм-. and the unchanging preposition in без конца, без смерти. Yet there is a limit to the degree of visual "distortion" allowed, e.g. old *безшумный*, new *бесшумный* but never бешшумный to show the real pronunciation. OCS spelling was apparently consistently phonemic at first, then began to make some use of morphophonemic principles.

3.3131 The obstruents behave variously. *S* and *z* remain (whereby *z* > *s* before *t*). Dental *t d* > *s* before *t*, but drop before *n* or *l*. Labial *p b* drop before *t*, remain before *l*, and do either before *n*. Velar *k g* combine with *t* in {šč}, remain otherwise.[13] That is:

a. Before *t*, the labials are deleted, while the dentals become *s*:
pt bt vt > *t*; *tt dt zt* > *st*. e.g. {tep-Ø+ti} > teti 'to beat', {živ-Ø+ti} > žiti 'to live'; {pad-Ø+ti} > pasti 'to fall', {lěz-Ø+ti} > lěsti 'go'.
Velar *k g* + *t* combine in *št*: {pek-Ø+ti} > pešti 'to cook', {mog-Ø+ti} > mošti 'to be able'. Note that this surface /št/–for underlying {šč}—is the special sequence that serves as a palatal unit.[14]

b. Before the *l* the labials and velars remain: {tep-Ø+l-i} > tepli '(they) beat', {greb-Ø+l-i} > grebli 'buried'.
The dentals are lost: *tl dl* > *l*: {plet-Ø+l-i} > pleli '(they) braided', {pad-Ø+l-i} > pali '(they) fell'. Note that this is a process limited to this particular morphological category; *tl* and *dl* occur in root-initial position.[15]

c. Before the *n* of {nǫ}, the labials either remain or are deleted, see §15.75.
The dentals are lost: *tn dn* > *n*.
The velars *k g x* remain, *kn gn xn*.

3.32 The possible CV combinations are defined by three groups of consonants (velars; *c* and *ʒ*; soft consonants, §2.51) and eight vowels which are limited as to which consonants they can follow. In specific grammatical morphemes these eight vowels are subdivided into *alternating* versus *non-alternating* morphophonemes. (The morphophonemes include units symbolized as i^2, $ě^2$, and y^2, which will be defined below.)

3.4 The major alternation in stem-final consonants is *palatalization* (or substitutive softening). There are two types: (I) a general or default process that occurs in derivation and inflection, and (II) a limited special process that occurs in declension (and rarely in conjugation) before morphophonemes that are specifically marked.

---

13 The preterite-marker *x* becomes *s* before *t*. See §10.11.

14 The historical process surely starts with voicing assimilation: **gt* > **kt*. The agreed-on formula for Middle Common Slavic is **tj*. For Southeast Late ComSl (or early Bulgaro-Macedonian) it is safe to posit *šč* and *žǯ* as the immediate forerunners of attested OCS *št*/*žd*.

15 For example, *dlъgъ* 'long', *dlanь* 'palm (of hand)'; *tlъkǫtъ* 'they drag'.

I. A velar {k g x} or {c ʒ} that stands before a front vowel {i ь e ě ę}, becomes palatal (č ž š) [*except that* {sk zg} > šč žǯ]

II UNLESS the front vowel is the marked {i²} or {ě²}, in which case {k g x} > c ʒ s [*whereby* {sk zg} > sc zʒ *or* st zd].[16]

Type I takes place before any front vowel that is not specially marked and it applies to *c* and *ʒ* as well as to *k g x*. Historically, it changed any velar before all front vowels; we may label it KI. At that time velars followed by a diphthong *ai* were not affected. Subsequently, *ai* became a front vowel (*i* or *ě*); the velars then adapted to these new front vowels, but in a different way. This second regressive palatalization (Type II) may be labelled KAI.

3.5 The *alternating* and *non-alternating* morphophonemes are these:

a. Three alternating morphophonemes are purely phonotactic: {ъ/ь}, {o/e}, and {y/i} choose the second or "soft" variant when they follow *c ʒ* or a soft consonant.

{otrok+ъ/ь}	>	otrokъ	'boy [Nsm]'	{měst+o/e}	>	město	'place [Nsn]'
{otьc+ъ/ь}	>	otьcь	'father [Nsm]'	{lic+o/e}	>	lice	'face [Nsn]'
{ključ+ъ/ь}	>	ključь	'key [Nsm]'	{morj+o/e}	>	morje	'sea [Nsn]'
{otrok+y/i}	>	otroky	'boys [Ip]'	{měst+y/i}	>	městy	'places [Ipn]'
{otьc+y/i}	>	otьci	'fathers [Ip]'	{lic+y/i}	>	lici	'faces [Ipn]'
{ključ+y/i}	>	ključi	'keys [Ip]'	{morj+y/i}	>	morji	'seas [Ipn]'

The tense jers or reduced *y/i*, (neutralization of *y* ~ ъ and *i* ~ ь in position before *j*, §2.61), also alternate in this way.

b. A fourth morphophoneme also has *y* as the basic or hard alternant; we will label it *y*², to show it belongs with the alternant *ę*: {y²/ę}. Thus, e.g.,

{otrok+y²/ę}	>	otroky	'boys [Apm]'	{rǫk+y²/ę}	>	rǫky	'hands [Apf]'
{otьc+y²/ę}	>	otьcę	'fathers [Apm]'	{ovьc+y²/ę}	>	ovьcę	'sheep [Apf]'
{ključ+y²/ę}	>	ključę	'keys [Apm]'	{duš+y²/ę}	>	dušę	'soul [Apf]'

These morphophonemes are lexical elements with specific grammatical meanings: for example, {o/e} serves as nominative singular neuter in the major declensional types, and as initial syllable in certain other substantival desinences (e.g. instrumental sing. {$^{o}/_{e}$mь}, {$^{o}/_{e}$jǫ}).

c. The vowel *ě* is idiosyncratic. Though a front vowel, it does not occur after the palatal consonants, but only after the neutral labials and

[16] The term for 'Easter' is spelled *Pasxa,* but surely was pronounced with /sk/, as in spoken Greek; the DL is *pascě* or *pastě*. The cluster *sx* occurs at a prefix-root boundary, eg. isxoditi {iz-xod-i+ti} 'go out', rasxytiti {raz-xyt-i+ti} 'steal, carry off'.

dentals and the special subgroup *c ʒ*. We may regard it as two underlying entities. The first is the basic or ("hard") alternant in {ě/a}, a morphophoneme that serves as a verb-making formant (§3.5c {sěd-ě/a+ti} > *sěděti* 'sit' vs. {stoj-ě/a+ti} > *stojati* 'stand') and in some derivational suffixes.

c1. This *ě*^{1} triggers KI (the First Regressive Palatalization) and then must become *a*: {kě gě xě} > *ča ža ša*. See §9.112.

c2. Underlying *ě*^{2} is correlated with *i*^{2} in {ě^2/i^2}, serving as the basic (or "hard") alternant. Both the non-alternating morphophoneme {i^2} and {ě^2/i^2} are specially marked to cause KAI palatalization in a preceding velar (*k g x*); {i^2} is the nominative plural masculine desinence of the twofold nominal declension and the singular imperative-marker in conjugation (§7.101); {ě^2/i^2} serves as the initial or only morphophoneme in several desinences of the HARD twofold nominal declension, and as a dual or plural imperative marker.

{otrok+i^2}	> otroci	'boys [Npm]'	{rǫk+ě^2/i}	> rǫcě	'hand [LDsf]'
{otьc+i^2}	> otьci	'fathers [Npm]'	{ovьc+ě^2/i}	> ovьci	'sheep [LDsf]'
{ključ+i^2}	> ključi	'keys [Npm]'	{duš+ě^2/i}	> duši	'soul [LDsf]'
{dъsk+ě^2/i}	> dъscě	'board [LDsf]'	{dręzg+ě^2/i}	> dręʒě	'woods [LDsf]'
or	> dъstě		or	> dręzdě	

Non-alternating {i^2} is distinct from nonalternating {i^1}, which is associated with KI mutation, the general type of palatalization ({ok-i} > *oči* Ndu 'eyes').

The surface sequences *cь ce cę cǫ ca cu* (and *ʒь ʒe* etc.) unambiguously signify stem-final *c ʒ* + vowel(-initial) desinence {ъ/ь, o/e, y/ę, ǫ, a, u}. The sequence *cě* (*ʒě*) is unambiguous in showing stem-final velar (*k g*) followed by the basic form of desinence-initial {ě^2/i^2}. In contrast, *ci* (*ʒi*) could be either a c/ʒ stem followed by {i^2} with the meaning Npm (e.g. *otьci, kъnęʒi* 'princes') or the soft alternant of a desinence with {ě^2/i^2} (e.g. Lp *otьcixъ, kъnęʒixъ*).[17]

d. These six alternating morphophonemes above evolved from single vowels or diphthongs that developed differently. The masculine vocative form has *-e* for "hard stems" **and** *c ʒ*, but *-u* for palatal stems. The {e/u} grammatical morpheme that belongs to OCS results from two historically diverse vocative desinences in pre-Slavic. For examples, see §4.11.

---

17 This assumes that forms like *cěna* 'price', *ʒělo* 'very', and *ocьtъ* 'vinegar' are based on lexically given stems of the type {cěn-a}, {ʒělo}, {ocьt-ъ). No verbal basic stem ends in *c ʒ*; the imperatives like *moʒi* 'be able' and *rьci, rьcěte* illustrate the singular vs. plural imperative marker, {i^2} vs. (ě^2/i^2}.

3.51 To summarize, here are the alternating vowel morphophonemes:

basic	o	ъ	y	y²	ě²	ě¹	e
"soft"	e	ь	i	ę	i²	a	u

3.6 A second process of substitutive softening is *iotation,* which involves the action of an underlying *j*. The *j* may be an underlying suffixal element, but in conjugation it is generated from an underlying *i, ě,* or *a* followed by a vowel. It is described in §6.13–6.23. Here is a summary:

pj	bj	vj	mj	tj	dj	cj	ʒj	sj	zj	kj	gj	xj	nj	lj	rj	stj	zdj	skj	zgj
пл̑	бл̑	вл̑	мл̑	щ	жд	ч	ж	ш	ж	ч	ж	ш	н̑	л̑	р̑	щ	жд	щ	жд

Notice that velars (*k g x*) and *c ʒ* are affected by iotation in precisely the same way as by KI (type I palatalization, §3.4).

3.61 A unique example shows *ǯʒ* for the expected *žd* (~ *d*). In Mk 1:6 the instrumental plural of the possessive adjective derived from *velbǫ**d**ъ* 'camel' is spelled *velьbǫ**žǯ**i* in Mar (but normal *velьbǫ**žd**i* in Zo As Sav).

3.62 The clusters *trj* and *drj* sometimes resisted iotation. Evidence is sparse, and complicated by the fact that scribes often fail to distinguish *rj* from *r*. Su has **съмоштрѫ** for expected sъmo*štrj*ǫ 'I look' {sъ-motr-i+ǫ}; 3p imperfect **съмотрааше** for -mo*štrj*aaše {-motr-i-ěaše}. The cluster *tvj* iotates to *štvlj,* though the *lj* often disappears in spelling (§2.521): e.g. from {u-mrьtv-i-aj+} 'mortify', pres. passive part. Npm *umrьštvlěemi* (Ps), but pres. act. part. Nsm *umrъštvěęi* (Euch). Variation doubtless reflects both regional and temporal dialect differences.

3.71 Labials (*p b m v*) are not themselves affected by *j*; it is the iod that changes—by becoming a unit liquid palatal, *lj,* see §2.521.

The clusters *plj blj mlj vlj* surely were standard OCS at the beginning, and efforts to spell *pj bj mj vj* in their place are to be interpreted as a change in scribal attitudes. Serbo-Croatian and Slovenian and East Slavic have this "epenthetic *l*" (to use the traditional term despite its misleading implication that *l* is inserted *between* labial and iod). Recorded West Slavic never had it, and modern Macedonian and Bulgarian lack it. The Vatican Cyrillic Gospel Lectionary generally avoids it. Post-OCS manuscripts from the Macedono-Bulgarian regions vacillate, but on the whole scribes tried to write *l* in accord with a tenacious tradition. Perhaps there were indeed regional dialects that supported such spellings; we lack unequivocal evidence for the history.

3.72 Underlying {v} usually behaves like a palatal obstruent, but the sequence {ov} generally becomes *u* before all consonants (cf. §15.841), including the *j* that is generated in the verbal classifier {ova/eva}. In i-verbs, *vj* has the same effect as the other labial consonants and the palatal *lj* results. See §6.21 with footnote.

3.721 Stem-final *xv* is unique to *vlъxvъ* 'magician'; the noun is subject to both types of palatalization: voc. *vlъšve*, Np *vlъsvi*. Before a suffixal front vowel in derivation, however, the two units become *š*: vlъšьba 'sorcery'.

3.8 The nominative singular desinence of comparatives, of certain participles (cf. §4.19), and of some anomalous substantives is a zero which has the effect of a consonant. Since a word must end in a vowel (§1.2301), the underlying final consonant must be deleted. Thus {nes-Ø+ъš-C} 'carrying' yields *nesъ*; {otrok-ęt-C} 'child [nom.-acc. sg. neut.]' > *otročę*. Sometimes the VC of the stem is modified before the final consonant is lost: {sěmen-C} 'seed [nom.-acc. sg. neut.]' > *sěmę*. These noun-forms are essentially irregular morphological forms that belong in the lexical definition of individual words. The masculine {kamen-C} 'stone' has Ns *kamy*. Other types are *ъv* ~ *y* ({crьk-ъv+C} > 'church' *crьky*), *er* ~ *i* ({mater-C} 'mother' > *mati*), *es* ~ *o* ({těl-es-C} 'body' > *tělo*. See pp. 73-74.

3.90 In the morphology of irregular verbs, and in derivation, there are many more alternations.[18] Here we will point out the chief vowel-alternations (and alternations involving both vowel and consonant) found in the various possible forms of a root which may occur in a single "family".[19] The majority of these root-vowel alternations exemplify an old process called vowel-gradation (or *ablaut* or *apophony*).

3.911 Perhaps the majority of roots have in some form the vowel *e*, which is taken as basic for the alternations; *e* may alternate on the one hand with *ě*, on the other with ь, and in still other forms there may be *o*. The *ě* and the *o* may in turn alternate with *a*, and the ь may alternate with *i*. Thus:

ě	←	**e**	→	ь	→	*i*
↓		↓				
a	←	*o*				

3.912 The alternations *e* ~ *o* and *ě* ~ *a* are {front ~ back}; *e* ~ *ě*, *o* ~ *a*, and ь ~ *i* are {lax ~ tense}; *e* ~ ь is {low ~ high}.[20] This is all complicated

18 Isolated alternations occur in the roots of irregular verbs: ъ ~ *u* (§15.643), *e* ~ ь (§15.644), o ~ ъ (§15.645), *o* ~ *ě* (§§16.53), *ě* ~ *ę* (§16.61), *e* ~ *ę* (§16.62), and perhaps *ъm* ~ *u* (§16.92).

19 "Family" is the term for all possible derivatives of a single root. The example of the root *rek-* given in § 3.1 above illustrates varying shapes of the root, but gives only a small percentage of the words in this particular family.

20 The historical terminology is different: *e* ~ *o* is the basic qualitative opposition, *ě* ~ *a* is "lengthened e-grade vs. lengthened o-grade"; *e* ~ ь is "normal vs. reduced grade", while ь ~ *i* is "reduced vs. lengthened reduced".

by the fact that if the theoretical vowel root was followed by a resonant (*r, l*; *m, n, nj*), forms with *e, o* and ь vary according to their position before vowel or consonant. Thus the combination *er* remained before vowel but became *rě* before consonant, i.e. *er/rě*; *em, en/ę*; *or/ra, ol/la, on/ǫ*; and *ьr/rь, ьl/lь, ьm/ę*. Cf. §16.5ff.

3.913 No root illustrates all the possibilities, and some roots have only one or two surviving forms. Here are some typical examples. Forms marked * are not attested in OCS but fit the old patterns and occur in slightly later mss.

*ved-: v**e**dǫtъ 'they are leading' – v**o**dętъ 'they lead' – v**ě**sъ 'I led' – prov**a**ždati sę 'be influenced'
*ber-: b**er**ǫ 'I gather' – br**ě**mę 'burden' – b**ьr**ati 'to gather' – sъb**ir**ati 'to gather' – sъb**or**ъ 'a gathering'
*mer-: um**rě**ti 'to die' – um**ьr**ǫ 'I shall die' – sъm**rь**tь 'death' – um**ir**ajǫ 'I'm dying' – um**or**iti 'kill' (P) – um**arj**ati 'kill' (I)
*pen: *p**ьn**ǫ 'I stretch' – prop**ę**ti 'crucify' (P) – prop**i**nati 'crucify' (I) – op**on**a 'curtain' – p**ǫ**ta 'fetter'
*zven-: zv**on**ъ 'a sounding noise' – *zv**ьn**ěti 'to sound' – *zv**ǫ**kъ 'sound'
*velk-: v**lě**kǫ 'I drag' – v**lь**kъ 'having dragged' – priv**la**čiti 'attract'

3.92 It is probable that this system was fairly vital in the language of Cyril and Methodius, although many of the alternations were represented only by a few lexical items. The jer-shift caused major readjustments, however, so that a number of the older relationships became obscured or lost entirely.

3.93 The alternations *o ~ a*, *ъ ~ y*, *ь ~ i*, and *e ~ ě* remained marginally productive in OCS in the formation of imperfective verbs. See the subdivisions of §5.7 for more examples:

o ~ a

u**kor**i-	u**karj**aj-	'reproach'	**kos**nǫ-	**kas**aj-	'touch'
o**moč**i-	o**mak**aj-	'moisten'	iz**bod**-	iz**bad**aj-	'stab'
svobodi-	**svobažd**aj-	'free'	sъ**gor**ě-	sъ**garj**aj-	'burn up'

ь ~ i

sъ**bьr**a-	sъ**bir**aj-	'collect'	sъ**zьd**a-	sъ**zid**aj-	'build'
po**mьn**ě-	po**min**aj-	'remember'	po**čьt**-	po**čit**aj-	'count, read'
vъ**zьm**-	vъz**im**aj	'take'	za**klьn**-	za**klin**aj-	'swear'

ъ ~ *y*

po**sъl**a-	po**syl**aj-	'send'	vъz**dъx**nǫ-	vъz**dyx**aj-	'sigh'

CHAPTER THREE

DECLENSION

4.00 The great majority of Old Church Slavonic words are inflected: their form changes to express different relationships. All inflected words consist of a *stem* plus an inflectional suffix—a *desinence*. (The stem may itself be complex—it must contain a *root,* and may contain prefixes and derivational suffixes—but this fact is not important for a discussion of inflection.) In the presence of different desinences, the stem may itself be modified; and conversely, certain desinences have different forms to adapt to different types of stems. Uninflected words are classified, on the basis of their syntactical functions, as adverbs, conjunctions, prepositions, particles, and interjections.

4.01 Inflected OCS words are of two major categories: *verbs* and *nouns*. The suffixes in both categories nearly always indicate **number**: *singular* (one), *dual* (two) or *plural* (three or more).

4.02 Nouns have different suffixes to express the relationships of the words to one another in the sentence, that is, **case**. There are six cases in OCS: *nominative, accusative, genitive, locative, dative,* and *instrumental*. Normally these are expressed by different desinences in singular and plural, but in the dual there are only three possible forms: a nominative-accusative, a genitive-locative, and a dative-instrumental. A separate *vocative* form exists for most masculine and feminine substantives in the singular; otherwise the nominative is used for an appeal.

4.021 Nouns are divided into three groups on the basis of their expression of gender and their declension-types: *substantives, adjectives,* and *pronouns*. Only substantives have an inherent, unchanging **gender** (*masculine, feminine,* or *neuter*). Other nouns have variable (or syntactic) gender, changing to agree with the substantives they modify in a given sentence. There are two types: *pronouns* do NOT follow the nominal declension, but have a special set of forms we call *pronominal* declension. Adjectives *may* follow the nominal declension and/or a compound declension combining elements of nominal and pronominal declension. Finally, there is the anomalous group of personal pronouns, which have no formal means of expressing gender, and which follow completely idiosyncratic declensions.

4.0211 A handful of words without declension or gender are defined as adjectives because of their syntactical use and their meanings: e.g. *isplьnь* 'full', *svobodь* 'free', *različь* 'different'. They all have synonyms which are inflected as adjectives (e.g. *plьnъ, svobodьnъ, različьnъ*).

4.03 The types of substantival declension generally correspond to gender, but there are outstanding exceptions. The dominant inflection-class, called here ***twofold nominal declension*** includes: (1) a masculine-neuter type and (2) a feminine type [with a few masculine members], both of which (a) may be used for adjectives as well as substantives, (b) have desinence-variants according to the palatal or non-palatal character of the stem-final consonant, and (c) are productive. Another inflection-class, (3) the ***simple nominal declension***, is restricted to substantives, most of them feminine. A series of minor types may be subsumed under this simple nominal declension, and called its ***anomalous*** *subtype*. Pronominal stems belong to another paradigm, (4) the ***pronominal declension***. Determined or compound adjectives have desinences combining those of (1+2 and 4); this paradigm may be called the ***compound*** or ***adjectival declension***.

The gender and declensional type of a substantive can usually be determined from the nom. sg. form. Substantives in *-o* or *-e* are neuter, twofold declension (e.g. *město* 'place', *srьdьce* 'heart'; exceptions in §4.414); those in *-a* are feminine [unless they refer to male persons], of the twofold declension (e.g. *žena* 'woman', *zemlja* 'land'; *vojevoda* 'general') . The few ending in *-nji* (usually spelled simply *-ni*) are also feminine, soft twofold, e.g. *rabynji* 'slave woman'. The nom. sg. desinence -ъ indicates masculine hard twofold. The front jer -ь implies masculine soft twofold (e.g. unless preceded by *-t,* in which case simple nominal feminine is probable (e.g. *kostь* 'bone') but masculine is possible (see list in §4.4032)—or else anomalous (listed in §4.412). The word-final letter *-i* preceded by a vowel-letter, indicates **j-ь* (§1.24), soft twofold masculine. Substantives in *-ę* are neuters of the anomalous type (e.g. *vrěmę* 'time'); those in *-y* are anomalous feminines (e.g. *ljuby* 'love').

4.04 The stem of every declinable word ends in a consonant. The stem is, by definition, the nominative singular of substantives or the nominative singular masculine (short form) of words with variable gender, minus the final vowel (*vlьk-ъ* 'wolf', *žen-a* 'woman', *měst-o* 'place', *on-ъ* 'he, that one'). If the removal of the final vowel-letter leaves a vowel-letter, then the phonological stem ends in *j* (kra*i* = *kraj-ь* 'edge'; pitь*e* = *pitьj-e* 'drink', stru*ě* строуꙗ = *struj-a* 'stream').

4.05 If the final stem-consonant is **š, ž, č, j, lj, nj, rj, c, +** *or the groups* ***št*** or ***žd***, the stem will be called *soft*; all other stems are *hard*. The desinences may vary accordingly. The basic underlying form is the *hard* (or neutral) desinence; the *soft* form is selected for soft stems. Here are the possible morphophonemes that occur in the twofold nominal and pronominal declensions:

invariable	a	u	ǫ	i^2	hard	o	ъ	ě^2	y	y^2	hard
					soft	e	ь	i^2	i	ę	soft

In addition there is the idiosyncratic *e/u* of the vocative (see §3.5d). When desinences beginning with *i*^{2} or *ě*^{2} are added to stems in *k, g, x, c,* or *ʒ*, the stem-consonant undergoes KAI (substitutive softening of type II); before the desinence *-e* these stem-consonants undergo KI (substitutive softening of type I), see §4.11, below.

4.1 The twofold nominal declension.

In the table the slash (/) separates the suffix for the *hard* declension (given first) from that of the soft, when there is any difference.

	SINGULAR			DUAL			PLURAL			
	masc	neut	fem	masc	neut	fem	masc	neut	fem	
Nom	**-ъ/-ь**	**-o/-e**	**-a**	**-a**	**-ě/-i**		**-i**	**-a**	**-y^2/-ę**	N
Acc			**-ǫ**				**-y^2/-ę**			A
Gen	**-a**		**-y^2/-ę**	**-u**			**-ъ/-ь**			G
Loc	**-ě/-i**		**-ě/-i**				**-ěxъ/-ixъ**		**-axъ**	L
Dat	**-u**			**-oma/-ema**		**-ama**	**-omъ/-emъ**		**-amъ**	D
Instr	**-omь/-emь**		**-ojǫ/-ejǫ**				**-y/i**		**-ami**	I
Voc	**-e/-u**	=N/A	**-o/-e**	= N/A			= N/A			V
	masc	neut	fem	masc	neut	fem	masc	neut	fem	

4.101 Note that in spelling, stem-final *j* + ь or *i* merges in "i" (§2.625): Nsm (and Gp) **krajь* > *krai,* **краи**, Np (and L sing. and pl.) **kraji* > *krai,* **краи.**

Velar stems undergo KAI-softening in Ls, Ds fem., NAdu. neut./fem., Lp masc./neut (before {ě/i}), and Np masc. (before {i}).

Velar and *c ʒ* stems undergo KI-softening in the vocative (sing.), because the basic shape of {e/u} is a front vowel, see §4.11, below.

4.1011 Historically the soft feminines contained a CV formant with the shape **jā*, and the soft masculines and neuters had a similar formant with a variable vowel *e* or *o*, **je*/**jo*. In early Slavic the morphemic segmentation changed; the **j* was perceived as part of the stem, and the vowel took on the role of desinence (or first unit of a desinence): e.g. pre-Slavic **lug-jā* became **lъg-j+a* > OCS *lъža* 'lie' (cf. infinitive {lъg-a+ti} 'to lie'). In traditional OCS descriptions therefore the hard feminines are *a*-stems, the soft are *ja*-stems. Similarly the masculines and neuters are *o*-stems (hard) and *jo*-stems or *je*-stems. Here we will speak of *a*-stems and *o*-stems, hard or soft.

4.102 Note that in stems ending in -ij-, the *i* of the stem represents the tense ь (cf. §2.61) and may be so written: pьsan*i*e/pьsanье "writing", gen. sg. masc. zm*i*ja/zmьja 'snake', gen. sg. fem. lad*i*ę/ladьę 'boat'.

4.1021 Here belong a few adjectives with stems in -*ьj*. The most important are *velьi*/*velii* 'great' and *božьi*/*božii* 'God's, divine'. Note that in nom. sg. masc. and gen. pl. the tense strong ь (*-**ь**jь) may be written *e*: *božei, velei* (cf. §2.51, 2.525).

4.1022 A number of formally singular substantives in *ье* or *ьja* are collectives, to be translated as plurals: e.g. *trьnье* 'thorns', *kamenье* 'stones', *korenье* 'roots', *roždье* or *raždье* 'branches', *bratrьja* or *bratьja* 'brothers'.

4.11 The formation of the *vocative*. Masc. and fem. nouns of this declension have special forms for calling or addressing—the vocative. The desinences are -*o*/-*e* for the feminine (*ženo* 'woman', *děvice* 'maiden'), and the highly unusual alternants *e*/*u* for the masculine.

The basic variant used with non-palatal stems is the front-vowel *e*, which is accompanied by KI mutation in velars and c and ʒ: e.g. *vlьkъ* ~ *vlьče, bogъ* ~ *bože, duxъ* ~ *duše; otьcь* 'father' ~ *otьče, kъnęʒь* 'prince' ~ *kъnęže*. Palatal stems regularly take -*u* (*mǫžь* 'man' ~ *mǫžu, cěsarjь* 'king' ~ *cěsarju, zmii* 'snake' ~ *zmiju*).

Masculine adjectives sometimes take the regular *e*-desinence, but more often the nominative of the compound declension is used in vocative function; cf. §17.1.

Some variation is to be explained by innovating forms. *Synъ* 'son' occasionally has archaic *synu* beside regularized *syne* (cf. §4.145). Su 155.18 has regular кнѧже, and in the same speech кнѧꙃоу (Su 156.8); apparently ʒ was in competition with a newer **ź* (§2.8) that calls for the "soft" desinence.

4.12 Foreign words of masculine gender (especially names) may have stems ending in a vowel. Probably a *j* was added in conformity with the requirement that declensional stems must end in a consonant. The vowels *ъ, y*, or *ě* cannot stand in post-vocalic position, and the soft variant regularly appears: 'Pharisee' (Greek [farise-os]) thus has *farisei* (Ns and Gp *-*ejь*; Ls, nom. and instr. pl. *-*eji*). The Ap *fariseę* surely—and Gs *farisea*, Ds *fariseu* probably—may represent -*eję* (-*eja*, -*eju*), but the Ds *fariseovi*, instr. sg. *fariseomь* and Dp *fariseomъ* seem to introduce a sequence of vowels not found in native words. The variegated spellings of such words indicate disagreements that very likely include pronunciation.

4.13 Masculine substantives indicating male persons use the genitive singular forms in accusative function, as do pronouns and adjectives referring to such substantives: *člověkъ* 'man' – gen./acc. *člověka*. Usage fluctuates with such words as *bogъ* 'god', *angelъ* 'angel', *duxъ* 'spirit', *rabъ* 'slave', *otrokъ* 'child, servant', and words referring to animals. See §18.21.[1]

4.14 Masculine substantives indicating persons may have beside the regular *-u* desinence of dat. sg. an alternative *-ovi/-evi*: *synu* or *synovi* 'son', *vraču* or *vračevi* 'doctor'. Sometimes this desinence appears with words that do not refer to persons (*mirovi* 'to the world', *adovi* 'to hell'), possibly conveying a sense of personification.

4.141 Certain masculine nouns with monosyllabic stems may have in the gen. or loc. sg. (or both) the desinence *-u* beside the normal *-a*. Attested with *-u* in these cases are chiefly: *synъ* 'son', *domъ* 'house', *volъ* 'ox', *polъ* 'half'; but also *vrьxъ* 'top', *glasъ* 'voice', *grъmъ* 'bush', *darъ* 'gift', *dlьgъ* 'debt', *dǫbъ* 'oak', *medъ* 'honey', *mirъ* 'world', *rodъ* 'race', *rędъ* 'row', *sanъ* 'rank', *stanъ* 'camp', *synъ* 'tower', *činъ* 'rank', *jadъ* 'poison'.

4.142 Certain monosyllabic masculines occasionally have (beside the normal nom. pl *-i* and the gen. *-ъ/-ь*) bisyllabic desinences, nom. *-ove/-eve*, gen. *-ъ/-ь*. Examples are attested for: *synъ* 'son', *domъ* 'house', *volъ* 'ox', *polъ* 'half', *vračь* 'doctor', *gadъ* 'vermin', *grozdъ* 'grape', *grěxъ* 'sin', *zmii* 'snake', *sadъ* 'planting'. Supr has several more words with such desinences, but it is probable that they belong to a later stage of development.[2]

4.143 Some of these same stems (§4.142) occur with *-oxъ* in Lp (beside normal *-ěxъ*), and/or *-ъmi* in Ip. (beside normal *-y*): *synoxъ, synъmi*.

4.144 The same stems rarely have alternate dual forms: NA *-y* (beside *-a*), GL *-ovu* (beside *-u*), DI *-ъma* (beside *-oma*): *syny, synovu, synъma*.

4.145 These optional suffixes (§§4.14-4.144) must be listed in the OCS lexical entries for the individual substantives. They are remnants of what in early Slavic was surely an independent paradigm, traditionally called "*u*-stems". Some of the desinences began to spread to former *o*-stems; comparative evidence from medieval manuscripts and modern dialects does not suffice to identify the early status of many items. *Synъ* 'son' is best attested and at the same time impeccably documented as an ancient *u*-stem (e.g. by Sanskrit *sūnuš*): NA sg *synъ*, GL *synu*, D *synovi*, I sg **synъmь*; Voc. *synu*; NA du. *syny*, GL *synovu*, DI *synъma*; Np

---

1 It is probable that the earliest texts used the gen.-acc. only for substantives indicating a healthy, free, male person; the sick, the crippled, the enslaved, and the supernatural did not count. Surviving manuscripts record a continuing expansion to include all animate masculine singulars; see §18.21.

2 Modern Bulgarian, Macedonian, and eastern Serbo-Croatian use the *-ov-/-ev-* suffix in forming the plural of the great majority of monosyllabic masculines.

synove, Ap *syny;* G *synovъ;* L *synoxъ* (for **synъxъ*), I *synъmi*. Some of these desinences were later lost, others redistributed differently in various dialects. Sometimes a desinence could acquire a special meaning, e.g. the "personal dative" of OCS (§4.14).[3]

4.15 Beside the regular instrumental sing. masc. neut. desinences *-omь/-emь,* there are occurrences of *-ъmь/-ьmь*. They are the only forms in the Kiev Folia; in other mss they are rare and may be simply scribal errors. It is likely that such desinences were characteristic of dialects in Morava and fairly certain for Rus' (they are normal in 11th-century Rus' mss). Neuter stems in *-ij* and adjectives like *božьi,* and *velьi* (§4.1021) occasionally have Is *-iimь* (< *-*ьjьmь*) or a contracted *-imь*.

4.16 A number of substantives that belong formally to the *a*-declension, which is the typically feminine paradigm, are necessarily of masculine gender because they signify grown male persons: *vladyka* 'ruler, lord', *sluga* 'servant', *junoša* 'young man', *prědъteča* 'forerunner', *ǫžika* 'relative' (also functions as feminine), *ubiica* 'murderer', *vinopiica* 'winebibber'. When the stem is in *-ij/-ьj-* the Ns is normally *-ii* (*sǫdii* 'judge', *balii* 'doctor'), while foreign personal names had *-ija/-ьja* (e.g. *Josija* 'Josiah', cf. also *mesija* 'messiah'). These words follow the *a*-declension, hard or soft (except that names in *-ьja/-ija* have Is in *-emь*; e.g. *Isaiemь* 'Isaiah'). Vocatives have *-o/-e*: *vladyko, junoše, sǫdije*.

They have the normal accusative in *-ǫ,* but note that the pronouns and adjectives referring to them take the genitive masculine form (cf. §4.13); e.g. самого владꙑкѫ 'the lord himself' Su 491/5, юношѫ красьна 'a handsome youth' Su 187.3.

When these *a*-masculines are in the plural, modifiers tend to be feminine in form, e.g. dat. pl. *starěišinamъ galileiskamъ* 'chiefs of Galilee' (Mk 6:21).

4.17 Beside the normal instr. sg. fem. desinence *-ojǫ/-ejǫ*, there are occasional forms in *-ǫ* (*rǫkojǫ* and *rǫkǫ*), especially in the Suprasliensis.

4.18 Some feminine substantives have Ns in *-i* (rather than *-a*). Here belong all with the derivative suffix *-ynj-* (e.g. *rabynji* 'female slave', *bogynji* 'goddess', *pustynji* 'desert, wilderness') and most with stems in *-ij/-ьj* (e.g. *ladii* 'boat', *krabii* 'box', *mlъnii* 'lightning'), although there are a few nominatives in *-ija/-ьja* (*bratrьja* 'brothers, brethren', and names like *Marija*).

The numeral *tysęšti* '1000' also belongs here.

Mati 'mother' and *dъšti* 'daughter' belong to another declension; see §4.423, below.

---

[3] Vaillant departs from his descriptive framework by treating these words separately, although he makes it clear that there is not a separate paradigm. He provides details of attestation for both hypothetical ancient *u*-stems and substantives of less clear provenience, §§58-59.

For adjectival forms with *-i* in nom. sg. feminine, see §4.19.

Twofold declension paradigms

Masculines: hard-stems *gradъ* 'city'; *člověkъ* 'man';
soft-stems: *mǫžь* 'man'; *otьcь* 'father'

Sing.	N	градъ	чловѣкъ	мѫжь	отьць
	A	градъ	чловѣка	мѫжа	отьца
	G	града	чловѣка	мѫжа	отьца
	L	градѣ	чловѣцѣ	мѫжи	отьци
	D	градоу	чловѣкоу -ови	мѫжоу -еви	отьцоу -еви
	I	градомь	чловѣкомь	мѫжемь	отьцемь
	V	граде	чловѣче	мѫжоу	отьче
Dual	NA	града	чловѣка	мѫжа	отьца
	GL	градоу	чловѣкоу	мѫжоу	отьцоу
	DI	градома	чловѣкома	мѫжема	отьцема
Plur.	N	гради	чловѣци	мѫжи	отьци
	A	грады	чловѣкы	мѫжѧ	отьцѧ
	G	градъ	чловѣкъ	мѫжь	отьць
	L	градѣхъ	чловѣцѣхъ	мѫжихъ	отьцихъ
	D	градѣмъ	чловѣцѣмъ	мѫжимъ	отьцимъ
	I	грады	чловѣкы	мѫжи	отьци

Neuters: hard-stem *město* 'place';
soft-stems: *srьdьce* 'heart'; *znamenьe* 'sign'

Sing.	NA	мѣсто	срьдьце	ꙁнаменье	-ие
	G	мѣста	срьдьца	ꙁнаменьꙗ	-иꙗ
	L	мѣстѣ	срьдьци	ꙁнаменьи	-ии
	D	мѣстоу	срьдьцоу	ꙁнаменью	-ию
	I	мѣстомь	срьдьцемь	ꙁнаменьемь	-иемь
Dual	NA	мѣстѣ	срьдьци	ꙁнаменьи	-ии
	GL	мѣстоу	срьдьцоу	ꙁнаменью	-ию
	DI	мѣстома	срьдьцема	ꙁнаменьема	-иема
Plur.	NA	мѣста	срьдьца	ꙁнаменьꙗ	-иꙗ
	G	мѣстъ	срьдьць	ꙁнаменьи	-ии
	L	мѣстѣхъ	срьдьцихъ	ꙁнаменьихъ	-иихъ
	D	мѣстомъ	срьдьцемъ	ꙁнаменьемъ	-иемъ
	I	мѣсты	срьдьци	ꙁнаменьи	-ии

Feminines: hard-stems *žena* 'woman, wife', *rǫka* 'hand';
soft-stem *duša* 'soul'; and the masculine *sǫdii* 'judge'.
(for fem. and a-masculines with Ns in *-ьji/-iji*)

Sing.	N	жена	рѫка	доуша	сѫдьи	-ии
	A	женѫ	рѫкѫ	доушѫ	сѫдьѭ	-иѭ
	G	жены	рѫкы	доушѧ	сѫдьѩ	-иѩ
	LD	женѣ	рѫцѣ	доуши	сѫдьи	-ии
	I	женоѭ	рѫкоѭ	доушеѭ	сѫдьеѭ	-иеѭ
	V	жено	рѫко	доушє	сѫдьє	-иє
Dual	NA	женѣ	рѫцѣ	доуши	сѫдьи	-ии
	GL	женоу	рѫкоу	доушоу	сѫдью	-ию
	DI	женама	рѫкама	доушама	сѫдьꙗма	-иꙗма
Plur.	NA	жены	рѫкы	доушѧ	сѫдьѩ	-иѩ
	G	женъ	рѫкъ	доушь	сѫдьи	-ии
	L	женахъ	рѫкахъ	доушахъ	сѫдьꙗхъ	-иꙗхъ
	D	женамъ	рѫкамъ	доушамъ	сѫдьꙗмъ	-иꙗмъ
	I	женами	рѫками	доушами	сѫдьꙗми	-иꙗми

Adjectives: hard-stem *novъ* 'new'; soft-stem *ništь* 'poor'.

<table>
<tr><th></th><th></th><th>masc.</th><th>neut.</th><th>fem.</th><th>masc.</th><th>neut.</th><th>fem.</th><th></th></tr>
<tr><td rowspan="6">Sing.</td><td>N</td><td>новъ</td><td rowspan="2">ново</td><td>нова</td><td>ништь</td><td rowspan="2">ништє</td><td>ништа</td><td>N</td></tr>
<tr><td>A</td><td>=N or G</td><td>новѫ</td><td>=N or G</td><td>ништѫ</td><td>A</td></tr>
<tr><td>G</td><td colspan="2">нова</td><td>новы</td><td colspan="2">ништа</td><td>ништѧ</td><td>G</td></tr>
<tr><td>L</td><td colspan="2">новѣ</td><td rowspan="2">новѣ</td><td colspan="2">ништа</td><td rowspan="2">ништи</td><td>L</td></tr>
<tr><td>D</td><td colspan="2">новоу</td><td colspan="2">ништоу</td><td>D</td></tr>
<tr><td>I</td><td colspan="2">новомь</td><td>новоѭ</td><td>ништємь</td><td colspan="2">ништєѭ</td><td>I</td></tr>
<tr><td rowspan="3">Dual</td><td>NA</td><td>нова</td><td colspan="2">новѣ</td><td>ништа</td><td colspan="2">ништи</td><td>NA</td></tr>
<tr><td>GL</td><td colspan="3">новоу</td><td colspan="3">нништоу</td><td>GL</td></tr>
<tr><td>DI</td><td colspan="3">новома новама</td><td colspan="2">ништєма</td><td>ништама</td><td>DI</td></tr>
<tr><td rowspan="6">Plur.</td><td>N</td><td>нови</td><td rowspan="2">нова</td><td rowspan="2">новы</td><td rowspan="2">ништи
ништѧ</td><td rowspan="2">ништа</td><td rowspan="2">ништѧ</td><td>N</td></tr>
<tr><td>A</td><td>новы</td><td>A</td></tr>
<tr><td>G</td><td colspan="3">новъ</td><td colspan="3">ништь</td><td>G</td></tr>
<tr><td>L</td><td colspan="2">новѣхъ</td><td>новахъ</td><td colspan="2">ништихъ</td><td>ништахъ</td><td>L</td></tr>
<tr><td>D</td><td colspan="2">новомъ</td><td>новамъ</td><td colspan="2">ништємъ</td><td>ништамъ</td><td>D</td></tr>
<tr><td>I</td><td colspan="2">новы</td><td>новами</td><td colspan="2">ништи</td><td>ништами</td><td>I</td></tr>
</table>

4.19 The comparatives, the present active participles, and the (first) past active participles follow the twofold nominal declension for their non-definite form (see §4.31 for definite forms), but their nominative and accusative forms in singular and plural are special. The feminine nom. sg. has the desinence *-i* (cf. §4.18) and the full stem; the masc. and neut. have a shortened stem. The following tables summarizes these cases:

Comparative

	m sg	n sg	f sg	m pl	n pl	f pl	
Nom	**-ьi (-ь)**	**-e**	**-ьši**	**-ьše**	**-ьša**	**-ьšę**	Nom
Acc	**-ьšь**		**-ьšǫ**	**-ьšę**			Acc
stem for other forms				**-ьš-**			stem

Past Active Participle

	m sg	n sg	f sg	m pl	n pl	f pl	
Nom	**-ъ**		**-ъši**	**-ъše**	**-ъša**	**-ъšę**	Nom
Acc	**-ъšь**	**-ъše**	**-ъšǫ**	**-ъšę**			Acc
stem for other forms				**-ъš-**			stem

Present Active Participle (*ǫ ~ e* present)

	m sg	n sg	f sg	m pl	n pl	f pl	
Nom	**-y**		**-ǫšti**	**-ǫšte**	**-ǫšta**	**-ǫštę**	Nom
Acc	**-ǫštь**	**-ǫšte**	**-ǫštǫ**	**-ǫštę**			Acc
stem for other forms				**-ǫšt-**			stem

Present Active Participle (*ę ~ i* present)

	m sg	n sg	f sg	m pl	n pl	f pl	
Nom	**-ę**		**-ęšti**	**-ęšte**	**-ęšta**	**-ęštę**	Nom
Acc	**-ęštь**	**-ęšte**	**-ęštǫ**	**-ęštę**			Acc
stem for other forms				**-ęšt-**			stem

4.191 When the comparative stem ends in *-ěj-*, the nom. sg. masc. is spelled *-ěi* (for **-ěj-ь*), neut. *-ěe*: *nověi nověe* 'newer', *starěi* starěe 'older'. The rest of the paradigm has the full suffix *-ěiš-* (**-ějьš-*) before the desinences (*nověiš-a*, etc.). Otherwise the nom. sg. masc. is spelled *-ьi* or *-ii* (for **-ьj-ь*), the neuter *-e, and* the rest *-ьš-*: e.g. *boljьi* or *boljii*, *bolje ~ boljьš-a* etc. 'bigger'; *vęštьi* or *vęštii vęšte ~ vęštьš-a* etc. 'greater'. For the formation of the comparative, see §4.7.

4.192 The two sets of formants for the present active participle are correlated to the shape of the present-markers (cf. §6.11). Verbs with *-ętъ* in the 3 pl pres. have *-ęšt-* as participial formant; in nom. sing. masc. (with *zero* desinence) it reduces to *-ę*. Verbs with *-ǫtъ* in 3 pl. pres. have *-ǫšt-* as participial formant, which is replaced in nom. sg. masc. by the variable {y/ę}: *-ę* appears after a soft (truncated) stem, *-y* otherwise. E.g. *prosi-ti prosętъ* 'beg' ~ *prosę* (mn) *prosęšti* (f.); *nes-ti nes-ǫtъ* 'carry' ~ *nesy* (mn) *nesǫšti* (f); *plaka-ti plačǫtъ* 'weep' ~ *plačę* (mn) *plačǫšti* (f).

4.193 In past active participial stems ending in a soft consonant, the -ъ- of the suffix is everywhere replaced by -ь-: *prošь, prošьši, prošьše,* etc.

4.194 Variants: Occasionally the accusative form of masc. and neut. participles is used as nominative. Conversely, the comparative nom. sing. masc. in *-ьi/-ii* often serves as acc. sg.; in both instances the tendency is to have a single form for nominative/accusative singular masculine, as do other declined words. In comparatives, the *-e* of nom. pl. is sometimes replaced by the usual nominal desinence *-i*, e.g. *lučьši* for *lučьše* 'better'.

Examples of **comparatives** (*vęštьi vęštьš-* 'bigger', *nověi nověiš-* 'newer'), **present active participles** (*nesy nesǫšt-* 'carrying', *vęžę vęžǫšt-* 'tying', *prosę prosęšt-* 'begging') and **past active partiple** (*nesъ nesъš-* 'having carried'). The other case-forms are like *ništь*, see above.

<table>
<tr><td></td><td>masculine</td><td>neuter</td><td>feminine</td><td>masculine</td><td>neuter</td><td>feminine</td><td></td></tr>
<tr><td>N sg</td><td>вѧштьи</td><td rowspan="2">вѧштє</td><td>вѧштьши</td><td>новѣи</td><td rowspan="2">новѣє</td><td>новѣиши</td><td>Nsg</td></tr>
<tr><td>A sg</td><td>вѧштьшь</td><td>вѧштьшѫ</td><td>новѣишь</td><td>новѣишѫ</td><td>Asg</td></tr>
<tr><td>N pl</td><td>вѧштьшє</td><td rowspan="2">вѧштьша</td><td rowspan="2">вѧштьшѧ</td><td>новѣишє</td><td rowspan="2">новѣиша</td><td rowspan="2">новѣишѧ</td><td>Npl</td></tr>
<tr><td>A pl</td><td>вѧштьшѧ</td><td>новѣишѧ</td><td>Apl</td></tr>
<tr><td></td><td colspan="2">stem for other forms</td><td>вѧштьш-</td><td colspan="2">новѣиш-</td><td>stem</td><td></td></tr>
</table>

<table>
<tr><td></td><td>masculine</td><td>neuter</td><td>feminine</td><td>masculine</td><td>neuter</td><td>feminine</td><td></td></tr>
<tr><td>N sg</td><td>несꙑ</td><td rowspan="2">несѫштє</td><td>несѫшти</td><td>вѧжѧ</td><td rowspan="2">вѧжѧ</td><td>вѧжѫшти</td><td>Nsg</td></tr>
<tr><td>A sg</td><td>несѫшть</td><td>несѫштѫ</td><td>вѧжѫшть</td><td>вѧжѫштѫ</td><td>Asg</td></tr>
<tr><td>N pl</td><td>несѫштє</td><td rowspan="2">несѫшта</td><td rowspan="2">несѫштѧ</td><td>вѧжѫштє</td><td rowspan="2">вѧжѫшта</td><td rowspan="2">вѧжѫштѧ</td><td>Npl</td></tr>
<tr><td>A pl</td><td>несѫштѧ</td><td>вѧжѫштѧ</td><td>Apl</td></tr>
<tr><td></td><td colspan="2">stem for other forms</td><td>несѫшт-</td><td colspan="2">вѧжѫшт-</td><td>stem</td><td></td></tr>
</table>

<table>
<tr><td></td><td>masculine</td><td>neuter</td><td>feminine</td><td>masculine</td><td>neuter</td><td>feminine</td><td></td></tr>
<tr><td>N sg</td><td>просѧ</td><td rowspan="2">просѧ</td><td>просѧшти</td><td>несъ</td><td rowspan="2">несъшє</td><td>несъши</td><td>Nsg</td></tr>
<tr><td>A sg</td><td>просѧшть</td><td>просѧштѫ</td><td>несъшь</td><td>несъшѫ</td><td>Asg</td></tr>
<tr><td>N pl</td><td>просѧштє</td><td rowspan="2">просѧшта</td><td rowspan="2">просѧштѧ</td><td>несъшє</td><td rowspan="2">несъша</td><td rowspan="2">несъшѧ</td><td>Npl</td></tr>
<tr><td>A pl</td><td>просѧштѧ</td><td>несъшѧ</td><td>Apl</td></tr>
<tr><td></td><td colspan="2">stem for other forms</td><td>просѧшт-</td><td colspan="2">несъш-</td><td>stem</td><td></td></tr>
</table>

4.2 The pronominal declension.

	Singular			Dual			Plural			
	masc.	neut.	fem.	masc.	neut.	fem.	masc.	neut.	fem.	
N	**-ъ/-ь**	**-o/-e**	**-a**	**-a**	**-ě/-i**		**-i**	**-a**	**-y/-e**	N
A			**-ǫ**				**-y/-ę**			A
G	**-ogo/-ego**		**-oję/-eję**	**-oju/-eju**			**-ěxъ/-ixъ**			G
L	**-omь/-emь**		**-oi/-ei**							L
D	**-omu/-emu**			**-ěma/-ima**			**-ěmъ/-imъ**			D
I	**-ěmь/-imь**		**-ojǫ/-ejǫ**				**-ěmi/-imi**			I

4.201 This is the declension of the pronouns *tъ* 'this', *onъ* 'that', *ovъ* 'this close by', *inъ* 'another', *kъ-žьdo* 'each', *samъ* 'self', *edinъ* 'one, alone', *eterъ* 'a certain', *kakъ* 'of what kind?', *nikakъ že* 'no (kind of)', *někakъ* '(of) some (kind)', *inakъ* 'of another kind', *jakъ* 'of this kind', *takъ* '(of) such (kind)', *vьsakъ* or *vьsěkъ* 'every', **jь* 'he' (*i-že* 'he who'), *moi* 'my', *tvoi* 'thy', *svoi* 'one's own', *našь* 'our', *vašь* 'your' *čii* 'whose', and the numerals which have only dual forms: *dъva* 'two' and *oba* 'both'.

The stems *s-* 'this' and *vьs-* 'all' are anomalous and seem to have a "soft" /ś/. See §4.21 for *vьsь* (**vьś-*) and *sicь* 'of this kind', §4.22 for *sь* (**śь*).

4.2011 *Tuždь* 'foreign, alien' has pronominal and compound forms: see §4.321.

4.2012 *Kotoryi* 'which', *někotoryi* 'a certain' and *nikotoryi* 'none' belong to the compound declension.

4.202 The desinences for nominative and accusative are the same as in the twofold nominal paradigm, but the other desinences are different.

4.203 Before desinences beginning with *ě* or *i,* stems in *k* undergo substitutive softening KAI: e.g. *takъ* ~ *tacěmь, tacěma, tacěxъ, tacěmi,* NA dual neuter and feminine *tacě,* Npm *taci.*

4.21 *Vьsь* 'all' and *sicь* 'of this sort, of (such) kind' take the basic desinences that begin with *ě,* otherwise the soft variant; i.e. {**ě**/i} ~ {ъ/**ь**, o/**e**, y/**ę**}. Thus soft *vьsego, vьsemu, vьsemь, vьsei, vьseę, vьsejǫ, vьseju; sicego,* etc. ~ *vьsěmь, vьsěmъ, vьsěma, vьsěmi, vьsěxъ; sicěmь,* etc. Forms with the desinence *-a* are written *vьsa* or *vьsě* in glagolitic, but only **вьса** (never ***вьсꙗ**) in cyrillic. Asf is usually *vьsǫ,* rarely *vьsjǫ* (never cyrillic ***вьсѭ**).

4.22 The pronoun *sь* (or possibly **ś-*) has a suppletive stem *sij-* that apparently was optional in certain nominative and/or accusative forms. In the following table the more common shorter form is given first, followed by slash and the longer form.

<table>
<tr><td></td><td colspan="3">Singular</td><td colspan="3">Dual</td><td colspan="3">Plural</td></tr>
<tr><td></td><td>masc.</td><td>neut.</td><td>fem.</td><td>m</td><td>n</td><td>f</td><td>masc</td><td>neut</td><td>fem</td></tr>
<tr><td>N</td><td rowspan="2">sь/sii</td><td rowspan="2">se/sie</td><td>si</td><td rowspan="2">sija</td><td rowspan="2" colspan="2">si</td><td>sii/si</td><td rowspan="2">si</td><td rowspan="2">się</td></tr>
<tr><td>A</td><td>sijǫ</td><td>się</td></tr>
</table>

The animate masculine accusative singular is *sego.*

4.23 The interrogative pronoun *kъto* 'who' has the normal hard pronominal declension except for the extra word-final suffix *-to* in the nom.; acc.gen. *kogo,* loc. *komь,* dat. *komu,* and (with mutated root-stem) instr. ***cěmь.***

Instr. *cěmь* early began to give way to *kyimь* 'which?', cf. §4.323).

Like *kъto* are declined *někъto* 'somebody' and *nikъtože* 'nobody'. The particle *že* follows the desinence. (Modern editors often write it as a separate word.)

4.24 The interrogative pronoun *čьto* 'what' has the following forms: nom. acc. *čьto,* gen. **česo,** loc. *čemь,* dat. **česomu,** instr. *čimь.* Similarly *něčьto* 'something', *ničьtože* 'nothing' (where the particle follows the desinence).

Alternate forms are found: gen. *čьso, česogo, č'sogo,* dat. *čьsomu, čemu,* loc. *ni* [o/pri] *česomьže. Ničьtože* is found, rarely, as gen. *Ničьže* appears once in Cloz, and four times in Vat.

4.25 The pronoun **jь* 'he' is not attested in the nominative; its function as third person pronoun is taken by a demonstrative, usually *tъ* 'that one', less often *onъ* 'that one yonder'. The other forms of **jь* all are attested, including acc. sg. *i* (**jь*)—but the root-consonant is never explicitly written (§1.24): **jego, *jeję* are spelled *ego, eę,* etc. After prepositions, *j* is replaced by the palatal nasal *nj*: *kъ njemu, sъ njimi, na njь* (acc. sg. masc.), etc.

With the suffixed particle *-že, *jь* serves as a relative pronoun 'who, which', and all forms are attested (*iže, eže, jaže,* etc.).

Note that acc. sg. m **jь* is enclitic and may affect a final jer of a verb form, cf. §2.61.

4.26 In rare instances, forms of the possessives *moi, tvoi, svoi* are written without the *e* of bisyllabic desinences: gen. sg. fem *moę* for *moeę,* inst. *mojǫ* for *moejǫ.* They may be simply errors.

		masc.	neut.	fem.	masc.	neut.	fem.	
Sing.	N	тъ	то	та	нашь	нашє	наша	N
	A	= N, G		тѫ	= N, G		нашѫ	A
	G	того		тоѧ	нашєго		нашєѧ	G
	L	томь		тои	нашємь		нашєи	L
	D	томоу			нашємоу			D
	I	тѣмь		тоѭ	нашимь		нашєѭ	I
Dual	NA	та	тѣ		наша	наши		NA
	GL	тою			нашєю			GL
	DI	тѣма			нашима			DI
Plur.	N	ти	та	ты	наши	наша	нашѧ	N
	A	ты			нашѧ			A
	GL	тѣхъ			нашихъ			GL
	D	тѣмъ			нашимъ			D
	I	тѣми			нашими			I

N	къто	чьто
A	кого	
G		чєсо
L	комь	чємь
D	комоу	чєсомоу
I	цѣмь	чимь

	Singular			Dual			Plural			
	m.	n.	f.	m.	n.	f.	m.	n.	f.	
N	(и)	(є)	(ꙗ)	ꙗ	и		(и)	ꙗ	ѧ	N
A	=N, G	є	ѭ				ѧ			A
G	єго		єѧ	єю			ихъ			G
L	ємь		єи							L
D	ємоу			има			имъ			D
I	имь		єѭ				ими			I

4.3 The compound or adjectival declension.

This declension has complex desinences that give to adjectival stems an additional meaning of definiteness roughly equivalent to the English definite article: *slěp***a** *žena* 'a blind woman' versus *slěp***aja** *žena* 'the blind woman'. The underlying forms combine the twofold desinence with the case- and gender-equivalent form of the pronoun **jь*, e.g. Nsf *slěp*-a+j-a, As *slěp*-ǫ+j-ǫ. Adjectives with these compound desinences are commonly called "long" or "definite" as opposed to the "short" adjectives that have only the twofold nominal desinences. For the use of long forms, see §17.

The ideal normalized OCS forms are obscured first by the inadequacy of both OCS alphabets in representing the glide *j* (for *j* plays a crucial role in these desinences) and second by the complex historical evolution that seems to be reflected in the variegated spellings in the oldest surviving manuscripts. As underlying forms for early OCS, the short adjectival forms plus the post-posed pronoun **jь* provide a solid descriptive basis. Thus, for example, the masculine dative singular of *starъ* 'old' is posited as {star-u+j-emu}, ideal OCS *starujemu,* attested also in a shape called "assimilated" and one called "contracted", *staruumu* and *starumu*. Similarly *ništь* 'poor' has *ništujemu, ništuumu, ništumu.*

4.301 The inflectional suffixes consist, in principle, of (a) the short or nominal desinence, plus (b) the pronominal root ***j**-, plus (c) the soft pronominal desinence.

4.3011 Two systematic processes of simplification apply to produce the ideal OCS forms.[1] **1**. a desinence-initial sequence *-oj-* or *-ej-* is deleted. **2**. a nominal desinence with more than one syllable is replaced by the single syllable *y* or *i*. This means that the compound desinence consists of VjV(CV)—two or three syllables.

4.3012 Within the history of OCS, the intervocalic glide *j* tended to disappear, and contraction could take place. Let us posit successive processes of "assimilation" and "contraction". (**3a**) The syllable *je* assimilates to a preceding tense vowel. (**3b**) *j* disappears between like vowels. In effect, *aja* and ***aje*** > *a**a***, *ě**je*** > *ě**ě**,* *uju* and ***uje*** > ***uu***, *i**ji*** > ***ii***, *ǫjǫ* > *ǫǫ*, *ę**ję*** > *ęę* (while *oje, ěji* and *yję* remain). Finally, (**4**) two like vowels coalesce.

4.30121 The sequence *yji* presumably lost the *j* and *yi* contracted to *y*. Spellings like новꙑимъ, новꙑихъ are not informative (§4.302), but the shorter spellings (новꙑмъ, новꙑхъ and the like) surely imply *y*.

4.3013 The role of *j* (and its absence) in these forms is crucial; the lack of an unambiguous device for representing *j* in either OCS alphabet obscures the problems. In the following table the theoretical *j* is written consistently (with no asterisks). The individual gender-case desinences are numbered in order to facilitate discussion; "s" stands for *soft* when needed. The feminine two-syllable nominal desinences *-ama, -axъ, -amъ,*

---

[1] These are special morphophonemic adjustments that occur only in this specific environment. The English alternants *don't* and *won't* instead of *do not* and *will not* are formed by similar special rules.

-ami—which by rule 2 are replaced by *y* or *i*—have been omitted from the table, where they might fit into ##14, 20–22; note that the compound desinences have no specifically feminine shapes in dual or plural.

		underlying	OCS	assimilated	contracted	processes
1.	NAsm 1s	ъ/ь+**j**-ь	ъjь ьjь		y I yj i I ij	see §4.3021
2.	NAsn 2s	o/e+**j**-e	oje eje	ee	e	exempt 3b, 4
3.	Nsf	a+**j**-a	aja	aa	a	3b, 4
4.	Gsmn	a+**j**-ego	ajego	aago	ago	3ab, 4
5.	Gsf 5s	y/ę+**j**-eję	yję ęję	ęę	ę	1 3b, 4
6.	Lsmn 6s	ě/i+**j**-emь	ějemь ijemь	ěěmь iimь	ěmь imь	3a, 4 3a, 4
7.	Dsmn	u+**j**-emu	ujemu	uumu	umu	3ab, 4
8.	LDsf 8s	ě/i+**j**-eji	ěji iji	ii	i	1 3b, 4
9.	Ismn 9s	omь+**j**-imь emь+**j**-imь	yjimь ijimь	yimь iimь	ymь imь	§4.30121 2, 3b, 4
10.	Isf 10s	ojǫ+**j**-ejǫ ejǫ+**j**-ejǫ	ǫjǫ	ǫǫ	ǫ	1+1, 3b, 4
11.	NAdm	a+**j**-a	aja	aa	a	3b, 4
12.	NAdnf 12s	ě/i+**j**-i	ěji iji	ii	i	exempt 3b, 4
13.	GLd	u+**j**-eju	uju	uu	u	1, 3a, 4
14.	DId 14s	yma+**j**-ima ima+**j**-ima	yjima ijima	yima iima	yma ima	§4.30121 3b, 4
15.	Npm	i+**j**-i	iji	ii	i	3b, 4
16.	Apm 16s	y/ę+**j**-ę	yję ęję	ęę	ę	exempt 3b, 4
17.	NApn	a+**j**-a	aja	aa	a	3b, 4
18.	NApf 18s	y/ę+**j**-ę	yję ęję	ęę	ę	exempt 3b, 4
19.	Gp 19s	ъ/ь+**j**-ixъ	ъjixъ ьjixъ	yixъ iixъ	yxъ ixъ	§4.30121 3b, 4
20.	Lp 20s	ěxъ+**j**-ixъ ixъ+**j**-ixъ	yjixъ ijixъ	yixъ iixъ	yxъ ixъ	§4.30121 3b, 4
21.	Dp 21s	ěmъ+**j**-imъ imъ+**j**-imъ	yjimъ ijimъ	yimъ iimъ	ymъ imъ	§4.30121 3b, 4
22.	Ip 22s	ěmi+**j**-imi imi+**j**-imi	yjimi ijimi	yimъ iimъ	ymi imi	§4.30121 3b, 4

4.302 The attested glagolitic and cyrillic spelling of variants is chaotic. Since a vowel-letter in unblocked position implies syllable-initial *j*, spellings like *novaa* and *novǫǫ* do not necessarily specify that *j* is not present. The sequences *ъj* and *yj*, *ьj* and *ij*, are neutralized (§2.61), and the spellings of sequences in desinences 1, 19; 6s, 8s, 9s, 14, 15, 19-22 fluctuate considerably. Normal spelling is *-yi/-ъi* or *-ii/-ьi*, cyrillic **-ъıи/-ии** or **-ъи/-ьи**. But often enough **-ъı** is found (and could be interpreted as two syllables), while **-и** in soft-stems is rare. Often it is impossible to know whether a graphic ъ + *i* (**ъı, ъи, ъї**) is to be read as two syllables (*ъji, ъjь, yji, yjь*) or one (*y*).

4.3021 In desinence #1, the first jer is both strong and tense (§2.525), **-ъ**jь or **-ь**jь, and presumably the final jer had disappeared, leaving word-final *j*—which can be represented only by an *i*-letter. Spellings with *-oi/-ei* are found, but they are uncommon.

4.3022 In desinence #6, the spelled sequence *-ěě-* is sometimes replaced by *-ěa-* (chiefly in As, e.g. *na krilě cr̂kovьněam* 'on the temple parapet' Mt 4:5, *vъ životě věčъněamь* 'in eternal life' J 23:25). Such spellings surely result from arbitrary orthographic rules.

4.303 OCS and post-OCS mss demonstrate ever stronger tendencies for the pronominal desinences to influence these compound desinences, or replace them. At the same time it appears that a variety of spelling rules tried to maintain a two-letter sequence (particularly *aa, uu, yi*) that implies disyllabic pronunciation; it is probable that church tradition of recitation required special syllabification.

4.304 Late OCS shows beginnings of replacement of Dsmn *-umu* by pronominal *-omu* (twice in Assem), which is found with ever greater frequency in 11th-12th century Rusian mss and "Middle Bulgarian". The forms *slěpoumu* J 11:37 and *prъvoumu* J 19:32 in Mar are very likely illustrations of scribal uncertainty as to the correct spelling of the words. Isolated examples of *-eimъ* (3 each in Zo Mar Sin, **ищѫщеїмъ** 'seeking [Dp]' Su) and *-eixъ* (2 in Sin) in participial forms are very likely artificial. The regular forms become *star**omu*** like ***tom**u*, *niš**temu*** like ***semu***, although by tradition the *-umu* forms occur also.

4.305 In contrast, the adjectival *-ago* (or *-aago*) is systematically opposed to pronominal *-ogo/-ego* both in South and East Slavic texts until considerably later.

There is a single exception in OCS: **єлѣ живого сѫща** L 10:30 Sav (**єлѣ жива** As).

4.31 The compound forms of the **comparative adjectives** and the **active participles** are somewhat irregular in nom. and acc. (cf. §4.191-192). The Ns masc. long form of the comparative is just like the short: *nověi*, *vęštii*. The NAs neuter long form of comparatives is based on the lengthened stem *-ěiš-* (for **-ějьš-*) or *-ьš-*, *nověišee, vęštee*: there are also occasional examples lacking **-ьš-* (*tačaee* 'better (sort of)' J 2:10 Zo; **въıшєк** 'higher' Su 303.20). The active participles use the longer stems: *prosęštee, nesъšee, prošьšee.*

The Ns fem. is made by adding *-ja* to the short form: *nověišija, vęštija; nesǫštija, nesъšija*. Ns masc. of the active participles is regularly formed by adding *-i* (for **-jь*) to the short form: *nesyi, glagoljęi, prosęi*. In the past active participle, the compound desinence *-ъi/-ьi* may appear as *-yi/-ii* (*nesyi, prošii*), but spellings with *-ei (prošei)* are not uncommon (for *-**ьj**ь, cf. §§2.51, 2.522).

Here are the NA long forms (compare the short forms in §4.19):

		Comparatives		Present Active Participle				Past. Act. Part.	
		nom.	acc.	nom.	acc.	nom.	acc.	nom.	acc.
Sg.	M	-i	-ьšьi	-yi/-ęi	-ǫštii	-ęi	-ęštii	-yi	-ъšii
	N	-ьšee		-ǫštee		-ęštee		-ъšee	
	F	-ьšija	-ьšǫjǫ	-ǫštija	-ǫštǫjǫ	-ęštija	-ęštǫjǫ	-ъšija	-ъšǫjǫ
Pl.	M	-ьšei	-ьšęę	-ǫštei	-ǫštęę	-ęštei	-ęštęę	-ъšei	-ъšęę
	N	-ьšaja		-ǫštaja		-ęštaja		-ъšaja	
	F	-ьšęę		-ǫštęę		-ęštęę		-ъšęę	

4.311 Beside the regular nom. sg. masc. pres. act. part. of the *nesyi* type, there are certain cases where *y* is replaced by *ǫ, ę,* or a rare glagolitic symbol which we transcribe *ǫ̈*: *živyi, živǫi, živęi, živǫ̈i*. This fluctuation is attested only in a few verbs (principally *živyi* 'living', *syi* 'being', *grędyi* 'coming') and is doubtless a reflection of different dialects and morphological innovation. See Koch 553-59.

4.312 Beside the expected *-ei* in nom. pl. masc., *-ii* (or, contracted, *-i*) is often found. It is to be regarded as a relatively late form.

4.313 Very rarely, participial forms in *-e* or *-i* stand for any gender-number-case form.

Compound declension paradigms: hard-stem *novyi*; soft-stem *ništii*:

<table>
<tr><td></td><td></td><td>masculine</td><td>neuter</td><td>feminine</td><td></td></tr>
<tr><td rowspan="6">Sing.</td><td>N</td><td>новꙑи, новꙑ</td><td rowspan="2">новоє</td><td>новꙗ, -аа</td><td>N</td></tr>
<tr><td>A</td><td>= Nom or Gen.</td><td>новѫѭ</td><td>A</td></tr>
<tr><td>G</td><td colspan="2">новаєго, новааго, новаго</td><td>новꙑѧ</td><td>G</td></tr>
<tr><td>L</td><td colspan="2">новѣємь, новѣмь, новѣѣмь, новѣамь</td><td rowspan="2">новѣи</td><td>L</td></tr>
<tr><td>D</td><td colspan="2">новоуємоу, новоуоумоу, новоумоу</td><td>D</td></tr>
<tr><td>I</td><td colspan="2">новꙑимь, новꙑмь</td><td>новѫѭ</td><td>I</td></tr>
<tr><td rowspan="3">Dual</td><td>NA</td><td>новии</td><td colspan="2">новѣи</td><td>NA</td></tr>
<tr><td>GL</td><td colspan="3">новоую</td><td>GL</td></tr>
<tr><td>DI</td><td colspan="3">новꙑима, новꙑма</td><td>DI</td></tr>
<tr><td rowspan="5">Plur.</td><td>N</td><td>новии</td><td rowspan="2">новꙗ, новаа</td><td rowspan="2">новꙑѧ</td><td>N</td></tr>
<tr><td>A</td><td>новꙑѧ</td><td>A</td></tr>
<tr><td>GL</td><td colspan="3">новꙑихъ, новꙑхъ</td><td>GL</td></tr>
<tr><td>D</td><td colspan="3">новꙑимъ, новꙑмъ</td><td>D</td></tr>
<tr><td>I</td><td colspan="3">новꙑими, новꙑми</td><td>I</td></tr>
</table>

<table>
<tr><td></td><td></td><td>masculine</td><td>neuter</td><td>feminine</td><td></td></tr>
<tr><td rowspan="6">Sing.</td><td>N</td><td>ништии, ништи</td><td rowspan="2">ништєє</td><td>ништꙗ, -аа</td><td>N</td></tr>
<tr><td>A</td><td>= Nom or Gen.</td><td>ништѫѭ</td><td>A</td></tr>
<tr><td>G</td><td colspan="2">ништаєго, ништааго, ништаго</td><td>ништѧѧ</td><td>G</td></tr>
<tr><td>L</td><td colspan="2">ништиимь, ништимь</td><td rowspan="2">ништии</td><td>L</td></tr>
<tr><td>D</td><td colspan="2">ништоуємоу, ништоуоумоу, ништоумоу</td><td>D</td></tr>
<tr><td>I</td><td colspan="2">ништиимь, ништимь</td><td>ништѫѭ</td><td>I</td></tr>
<tr><td rowspan="3">Dual</td><td>NA</td><td>ништꙗ</td><td colspan="2">ништии</td><td>NA</td></tr>
<tr><td>GL</td><td colspan="3">ништоую</td><td>GL</td></tr>
<tr><td>DI</td><td colspan="3">ништиима, ништима</td><td>DI</td></tr>
<tr><td rowspan="5">Plur.</td><td>N</td><td>ништии</td><td rowspan="2">ништꙗ, ништаа</td><td rowspan="2">ништѧѧ</td><td>N</td></tr>
<tr><td>A</td><td>ништѧѧ</td><td>A</td></tr>
<tr><td>GL</td><td colspan="3">ништиихъ, ништихъ</td><td>GL</td></tr>
<tr><td>D</td><td colspan="3">ништиимъ, ништимъ</td><td>D</td></tr>
<tr><td>I</td><td colspan="3">ништиими, ништими</td><td>I</td></tr>
</table>

Compound declension of comparatives and participles, nominative and accusative. Note that the masc. accusative sing. may also have the genitive form, which like all other declensional forms has the variations listed for *ništii,* above.

		masculine	neuter	feminine	
Sg.	N	вѧштьи	вѧштьшее	вѧштьшиꙗ	N
	A	вѧштьшии		вѧштьшѫѭ	A
Pl.	N	вѧштьшеи	вѧштьшаꙗ	вѧштьшѧѧ	N
	A	вѧштьшѧѧ			A
Sg.	N	новѣи	новѣишее	новѣишиꙗ	N
	A	новѣишии		новѣишѫѭ	A
Pl.	N	новѣишеи	новѣишаꙗ	новѣишѧѧ	N
	A	новѣишѧѧ			A

		masculine	neuter	feminine	
Sg.	N	несꙑи	несѫштее	несѫштиꙗ	N
	A	несѫштии		несѫштѫѭ	A
Pl.	N	несѫштеи	несѫштаꙗ	несѫштѧѧ	N
	A	несѫштѧѧ			A
Sg.	N	просѧи	просѧштее	просѧштиꙗ	N
	A	просѧштии		просѧштѫѭ	A
Pl.	N	просѧштеи	просѧштаꙗ	просѧштѧѧ	N
	A	просѧштѧѧ			A
Sg.	N	несꙑи, несꙑ	несъшее	несъшиꙗ	N
	A	несъшии		несъшѫѭ	A
Pl.	N	несъшеи	несъшаꙗ	несъшѧѧ	N
	A	несъшѧѧ			A

4.32 Mixture of the twofold nominal, pronominal, and compound declensions.

4.321 Some stems occur with desinences that belong to more than one paradigm. Compound-declension forms of such words are not necessarily definite in meaning.

Tuždь (with alternate shapes *štuždь* and *stuždь*) 'alien, foreign' (the antonym of *svoi* 'own') is chiefly a soft pronominal stem, but it sometimes appears with twofold nominal or compound desinences. *Edinъ* 'one; only, sole' has predominantly pronominal desinences, but compound desinences are well attested (see SJS, p. 976).

4.322 The words *mъnogъ* 'many, numerous', *kolikъ* 'how big?', *tolikъ* 'so big', *selikъ* 'as big as this', *elikъ*, 'so big (relative)', have a mixture of nominal and pronominal forms. The prominal desinences that begin with *-ě-* are selected, accompanied by mutation of stem-final velar (*k g* > *c ʒ*): instr. sg. masc. neut. *kolicěmь,* gen. loc. pl. *tolicěxъ,* dat. pl. *tolicěmъ,* instr. pl. *tolicěmi*. *Mъnogъ* has both the regular nominal forms and these pronominal *ě*-forms: *mъnogomь/mъnoʒěmь, mъnogъ/mъnoʒěxъ, mъnogomъ/mъnoʒěmъ, mъnogy/mъnoʒěmi*. All of these words have regular definite forms according to the compound declension.

4.323 The adjectival interrogative *kyi, koe, kaja* 'which', and also *nikyi, nikyiže* 'none' and *někyi* 'a certain' have the stem *k-* with (1) long desinences (hard) in nominative and accusative forms, and (2) long desinences beginning with *y*; and the stem *koj-* with soft pronominal desinences that begin with *e*.

In the table below, *j* is written but the forms are not asterisked.

<table>
<tr><th></th><th colspan="3">Singular</th><th colspan="3">Dual</th><th colspan="3">Plural</th><th></th></tr>
<tr><th></th><th>masc.</th><th>neut.</th><th>fem.</th><th>masc.</th><th>neut.</th><th>fem.</th><th>masc.</th><th>neut.</th><th>fem</th><th></th></tr>
<tr><td>N</td><td rowspan="2">kyjь</td><td rowspan="2">koje</td><td>kaja</td><td rowspan="2">[kaja]</td><td colspan="2" rowspan="2">cěji?</td><td>ciji</td><td rowspan="2">kaja</td><td rowspan="2">kyję</td><td>N</td></tr>
<tr><td>A</td><td>kǫjǫ</td><td>kyję</td><td>A</td></tr>
<tr><td>G</td><td colspan="2">kojego</td><td>kojeję</td><td colspan="3" rowspan="2">[kojeju]</td><td colspan="3" rowspan="2">kyjixъ</td><td>G</td></tr>
<tr><td>L</td><td colspan="2">kojemь</td><td rowspan="2">kojeji</td><td>L</td></tr>
<tr><td>D</td><td colspan="2">kojemu</td><td colspan="3" rowspan="2">kyjima</td><td colspan="3">kyjimъ</td><td>D</td></tr>
<tr><td>I</td><td colspan="2">kyjimь</td><td>kojejǫ</td><td colspan="3">kyjimi</td><td>I</td></tr>
</table>

Forms with *ko-* instead of *ky-* are attested but rare; they are common in post-OCS mss.

4.4 The simple nominal declension.

Two groups of stems belong to this declension: one is regular and productive; the other amounts to a list of individual nouns that are anomalous in varying manners, but includes derivational formants that are productive. The regular type is made up predominantly of feminine substantives (counting also the numerals *pętь* '5', *šestь* '6', *sedmь* '7', *osmь* '8', *devętь* '9'), but includes some masculines, and one numeral with syntactic gender, *trьe* '3'. They are usually called, on historical grounds, *i*-stems.

The anomalous stems include substantives of all three genders (counting one numeral of feminine gender, *desętь* '10') and one numeral with syntactic gender, *četyre* '4'.

The normal i-stems have these underlying desinences:

<table>
<tr><th></th><th colspan="2">Singular</th><th colspan="2">Dual</th><th colspan="2">Plural</th><th></th></tr>
<tr><th></th><th>masc.</th><th>fem.</th><th>masc.</th><th>fem.</th><th>masc.</th><th>fem.</th><th></th></tr>
<tr><td>N</td><td colspan="2" rowspan="2">-ь</td><td colspan="2" rowspan="2">-i</td><td>-ьje</td><td rowspan="2">-i</td><td>N</td></tr>
<tr><td>A</td><td>-i</td><td>A</td></tr>
<tr><td>G</td><td colspan="2" rowspan="3">-i</td><td colspan="2" rowspan="2">-ьju</td><td colspan="2">-ьjь</td><td>G</td></tr>
<tr><td>L</td><td colspan="2">-ьxъ</td><td>L</td></tr>
<tr><td>D</td><td colspan="2" rowspan="2">-ьma</td><td colspan="2">-ьmъ</td><td>D</td></tr>
<tr><td>I</td><td>-ьmь</td><td>-ьjǫ</td><td colspan="2">-ьmi</td><td>I</td></tr>
<tr><td>V</td><td colspan="2">-i</td><td colspan="2"></td><td colspan="2"></td><td></td></tr>
</table>

4.401 The tense *ь* in Isf, in GL dual, and Gp usually is spelled *i*. The underlying Gp desinence has a strong and a weak jer (-**ьj**ь) and therefore can be spelled *-ьi* or *-ii* in normalized OCS, or *-ei* and sometimes merely *-i* in the mss. Thus Gp **ljudьjь* appears as *ljudьi, ljudii; ljudei, ljudi*. The strong jer of Ism and Dp may also be spelled *e*: *ljudьmь* or *ljudemь*. Cf. §§2.61, 2.625.

4.402 The numeral *trьe* (*trie*) is inherently plural. The NA form *tri* is used for both neuter and feminine agreement. The genitive is *trьi* (*tr**ьj**ь), spelled also *trei, tri*; loc. *trьxъ* (*trexъ*); dat. *trьmъ* (*tremъ*); instr. *trьmi*.

4.4031 The majority of substantives of this pattern were feminine, and some foreign names of women were adapted to it (e.g. *Agarь, Tamarь*). The productivity of this type is assured in part because of the suffix *-ostь,* used to form abstract nouns from adjectival roots or stems (e.g. *bělostь* 'whiteness' ~ *bělъ* 'white'; *světьlostь* 'brightness' ~ *světьlъ* 'bright').

4.4032 Masculine substantives are well attested, but the number is restricted and many individual stems tend to take twofold nominal desinences. Most important are: *bolь* 'sick man', *gvozdь* 'nail', *golǫbь* 'dove', *gostь* 'guest', *grъtanь* 'throat', *zętь* 'bridegroom', *lystь* 'calf (of leg)', *pǫtь* 'road', *tatь* 'thief', *tьstь* 'wife's father', *ušidь* 'fugitive', *črьvь* 'worm', *ǫglь* 'coal', and *ljudьe* (plural only).

Gladь 'hunger, famine' (Ns *gladь krěpъkъ* Zo L 15:14; Is *glademь* Sin [Deuteronomy 32:24]) is in competition with a better-attested twofold nominal *gladъ*.

Zvěrь 'beast', *ognjь* 'fire', and *gospodь* 'lord' are treated in §4.51 below.

Malomoštь 'cripple; beggar' takes masculine modifiers, but unexpectedly has the Is feminine desinence, *malomoštijǫ*, Mk 9:43.

Lakъtь 'elbow; ell', *nogъtь* 'fingernail', *paznegъtь* 'claw' and *pečatь* 'seal' seem to belong to the anomalous type (cf. Vaillant §70).

Simple nominal declension paradigms:

feminine *kostь*'bone' and masculine *pǫtь* 'road'.

Sing.	NA	кость		пѫть		NA
	GLD	кости		пѫти		GLD
	I	костьѭ	-иѭ	пѫтьмь	-(ємь)	I
Dual	NA	кости		пѫти		NA
	GL	костью	-ию	пѫтью	-ию	GL
	DI	костьма		пѫтьма		DI
Plur.	N	кости		пѫтьє	-иє	N
	A			пѫти		A
	G	костьи	-ии (-єи)	пѫтьи	-ии (-єи)	G
	L	костьхъ	(-єхъ)	пѫтьхъ	(-єхъ)	L
	D	костьмъ	(-ємъ)	пѫтьмъ	(-ємъ)	D
	I	костьми		пѫтьми		I

4.410 The anomalous subtypes of simple nominal declension

About fifty substantives (the most clearly attested of which are listed in the next two pages) have, ***in addition to the regular forms*** *given above,* other—older—desinences. From the point of view of OCS, the variant desinences are simply irregularities that must be listed in the lexicon, but in terms of linguistic history they are remnants of formerly distinct paradigms, known as *consonant-stems*. These stems tended to replace the old distinctive endings with simple-stem desinences. Masculines and neuters tend to become even more regular by substituting twofold nominal desinences.

The most striking characteristic is special stems in nominative singulars; they may be described in terms of an underlying zero desinence, see §4.415.

<table>
<tr><th></th><th colspan="3">Singular</th><th colspan="3">Dual</th><th colspan="3">Plural</th><th></th></tr>
<tr><th></th><th>masc.</th><th>neut.</th><th>fem.</th><th>masc.</th><th>neut.</th><th>fem.</th><th>masc.</th><th>neut.</th><th>fem</th><th></th></tr>
<tr><td>N</td><td>-ь, -Ø</td><td rowspan="2">-Ø</td><td>-Ø</td><td rowspan="2">-i</td><td rowspan="2">-ě? -i?</td><td rowspan="2">-i</td><td>-e</td><td rowspan="2">-a</td><td rowspan="2">-i</td><td>N</td></tr>
<tr><td>A</td><td>-ь</td><td>-ь</td><td>-i</td><td>A</td></tr>
<tr><td>G</td><td colspan="3" rowspan="2">-e</td><td colspan="3" rowspan="2">-u</td><td colspan="3">-ъ</td><td>G</td></tr>
<tr><td>L</td><td colspan="3">-exъ</td><td>L</td></tr>
<tr><td>D</td><td colspan="3">-i</td><td colspan="3" rowspan="2">-ьma</td><td colspan="3">-emъ</td><td>D</td></tr>
<tr><td>I</td><td colspan="2">-ьmь</td><td>-ьjǫ</td><td colspan="2">-y? -ьmi?</td><td>-ьmi</td><td>I</td></tr>
</table>

4.4111 The GL singular has *-e,* and the nominative plural masculine has *-e*; these desinences are unique to anomalous stems and they are frequently used. Thus the masculine stem *dьnь* 'day' has *dьne* as Gs and Ls (while *dьni* is the only Ds form, but appears also as Gs and Ls). Np is also *dьne* (beside *dьnьe, dьnie, denьe,* §2.65).

4.4112 The Gp *-ъ* and the GL dual *-u* are shared with the hard twofold paradigm. *Dьnь* normally has i-stem Gp *dьnьi* (*dьnii, dьnei*), but after numerals almost always *dьnъ* (*denъ*).

4.4113 The disyllabic desinences of masc. sg. instrumental (*-ьmь* ~ *-emь*), Lp (*-ьxъ* ~ *-exъ*), and Dp (*-ьmъ* ~ *-emъ*), are somewhat uncertain. The Is might represent i-stem or soft o-stem desinences: there is no way to distinguish whether written *-e-* represents historical *ь* or not. The attested plural forms are predominantly spelled *-emъ* and *-exъ*; the historically expected desinences have *ь*.

4.4114 The numeral *četyre* '4' has a single neuter-feminine NA (pl) form, *četyri*. (All anomalous neuter substantival stems have NAp *-a,* like o-stems.)

4.412 Masculines are few: *dьnь* 'day', *korenь* 'root', *remenь* 'strap', *elenь* 'stag', *stepenь* 'degree'. *Kamenь* 'stone' and *plamenь* 'flame' have alternate NAs forms, *kamy* and *plamy* (only in Su).

4.413 Most feminines and neuters have a nominative sg. form with a stem that is shorter than the usual stem. Feminines are of two types, traditionally called "long u-stems" and "r-stems".

The former have a full stem ending in *-ъv-*, but Ns in *y*: e.g. *ljuby* 'love', Gs *ljubъve*. Here belong: *crьky* or *cirъky* 'church', *neplody* 'barren woman', *smoky* 'fig', *svekry* 'husband's mother', *loky* 'pond', *brady* 'ax', *žrьny* 'millstone', *cěly* 'cure', *xorǫgy* 'flag' (Gs *crьkъve* or *cirъkъve, neplodъve,* etc.). Expected Ns **kry* 'blood' is by chance not attested: the accusative form *krъvь* functions as nom. The acc. sg. of other stems is also found in nominative function. *Bukъvi* 'writing, letter' is attested only in the plural, with collective meaning.

The two r-stems *mater-* 'mother' and *dъšter-* 'daughter' have *mati* and *dъšti* in Ns (and vocative), As *materь, dъšterь*, Gs *matere, dъštere,* etc. The genitive form functions as accusative in Sav and Su.

4.414 Neuters of the anomalous group are "n-stems", "nt-stems", and "s-stems". Stems in *-en-* have NAs in *-ę*: e.g. *vrěmę* 'time'~ Gs *vrěmene,* etc. Also *brěmę* 'burden', *čismę* 'numeral', *imę* 'name', *pismę* 'letter', *plemę* 'tribe', *sěmę* 'seed'.

Stems in *-ęt-* also have NAs in *-ę*: e.g. *otročę* 'child' ~ Gs *otročęte*, etc. This formant was surely productive, serving to create words denoting young living creatures; the list of stems that happen to be attested in OCS is short: *osьlę* 'young ass', *ovьčę* 'lamb', *kozьlę* 'kid', *žrěbę* 'foal', *kljušę* 'draft animal'.

Neuters like NAs *slovo* ~ G *slovese* 'word' are always paralleled by forms without *-es-*; they will be discussed below, §4.55.

4.415 The shorter nominative shapes represent underlying forms with a *zero* desinence that is in effect a word-boundary. Stem-final C + desinential Ø violates the requirement that every word must end in a vowel. The productive *nt*-type ({otrok-ęt+Ø} > *otročę*) and the closed group of neuter *n*-stems ({sěm-en+Ø} > *sěmę*) involve morphophonemic rules that are required elsewhere in the system. The *ū*-stems ({crъk-ъv+Ø} > *crьky*) are subject to a special alternation that recurs in certain verbal stems (§11.341). The two fundamental kinship terms that constitute the class of *r*-stems ({mat-er+Ø} > *mati,* {dъšt-er+Ø} 'daughter') are isolated relics. The masculine *n*-stems ({plam-en+Ø} > *plamy*) and the extremely variable *s*-stems ({těl-es+Ø} > *tělo*) are irregularities that must be listed in the lexicon.

4.5 Mixture of the two nominal declension types.

A number of substantives are attested with forms from the twofold nominal and the simple declension (including its anomalous subtypes). From the historical point of view, the variation illustrates the general tendency for the simple nominal declension to be restricted to feminines, and for masculines and neuters to follow the twofold paradigm.

4.51 Masculine i-stems frequently have singular desinences of the soft twofold declension: *zvěrь* 'wild beast' has Ds and Ap *zvěri,* but Gs *zvěrja* and Np *zvěrьje*. *Ognjь* 'fire' also uses chiefly i-stem desinences, but also occasionally twofold soft nominal forms. The extremely common *gospodь* 'lord' shows great variation, in part obscured by the fact that the stem is abbreviated (e.g. г҃ь, гс҃амь). It is clear that i-forms and hard twofold forms are used, e.g. Ds *gospodi* ~ *gospodu*, but spellings like г҃ю, implying *gospodju*, raise problems of phonological innovation that cannot be treated here.

4.52 Masculine substantives with the suffixes *-telj-* and *-arj-* (both indicating agent or actor) have the normal soft twofold desinences in the singular, but in the plural the stem seems to have been hard (*-tel-, -ar-*), and desinences are usually those of the anomalous type of simple-declension. With rare exceptions, the Np is *-e* (*učitele* 'teachers', *rybare* 'fishermen'), but often the spelling indicates the palatal stem of the singular here as well, at least for *-telje*, -телѥ. The Gp *-telъ, -arъ* is less common than the softened stem type *-teljь, -arjь* (although we must be cautious in interpreting the spelling). Ap has only the soft twofold *-ę*. Instr. pl. is found both with *-ly, -ry* and with *-li* (*-lji*). (Note that many scribes do not distinguish *li* from *lji*, and very few distinguish *r* from *rj* before any vowel, cf. §§1.31–1.331.)

4.53 A number of plural nouns with stems in *-an-/-ěn-* ordinarily have the anomalous simple-declension desinences: *izmailitěne* 'Ishmaelites' ~ Lp *izmailitěnexъ*; *graždane* 'townsmen' ~ Lp *graždanexъ*. Twofold desinences are also found, notably the Ap in *-y*. (Cf. Vaillant, §71.)

These nouns denote national groups and classes. The corresponding singular and dual forms normally have the derivational suffix *-in-*, followed by the regular hard twofold desinences: **izmailitěninъ, graždaninъ*.

4.54 The feminines with stems in *-ъv-* (Ns *-y*, §4.413) regularly have the singular and NAp of the anomalous declension, but other plural forms from the hard twofold feminine (a-stem) paradigm: *crьky* 'church', Gs *crьkъve* ~ NAp *crьkъvi*, Gp *crьkъvъ*, Lp *crьkъvaxъ*, Dp *crьkъvamъ* (Ip **crьkъvami*, attested in post-OCS mss).

4.55 Neuter "s-stems" exhibit anomalous simple desinences added to the suffix *-es-* beside twofold endings without this suffix: NAs *tělo* 'body' ~ Gs *těla/tělese*, Ls *tělě/tělese*, Ds *tělu/tělesi*, etc. Usage varies with different words and mss (cf. Vaillant §73). Here belong: *nebo* 'sky, heaven', *tělo* 'body', *drěvo* 'tree', *slovo* 'word, speech', *čudo* 'wonder', *divo* 'miracle', *dělo* 'work', *kolo* 'wheel', *ljuto* 'misdeed', *istesě, istesa* (dual and pl. only) 'kidneys, loins', *lice* 'face', *oko* 'eye', *uxo* 'ear'. Before *-es-* the stems of *lice, oko, uxo* undergo substitutive softening: *ličese, očese, ušese*.

4.551 *Oko* and *uxo* have special dual forms: *oči uši*, GL *očьju/očiju*, DI *očima ušima*. They may take feminine modifiers. Both words are rare in the plural.

4.6 Declension of the personal pronouns.

The personal pronouns have no formal expression of gender, and their declensions are unique, with little resemblance to the other declension types. For the third person, the demonstrative **j-* is used (cf. §4.25), suppleted by nominative forms of *tъ* (or, less commonly, *onъ*).

<table>
<tr><th></th><th>N</th><th>A</th><th>G</th><th>L</th><th>D</th><th>I</th><th></th></tr>
<tr><td>1st pers. sg.</td><td>azъ</td><td>mę</td><td>mene</td><td colspan="2">mьně</td><td>mъnoju</td><td>‘I’</td></tr>
<tr><td>2nd pers. sg.</td><td>ty</td><td>tę</td><td>tebe</td><td colspan="2">tebě</td><td>tobojǫ</td><td>‘thou’</td></tr>
<tr><td>reflexive</td><td>–</td><td>sę</td><td>sebe</td><td colspan="2">sebě</td><td>sobojǫ</td><td>‘self’</td></tr>
<tr><td>1st pers. du.</td><td>vě</td><td>na</td><td colspan="2">naju</td><td colspan="2">nama</td><td>‘we two’</td></tr>
<tr><td>2nd pers. du.</td><td colspan="2">va</td><td colspan="2">vaju</td><td colspan="2">vama</td><td>‘you two’</td></tr>
<tr><td>1st pers. pl.</td><td>my</td><td>ny</td><td colspan="2">nasъ</td><td>namъ</td><td>nami</td><td>‘we’</td></tr>
<tr><td>2nd pers. pl.</td><td colspan="2">vy</td><td colspan="2">vasъ</td><td>vamъ</td><td>vami</td><td>‘you’</td></tr>
<tr><td></td><td>N</td><td>A</td><td>G</td><td>L</td><td>D</td><td>I</td><td></td></tr>
</table>

4.61 Beside *mьně* and *mъnojǫ* there are enough cases of *mъně* and *mьnojǫ* (beside many with *m'n-/mn-*) to make it impossible to decide which form was really normal. Beside Gs *mene,* Euch and Sin have a number of cases of *mne/m'ne*.

4.62 In KF, *ny* functions as Np as well as acc. (According to comparative evidence, this seems to be a Bulgarian-Macedonian feature.)

4.63 The dative forms *mьně, tebě, sebě* are paralleled by *mi, ti, si*. The difference seems to be that the longer forms are independent, while the short forms are enclitic, and stand after the first accented word of a clause. In a few rare instances short dual and plural forms are found, Ddu *va,* Dp *ny, vy*.

4.64 The genitives *mene tebe nasъ vasъ* commonly function as accusative, but this usage is apparently an innovation within the OCS period. Cf. Mt 4:6 pusti *sebe* dolu ‘throw thyself down’ Zo (As vrъʒi *sę*, cf. §21.61)

4.65 The NA dual forms are not needed often; acc. *na* appears only five times. The specifically dual NA *va* and *na* are, on the whole, replaced by the plurals *vy* and *ny*.

Excursus

Formation of the comparative.

4.70 Comparatives of OCS adjectives end either (1) in **-ьi** (neut. **-e**, fem. **-ьši**) or (2) in **-ěi** (neut. **-ěe**, fem. **-ěiši**). They reflect either (1) the unproductive underlying suffix {jьj-ьš} or (2) the productive {ěj-ьš-}.

The declensions are treated in §4.19 and §4.31. The NA short neuter form may be used as an adverb.

OCS has no morphological superlative; the sense of English superlatives is achieved by phraseological means, e.g. L 9:48 iže bo estъ mьnjii vьsěxъ vasъ, lit. 'for he who is the *lesser* one *of* you *all*, i.e. the least; L 13:2 grěšьněiše pače vьsěxъ člověkъ 'more sinful than all men'.

4.71 The suffix {jьj-ьš} is found with a limited but important group of stems. Before the suffix, the stem-final consonant undergoes iotation if possible. Nsm may be analyzed as taking a zero desinence; stem-final *š* is deleted (cf. §4.415). The NA neuter is unique; the soft desinence *-e* is added to a shortened suffix {j}. Thus {vęt-jьj-ьš+Ø} > *vęštьjь,* {vęt-j[ьj-ьš]+e} > *vęšte.*

(**1**) The comparative stem is unlike the corresponding positive stem: *boljьi bolje boljьši* 'bigger', *vęštьi vęšte vęštьši* 'greater' (~ *velьi* or *velikъ* 'big, great'); *mьnjьi mьnje mьnjьši* 'smaller, lesser' (~ *malъ* 'small'); *lučьi luče lučьši* 'better', *unjьi, unje, unjьši* 'better' (~ *dobrъ* 'good'); *gorjьi gorje gorjьši* 'worse' (~ *zъlъ* 'bad').

(**2**) The positive exists either (**a**) with a derivational suffix in *-k-* which is lost in the comparative: *tęžьkъ* 'heavy' ~ *tęžьi tęže tęžьši*; *krěpъkъ* 'strong' ~ *krěpljьi krěplje krěpljьši*; *sladъkъ* 'sweet' ~ *slaždьi*; *vysokъ* 'high' ~ *vyšьi*; *širokъ* 'wide' ~ *širjьi*; and the neuter form functioning as an adverb *daleče* 'far' ~ *dalje*: or (**b**) without derivational *-k-*: *xudъ* 'poor, insignificant' ~ *xuždьi xužde xuždьši*; *ljutъ* 'fierce' ~ *ljuštьi ljušte ljuštьši*; *grǫbъ* 'rough, rude' ~ *grǫbljьi grǫbljьši*; *dragъ* 'dear, valuable' ~ *draže; lixъ* 'superfluous' ~ *liše.*

Some comparatives are attested only as adverbs, e.g. *niže* 'lower' (the positive *nizъkъ* 'low' by chance is not recorded in OCS).

4.72 The suffix *-ěi* (neut. *-ěe,* fem. *-ěiši*) is used with all other stems. It causes KI mutation, with automatic shift of *ě* to *a* after palatal consonant (§3.5 c1): *starъ* 'old' ~ *starěi starěe starěiši*; *dobljьi* 'brave' ~ *dobljai dobljae dobljaiši*; *mъnogъ* 'much, many' ~ *mъnožai*; *gorjьkъ* 'bitter' ~ *gorjьčai,* and the like.

The underlying suffix is {ěj-ьš}. The masculine zero-desinence applies (as in §4.71 above). The NA neuter singular also is shorter; it omits the two units *ьš*.

The underlying {ě} sometimes is spelled with "ě" (cyr. ѣ) instead of "a" (e.g. Mt 21:36 множѣиша 'a larger number of [Apm]' Sav; J 4:1 mъnožaišę ZoMar).

On the formation of certain adverbs

4.80 A large percentage of OCS adverbs must be regarded as given lexical items, historically of diverse formation. Here the adverbs based on pronominal stems will be listed; they constitute an important subsystem. The productive types of adverbs formed from adjectives will be mentioned.

4.81 Adverbs may be formed by adding special suffixes to the pronominal roots *k-* (interrogative), *t-* (pointing, general), *s-* [or *ś-*] (close by), *ov-* (pointing, distant), **j-* (relative, usually with added *že,* cf. *iže* 'he who'), *in-* 'another', *vьs-* [or *vьś-*] 'all' (general), *nik-* (negative).

4.811 Expressing positional relations:

kъde	where	**kamo**	whither, to what place	**kǫdu, kǫdě, otъ kǫdu**	whence, from what place
tu	there	**tamo**	thither, to that place	**tǫdu, tǫdě otъ tǫdu**	thence, from that place
sьde	here	**sěmo**	hither, to this place	**sǫdu, sǫdě, otъ sǫdu**	hence, from this place
ovъde	there, here	**ovamo**	thither, hither	**ovǫdu**	there
onъde	yonder, over there	**onamo**	to that place	**onǫdu**	over there
ide **ideže**	in the place where	**jamo** **jamože**	to the place where	**jǫdu,** **jǫduže**	from the place where
inъde	elsewhere, in another place	**inamo**	to another place	**inǫdu,** **inǫdě**	from another place
vьsьde	everywhere	**vьsěmo**	to all places	**vьsǫdu, vьsǫdě; otъ vьsǫdu**	everywhere; from everywhere
nikъde(**že**)	nowhere	**nikamo**	to no place		

The forms with suffix *-ǫdu/-ǫdě* are rare without the preceding *otъ,* and can mean movement about a place, rather than 'from'.

The meaning of motion is often lost in *tamo,* and it is contrasted to *tu* as more general and distant. Some of the *-de* forms have variants in *-žde* (Su); *vьsьžde, inъžde, ižde* or *iždeže*. Note the compounds *doideže, donjьdeže* (rarely *donjьžde, doižde*) 'to the place where, up to, until; during'.

To these series may be added *vъně* 'outside', *vъnъ* '(to) outside', *vъnějǫdu/vъnějǫdě* 'outside'; *ǫtrь* 'inside', *ǫtrь/vъnǫtrь* '(to) inside', *izǫtrь, ǫtrьjǫdu, ǫtrьjǫdě* 'from within'; *otъ obojǫdu* 'from both sides' (cf. *oba* 'both').

4.812 Expressing time: *kogda* 'when', *togda* 'then', *ovogda* 'at this time, now', *egda* 'when' (and *vъnjegda,* cf. §3.3103, 'during'), *vьsegda* 'always', *nikogdaže* 'never', *někogda* 'at one time, formerly', *togdaže* 'at the same time', and *inogda* 'another time; once'. Beside the forms in *-ogda* are forms in *-ъgda* (*kъgda, tъgda,* etc.); this is not a phonetic change of ъ to *o,* but a replacement of the old rooots *ko-, to-* by contemporary *k-ъ, t-ъ* (as in *kъto* and *kyi*).

4.813 Expressing manner: *kako* 'how', *tako* 'thus', *jako/jakože* 'in the manner that', *inako* 'otherwise', *vьsěko/vьsako* 'in all manners', *sice* 'in this way, thus'.

4.814 Three productive types of adverbs are formed from adjectives.

(**a**) The short neuter singular accusative and (**b**) the short neuter locative may function as adverbs. Some stems prefer one or the other, and some stems allow both: *dobro* or *dobrě* 'well', *gorjьko* or *gorjьcě* 'bitterly', *različьno* or *različьně* 'differently'. Comparative evidence shows that both types were current in the oldest forms of Czech and of Balkan Slavic, but it is probable that the usage with individual words varied from dialect to dialect.

(**c**) Adjectives with the derivational suffix *-ьsk-* (§28.41) form adverbs of manner in *-ьsky*. Relatively few are attested: e.g. *vražьsky* 'inimically', *rabьsky* 'slavishly', *mǫžьsky* 'like a man, courageously', *pьsьsky* 'like a dog', *mirьsky* 'in a worldly (secular) manner', *grьčьsky* 'in Greek', *evrěisky* 'in Hebrew', and *latinьsky* 'in Latin'.

CHAPTER FOUR

CONJUGATION

5. *Fundamental notions*

5.1 Every OCS verb belongs to one of two **aspects**, *perfective* or *imperfective*: the former indicates that the action of the verb is limited by an absolute boundary (that is, that the action or process reaches its culmination), while the latter denotes no absolute boundary of the action. Verbs of motion have a further subdivision within the imperfective aspect: *determined* verbs denote a motion being carried out at one time in one direction, while *non-determined* verbs do not have this denotation. Verbal aspect is inherent (like the gender of nouns), and is not necessarily expressed by any formal means (see §5.70).

5.2 The system of forms includes three **tenses**—a *present* (which may function also as future) and two past tenses, *imperfect* (or coordinate past) and *aorist* (simple past); **imperative**; five **participles** (*present active* and *passive, past active, resultative, past passive*); a verbal **substantive**; and two inflexible forms, **infinitive** and **supine**. In each tense three **persons** in **singular**, **dual** and **plural** may be expressed, although in certain instances a single form may function for two persons. The imperative has no first person singular, and the third person forms are rare. The participles, except the resultative (§11.2), have full adjectival declensions, both according to the twofold nominal and the compound declensions (cf. §§4.19, 4.31), and the verbal substantive has a full declension, although the dual and plural forms are little used.

5.3 Every verbal form consists of a *stem* plus a *desinence*—an inflectional suffix. The desinence may be simple, a single suffix, or it may be complex, made up of a terminal suffix (which is in final position) and a non-terminal suffix. Definitions of the various suffixes will be given in the following paragraphs. The stem of any given form is obtained by subtracting the suffix (simple or complex).

In some verbs, one invariable stem is found in all forms (e.g. ‘carry’; infinitive *nes*-ti; 1 sg. pres. *nes*-ǫ, 3 pl. *nes*-ǫtъ; imperfect *nes*-ěaxъ; aorist *nes*-oxъ; past act. participle *nes*-ъ; l-participle *nes*-lъ); in others there are two stems (*dělaj*-ǫtъ 'they do' ~ *děla*-ti 'to do'; *plač*-ǫtъ 'they weep' ~ *plaka*-ti 'to weep'); and in still others there are three stems (*vidě*-ti ~ *vižd*-ǫ 'I see' ~ *vid*-ętъ 'they see'; *dvignǫ*-ti 'to move' ~ *dvign*-etъ 'he moves' ~ *dvig*-oxъ 'I moved').

Many verbs have prefixes. For the purposes of conjugation, the prefixes may be ignored. The term *verb,* therefore, will be used in the description of conjugation to refer to all lexical items which have the same stem (as defined above), regardless of prefixes. Thus a statement about the treatment of "the verb *nes-ǫtъ* 'carry'" applies equally to *vъ*-nesǫtъ 'bring in', *iz*-nesǫtъ 'carry out', and other prefixed stems. Many verbs do not occur without prefixes. This will be indicated by writing a hyphen before the stem, e.g. *-věštaj-ǫtъ* stands for *vъz*-věštajǫtъ 'announce', *otъ*-věštajǫtъ 'answer', *pro*-věštajǫtъ 'proclaim', and others. Occasionally the hyphen can be used to show that the forms with prefix behave somewhat differently than the unprefixed verb.

5.31 The prefixes are: *vъ, vъz, do, za, iz, mimo, na, nadъ, nizъ, o(b), ot(ъ), po, podъ, pri, pro, prě, prědъ, raz, sъ,* and *u*. On the variant shapes of the prefixes ending in consonants, see §3.311 (*vъz, iz, raz*), §3.312 (*ob*), and §3.3121 (*ot*). Note that in a very few verbs the particle *ne* is prefixed to a verb: *viděti* 'see', *nenaviděti* 'hate'; *mošti* 'be able', *nemošti* 'be weak, ill'.

PsSin attests ten forms with the prefix *vy-*, surely an early western dialect morpheme that was replaced in usual OCS by *iz-*. cf. Lunt *IJSLP* 39–40 (1996): 283–84; Koch p 545.

5.4 The whole conjugation can be described in terms of stems, desinences, and rules governing their combination. Regular verbs are those whose forms can all be predicted from a *basic stem,* with the aid of appropriate rules. The basic stem is to be found either in the infinitive or in the third person plural present. In the great majority of cases it is the longer of the two stems: for example **moli**-*ti* 'to beg' ~ *mol-ętъ*; **sěja**-*ti* 'to sow'~ *sěj-ǫtъ*; but *děla-ti* 'to do' **dělaj**-*ǫtъ*; *gre-ti* 'to bury' ~ **greb**-*ǫtъ* (the desinences here are *-ti* for infinitive and *-ǫtъ*/*-ętъ* for 3rd person plural present). In some verbs, however, the two stems are the same length; in such cases the basic stem is the one from which we can gain the most information. For example, the two infinitives *ves-ti* 'lead' and *lěs-ti* 'go' both have stems ending in *-s*; the corresponding 3 pl. forms are **ved**-*ǫtъ* and **lěz**-*ǫtъ,* respectively. Now, the sequences *dt* and *zt* do not occur: *st* is found instead. If we regard these infinitive forms as **ved**-*ti* and **lěz**-*ti,* we can predict that in the overt or surface form they will have *-sti* (§3.3131). Since the third plural present is the form that gives the most information, it is the basic stem. This goes for the distinctive forms of the 3 pl. **žeg**-*ǫtъ* 'burn' and **rek**-*ǫtъ* 'say': we can predict the infinitives *žešti* and *rešti,* but not vice versa (§3.3131a).

In citing verbs, only the basic stem (inf. *or* 3p pres) will be given; for example, *moli-ti, mьně-ti, kriča-ti, rinǫ-ti, věrova-ti, kaza-ti, plaka-ti* ~ *tep-ǫtъ, greb-ǫtъ, plěv-ǫtъ, čuj-ǫtъ, uměj-ǫtъ, kopaj-ǫtъ, žeg-ǫtъ, pьn-ǫtъ.*

Thus far we have been dealing with the "real words" as we perceive them in written form and interpret them as strings of morphophonemes. Now we will reanalyze them as theoretical underlying strings of morphemes.

5.41 Every basic stem may be regarded as containing a suffix that specifies that the stem is a verb and at the same time determines the set of forms that can be derived from the stem. These verb-forming suffixes will be called *classifiers*. There are five overt classifiers that end in a vowel, *-i+, -ě+, -a+, -ova+,* and *-nǫ+,* and two that end in the consonant /j/, *-aj+* and *-ęj+*. Further there is a zero-classifier, *-Ø+*; it has no phonetic value. The symbol + is used to mark the end of the basic stem.

The lexical shape of the basic stems written above in terms of real words is then: *mol-i+, mьn-ě+, krič-a+, ri-nǫ+, věr-ova+, glagol-a+, plak-a+* ~ *tep-Ø+, greb-Ø+, plěv-Ø+, čuj-Ø+, um-ěj+, kop-aj+, žeg-Ø+, pьn-Ø+.*

5.5 Basic stems end either in a consonant or in a vowel and they are accordingly called *consonantal* or *vocalic* basic stems. (Stems with the classifiers *-aj+, -ěj+,* or *-Ø+* are consonantal.) Similarly, some desinences begin with a consonant (*consonantal suffixes*) and others with vowels (*vocalic suffixes*). Since OCS structure does not permit certain successions of phonemes, the addition of suffix to stem may entail a change: most frequently the stem is altered, but some suffixes may adapt to the stem. For instance, the consonantal basic stem *ved-Ø+* (*vedǫtъ* 'they lead') appears as *ves-* before the consonantal infinitive desinence *-ti* (*vesti*) and *ve-* before the consonantal suffix *-l-ъ* of the resultative participle (*velъ*). The vocalic basic stem *kaz-a+* (*kaza-ti* 'to show') is *kaž-* before vocalic suffixes of the present tense (e.g. 3 pl. *kažǫtъ*) but it causes the vocalic imperfect suffix *-ěax-* (compare *veděaxǫ* 'they were leading') to become *-ax-* (kaza*axǫ* 'they were showing'). The shortening or modification of the stem is called *truncation.*[1]

---

1 Some rules of truncation are not simply phonological in nature, for they require special morphological marking for certain morphemes, e.g. the imperfect {ěa}.

5.6 Truncation adjusts the theoretical underlying form to a shape that conforms to the structural constraints of the (C)VCVCVCV surface structure (see pp. 32-34). If a vocalic suffix is added to a vocalic stem, the {VV} **must** be modified, usually by change or elimination of the first vowel. If a consonantal suffix is added to a consonantal stem, the {CC} sequence remains if it fits the patterns for permitted clusters (§2.522), but impermissible sequences are modified. The exact processes to be called for depend on the individual morphemes. The desinences specify the following categories:

(1) the infinitive and supine;
(2) the aorist and the resultative (or *l*-) participle;
(3) the past active participle;
(4) the past passive participle and the verbal substantive;
(5) the imperfect tense;
(6) the first person singular present;
(7) the other forms of the present tense, the imperative, and the present active and passive participles.

The first three call for C-desinences and the last three for V-desinences, but (4) includes both consonantal and vocalic allomorphs. This structural fact results in pervasive surface formal distinctions traditionally defined as the *present* versus the *infinitive/aorist* stems.

5.601 The underlying formulas may look very like or very unlike the surface forms they generate. For example, here are the infinitive, the 3rd person singular aorist (both formed with C-desinences), and the 1st person singular present (with a V-desinence) of 'to beat' and 'to testify'. The stem in one is the root with a zero suffix. In the other the root with a suffix and prefix make a verbal stem that is converted into an actor/agent by a noun-forming suffix (*telj*); this in turn becomes an abstract noun (*sъvědětelјьstvo* 'testimony') that is made into a verb (by *-ova+*), and that complex stem is perfectivized by another prefix (*za-*).

{bьj-Ø+ti} >**biti** {(za-(((sъ-((věd)-ě+))telj-)ьstv-)ova)+ti > **zasъvědětelјьstvovati**
{bьj-Ø+x-Ø}>**bi** {(za-(((sъ-((věd)-ě+))telj-)ьstv-)ova+x-Ø > **zasъvědětelјьstvova**
{bьj-Ø+Ø-ǫ}>**bьjǫ** {(za-(((sъ-((věd)-ě+))telj-)ьstv-)ova)+Ø-ǫ} > **zasъvědětelјьstvujǫ**

Keep in mind that in the surface forms the desinences are usually recognizable; by definition, the stem (whether truncated or full) is what remains when the desinence is removed. Homographs may represent different words with different underlying structure. Thus *prosi* can be 3rd singular aorist '(he) begged' or 2 sg. imperative 'beg!'; the context will usually indicate which is more plausible. The aorist 3 sg has past-marker {x} and zero desinence; the imperative sg. has non-terminal -i- plus zero for person: therefore

{pros-i+x-Ø} > *prosi* ~ {pros-i+i-Ø} > *prosi*.

The former contains the full basic stem—the theoretical {x} of the complex desinence is deleted because a consonant cannot stand at the end of a word. The latter has a VV sequence; the general rule is that the second vowel prevails—the first is either lost (as here) or converted to *j*. The segmentation is therefore aorist *prosi* versus imperative *pros-i*. Similarly, 1 sg present *rinǫ* 'I push' is *rin*-ǫ < {ri-nǫ+Ø-ǫ}, while 3 sg aorist is *rinǫ* < {ri-nǫ+x-Ø}.

5.602 The theoretical basic stems with the desinences and generative rules allow prediction of the number and types of truncated stems. There is a primary division between vocalic and consonantal basic stems. Two other factors affect the classification of conjugational types. First, vocalic stems ending in a front vowel (*i* or *ě*) require a non-terminal vocalic present-marking morpheme **ę/i**; all other basic stems take **ǫ/e**. And second, some basic stems end in *j* and others when truncated end in a palatal consonant: this affects the selection of certain allomorphs in conjugation. The remaining basic stems are those that have the classifier *-nǫ+* or consist of a root ending in a consonant other than *j* plus zero classifier—thus effectively having stem-final C. Types 6–7 below will be referred to as *hard*, types 8–9 as *soft*.

Here are the possible types of regular verbs (the numbers are for reference to the following illustrative synopses of forms):

A. Basic stem ends in a vowel

1. -i+	**i-verbs**; e.g. *prositi* 'beg', *mǫčiti* 'torment'	**ę/i**
2. -ě+	**ě-verbs**; e.g. *mьněti* 'think'	**ę/i**
2b. {X-ě+} = /š-a/	**ša-verbs**; e.g. *slyšati* {slyx-ě+} 'hear'	**ę/i**
	: surface *ča ža ša šta žda* = {kě gě xě skě zgě}	
3. *j*-a+	**ja-verbs**; e.g. *dějati* 'do'	**ǫ/e**
[*2b*]	NB: *bojati sę* 'fear' and *stojati* 'stand' belong with 2b, *ša*-verbs	*ę/i*
4. -ova+	**ova-verbs**; e.g. *milovati* 'have mercy	**ǫ/e**
5. C-a+	**Ca-verbs**; e.g. *glagolati* 'speak', *vęzati* 'tie'	**ǫ/e**
6. -nǫ+	**nǫ-verbs**; e.g. *rinǫti* 'push', *dvignǫti* 'move'	**ǫ/e**

B. Basic stem ends in a consonant

7. other than *j*-Ø+	**C-verbs**; e.g. *nesǫtъ* 'carry', *rekǫtъ* 'say	**ǫ/e**
8a. aj+	**aj-verbs**; e.g. *dělajǫtъ* 'do'	**ǫ/e**
8b. ěj+	**ěj-verbs**; e.g. *uměјǫtъ* 'know how to'	**ǫ/e**
9. *j*-Ø+	**j-verbs**; e.g. *bьjǫtъ* 'beat', *kryjǫtъ* 'cover'	**ǫ/e**

The table gives samples of typical forms of the major types: a = infinitive, b = 1 sg aorist, c = past passive participle (nom. sg. masc.), d = 1 sg. imperfect, e = 1 sg present, f = 3rd plural and 3rd sing. present, g = present active part., nom. sing. masc.-neuter and feminine, h = present passive participle, i = 2nd person singular imperative

	a inf	b 1s aor	c past pass participle	d 1s imperf	e 1s pres	f 3p/3s pres	g Ns mn/f	h pres pass participle	i 2s imv
1	**prosi**ti	**prosi**xъ	**proš**enъ	**proš**aaxъ	**prošǫ**	**pros**ętъ *pros*itъ	**prosę** -ęšti	**pros**imъ	**prosi**
2	**mьně**ti	**mьně**xъ	**mьně**nъ	**mьně**axъ	**mьnj**ǫ	**mьn**ętъ *mьn*itъ	mьnę -ęšti	**mьn**imъ	**mьni**
2b	**slyša**ti	**slyša**xъ	**slyša**nъ	**slyša**axъ	**slyš**ǫ	**slyš**ętъ *slyš*itъ	**slyšę** -ęšti	**slyš**imъ	**slyš**i
3	**děja**ti	**děja**xъ	**děja**nъ	**děja**axъ	dějǫ	**děj**ǫtъ *děj*etъ	**děję** -ǫšti	**děj**emъ	**děj**i
4	**milova**ti	**milova**xъ	**milova**nъ	**milova**axъ	**miluj**ǫ	**miluj**ǫtъ *miluj*etъ	**miluję** -ǫšti	**miluj**emъ	**miluj**i
5	**vęza**ti	**vęza**xъ	**vęza**nъ	**vęza**axъ	**vęž**ǫ	**vęž**ǫtъ *vęž*etъ	**vęžę** -ǫšti	**vęž**emъ	**vęž**i
6	**rinǫ**ti	**rinǫ**xъ	**rin**ovenъ	**rin**ěaxъ	**rin**ǫ	**rin**ǫtъ *rin*etъ	**rin**y -ǫšti	**rin**omъ	**rin**i
7	**nes**ti	**nes**oxъ **něs**ъ	**nes**enъ	**nes**ěaxъ	**nes**ǫ	**nes**ǫtъ *nes*etъ	**nes**y -ǫšti	**nes**omъ	**nes**i
	rešti	**rek**oxъ **rě**xъ	**reč**enъ	**reč**aaxъ	**rek**ǫ	**rek**ǫtъ *reč*etъ	**rek**y -ǫšti	**rek**omъ	**rьc**i
8a	**děla**ti	**děla**xъ	**děla**nъ	**děla**axъ	**dělaj**ǫ	**dělaj**ǫtъ *dělaj*etъ	**dělaję** -ǫšti	**dělaj**emъ	**dělaj**i
8b	**umě**ti	**umě**xъ	**uměnъ**	**umě**axъ	**uměj**ǫ	**uměj**ǫtъ *uměj*etъ	**uměję** -ǫšti	**uměj**emъ	**uměj**i
9	**bi**ti	**bi**xъ	**bьj**enъ	**bьj**aaxъ	**bьj**ǫ	**bьj**ǫtъ *bьj*etъ	**bьję** -ǫšti	**bьj**emъ	**bьj**i

Notice that in this table ***j*** is written before front vowel: *ję je ji* (instead of the unblocked "ę e i" of the mss.; cf. §1.24).
The C-verbs (type 7 here) have many idiosyncratic variations and irregularities, see §15.8.

5.70 Before proceeding to the description of the morphology of the verbal categories, let us survey what may be called aspect-morphology, an important part of the word-formation of verbal stems.

The aspect of individual verbs cannot always be determined, since there is no formal criterion, and most contexts permit the use of either aspect, with appropriate modification of the meaning. Indeed, variant readings of a single passage may show different aspects—or at least varying spellings that scholars interpret as signifying different aspects. Even in the earliest OCS period there must have been dialect differences both as to the aspect of certain verbs and as to the details of aspect-morphology, and some variation must have been in the original texts. Further variants were doubtless introduced by scribes from different regions and later periods. But the system as a whole is clear, despite variations and doubtful cases.

(Modern scholars, including native speakers of Slavic languages, not infrequently disagree about the aspect-definition of some OCS verbs.)

5.71 Verbs generally appeared in pairs, one perfective (P) and one imperfective (I). Exceptionally a verb could function in both aspects, and surely there were a few verbs which had no exact mates of the opposite aspect. The relationship between the two members of an aspect pair may be that of a prefixed form opposed to a non-prefixed one (*tvoriti* I ~ *sъtvoriti* P 'to do'), difference in verbal classifier (*stǫp*-i-*ti* P ~ *stǫp*-aj-*ǫtъ* I 'tread'), difference in classifier plus modification of the root (*prost*-i-*ti* P ~ *prašt*-aj-*ǫtъ* 'forgive'), or, in rare and not altogether certain cases, of suppletion, i.e. completely different stems (glagola-*ti* I ~ rek-*ǫtъ* 'say', meta-*ti* I ~ vrьg-*ǫtъ* 'throw').

[In the following paragraphs, verbs will be cited in basic-stem form without the *-ti* or *-ǫtъ* used elsewhere in the book; e.g. *prost-i* ~ *prašt-aj* for *prostiti* ~ *praštajǫtъ*. Hyphens set off prefix and the verbal derivational suffix under discussion.]

The most easily definable types are those where the prefixed verbs have different classifiers, often with a variation in the root as well. In the vast majority of pairs the imperfective has the classifier *-aj*. The most important pattern shows *-i* in P versus *-aj* (with possible root modifications) in I; the underlying structure has two classifiers {-i+aj+} plus rules of root-vowel alternation. In other major patterns the imperfectivizing {-aj+} takes the place of the {-Ø+}, {-nǫ+}, {-a+}, or {-ě+} of the perfective. And finally there are some minor types and some individual stems that allow competing forms in one or both aspects.

5.711 Classifier ***-i+*** *followed by* imperfectivizing classifier ***-aj+***, plus a rule that root-vowel *o* is to be replaced by *a* (and *e* by *ě*, though examples are rare). The underlying sequence of vowels (*i-a*) provides the conditions for iotization (§6.13) if mutation is applicable. This is the most widespread and most certainly productive group. Over 180 pairs are attested, while many more are clearly implied by the presence of the two aspect-stems compounded with different prefixes (e.g. on the pattern sъ-klěst-i ~ sъ-klěšt-aj, is-tъšt-i ~ is-tъšt-aj and many others, the forms *po*-těšt-i and *u*-těst-aj imply both **potěštaj* and **utěšti*). It seems safe to surmise that many verbs attested in only one aspect-stem belonged to this type.

5.7111 Here are typical examples of possible stem-alterations:

pri-bliž-i	pri-bliž-aj	near	u-tvrьd-i	u-tvrьžd-aj	make firm
raz-lǫči	raz-lǫč-aj	separate	vъ-gnězd-i	vъ-gněžd-aj	make nest
ostruj-i	ostruj-aj	ruin	u-god-i	u-gažd-aj	please
ras-toč-i	rastač-aj	disperse	pri-gvozd-i	pri-gvažd-aj	nail to
na-poj-i	na-paj-aj	give drink to	pri-měs-i	pri-měš-aj	join
u-krěp-i	u-krěplj-aj	strengthen	vъ-pros-i	vъ-praš-aj	ask
o-krop-i	o-kraplj-aj	sprinkle	pro-obraz-i	pro-obraž-aj	prefigure
pro-slav-i	pro-slavlj-aj	extol	sъ-xran-i	sъxranj-aj	preserve
iz-bav-i	iz-bavlj-aj	save	sъ-blazn-i	sъ-blažnj-aj	offend
u-mrьtv-i	u-mrьštvlj-aj	mortify	po-xval-i	po-xvalj-aj	praise
u-lov-i	u-lavlj-aj	catch	po-mysl-i	po-myšlj-aj	intend
u-strьm-i	u-strьmlj-aj	rush	ra(z)-šir-i	ra(z)-širj-aj	extend
sъ-mǫt-i	sъ-mǫšt-aj	disquiet	raz-or-i	raz-arj-aj	ravage
o-cěst-i	o-cěšt-aj	purify			

5.7112 A few non-prefixed aspect pairs belong to this class:

av-i	avlj-aj	manifest	prost-i	prašt-aj	forgive
var-i	varj-aj	anticipate	pust-i	pušt-aj	let go
vrěd-i	vrěžd-aj	harm	rod-i	ražd-aj	give birth
gonoz-i	gonaž-aj	free	svobod-i	svobažd-aj	liberate
mьst-i	mьšt-aj	avenge			

5.7113 Several more pairs of verbs fit this pattern in form, but the meaning of the i-verb is sometimes or always imperfective; thus the formal contrast is not a clearcut reflection of an aspectual opposition. Now, aj-verbs as a class are imperfective (with very few exceptions), while unprefixed i-verbs may belong to either aspect—and some to both. Therefore the presence of an unprefixed aj-verb beside an unprefixed imperfective (or ambiguous) i-verb with the same root represents either a lexical doublet (perhaps reflecting different dialects), or possibly a special aj-verb whose lexical meaning includes iteration of the basic action expressed by the root.[2]

Pairs where both verbs are attested only as imperfectives: *val-i ~ valj-aj* 'roll', *velič-i ~ velič-aj* 'magnify', *glas-i glaš-aj* 'call', *klon-i ~ klanj-aj* 'bow', *tvor-i ~ tvarj-aj* 'make'.

---

[2] Note that the term "iterative" is often used for the aj-verbs in varying senses: (1) the *forms* made by this derivational suffix (with or without modifications of the root), (2) the imperfective *meaning* conveyed by such derivatives, and (3) a special *aspect*, a subdivision of the imperfective, characterized by the meaning of iteration or frequentativeness. The evidence is insufficient to posit such a sub-aspect, since the iterative meaning is not always present, although it cannot be denied that this meaning is indeed the characteristic of certain aj-verbs: it is simply a part of their lexical meaning.

Pairs where the i-verb usually, but not always, is perfective: *živ-i* ~ *življ-aj* 'give life',[3] *krьst-i* ~ *krьšt-aj* 'baptize', *liš-i liš-aj* 'deprive', *plěn-i* ~ *plěnj-aj* 'take prisoner', *protiv-i sę* ~ *protivlj-aj sę* 'resist', *svęt-i* ~ *svęšt-aj* 'sanctify', *stav-i* ~ *stavlj-aj* 'place', *trud-i* ~ *tružd-aj* 'exert'.

5.7114 In a few verbs the root in the imperfective does not show the expected changes. *O-pravьd-i* ~ *o-pravьd-aj* 'justify' and *stǫp-i* ~ *stǫpaj* (and prefixed forms) apparently have {-aj+} instead of, rather than added to, {-i+}. An unchanged root-vowel is found in *pri-gotov-i* ~ *pri-gotovlj-aj* 'prepare'; a changed vowel but no iotation in *na-lož-i* ~ *na-lag-aj* 'put on', and *o-moč-i* ~ *o-mak-aj* 'wet'.[4] Doublets are attested in *vъs-xyt-i* ~ *vъs-xyšt-aj* / *vъs-xyt-aj* 'steal'; (*sъ*)*-lom-i* ~ (*sъ*)*-lamlj-aj* / (*prě*)*-lam-aj* 'break', *sram-i* ~ *sramlj-aj* / *sram-aj* 'shame';[5] *sъ-motr-i* ~ *sъ-motrj-aj* / *sъ-matrj-aj*, cf. *ra-sъ-maštrj-aj* 'view'; *u-mǫdr-i* ~ *u-mǫdrj-aj* 'make wise', cf. *prě-mǫždrj-aj*.[6] Also *vъ-sel-i* ~ *vъ-sělj-aj* / *vъ-selj-aj* 'settle'. Other attested variants: *vъz-běs-i* ~ *vъz-běš-aj*/*vъz-běs-ova* 'make frantic', *iz-měn-i* ~ *iz-měnj-a* / *iz-měn-ova* 'change', *prě-lьst-i* / *prě-lьšt-aj* / *prě-lišt-aj* 'deceive'; and *o-svět-i* ~ *o-svěšt-aj* / *o-svěšt-av-aj* 'illuminate'.

5.712 The imperfective is formed from the perfective stem by *replacing* the verbal classifier with **-*aj*+**; vowel alternation (tense *a ě i y* for lax *o e ь ъ*) if possible, and—with velar roots—mutation (*c* for *k*, *ʒ* for *g*).[7]

a. Perfective stem has **zero** classifier; a number of these perfective stems are somewhat irregular. Over 40 pairs are attested, many of them very common verbs. The following list gives examples of all the roots attested in OCS. For irregular or special stems, paragraph references to the discussion of each stem are provided. Roots ending in *j* may replace the stem-final glide with *v*; see section **e**, below.

sъ-bljud-Ø+ ~ *sъ-bljud-aj+* 'watch', *po-ěd-Ø+* (§16.22) ~ *po-ěd-aj+* 'eat', *na-klad* ~ *na-klad-aj* 'load', *pad* ~ *pad-aj* 'fall', *po-tręs* ~ *po-tręs-aj* 'shake', *otъ-sěk* ~ *otъ-sěk-aj* 'cut off', *po-čгьp* (§15.72) ~ *po-čгьp-aj* 'draw

---

3 The sole example is Mar *živlěatъ* in J 6:63, where As has *živetъ* 'lives' and Zo the same, corrected by a later cyrillic hand to *živitъ* (the expected reading). It is highly probable that the scribe of Mar (or one of his immediate predecessors) found this same erroneous intransitive verb in his model, and invented **živlajetъ* to make sense of the clause. Many other forms listed in these paragraphs are very likely *ad hoc* inventions of translators or copyists.

4 Underlying {na-log-i+} ~ {nalag-aj+}, {na-mok-i+} ~ {na-mak-aj+}.

5 These may rest on the presence or absence of "epenthetic l" (§3.71).

6 The expected palatal clusters may not appear because a scribe lacked /rj/ or because he expected the reader to derive the proper pronunciation from a morphophonemic spelling. The stem *jazv-i* 'wound' implies {jazv-i+ъš-} > *ja**žvlj**ьš- and an imperfective **ja**ž**vlj**-aj*: the only attested forms (Su 499.28 ꙗꙁвьшее сѧ, 436.12 ꙗꙁвѣѥмꙑи) fail to express *j* or mutation of *-zv-*.

7 In effect, this is Type II palatalization (§3.4), but it has become fully morphologized, see §44.361.

(water)', *otъ-vrьz-* (§15.72)[8]~ *otъ-vrьz-aj* 'open', *sъ-rět* (§16.74) ~ *sъ-rět-aj* 'meet', *sъ-sěd* (§16.61) ~ *sъ-sěd-aj* 'coagulate'.

iz-bod- ~ *iz-bad-aj* 'stab', *po-mog* ~ *po-mag-aj* 'help'; *po-gnet* cf. *u-gnět-aj* 'press, oppress'; *pro-cvьt* (§15.871) ~ *pro-cvit-aj* 'bloom', *po-čьt* (§15.871) ~ *po-čit-aj* 'read', *za-čьn* ~ *za-čin-aj* 'begin', *pro-klьn* ~ *pro-klin-aj* 'curse', *u-mьr* ~ *u-mir-aj* 'die', *pro-pьn* ~ *pro-pin-aj* 'crucify', *is-tьr* ~ *is-tir-aj* 'erase', *sъ-žъm* ~ *sъ-žim-aj* 'squeeze'; *na-dъm sę* ~ *na-dym-aj sę* 'puff up'; here also *za-kolj* (§16.513) ~ *za-kal-aj* 'slaughter'.

na-lęk ~ *na-lęc-aj* 'draw (bow)', *is-tek* ~ *is-těk-aj* 'run out'.

With variants: *po-greb* ~ *po-grěb-aj/po-grib-aj* 'bury'; *sъ-plet* ~ *sъ-plět-aj/sъ-plit-aj* 'braid'; *po-strig* (§15.874) ~ *po-strig-a/po-striʒ-aj* 'tonsure'; *sъžeg* (*žьg*; §15.875) ~ *sъ-žag-aj* (*a* for *ě*, §3.5c1)/*sъ-žiʒ-aj* 'burn up'.

b. Perfective has the classifier **-nǫ+**. Only 23 pairs are attested, although there were surely more.

iz-běg-nǫ ~ *iz-běg-aj* 'flee', *u-vęz-nǫ* ~ *u-vęz-aj* 'be caught', *u-gas-nǫ* ~ *u-gas-aj* 'be quenched', *iz-gyb-nǫ* ~ *iz-gyb-aj* 'perish', *pro-zęb-nǫ* ~ *pro-zęb-aj* 'sprout', *otъ-rig-nǫ* ~ *otъ-rig-aj* 'spew forth'.

kos-nǫ ~ *kas-aj sę* 'touch', *u-top-nǫ* ~ *u-tap-aj* 'sink'; *i-čez-nǫ* ~ *i-čaz-aj* (*a* for *ě*, §3.5c1) 'disappear'; *vъz-dъx-nǫ* ~ *vъz-dyx-aj* 'sigh', *po-tъk-nǫ* ~ *po-tyk-aj* 'knock'; *na-vyk-nǫ* ~ *na-vyc-aj* 'study, learn', *sъtęg-nǫ* ~ *sъ-tęʒ-aj* 'gain'

c. Perfective has classifier **-a+**. Seventeen pairs are attested. Most of the perfective stems have an unpredictable vowel alternation in the root, see §15.643–.65.

po-maz-a ~ *po-maz-aj* 'anoint', *prě-pojas-a* ~ *prě-pojas-aj* 'gird'; *ob-lobъz-a-* ~ *ob-lobyz-aj* 'kiss'; *iz-bьr-a iz-bir-aj* 'select', *raz-dьr-a* ~ *raz-dir-aj* 'rend', *sъ-zьd-a* ~ *sъ-zid-aj* 'build', *po-pьr-a* ~ *po-pir-aj* 'trample', *po-sъl-a* ~ *po-syl-aj* 'send', *sъ-lъg-a* cf. *ob-lyg-aj* 'lie, deceive'; and with variant, *po-kaz-a* ~ *po-kaz-aj/po-kaz-ova* 'show'.

d. Perfective has classifier **-ě+**. A small group: *sъ-gor-ě* ~ *sъ-gar-aj* 'burn up', *po-mьn-ě* ~ *po-min-aj* 'remember', *prě-pьr-ě* ~ *prě-pir-aj* 'convince', *pri-zьr-ě* ~ *pri-zir-aj* 'view'. In other prefixed forms of *zьr-ě+ti* 'to see', there is doubt as to whether the *ě*-verbs are always perfective. (L 6:7 Mar *nazьrěaxǫ i kъnižnici*, if perfective imperfect, would mean that the scribes made a continued series of completed observations; Zo As *naziraaxǫ* is simpler: 'they continually observed him' [Jesus].)

---

[8] The spelled *rь* in *črьp* and *vrьz* doubtless represents syllabic *r* (cf. §2.631). It is highly probable that it was short in the perfectives but long in the imperfectives.

e. Perfective stem ends in **j**, which is replaced by *v* before the *-aj+* classifier. In an older formation, the *j* is the root-final consonant, followed by the zero classifier. A younger formation, surely productive in the innovating type of language attested in Supr, adds the classifier *-aj+* to a stem that already has *-aj+* or *-ěj+*; the first glide is replaced by *v,* producing *-avaj-* or *-ěvaj-* (with, however, no apparent change of meaning). The *-vaj* forms are far more common in the mss.

Some older forms survive beside the new: *u-bьj-Ø+* ~ *u-bij-aj+* and *u-bivaj* 'beat, kill'; *po-vьj* ~ *po-vij-aj* and *po-vivaj* 'wrap'; and *iz-lьj-Ø+* beside *iz-lьj-a+* (§15.46) ~ *iz-livaj* 'pour out'.

sъ-kryj ~ *sъ-kryvaj* 'hide', *o-myj* ~ *o-myvaj* 'wash', *u-nyj* ~ *u-nyvaj* 'lose courage'; *u-pьj* (§15.93) ~ *u-pivaj sę* 'become intoxicated', *vъz-ъpьj-* cf. *pri-v-ъpivaj* (§3.25) 'call out to'; also the irregular *vъs-pě* (§16.53) ~ *vъs-pěvaj* 'sing forth', prefixed forms of *byti* (§16.11) like *iz-by* ~ *iz-byvaj* 'be left over'; *o-pljьv-a* (§15.52) ~ *o-pljьvavaj.*

o-del-ěj or *o-dol-ěj* ~ *o-delěvaj* or *o-dol-ěvaj* 'win, be victorious'; *u-spěj* ~ *u-spěvaj* 'be of use', *o-cěpěn-ěj* ~ *o-cěpěněvaj* 'become rigid'; *po-znaj-* ~ *po-znavaj* 'know', *o-klevet-aj* ~ *o-klevetavaj* 'slander', *sъ-konьč-aj* ~ *sъ-konьčavaj* 'finish', *podъ-kopaj-* ~ *podъ-kopavaj* 'dig (under)', *ob-lъgъč-aj* ~ *ob-lъgъčavaj* 'ease', *o-tęžьč-aj* ~ *o-tęžьčavaj* 'become heavy'.

Some common stems are both P and I, with corresponding *-vaj* forms that are only I: *razum-ěj* 'understand' (IP), *po-razuměj* (P); *razum-ěvaj* and *pro-raz-uměvaj* (I); *konьč-aj* {kon-ьc-ěj+} 'finish' (IP), prefixed *sъ-konьč-aj* is P and *sъkonьčavaj* is I; *otъ-věšt-aj* (IP) 'answer' *otъ-věšt-avaj* (I)—also *sъ-věšt-aj* 'convince', *u-věšt-aj* 'counsel', *oběšt-aj* 'promise' (§3.312), *za-věšt-aj* 'bequeath'.[9]

5.713 *Isolated types*

a. The small group of verbs having *determined* ~ *non-determined* forms (within the imperfective aspect, cf. §5.1) are: *ved* ~ *vod-i* 'lead', *nes* ~ *nos-i* 'carry', *per* ~ *par-i* 'fly', *gъn-a* ~ *gon-i* 'drive, chase', *vlěk* ~ *vlač-i*

---

9 These well attested verbs seem to fall into patterns that allow us confidently to predict forms, here the type *-svęt-**i**+* ~ *-svět-**i-aj**+* *-svěšt**avaj**+* (§5.7114). The root *vět* 'solemn speech' underlies synchronic {-vět-i+aj+}; yet the mediating formation *-vět-i+* is hypothetical. Although nouns like *otъvětъ* and *otъvěštanьe* are in common usage, no i-verb is found in early medieval Slavic. The isolated infinitive **кръ҆млгавати** Su 188.4 'to traffic dishonestly' suggests a noun *krъčьma* 'tavern' (SC *krčma*) and a formation {kъrčьm-i-aj}—which may never have existed—while the meaning is derived from the Gk and the context.

'drag', *id* (§16.3) ~ *xod-i* 'go, walk', and perhaps *plov* ~ *plav-aj* 'go (by boat)'. With prefixes these pairs become normal P ~ I pairs, e.g. *vъ-ved* (P) ~ *vъ-vod-i* (I) 'lead in', *iz-id* (P) ~ *is-xod-i* (I) 'go out'. The pair *-lěz* ~ *-laz-i* 'go, clamber' is by chance not attested without prefix, cf. *sъ-lěz-* ~ *sъlaz-i* 'climb down'.

The rare prefixed stems with *-važd-aj, -ganj-aj,* and *-xažd-aj* do not seem to be semantically opposed to the normal imperfectives in *-vod-i, -gon-i,* and *-xod-i*. Perhaps some instances represent lexical iteratives (cf. §5.7113), they do not show a systematic opposition of aspect.

b. Other types of relationship (P is given first):

kup-i ~ *kup-ova* 'buy', *obraz-i* ~ *obraz-ova* 'form', *obьšt-i* ~ *obьšt-eva* 'associate' (but *pri-obьšt-i* ~ *pri-obьšt-aj/pri-obьšt-avaj*).

prě-minǫ {prě-min-nǫ+} ~ *prě-min-ova* 'pass', *po-vinǫ* {po-vin-nǫ+} ~ *po-vin-ova* 'be subject to' (and *obinǫ* {ob-vin-nǫ} ~ *obinova* 'avoid', §3.312).

otъ-rěz-a ~ *otъ-rěz-ova* 'cut off', *vъz-isk-a* (§15.641) ~ *vъz-isk-ova* 'seek out'; perhaps *znamen-aj* ~ *znamen-avaj/znamen-ova* 'signify'.

skoč-i ~ *skak-a* 'jump', *tlьk-nǫ* ~ *tlьk* (§15.874) 'knock'; *kanǫ* {kap-nǫ} ~ *kap-a* 'drip'; *pljunǫ/plinǫ* ~ *pljьv-a* 'spit'; *otъ-ri-nǫ* ~ *otъ-rěj/otъrivaj* 'push away'; *po-manǫ* {po-maj-nǫ+} ~ *po-maj-a/po-mavaj* 'beckon'; *prě-sta-n* ~ *prě-staj-a* 'stop'; *dad-* (§16.21) ~ *daj-a* (but with prefixes *-dad* ~ *-daj-a* or *-davaj*); *imǫtъ ęti* ({ьm-Ø+} §15.83) ~ *im-a jemlj-ǫtъ* (§15.643) 'take' (with consonantal prefixes *vъz-ьm-* ~ *vъz-ьm-a* or *vъz-ьm-aj*).

5.721 It is more difficult to determine aspect-pairs whose formal relationship is that of non-prefixed imperfective ~ prefixed perfective (e.g. tvoriti ~ *sъ*-tvoriti 'do'), for similarity in *form* must be supported by identity in lexical *meaning*. Now, the addition of any prefix to any verb (except the non-determined ones and most imperfectives with the classifier *-aj*+) produces a perfective, but the prefix also adds a semantic element. Thus *prě*-tvoriti and *ras*-tvoriti are perfective, but they mean 'transform' and 'dissolve', respectively, and hence are opposed to the simplex *tvoriti* in lexical meaning as well as in form. In *sъ*-tvoriti, however, the prefix *sъ*- has no force other than to perfectivize the verb; it is an "empty prefix". Nearly all of the prefixes serve with one verb or another in this purely perfectivizing function (e.g. *u-slyšati* 'hear', *po*-gasiti 'quench', *vъs*-plakati 'weep'), so that only a semantic analysis of each group of formally related verbs can separate out the prefixed perfective which corresponds in meaning to the simplex imperfective. Information of this kind is often too meager in the texts to permit a clearcut decision.

5.722 The formation of new prefixed forms and of mates of the opposite aspect for various newly-created or already extant verbs must have been an active process in OCS as it is in all modern Slavic languages. It is certain that the classifier *-aj* (with or without modification of the root), and, to a lesser extent *-ova+*, were productive for making imperfectives to various other classes of verbs, and it is probable that *-nǫ+* was productive for making perfectives. Patterns of like formations could easily be extended. For example, the pairs *prě*-tvor-i+ ~ *prě*-tvarj-aj+, *pri*-tvor-i+ ~ *pri*-tvarj-aj+, and u-*tvor-i+* ~ u-*tvarj-aj+*, originally opposed to *sъ-tvor-i+* ~ *tvor-i+*, gave rise both to a new imperfective *sъ-tvarj-aj+*, and to an unprefixed *tvarj-aj+*. The preference of different dialects (regional and historical) for specific forms in given contexts doubtless accounts for such doublets in our texts.

5.8 The possible verb-forms are most economically described in terms of separate morphological categories. After preliminary remarks on the personal suffixes in the next section (§5.9), the present tense will be described (§6), then the imperative (§7) and the present participles (§8). The two past tenses, imperfect (§9) and aorist (§10), are followed by the three past participles (§11), the verbal substantive (§12), the two invariable forms, infinitive and supine (§13), and finally a note on the formation of compound tenses (§14).

NB: the sections on the infinitive and present tense are of particular importance to students because traditionally it is the infinitive, with or without the first person singular present and/or the second or third person singular present, that is cited as the "name-form" in dictionaries and grammars. One must therefore know the relationship of these forms to the *basic stems* used in this book.

A survey of the verbs by classes (§15) will include the enumeration of irregular verbs; minor irregularities are mentioned in §6–§13.

An index of irregular verbs is at the end of the book.

5.9 The *terminal desinences* expressing the three persons of the dual and the 2nd plural are constant throughout all categories that specify person (present, imperative, imperfect, aorist), while the other persons are expressed by two or more desinences which vary according to the category.

Here is a summary table of all person-number desinences. The term *past* includes the *imperfect* (coordinated past) and the *aorist* (simple past).

	Singular		Dual	Plural		
	present	*past*		*present*	*past*	
1	**-ǫ** (-mь, -ě)	**-ъ**	**-vě**	**-mъ**	**-omъ**	1
2	**-ši** (-si)	-Ø (-tъ)	**-ta**	**-te**		2
3	**-tъ**	-Ø (-tъ)	**-te**	**-tъ**	**-ǫ, -ę**	3

1sg **-mь** appears in the present of 5 verbs, **-ě** is an alternative for one: *esmь, damь, ěmь, věmь/vědě, imamь* (§16.2).
-ǫ is otherwise the universal 1 sg present desinence.
-ъ is used for *past* (i.e. imperfect and aorist).

2sg **-si** is present, used with 4 verbs: *esi, dasi, ěsi, věsi* (§16.2).
-ši is the terminal present desinence for all other verbs.
-tъ is used in presence of *-imperfect* (i.e. the aorist) in a limited group of specially marked verbs (including some where it is optional); it always is homonymous with 3sg (§10.51-2).
-**Ø** is normal in presence of *past* (i.e. imperfect and aorist, §9.1, 10.1).

3sg **-tъ** is universal in the present tense; it is special in the aorist of certain verbs (§10.51–2).
-**Ø** is normal in presence of *past* (and the same as 2sg). See also §6.61

3pl **-tъ** is universal in the present tense.
-ǫ is used in the imperfect (hence *-xǫ*).
-ę is used in the aorist (whereby *-xę* > *-šę*).

5.91 The third person dual desinence **-te** ('they two') is for the most part clearly opposed to the second person dual **-ta** ('you two'). Thus *third* person dual has the same form as *second* person plural—a distinction maintained in Mar, Ps, Euch, and Cloz. In Zo and As, *-ta* occasionally functions as 3rd person dual, while in Sav and Su *-te* in 3 du is rare.

This means that in late OCS *-te* signifies 2nd person plural, while 2–3 dual is only *-ta*; the same form is used for second and third persons in all duals as well as in the imperfect and aorist singular.

Therefore: *in* **every** *tense-paradigm the third dual desinence should be understood to be* **-te/-ta**.

5.911 Supr (twice) and Sav (6x) use the suffix *-tě* for 3 person dual with non-masculine subjects, e.g. **текостѣ** 'they (the two Marys) ran' (Mt 28:8 Sav), Vaillant 228.

6.0 The present tense

6.10 The desinences of the present tense are complex; a vocalic present-marker preceeds the terminal desinences that indicate person and number, except in the first person singular (where the marker is zero).

6.11 The present-marker is either general, **ǫ** in 3 pl and **e** elsewhere, or specific, **ę** in 3 pl, and **i** elsewhere. The specific *ę/i* is used with basic stems that end in a front vowel (therefore *-i+*, *ě+*, and the *ša*-verbs, where surface *a* represents underlying {ě}, §15.31); *ǫ/e* is used with all other verbs. E.g.:

	nosi-ti 'carry' and	*mьně-ti* 'think' + *ę/i*	~	*nes-ǫtъ* 'carry' and	*dělaj-ǫtъ* 'do' + *ǫ/e*
3pl	{nos-i+ę-tъ}	{mьn-ě+ę-tъ}	~	{nes-Ø+ǫ-tъ}	{děl-aj+ǫ-tъ}
3 sg	{nos-i+i-tъ}	{mьn-ě+i-tъ}	~	{nes-Ø+e-tъ}	{děl-aj+e-tъ}
1sg	{nos-i+Ø-ǫ}	{mьn-ě+Ø-ǫ}	~	{nes-Ø+Ø-ǫ}	{děl-aj+Ø-ǫ}

6.12 Person-number desinences:

	singular	dual	plural
1st person	**-ǫ**	**-vě**	**-mъ**
2nd person	**-ši**	**-ta**	**-te**
3rd person	**-tъ**	**-te**	**-tъ**

6.13 Vocalic basic stems are truncated before the vocalic desinences: the first vowel (V_1) either disappears or is replaced by *j*.

(**A**) V_1 is replaced by *j*

(1) if it is **a**, and (2) if V_1 is **i** or **ě** and V_2 is *not* **i** or **ę**. Otherwise

(**B**) V_1 is deleted.

The *j* resulting from the action of rule **A** creates a new Cj cluster that requires further adjustment.

6.21 The classifier *-ova/-eva* and two stems with *-ьv-a+* become *ovj, evj, ьvj,* and then *uj*: e.g. věr-*ova*+ti 'to believe' ~ 3 pl {věr-ova+ǫ-tъ} > věrovjǫtъ > věr*uj*ǫtъ; nepьšt-*eva*+ti 'to suppose' ~ nepьšt*uj*ǫtъ; plj*ьv-a*+ti 'to spit' ~ plj*uj*ǫtъ.[10]

6.22 A-verb presents have iotation: *vęz-**a**+ti* 'to tie' ~ {vęz-a+ǫ-tъ} > *vęz**j**ǫtъ* > *vę**ž**ǫtъ*, 2 sg {vęz-a+e-ši} > *vęz**j**eši* > *vę**ž**eši*; *plak-**a**+ti* 'to weep'

---

10 This is a morphological rule that occurs with these specially-defined morphemes. Like many morphological rules, it has specific phonological effects. Elsewhere in OCS it is normal for *ovj* to become *ovlj*: the *j* after labial consonant becomes palatal *lj*, cf. §6.23: *loviti* 1 sg pres *lovljǫ* like *lomljǫ* from *lomiti*.

~ 3 pl {plak-a+ǫ-tъ} > *plakjǫtъ* > *plačǫtъ*, 2 sg {plak-a+e-ši} > *plakješi* > *plačeši*. (For a-verbs that have an unpredictable alternation of root-vowel in the present stem, see §15.642.)

In *sěj-a+ti* 'to sow' {sěj-a+ǫ-tъ} > *sěj-j-ǫtъ*; double consonants reduce to one: *sějǫtъ*.

6.23 In i-verbs and ě-verbs *j* is generated from *i* or *ě* before the first person singular desinence, creating Cj, and triggering iotation: {kup-i+Ø-ǫ} > kupjǫ by rule A, while {kup-i+ę-tъ} > kupętъ by rule B.

kupi-ti ku*p*-ętъ	~ ku*plj*ǫ	'buy'	ljubi-ti lju*b*-ętъ	~ lju*blj*ǫ	'love'
lovi-ti lo*v*-ętъ	~ lo*vlj*ǫ	'hunt'	lomi-ti lo*m*-ętъ	~ lo*mlj*ǫ	'break'
svęti-ti svę*t*-ętъ	~ svę*št*ǫ	'sanctify'	vidě-ti vi*d*-ętъ	~ vi*žd*ǫ	'see'
nosi-ti no*s*-ętъ	~ no*š*ǫ	'carry'	obrazi-ti obra*z*-ętъ	~ obra*ž*ǫ	'form'
mьně-ti mь*n*-ętъ	~ mь*nj*ǫ	'think'	mysli-ti my*sl*-ętъ	~ my*šlj*ǫ	'think'
kъsně-ti kъ*sn*-ętъ	~ kъ*šnj*ǫ	'be late'	blazni-ti bla*zn*-ętъ	~ bla*žnj*ǫ	'offend'
pusti-ti pu*st*-ętъ	~ pu*št*ǫ	'let go'	xvali-ti xva*l*-ętъ	~ xva*lj*ǫ	'praise'
umori-ti umo*r*-ętъ	~ umo*rj*ǫ	'kill'	sъmotri-ti sъmotr-ętъ	~ sъmo*štrj*ǫ	'look'

6.3 Root-final velars in C-verbs undergo KI-mutation before the present-marker *e*: this produces an alternation of consonants within the paradigm.

{tek-Ø+ǫ-tъ} > *tekǫtъ*, 1 sg *tekǫ* ~ 2 sg {tek-Ø+e-ši} > *tečeši* etc. 'run'
{mog-Ø+ǫ-tъ} > *mogǫtъ*, 1 sg *mogǫ* ~ 2 sg {mog-Ø-e-ši} > *možeši* 'be able'

6.41 The verb *xotěti* 'want' (and prefixed forms) takes the non-terminal e-marker in all forms but 3 pl and 1 sg: {xot-ě+ę-tъ} by rule B > *xotętъ*, while {xot-ě+Ø-ǫ} by rule A2 > *xotjǫ*, whence *xoštǫ*. The other forms have {xot-ě+e-}, which by A2 produces *xotje-*; therefore *xošteši*, *xoštemъ*, etc.

In Su, the root vowel *ъ* is found exceptionally for *o*: 1 sg χъштѫ 169.3, 534.11, 3 sg χъштє 153.7, 169.21. These are doubtless dialectal forms; note omission of the 3 sg desinence *-tъ* (cf. §6.61).

6.42 The verb *dovьlěti* 'suffice', which has only 3rd person forms, is attested with 3 pl *dovьlętъ* and *dovьlějǫtъ*, implying competing classifiers, -ě ~ -ěj. The 3 sg *dovьljetъ* implies irregular selection of the e-marker {dovьl-ě+e-tъ} > -lje- (cf. Vaillant 263).

6.431 The verb *iska*-ti 'seek' has the mutated forms 3 pl *ištǫtъ* and 1 sg *ištǫ* (< iskj- < isk-a+) beside unmutated *iskǫtъ* and *iskǫ*. This implies an alternate underlying {isk-Ø+}; in the rest of the present, *ište-* results from KI-mutation {isk-Ø+e-}.

6.432 The root *met* 'throw' also forms alternate basic stems, {met-Ø+} ~ {met-a+} and therefore *metǫ meteši* etc., beside *meštǫ mešteši* etc.

6.5 Verbs with present stems in *-aj-* or *-ěj-* have spelled *-ae-/ěe-* in all forms except 1 sg and 3 pl: děl*ae*ši, děl*ae*tъ; d*ae*ši, d*ae*tъ; um*ěe*tъ, um*ěe*te; s*ěe*tъ, etc. In Mar such forms (particularly 3 sg and 2 pl) are often written with *-aa-/-ěa-,* and occasionally (for *-aa-*) simply *-a-*: dělaatъ, dělatъ, uměatъ, sěatъ. This kind of change is extremely rare in other mss.

Similarly, stems in *-uj-* appear in Mar with *-uu* (rarely, for expected *-ue-*): trěb*uu*tъ for trěb*ue*tъ (from trěbova-ti 'demand') and the like.

6.61 The 3rd person desinence *-tъ* (sg and pl) is occasionally omitted. For *estъ* and *něstъ* (§16.101), *e* and *ně* occur. These are surely dialect features. Cf. Vaillant 227.

6.62 The jer in desinences *-mъ* and *-tъ* may be affected by the following enclitic **jь* 'him' (§4.25), for the ъ is both tense and strong. It may be written *y* (*-tyi, -myi*), e.g. *osǫdętyi* 'they will condemn him', *ostavimyi* 'we will leave him'. Spellings with *-oi* also occur, but rarely: e.g. *izbavitoi* 'he will save him'. Cf. Vaillant 43–4.

6.7 Five common verbs have quite irregular present forms; they lack a present-marker (except for *ę* in 3 pl), adding desinences directly to the consonantal root. The 1st and 2nd sg desinences are special: *-mь* and *-si*.

6.71 *Dati* 'give' (P), *ěsti* 'eat', and *věděti* 'know' and their prefixed forms have roots in *d* (*dad-, ěd-, věd-*). The *d* is retained only before the tense-marker *ę* of the 3 pl; it becomes *s* before desinences beginning with *t* (§3.3131a) and drops elsewhere (see §16.2 for details):

*damь dasi dastъ, *davě dasta daste, damъ daste dadętъ; ěmь věmь, ěsi věsi, ěstъ věstъ, *ěvě věvě … ědętъ vědętъ.*

The archaic and morphologically isolated 1 sg *vědě* 'I know' is a less frequent equivalent of *věmь*.

6.72 The verb *iměti* 'to have' forms its present (except for 3 pl) on a stem *ima-* to which desinences are added directly, including the special 1 sg *mь*. The 3 pl is *imǫtъ* (with a preferred alternant **имѣѭтъ** in Su):

imamь imaši imatъ, imavě imata imate, imamъ imate imǫtъ (iměјǫtъ).

6.73 *Byti* 'to be' has a present stem *es-* except for 3 pl *s-*: *esmь esi estъ, esvě esta este, esmъ este sǫtъ.*

The negated form is special except in 3 pl: *něsmь něsi něstъ, něsvě něsta něste, něsmъ něste,* but *ne sǫtъ.*

6.74 The present forms of *bǫd-ǫtъ* express the future 'will be'. For other future expressions, see §14.4, and more especially §21.11.

6.75 Prefixed derivatives of *byti* (§16.11) use *-bǫd-* for the present stem; e.g. *zabyti* 'forget' *zabǫdǫtъ, pribyti* 'join' *pribǫdǫtъ.*

6.8 The completely isolated form *sętъ* may be a relic present or aorist, 'he says/said', but in OCS it functions as an adverb meaning 'allegedly'. See SJS.

7.0 The imperative

7.100 The imperative desinences are complex, consisting of an imperative-marker **i²** or **e²** plus the personal desinences (including zero).

	singular	dual	plural
1st person	–	**-vě**	**-mъ**
2nd person	Ø	**-ta**	**-te**
3rd person	Ø	**-te**	Ø

Before the vocalic imperative-markers, vocalic basic stems are truncated by processes described above in §§6.13-23.

7.101 The marker *ě* appears in the dual and plural of basic stems in *-nǫ+* or *-Ø+* (unless preceded by *j*); *i* is used elsewhere—that is, in all singular forms and in the dual and plural of all stems ending in a consonant other than *j* or a vowel other than *ǫ*.

7.11 Because these vowels are specifically marked ({**i²**}, {**e²**}), they trigger KAI-mutation; stem-final velars (*k, g*) are replaced by *c ʒ* (§3.4): *mog*-ǫtъ 'be able' ~ *moʒi moʒěte*; *vrьg*-ǫtъ 'throw' ~ *vrьʒi vrьʒěte*; *strěg*-ǫtъ 'protect' ~ *strěʒi strěʒěte*.

7.111 Stems in *-ek* and *-eg* change to *ьc/ьʒ*: *rek*-ǫtъ 'say' ~ *rьci rьcěmъ rьcěte*.

7.2 *Irregularities*. The verb 'to be' forms the imperative on the stem *bǫd-*: *bǫdi bǫděmъ bǫděte*. (The 3 sg *bǫdi* 'may it be, may it happen' is the chief representative of third person imperatives.)

The irregular verbs *dati* 'give', *ěsti* 'eat', *věděti* 'know', and the otherwise regular *vidě*-ti 'see' have *daždь, ěždь, věždь* and *viždь*. (This implies underlying {-d-jь}, and iotation.) In the dual and plural the imperative-marking vowel is *i*: thus *dadimъ dadite, ědite, vědite*.

7.201 In Euch, these forms have final *i*: *daždi, viždi, pověždi* ('tell', from *pověděti*).

7.202 KF has the presumably Czech forms with *z* < {dj}, *podazь, otъdazь*.

7.21 C-a+ verbs and root *j*-verbs have plural imperative forms with the marker *ě* beside regular forms with *i*: *pokaza*-ti 'show' *pokažite* ~ *pokažěte* покажѣте, покажате, *pьj*-ǫtъ 'drink' *piite* ~ *piěte* пиꙗте. The *a/ě* is exclusive in Sav, frequent in As, Zo and Supr, less so in Mar, infrequent in Ps, and unknown in Euch and Sav. The spellings are not unambiguous, but the letter-sequence *žě* in glagolitic and жѣ in cyrillic violates a fundamental OCS rule (§2.413), and *ža* (жа) and the like suggest that underlying {ě[2]} (which alternates with {i[2]}) is being replaced with {ě[1]} (which alternates with {a}), cf. §3.5c. Compare Vaillant §149.

7.3 The third plural imperative is attested only by *bǫdǫ* 'may they be'. It occurs in L 12:35 (in Zo, Mar, As, Sav), three times in psalm 108, and once in KF.

7.4 The form *otъpaděmь* 'may I fall away' (Ps 7:5), supported by scraps of testimony from post-OCS mss, suggests that in early OCS such forms (with *-mь*) were more freely used. See Vaillant 232.

7.5 Third person imperative (and occasionally also first person) can be expressed by *da* plus the present tense: *da pridǫtъ* 'may they come, let them come'. See also §22.11.

8.0 The present participles

8.10 The declensional stem of the *present* **active** *participle* has a derivational suffix **-ęšt-** or **-ǫšt-** that is correlated to the shape of the present-markers (§6.11). Verbs with *-ętъ* in 3 pl. pres. have *-ęšt-* in pres.act. part., but *-ę* in masc./neut. nom. sg. Verbs with *-ǫtъ* in 3. pl. pres. have *-ǫšt-* in pres. act. part., but a variable {y[2]/ę} in nom. sg masculine/neuter; *-ę* is used if the (truncated) verbal stem ends in a palatal consonant, *-y* otherwise. Cf. §5.602.

The formant of the *present* **passive** *participle* is **-im-**, or **-em-/-om-**, underlying {i-m-} or {e/o-m}.

For the declension of the active participles see §4.19 and §4.31. The passive participles are regular adjectives that belong to the hard twofold nominal and compound declensions.

8.11 Verbs forming their present tense with the present-marker *i* (i.e. i-verbs, ě-verbs, and ša-verbs, §6.11) have present participles in **-ę** and **-im-ъ**: *kupi*-ti 'buy' *kup-i*-ši ~ *kupę kupimъ*; *vidě*-ti 'see' *vid-i*-ši ~ *vidę vidimъ*; *slyša*-ti 'hear' *slyš-i*-ši ~ *slyšę slyšimъ*. (For these verbs the nom. sg fem. of the active participle is in **-ęšti**: *kupęšti, vidęšti, slyšęšti*.)

8.12 Other soft present-stems (§5.602) have **-ę** and **-em-ъ**: *vęz-a*-ti *vęž*-ǫtъ 'bind' ~ *vęžę vęžemъ*; *milova*-ti 'have mercy' *miluj-e*-ši ~ *milueę miluemъ*; *dělaj*-ǫtъ 'do' ~ *dělaę, dělaemъ*; *sěja*-ti 'to sow' ~ *sěę, sěemъ*. (For these verbs the nom. sg. fem. of the active participle is in **-ǫšti**.)

8.13 All other stems (i.e. C-verbs and nǫ-verbs) take the suffixes -**y** and **-om-ъ**: *nes*-ǫtъ 'carry' ~ *nesy, nesomъ*; *dvignǫ*-ti 'move' ~ *dvigny, dvignomъ*. (For these verbs the nom. sg. fem. of the active participle is in **-ǫšti**.)

8.131 Exceptionally, the suffix **-y²** (masc.-neut. nom sg., alternating with **-ǫšt-** of the rest of the paradigm) is written with a special glagolitic letter we transcribe *ꙁ*: e.g. *nesꙁ*. Such spellings are more commonly found for the *-yi* of the definite participles. The special letter occurs only for this particular morpheme; the phonetic value is a subject for speculation.

8.2 The verb *byti* 'to be' forms the participles *sy* (f. *sǫšti*) 'being' and also *bǫdy* (f. *bǫdǫšti*), which means 'future, that to come'. *Věděti* 'know' has *vědy* (f. *vědǫšti*).

Gorěti 'burn' has beside regular *gorę* (*goręšti*) some forms of *gorǫšt-*: cf. Vaillant §180.

9.0 The imperfect.

9.1 The desinences of the imperfect are complex: the imperfect-marker {ěa} + the past-marker {x} + past person-number desinences. The surface forms are:

	singular	dual	plural
1st person	**-ěaxъ**	**-ěaxově**	**-ěaxomъ**
2nd person	**-ěaše**	**-ěašeta**	**-ěašete**
3rd person		**-ěašete**	**-ěaxǫ**

9.111 The sequence of vowels (*ě*[1]*a*) interacts with the stem-final vowels as follows:

A. The classifier *-i+* before {ěa}- becomes *j*; the resulting iod-cluster (Cj-ěa) undergoes iotation.

B. If the {ěa} follows *ě, ěj, a,* or *aj,* the sequence *jě* or *ja* is deleted: e.g. *mьn-ě+***ěa***-* > *mьn-ěa-*; *děl-a***j+ěa***-* > *děl-aa-*; *um-ě***j+ěa** > *um-ěa-*.

9.112 After consonants, the *ě*[11] behaves as usual (§3.5 c1): (1) it effects KI mutation in velars, and (2) itself becomes *a*. Thus *rek-Ø*+ěa- > reč-ěa- > reč*a*a-; *mog-Ø*+ěa > mož-ěa- > mož*a*a-.

9.12 The desinences are in effect **-ěax-** plus the desinences of the root aorist, see §10.601.

9.121 Beside the **-šet-** in the dual and pl. desinences, the innovative forms **-ěa-sta** and **-ěa-ste** are used (see also §5.91). The *-šet-* forms are

---

[11] The two-syllable person-number desinences of dual and plural may be regarded as /**ově**, **omъ**/ and /**eta**, **ete**/ with a variable "thematic vowel": (**1**) *e* is added (**a**) before *t* (**eta**, **ete**), and (**b**) before the Ø of 2nd–3rd sing.; (**2**) *o* is added otherwise. The past-marker *x* remains before *o* (-xově -xomъ) but by KI-mutation yields *š* before *e* (-šeta -šete). A modification of the rule deletes **1a**, and *xta* and *xte* (by a more general rule of consonant clustering) yield *sta* and *ste*. (In later Serbian dialects, the reformulated rule (1) inserts *o* before any C, while (2) *e* is added before Ø; this results in *-xota* and *-xote*.)

exclusive in Zo, nearly so in Mar, but only a bare majority in As; in Su they are clearly exceptional. Sav has only *-sta* and *-ste*.[1]

9.211 Contrary to §9.111 A, the classifier *-i+* in a few examples in Su is simply deleted. Thus prixod*ěa*xъ for prixo*žda*axъ (*prixodi*-ti 'come'), ra*dě*axъ *for ražd*aaxъ (*radi*-ti 'be pleasing'). This type of form increases in post-OCS mss.

9.212 The classifier *-ě+* appears to convert to *j* and trigger iotation in one isolated example: the form spelled *kъšněaše* in L 1:21 Mar appears to represent **kъšnjaaše* (*kъsně*-ti 'delay'). This type of form is better illustrated in post-OCS Serbian mss.

9.22 Stems in *-nǫ+* truncate before the *-ěa-* suffix: *podvignǫ*-ti 'move' ~ podvigněaxъ. Only five examples are attested (four in Su, 1 in Cloz), probably because nearly all nǫ-verbs are perfective, and perfective imperfects are rarely required (cf. §21.2).

9.3 In all texts there are forms spelled with only the initial *ě* or *a* of the suffix: *vėděaxъ* ~ *vėděxъ* 'knew', *boěaxǫ sę* ~ *boěxǫ sę* 'feared', *xotěaše* ~ *xotěše* 'wanted'. The longer forms usually predominate, but in Sav they are rare exceptions. These spellings apparently indicate that contraction of the two vowels into a single syllable began during the OCS period; most scribes considered it proper to write two vowels.

In Su there are spellings with *ěě* and *jaja* (начьнѣѣхомъ 'we began', строıаıаше 'set') that probably represent artificial attempts at restoring the older, non-contracted forms.

9.4 Verbs whose forms are not predictable from a basic stem (§16) usually use the present stem for the imperfect: *obrěsti obręštǫtъ* 'find' *obręštaaxъ*; *idǫtъ iti* 'go' ~ *iděaxъ*; *dadętъ dati* 'give' ~ *daděaxъ*; *duti dъmǫtъ* 'blow'' *dъměaxъ*; *žrьti žьrǫtъ* 'sacrifice' ~ *žьrěaxъ*; *gъnati ženǫtъ* 'drive' ~ *ženěaxъ*; *pěti pojǫtъ* 'sing' ~ *pojaaxъ*; *mlěti meljǫtъ* 'grind' ~ *meljaaxъ*; *klati koljǫtъ* 'stab' ~ *koljaaxъ*; *brati borjǫtъ* 'fight' ~ *borjaaxъ*; **ěxati ědǫtъ* 'ride' ~ *ěděaxъ*.

9.5 A few verbs have competing forms from the infinitive/aorist and from the present stem: 'spit' *plьvati pljьvaaxǫ* (Zo Mar) ~ *pljujǫtъ pljujaxǫ* (As; Mk 15:19); *besědovati* 'converse' ~ бесѣдоугıаше Su 304.18, 569.30; *trěbovati* 'need' ~ трѣбоугıаше Su 307.19; *radovati sę* 'rejoice' ~ радоугıаше сѧ Su 550.11 [all other imperfects from ova-verbs, even in Su, have *-ovaa-*]; 'call' *zъvati zъvaaxǫ* etc., Su зъваше ~ *zovǫtъ* зовѣахѫ Su 322.12; 'receive' *priemljǫtъ* прикмыıаше Su 274.24 ~ *priimati priimaše* etc.

9.6 The imperfect of *byti* is defective, being found only in the third person: *běaše, běašete, běaxǫ* (contracted *běše, běxǫ*). There is some confusion of these forms with the imperfective aorist *bě, běste, běšę* (§10.91).

Samples of typical imperfect derivation:

underlying	i > j	iotation	ějěa > ěa	KI	ě > a	OCS
pros-i+ěa-xъ	pros-j-ěa-xъ	proš-ěaxъ	>	>	prošaaxъ	prošaaxъ
mьn-ě+ěa-xъ	>	>	mьn-ě+a-xъ	>	>	mьněaxъ
děl-aj+ěa-xъ	>	>	děl-a+a-xъ	>	>	dělaaxъ
daj-a+ěa-xъ	>	>	daj-a+a-xъ	>	>	dajaaxъ
mil-ova+ěa-xъ	>	>	mil-ova+a-xъ	>	>	milovaaxъ
vęz-a+ěa-xъ	>	>	vęz-a+a-xъ	>	>	vęzaaxъ
rek-Ø+ěa-xъ	>	>	>	reč-ěa-xъ	rečaaxъ	rečaaxъ
bьj-Ø+ěa-xъ	>	>	>	>	bьjaaxъ	bьjaaxъ
						bijaaxъ
nes-Ø+ěa-xъ	>	>	>	>	>	nesěaxъ

10. Aorists

There is one productive type of aorist in OCS that is used in nearly all verbs, plus two archaic formations that are (or may be) used with C-verbs. The older aorists were apparently in use in Croatia and Macedonia well into the fifteenth century, though they seem to have become obsolete in eastern Bulgaria during the OCS period. See §10.7, below.

10.1 The desinences are:

	singular	dual	plural
1st person	**-(o)xъ**	**-(o)xově**	**-(o)xomъ**
2nd person	-(e)ø	**-(o)sta**	**-(o)ste**
3rd person	-(e)ø	**-(o)ste**	**-(o)šę**

10.11 The vowels given in parentheses appear only when the basic stem ends in an obstruent (*p b t d k g s z x*): *nes*-ǫtъ 'carry' ~ *nesoxъ nese*. (Cf. also §10.4 below).

The past-marker *x* ~ *s* ~ *š* is underlying {x}: it becomes *s* before *t* but *š* before *ę*.
2–3 sg. underlying {nes-Ø+x} > nes-e-x > *nese* (because no word-final C is allowed.)

10.12 Otherwise (i.e., for the vast majority of verbs), the suffixes (including the zero of 2-3 sing.) are consonantal. They are added directly to vowel-stems: *prosi*-ti 'beg' ~ *prosixъ prosi*; *mьně*-ti 'think' ~ *mьněxъ mьně*; *vęza*-ti 'bind' ~ *vęzaxъ vęza, daja-ti* 'give' *dajaxъ daja*.

10.2 Sonorant-stems are truncated as follows:

10.21 *j* is deleted: *dělaj*-ǫtъ 'do' ~ *dělaxъ děla*; *razuměj*-ǫtъ 'understand' ~ *razuměxъ razumě*; *bьj*-ǫtъ 'beat' ~ *bixъ bi bišę*; *kryj*-ǫtъ 'hide' ~ *kryxъ kry*; *po-ču*-ǫtъ *'feel'* ~ *počuxъ poču*.

10.22 stem-final *ь* + *nasal sonorant* is replaced by *ę*: *raspьn*-ǫtъ {raz-pьn+Ø} 'crucify' *raspęxъ raspę*; *po-žьnj*-ǫtъ 'reap' *požę*; *vъzьm*-ǫtъ {vъz-ьm-Ø+} take' ~ *vъzęxъ vъzę vъzęšę*.

10.23 stem-final *ьr* is replaced by *rě*: *umьr*-ǫtъ 'die' ~ *umrěxъ umrěšę*.

10.24 stem-final *ov* is replaced by *u*: *natrov*-ǫtъ 'feed' ~ *natruxomъ natru*.

10.25 The isolated verbs *melj*-ǫtъ 'grind', *borj*-ǫtъ 'fight', *kolj*-ǫtъ 'slaughter' become *mlěxъ, braxъ, klaxъ* (§16.511–3).

10.3 Before the *-e* of 2-3 sg., stem-final *k g x* become *č ž š* (§3.4 I): *rek*-ǫtъ 'say' ~*rekoxъ reče*; *mog*-ǫtъ 'be able' ~ *mogoxъ može*.

10.4 Some nǫ-verbs with consonantal roots drop the classifier before the aorist desinences: *pogybnǫ*-ti 'perish' ~ *pogyboxъ pogybe*; *dvignǫ*-ti 'move' ~ *dvigoxъ dviže* (cf. §10.3). Some other verbs retain the *nǫ*: *umlьknǫ*-ti 'be silent' ~ *umlьknǫ*. A number of verbs are attested with both types; the *nǫ* is particularly likely to be omitted in 2–3 sg. See §10.812 and §15.72–6.

10.41 Note that there are a few cases where the surface stem in *-nǫ* does not contain the root-final C of the underlying form; when *nǫ* is dropped, the C appears in the surface form, e.g. {-sъp-nǫ-ti} > *u-sъnǫ-ti* ~ *usъpe* '(he) went to sleep'. See also §15.73, 17.75.

10.51 Three verbs regularly have the anomalous desinence *-stъ* in 2–3 sg.; *byti* 'be' ~ *bystъ, dati* 'give' ~ *dastъ, ěsti* 'eat' ~ *ěstъ*. Both *dastъ* and *estъ* are ambiguous forms, since they are identical with 3 sg. present (cf. §66.21–2).

10.52 A few root-verbs whose stem ends in a sonorant (and aorist-stem ends in a vowel) usually take a terminal desinence *-tъ* in 2–3 sg.:[12] *pьj*-ǫtъ 'drink' ~ *pitъ*, po-*vьj*-ǫtъ 'wrap' ~ *povitъ*, {ob-vьj-Ø+} *obьj*-ǫtъ 'wind' ~ *obitъ*; *{nьr-} ~ *ponrětъ* 'sank'; u-*mьr*-ǫtъ 'die' ~ *umrětъ*; pro-*stьr*-ǫtъ 'spread' ~ *pro-strětъ*; po-*žьr*-ǫtъ 'consume' ~ *požrětъ*; vъz-*ьm*-ǫtъ 'take' ~ *vъzętъ* (and the simplex {ьm-} *im*-ǫtъ ę-ti ~ *ętъ*); na-*čьn*-ǫtъ, za-*čьn*-ǫtъ 'begin' ~ *-čętъ*; *klьn*-ǫtъ 'swear' ~ *klętъ*; {raz-pьn-} 'crucify' ~ *raspętъ*.

---

[12] Comparative materials from many sources establish that such root-verbs were inherently unaccented (or, in traditional terms, were "circumflex", presumably with a long vowel with falling intonation). The same verbs also had *-t-* in the past passive participle (cf. §11.321). Accented stems (called "acute"; presumed to have rising intonation) had no *-tъ* in 2–3 sg. aor. and *-en-* in past pass. part. Thus *pьj-* 'drink' had *pitъ*, but *bьj-* 'strike, beat' had only *bi* and *bьjen-/bijen-*. These relationships are somewhat obscured in some OCS examples, particularly in Supr.

Here also the irregular *pojǫtъ pěti* 'sing' ~ *pětъ* (and *vъspětъ* 'started to sing'). *Živ*-ǫtъ 'live' has 2-3 sg. *žive,* but also (Su) жи and прижитъ 'bore'.

10.53 The verb *trьti tьrǫtъ* 'rub' has the expected form *-trь* and also *-tьre* (cf. §16.522).

10.60 *The unproductive types of aorist*

10.601 The most widespread type of older aorist is the "***root**-aorist*", attested by over 650 examples with some 28 verbs (listed below, §10.81–.84), including the common *idǫtъ* 'go'. They have no aorist-marker, only the following person-number desinences:

	singular	dual	plural
1st person	**-ъ**	***-ově**	**-omъ**
2nd person	**-e**	***-eta**	**-ete**
3rd person		**-ete**	**-ǫ**

The stem is a root ending in an obstruent, with zero-classifier or a basic stem followed by -nǫ+ (which is deleted in the aorist): e.g. ***pad***-ǫtъ 'fall' ~ *padъ pade padǫ*; *mog*-ǫtъ 'be able' ~ *mogъ može mogǫ*; *vъz-**dvig**nǫ-ti* 'lift' ~ *vъzdvigъ vъzdviže vъzdvigǫ*.

10.602 The forms of the *"**s**-aorist"* occur with certain C-stems (in *b, t, d, s, z)* and those in ь + *nasal* (see below, §10.82). The desinences are like the normal type except that they have *s* instead of *x* or *š*:

	singular	dual	plural
1st person	**-sъ**	***-sově**	**-somъ**
2nd person	**-(e)s**	***-sta**	**-ste**
3rd person		**-ste**	**-sę**

The desinences are consonantal; stem-final consonants are therefore subject to truncation.

10.6021 Nasal stems truncate per §10.22: {ьm} vъz-*ьm*-ǫtъ *im*-ǫtъ 'take' ~ *vъzęsъ vъzę vъzęsę, ęsъ ę ęsę*; {raz-pьn-} *raspьn*-ǫtъ 'crucify' ~ *raspęsъ raspę raspęsę*.

10.6022 Stem-final obstruents are deleted except in 2–3 sg., where the vowel *e* is inserted: {sъbljud-Ø-s-ъ} 'I observed' > *sъbljusъ*; {-bljud-Ø+s} > -bljudes > *sъbljude*.

Moreover, the low lax root-vowels *e* and *o* are replaced by tense *ě* and *a*: *ved*-ǫtъ 'lead' ~ *věsъ, vede, věsomъ, věsę*; *bod*-ǫtъ 'pierce' ~ *basъ, bode, basomъ basę*.

10.603 The "**x**-*aorist*" is attested for stems in *k* and *g* (§10.84). The desinences are those of the normal aorist except that they do not admit the initial vowel *o*. Stem-final obstruents are deleted, and root-vowel *e* becomes *ě* (except in 2–3 sg., where the vowel *e* is inserted): *rek*-ǫtъ 'say' ~ *rěxъ, reče, rěste, rěšę*.

10.604 NOTE that the 2–3 singular has the same form in all types of aorist.

10.7 Historically, there were two aorist formations. The "root aorist" added special non-present person-number desinences directly to the verbal root; the OCS examples are archaic relics that have survived in very common verbs. The "sigmatic aorist" had an explicit tense-sign *s* (written with the letter *sigma* in Greek) before the desinences: OCS displays two obsolescent forms of this paradigm, the "*s*-aorist" and the "*x*-aorists", and a productive type, the "*ox*-aorist".[13] During the OCS period some dialects were eliminating most of the unproductive forms. The root-aorists and the s- and x-aorists of consonantal stems were replaced by the ox-type (*padъ, věsъ, rěxъ ~ padoxъ, vedoxъ, rekoxъ*), while s-aorists of nasal stems gave way to the x-type (*ęsъ ~ ęxъ*). For example:

Root > ox: идъ > идохъ; 2-3s идє, 3du идєтє > идостє (-та); идомъ > идохомъ, идєтє > идостє, идѫ > идошѧ. двигъ > двигохъ, 2-3s движє; 3du движєтє > двигостє (-ста); двигомъ > двигохомъ, двигѫ > двигошѧ

S > ox: вѣсъ > вєдохъ, 2-3s вєдє; 3du вѣстє > вєдостє (-ста), вѣсомъ > вєдохомъ, вѣстє > вєдостє, вѣсѧ > вєдошѧ

S > x: ѧсъ > ѧхъ, 2-3s ѧтъ (ѧ); 3du ѧстє (ѧста), ѧсомъ > ѧхомъ, ѧстє, ѧсѧ > ѧшѧ

S > ox: рѣхъ > рєкохъ, 2-3s рєчє; 3du рѣстє > рєкостє (-ста), рѣхомъ > рєкохомъ, рѣстє > рєкостє, рѣшѧ > рєкошѧ

To illustrate the distribution of these forms in the texts, here are the percentages of the non-productive forms in each ms. Figures in parentheses are based on fewer than five examples.[14]

---

[13] What we call the s-aorist represents the inherited sigmatic form, with the x-aorist as a variant that utilized the Slavic reflexes of old *s* (s before *t*, *š* before front vowel, *x* otherwise). The ox-aorist is a further development that inserts a vowel between stem-final obstruent and the x/š/s desinences.

[14] It is worth noting that the common verb *rekǫtъ* 'say' accounts for all of the old x-forms in Su and more than 95% of them everywhere but Ps, which has 40 x-forms from *rek-* and 16 from 5 other roots. Of all attested root-aorists, the verb *idǫtъ* accounts for a full two-thirds, *-rět-* 'come upon' (§16.55) another 12.5%, *mog-*, *pad-* and *vrъg-* another 10%, while the last 10% includes 26 verbs. These facts are an excellent illustration of the principle that irregularities persist in words of highest frequency.

	Ps+2N	Mar	Cloz	Euch	As	Zo	Sav	Supr
type *rěxъ*	100	100	(100)	100	99	99+	89+	72
type *idъ*	100	100	100	76	85+	70	66	–
type *něsъ*	100	100	100	(50)	96	43	7+	–
type *ęsъ*	95+	93	(–)	(75)	64+	10	–	–

10.80 The following lists signal the attested forms of the unproductive aorists. When no specific reference is given after a form, it means that more than five occurrences are attested; further, the forms may have different prefixes. Chapter-verse citation without indication of ms means that the form occurs in more than one of the Gospel texts in the given passage. A citation followed by + means that there are one to three other occurrences. Otherwise the lists are exhaustive.

10.81 *Root-aorists*

10.811 *pad-ǫtъ* 'fall': **падѫ**. *krad-*ǫtъ 'steal': **оукрадѫ** Mt 28:13 Mar, *-lěz-*ǫtъ 'go' **излѣзѫ** J 21:9, **вълѣзѫ** J 6:24. *tręs-*ǫtъ 'shake': **сътрѧсъ сѧ** Ps 108:23 (see also §10.84). *-gręz-*ǫtъ 'sink' **погрѧзѫ** Ps 2N Ex 15:5, 8. *mog-*ǫtъ 'be able': **възмогъ** Ps 39:12; 3du **изнеможете** Ps 17:37, 87:10, 108:24; **възмогомъ** Mk 9:28+; **могѫ**. *-rět-* 'come upon': **обрѣтъ**; 3du **обрѣтете**, **сърѣтете**; **обрѣтомъ** J 1:42+; **обрѣтѫ**; **сърѣтѫ** J 4:51. *sěsti sędǫtъ* 'sit down': **сѣдъ** Ps 25:4, **сѣдомъ** Ps 136:1, **сѣдомъ** Ps 136:1, **сѣдѫ** Ps 118:23+. *-lešti -lęgǫtъ* 'lie down': **възлегѫ** Mk 6:40 Mar. *vrьgǫtъ vrěšti* 'throw': **-врьгѫ**. *idǫtъ iti* 'go': **-идъ**; 3du **иѕидете**; **идомъ**; **идете**; **идѫ**. *ědǫtъ *ěxati* 'ride' **прѣѣдѫ** Zo = **въѣдѫ** Mar. u-*nьz-*ǫtъ *'pierce':* **оунь ѕѫ** Ps 37:3 = Euch 76a4. *o-*xrъm-* 'get lame' (§15.771): **охръмѫ** Ps 17:46.

10.812 u-*glьb-nǫ*-ti 'get stuck' (**оуглебъ** Ps 68:3; **оуглъбѫ** Ps 9:16); *vъs-*kys-nǫ*-ti 'get sour' (**въскысѫ** L 13:21 As); and *{svęd-nǫ+} 'be scorched' (**присвѧдѫ** Mt 13:6) happen to be attested with no alternate forms.

With root and regular forms: *-běg-nǫ*-ti 'flee' (**прибѣгъ** Euch 85a6, **иѕбѣгъ** Cloz 6b34; **отъбѣгъ** Eu 48a6 ~ **отъбѣгоша** Su 229.20). na-*vyk-nǫ*-ti 'learn' (**навыкнѫ** Ps 105:35 ~ **навыкошѧ** Su 488.12). vъs-*krьs-nǫ-* 'be resurrected' (**въскрьсѫ** Su 471.4 ~ **въскръсошѧ** 386.16). *-nik-nǫ*-ti (**възнікѫ** Ps 91:8 ~ **възникоша** Su 39.12), {iz-čez-nǫ+} (§3.311) 'disappear' (1 sg **іщеѕъ** Is 38:12, 3du **іщеѕете** Ps 68:4, **іщеѕѫ** Ps 36:20, 63:7, Cloz 13a33, **ичеѕѫ** Ps 101:4 ~ **ищеѕошѧ** Euch 62a22).

With root forms, regular forms without *nǫ*, and regular forms with *nǫ*: *dvig-nǫ*-ti 'move' (**въѕдвигъ** Euch 58b3, 17b7 = Ps 24:1; **въѕдвигѫ** L 17:3 Sav; Ps 82:3, 92:3 bis ~ 3 sg **въѕдвигнѫ** ~ **въѕдвиже**; **въѕдвигошѧ**). pro-*zęb-nǫ*-ti 'sprout' (**проѕѧбѫ** Mar ~ **проѕѧбошѧ** Zo Mt 13:5 ~ **проѕѧбнѫшѧ** Ps 91:8). u-*žas-nǫ*ti sę 'be terrified' (3 du. **оужасете** L 8:56 Mar ~ **оужасосте** As ~ **оужаснѫста** Zo Sav; **оужасѫ** Mk 16:5 Zo Mar As, Mk 1:27, 9:15 Zo Mar ~ **оужасоша** Su 269.1 ~ **оужаснѫшѧ** Mk 5:42 Zo Mar, Su 32.8, 33.17, 466.9). *-mlьk-nǫ* 'fall silent' (**оумлъкѫ** Ps 106:29, 30 ~ **прѣмлькоша** Su 331.19; 3 sg **оумлъкнѫ** Su 570.18 ~ **оумльче** Su 208.2). *-sъx-nǫ*-ti 'dry out' (1 sg **исохъ** Ps 101:2, **сосъхъ** Ps 101.4; **исъхѫ** Mt 13:6 Mar ~ Zo **исъхошѧ**

~ 3 sg оусъхнѫ Su 343.28+). *-top-nǫ*-ti 'drown' (истопѫ Mt 8:32 Sav = оутопѫ Mar As ~ оутопоша Zo, истопоша Su 401.3 ~ истопнѫша Su 197.10). po-*tъk-nǫ*-ti sę 'stumble against' (потъкѫ сѧ Mt 7:25, 27 Sav; Cloz 12b20, 23 ~ потъкнѫша сѧ Su 448.16).

10.82 *S-aorist*. *bljud*-ǫtъ 'watch': съблюсъ J 15:10, съблюсомъ Ps 2N Deut 3:30, съблюсѧ J 15:20. *bod*-ǫtъ 'pierce': пробасѧ J 19:37+. *nes*-ǫtъ 'carry' възнѣсъ Ps 65:17+; 3 du. възнѣсте Ps 103:1, L 2:27 As; възнѣсѧ L 2:22+; принѣсѧ. *ved*-ǫtъ 'lead': привѣсъ Mk 9:17+; 3 du. привѣсте Mt 21:7+, вьвѣсте L 2:27 Zo Mar, Ps 42:3, ізвѣсте Ps 118:136; въвѣсомъ Mt 25:38; привѣсте L 23:14, J 7:45; вѣсѧ, привѣсѧ. *cvьt*-ǫtъ cvisti 'bloom': процвисѧ Cloz 13b4. *-vrьz*-ǫtъ -vrěsti 'tie' отъврѣсъ Ps 38:10, 118:131; 3 du. отврѣсте сѧ J 9:10+; отврѣсѧ. {raz-sup-} 'scatter': расоусѧ сѧ Ps 140:7 2N. *greb*-ǫtъ 'bury': погресѧ Mt 14:12+. *klьn*-ǫtъ 'curse': клѧсъ сѧ Ps 88:4+. *-pьn*-ǫtъ 'stretch, crucify': пропѧсѧ, распѧсѧ. *-čьn*-ǫtъ 'begin': начѧсъ Ps 76:11; начѧсѧ Ev. {ьm-} *im*-ǫtъ ęti 'take': ѩсъ Ril VIII[1] 17; поѩсъ L 14:20 Mar; приѧсъ J 10:18 Mar As, приѧсъ Vat, ѩсомъ L 5:5 Mar; ѩсѧ, възѧсѧ Ev, Ps.

For *męt*-ǫtъ, *čьt*-ǫtъ, *ěd-* 'eat', and *tręs*-ǫtъ, see §10.84.

10.83 *X-aorists*. *rek*-ǫtъ 'say': рѣхъ; 3du рѣсте/рѣста; рѣхомъ, рѣсте, рѣшѧ. *tek*-ǫtъ 'run': тѣхъ Ps 58:5, 118:32; 3du тѣсте Mt 28:8; тѣшѧ. *vlěk*-ǫtъ 'drag': вьвлѣхъ Ps 118:131, съвлѣшѧ, извлѣшѧ, облѣшѧ. *-lęk*-ǫtъ 'bend': сълѧхъ Ps 37:7 = Euch 76a5; сълѧшѧ Ps 55:7, налѧшѧ Ps 10:2, 36:14, 63:4. *sěk*-ǫtъ 'cut': расѣшѧ Ps 73:5. vъz-*žeg*- 'enkindle': вьжѣшѧ Ps 73:7 (for expected *vъžašę*, §3.5c1).

10.84 A few verbs have more than one attested unproductive aorist.

tręs-ǫtъ 'shake': root-form сътрѧсѫ сѧ Mt 28:4 As, s-form сътрѧсѧ сѧ Mar ~ сътрѧсошѧ сѧ Zo Sav.

męt-ǫtъ 'stir, disturb': s-forms съмѧсъ сѧ Ps 76:5+; съмѧсомъ Ps 89:7; възмѧсѧ, съмѧсѧ сѧ Ps ~ x-forms възмѧшѧ Mk 6:50 Mar, съмѧшѧ Mt 14:26+.

čьt-ǫtъ čisti 'read': s-forms чисѧ Ps 21:18, чисѧ J 19:20 Mar As ~ x-form чишѧ Zo (~ чьтоша Sav).[15]

ěd-ętъ 'eat': s-forms ѣсъ Ps 101:10, ѣсмь [for ѣсомъ? L 13:26 Mar], ѣсѧ Mk 8:8 Mar, поѣсѧ Ps 77:45+, сънѣсѧ Ps 105:28+.

---

[15] SJS lists отъвѣ, отъвѣшѧ 'answer' as a defective verb with only 3rd pers. aor. forms. No root-final C is deleted in 2–3 sg aor (except for irregular *dad-*, *ěd-* ~ *dastъ/da*, *ęstъ/ě*), and, moreover, no C-verb with the root *vět* is otherwise attested; it is safe to regard the 4 examples from As and the 2 from Sav as scribal errors—both scribes are prone to omit syllables. All six instances correspond to normal *otъvěšta(šę)* forms in the corresponding verses in other mss, and both forms are correctly written scores of times.

10.90 In irregular verbs, the aorist stem is normally (i.e. except as noted above) the same as the infinitive stem: *bьra*-ti berǫtъ ‘gather’ ~ *bьraxъ*. gъna-*ti ženǫtъ ‘drive’* ~ gъnaxъ; *bra*-ti borjǫtъ ‘fight’ ~ *braxъ*: *pě*-ti pojǫtъ ‘sing’ ~ *pěxъ*: {leg-Ø+} lešti lęgǫtъ ‘lie down’ ~ *legoxъ*; {sěd-Ø+} sěsti sędǫtъ ‘sit down’ ~ *sědoxъ*; {-rět/ręt} -rěsti -ręštǫtъ ‘come upon’ ~ *-rětoxъ*. But the present stem serves for at least the regular aorist in: *vrьg*-ǫtъ vrěšti ‘throw’ ~ *vrьgoxъ* (and *vrьgъ*), *čьt*-ǫtъ čisti ‘read’ ~ *čьtoxъ* (but *čisъ*), *cvьt*-ǫtъ cvisti ‘bloom’ ~ *cvьtošę* (but *cvisę*), *-vrьz*-ǫtъ -vrěsti ‘tie’ ~ *vrьzoxъ* (but *-vrěsъ*).

10.91 The unprefixed verb *byti* ‘to be’ has two sets of aorist forms: from the stem *bě-* (*běxъ bě … běšę*) and from the stem *by-* (*byxъ bystъ … byšę*). The *bě*-forms were imperfective and the *by*-forms perfective (see also §16.1, §21.21). 2–3 sg *by* is occasionally found for *bystъ*.

10.911 Prefixed forms *-byti* (e.g. *zabyti* ‘forget’, *prěbyti* ‘remain’) have only *-byxъ*, *-bystъ*, etc.

11. Past participles

OCS has a *past active participle*, a *resultative participle* (often called “second past active participle”) and a *past passive participle*.

11.11 **The (first) past active particple** has the formant **-ъš-** or **-vъš-** plus the soft twofold nominal or compound desinences. The nominative singular masculine-neuter surface forms end in *-ъ*, *-ь*, or *-vъ* (representing underlying -š-Ø; word-final consonant is deleted). For the declension see §4.18–10, 4.31.

11.12 The vocalic suffix *-ъš-* is used with i-verbs, and with C-verbs (including nǫ-verbs that lose the *nǫ*), excepting stems in *j* or the group *ov*. The consonantal suffix *-vъš-* is used with all other verbs (i.e. those in *-ov*, *-j*, *-nǫ*, *-ě*, *-a*).

11.13 The classifier *-i+* becomes *j* before the vocalic suffix *-ъš-*, triggering iotation in the stem-final consonant(s), and the back ъ becomes front ь: {pros-i+ъš-i} > prosj-ьši > *prošьši* ‘having begged (Nsg fem)’.

Before the consonantal suffix, stem-final *j* is deleted, and *-ov* > *u*: {děl-aj+vъš-i} > *dělavъši* ‘having done (N sg fem)’, {kryj-Ø+vъš-i} > *kryvъši* ‘having hidden (Nsg fem)’, {ot-plov-Ø+vъš-i} > *otъpluvъši* ‘having sailed away (Nsg fem)’.

Note: roots like *čьt*-ǫtъ ‘read’, *-čьn*-ǫtъ ‘begin’, {ьm} *im*-ǫtъ ęti ‘take’, u-*mьr*-ǫtъ ‘die, have strong jers before the ъš and are often written with *e*: **начєнъшє**, **ємъ**, **възємъши**, **оумєръшаага**.

11.14 An innovation within the OCS period is that i-verbs could (like other vocalic stems) take the consonantal suffix *-vъš-*: *pusti-ti* 'abandon' *puštьši* Mk 10:12 Mar ~ *pustivъši* Zo. Such forms are rare except in Supr, where they constitute the norm.

-ivъ (*š-*) is absent from As, Ps, Cloz; occurs once in Mar (~ 186x -ь[*š*-]), 4x in Zo (~ 163), 3x in Sav [погоубивъı Mt 10:39, in 2 different lections, As *iže pogubitъ*], помъısливъ [in a reworded phrase] (~ 69x), under 10% in Euch. In Su, however, 598x ~ 117x, whereby the older forms occur only in a few of the 48 component texts. Further, younger forms of masc. neut nom. sg (*sъtvorivъ*) seem to have been favored over the old forms (*sъtvorjь*).

11.15 *Irregularities*. *Trьti tьrǫtъ* 'rub' has *tьrъ*. *Vlěkǫtъ* 'drag' has regular *-vlěkъ* beside *-vlьkъ*. *Nebrěgǫtъ* 'neglect' has *nebrьgъ* (only in Su) or *nebrěgъ*. *Pro-stьr-ǫtъ* 'spread' seems to have **prostrьvъ* (Su 311.16 **простръвъ**) beside regular *prostrěvъ*. *Byti* 'to be' has *byvъ*. *Idǫtъ iti* 'go' has *šьdъ* (*prišьdъ*, etc.). *Dadętъ* 'give' has *davъ*, *ědęt* 'eat' has *ědъ*; *ědǫtъ* 'ride' has both *-ěvъ* and *-ěxavъ*.

11.2 **The resultative participle**, conveniently called the l-participle, is formed by means of the suffix **-l-** plus the hard desinences of the twofold nominal desinences. It is found only in nominative short forms.

11.211 The suffix is added directly to the basic stem; since it is consonantal, it may cause truncation of consonantal stems. Stem-final obstruents, except the dental stops (*t d*, §3.3131), remain. E.g. *greb*-ǫtъ 'bury' *greblъ*; *nes*-ǫtъ 'carry' *neslъ*; *rek*-ǫtъ 'say' *reklъ*; *mog*-ǫtъ 'be able' *moglъ*.

11.212 Stem-final *t d j* is dropped; *ь* + *nasal consonant* > *ę*; *ov* > *u*; *ьr* > *rь*:[16] *plet*-ǫtъ 'braid' *plelъ*: *ved*-ǫtъ 'lead'; *klьn*-ǫtъ 'curse' *klęlъ*; *vъzьm*-ǫtъ 'take' *vъzęlъ*; *plov*-ǫtъ 'sail' *plulъ*; *tьr*-ǫtъ 'rub' *trьlъ*.

11.213 Nǫ-verbs that lose the classifier in other past forms (§15.76) may lose it here too: *vъzdvignǫ*-ti 'lift' *vъzdvignǫlъ* or *vъzdviglъ*; *obyknǫ-ti* 'learn' *obyklъ*.

11.221 Irregular verbs normally use the infinitive stem for the l-participle: *bra*-ti borjǫtъ 'fight' *bralъ*: {leg} *le*šti lęgǫtъ 'lie down' *leglъ*; {sěd} *sě*sti sędǫtъ 'sit down' *sělъ*; {ěd} *ěsti ědętъ* 'eat' *ělъ*.

However: *vrьg*-ǫtъ vrěšti 'throw' *vrьglъ*; *čьt*-ǫtъ čisti 'read' *čьlъ*.

---

[16] Note that the l-participle stem is identical with the aorist stem (aside from the automatic loss of *t*/*d* before *l*) except for the 6 verbs in *ьr* which alternates with *rě* before all other consonantal suffixes (u*mьr*ǫtъ u*mrě*ti; §15.86), the irregular *vlěkǫtъ vlьklъ*, and the anomalous *idǫtъ iti*.

11.222 The irregular *idǫtъ iti* 'go' uses the suppletive root *šьd*: *šьlъ*.

11.23 The l-participle is used only in compound verb-forms: the perfect (cf. §14.1), the pluperfects (§14.2), the conditional (§14.3), and the future perfect (§14.4).

The traditional name "second past active participle" is better applied to some usages in post-OCS texts where non-nominative declensional forms are used. The sole example in OCS is acc. sg fem. [*агодѫ] изгнилѫ '[make its fruit] rotten' (cf. **izgnijǫtъ* 'to rot') in Sav, Mt 12:33, where the other mss have [*plodъ*] *zъlъ* '[make its fruit] bad'.

11.30 The past passive participle

Only transitive verbs can form this participle, and it is rare in imperfective verbs.

11.31 The suffixes are **-t-, -n-** or **-en-** plus the hard desinences of the twofold nominal or the compound declensions.

11.32 The suffix **-t-** is restricted to certain sonorant-stems, and it effects truncation. It is regular with stems in ь + *nasal*: *-pьn-*ǫtъ 'crucify' *raspętъ, propętъ*: {ьm} *imǫtъ ęti* 'take' *ętъ*, vъz-*ьm*-ǫtъ vъz-*ę*-ti ~ *vъzętъ*.

It is used also with *-vьj*-ǫtъ 'wind' ~ *-vitъ*, pro-*lьj*-ǫtъ 'pour out' ~ *prolitъ*; *pěti* pojǫtъ 'sing' ~ *pětъ*; *požьr*-ǫtъ 'swallow' ~ *požrьtъ* (§15.86: but *požrenъ* 'sacrificed' §16.521); *-vrьz*-ǫtъ -vrěsti 'tie' ~ *otvrьstъ* 'open'; and *uvęstъ* 'crowned' from *uvęzǫtъ*.

11.33 The suffix **-n-** is used with the classifiers *a, aj, ě*, and *ěj*, whereby the *j* is truncated: *vęza*-ti 'tie' ~ *vęzanъ, sěja*-ti 'sow' ~ *sějanъ*; *pomьně*-ti 'remember' ~ *pomьněnъ*; *dělaj*-ǫtъ 'do' ~ *dělanъ*: *razuměj*-ǫtъ 'understand' *razuměnъ*.

11.34 The suffix **-en-** is used with all other stems.

It effects the generation of *j* from the -i+ classifier, and therefore iotation: *pros-i+* 'beg' ~ *prošenъ*; *sъ-lom-i+* 'smash' ~ *sъlomljenъ*; *mǫč-i+* 'torment' ~ *mǫčenъ*.

Note that the "epenthetic l" does not always develop and the spellings may fail to indicate the /j/ we expect, see §2.4521.

11.341 In a few verbs the vocalic suffix is preceded by a *v* (which may be interpreted as a variant of stem-final *j* in some stems):

Nǫ-verbs that retain the *nǫ* in past forms have *-nov-en*: *rinǫ*-ti 'push' ~ *rinovenъ*. Root-verbs ending in back-vowel +*j*: *kryj*-ǫtъ/*krъj*-ǫtъ 'hide' ~ *krъvenъ, myj*-ǫtъ/*mъj*-ǫtъ 'wash' ~ *u-mъvenъ, obuj*-ǫtъ 'put on shoes' ~

obuvenъ. The verb *šьj-/šij-* ‘sew’ has *šьvenъ*. *Zabyti* ‘forget’ (§16.11) has *zabъvenъ*.

11.351 Irregular verbs normally form the past passive participle on the infinitive stem: *stьla*-ti steljǫtъ ‘spread’ ~ *postьlanъ*; *bьra*-ti berǫtъ ‘collect’ ~ *-bьranъ*; *gъna*-ti ženǫtъ ‘drive’ ~ *-gъnanъ*.

11.352 However, the verbs *dъm*-ǫtъ duti ‘blow’, *vrьg*-ǫtъ vrěšti ‘throw’, and *tlьk*-ǫtъ tlěšti ‘knock’ use the present stems: *nadъmenъ, -vrьženъ, -tlьčenъ*. *Vlьk*-ǫtъ *vlě*šti ‘drag’ has both *-vlьčenъ* and *-vlěčenъ*. *Kla*-ti *kolj*-ǫtъ ‘stab’ has both *zaklanъ* and *zakolenъ* ‘slaughtered’.

12.0 Verbal substantive

The verbal substantive is a neuter; it follows the soft type of the normal twofold nominal declension.

12.1 The formant **-ьj-/-ij-** is added to the stem of the past passive participle to make the substantival stem.

raspьn	crucify	*raspętьe*	crucifixion	*děl-aj*	do	*dělanьe*	doing
um-ěj	know	*uměnьe*	ability	*glagol-a*	speak	*glagolanьe*	speaking
mьn-ě	think	*mьněnьe*	opinion	*rek*	say	*rečenьe*	statement
pros-i	beg	*prošenьe*	plea	*dvig-nǫ*	move	*dviženьe*	movement
rod-i	bear	*roždenьe*	birth	*ri-nǫ*	push	*rinovenьe*	throwing

Keep in mind that the spelling *-ьe* means *-ьje* or *-ije*.

12.2 The verbal substantive or name of the action may have variants (perhaps with slightly different meaning) involving the distribution of “participial” *-t-* and *-v-*. E.g.:

sěj-a	sow	*sějanьe* *sětie*	sowing; planting	*u-mьr*	die	*umrьtie*	death
trov	feed	*otrovenьe*	poisoning	*slov*	be known	*slutie*	fame
by	be	*bytьe*	being	*rek*	say	*rečenьe*	statement
za-by	forget	*zabytьe* *zabъvenьe*	oblivion, forgetting	*pě-ti* *poj-ǫtъ*	sing	*pětьe* *pěnьe*	singing
bьj	strike	*bьenьe*	striking	*u-bьj*	kill	*ubitie*	murder
bra-ti *borj-ǫtъ*	fight	*branьe* *borjenьe*	fighting	*žьr-ǫtъ* *žrь-ti*	sacrifice	*žrьtie*	sacrifice
vrьz- *vrěz*	untie	*otvrьstie* *razvrьzenie* *pouvrьzenie*	opening	*i- id-,* *šьd-*	go	*sъn-itьe* *šьstьe* *šьstvьe*	descent; going

It is probable that dialects differed in how they created and retained this kind of derivative; in particular Supr has many distinctive formations.

13.0 Infinitive and supine

13.1 The infinitive desinence is **-ti;** the supine desinence is **-tъ.** Since the only consonant that can stand before *t* is *s,* these t- suffixes cause truncation in consonantal stems (except *s*).

13.2 Some stems ending in vowel plus glide (*j v*) or sonorant replace the VC with a vowel:

a. *ov > u* (cf. §3.72): *slov*-ǫtъ ~ *sluti slutъ* 'be renowned'; *plov*-ǫtъ ~ *pluti plutъ* 'sail'; *vъzdrov*-ǫtъ 'bellow' ~ *vъzdruti vъzdrutъ* (§15.841).

b. *ьj/ъj > i/y* (§3.313): *bьj*-ǫtъ or *bij*-ǫtъ ~ *biti bitъ* 'strike'; *mъj*-ǫtъ or *myj*-ǫtъ ~ *myti mytъ* 'wash'.

c. Otherwise, *j* and *v* are deleted: *čuj*-ǫtъ ~ *čuti čutъ* 'sense, hear'; *živ*-*ǫtъ* ~ *žiti žitъ* 'live' (§15.842).

d. *ь + nasal > ę* (§3.313): *klьn*-ǫtъ ~ *klęti klętъ* 'curse'; *žьnj*-ǫtъ ~ *žęti žętъ* 'reap'; *žьm*-ǫtъ ~ *žęti žętъ* 'squeeze'(§15.83).

e. *ьr > rь* (§16.521): *žьr*-ǫtъ ~ *žrьti žrьtъ* 'sacrifice'

13.3 Root-final velar (*k g*) combines with desinential *t* in the group *št* that functions as a palatal unit (§3.3131a). The final ъ of the supine desinence automatically becomes ь: *rek*-ǫtъ ~ *rešti reštь*; *mog*-ǫtъ ~ *mošti moštь* 'be able' (§15.85).

13.31 The stems *tlьk*-ǫtъ 'knock' and *vrьg*-ǫtъ 'throw' have infinitives *tlěšti* and *vrěšti*. Cf. §15.874.

13.32 The stem *strig*-ǫtъ 'shear' has *postrěšti*.

13.4 Root-final labial *p* and *b* are deleted: *tep*-ǫtъ ~ *teti tetъ* 'beat', *greb*-ǫtъ ~ *greti gretъ* 'dig' (§15.824).

13.5 There are some cases where the same written form serves as infinitive for two basic stems: *Pomazati* 'anoint' may contain the full basic stem of perfective {po-maz-a+}, or represent a truncated shape of imperfective {po-maz-aj+} (derived by §13.2c above). The corresponding third person plurals are *pomažǫtъ* and *pomazajǫtъ*.

14. Compound tenses

14.01 The resultative (l-)participle may be used with the forms of the verb byti *'to be'* in constructions which can be considered compound tenses; the perfect, the pluperfects, the conditional, and the rare future perfect.

14.02 The past passive participle frequently occurs with forms of *byti* in constructions which may translate a Greek passive and be rendered by an English passive, but they cannot be regarded as compound tenses. Similarly the active participles with *byti* are not compounds, but merely copula plus verbal adjective. For example, *bě* že eterъ *bolę* Lazarь (J 11:1) "there *was* a certain *ailing man* Lazarus" ~ Marija … eęže bratrъ Lazarь *bolěaše* (J 11:3) "Mary … whose brother Lazarus *ailed*."

14.1 The perfect

The forms of the l-participle are frequently used with the present forms of *byti* (*esmь*, etc., §6.73) to express an action which took place in the past, but whose results are still significant: e.g. ašte ty *esi vъzęlъ* i, pověždь mьně kъde i *esi položilъ* (J 20:15) "if thou have borne him hence, tell me where thou hast laid him"; otrokovica *něstъ umrьla* nъ sъpitъ (Mk 5:39) "the damsel is not dead, but sleepeth"; *něste* li *čьli* jako sъtvorjьi iskoni mǫžьskъ polъ i ženьskъ *sъtvorilъ* ja *estъ* (Mt 19:4) "have ye not read that he which made them at the beginning made them male and female?"

In the third person singular the auxiliary is omitted fairly frequently in certain of the texts within the Suprasliensis, but there are no parallels in the other codices.

The perfect is not common, chiefly because the texts which we have do not need to express this particular relationship very often.[17]

14.2 The pluperfects

Two pluperfect tenses are formed by the l-participle in conjunction with the imperfect or imperfective aorist of *byti* (*běaše*/*běaxǫ* or *běxъ* etc.). E.g. mъnoʒi že otъ ijudei *běaxǫ prišьli* kъ Martě i Marii da utěšętъ i (J 11:19) "and many of the Jews were come to Martha and Mary to comfort them"; ne *bě* že ne u Isusъ *prišьlъ* vъ vьsь (J 11:30) "now Jesus *was* not yet *come* into the town". The use of the imperfect auxiliary shows that the past moment is coordinated with some other moment, mentioned or simply

---

17 There are about 600 attested examples of the perfect, against some 10,000 aorists and 2300 imperfects. The precise meaning in individual cases is open to a variety of interpretations, depending on assumptions about aspect, tense, and the degree of dependence on (or independence from) the Greek verb-form underlying the OCS translation. For data, literature, and discussion, see Dostál (Studie, pp. 603 ff.); also K. Trost, *Perfekt und Konditional im Altkirchenslavischen* (Wiesbaden, 1972).

implied by the context; the use of the aorist states an independent action, simply a moment in the past. The participle in both cases shows an action which had started even previous to the past moments implied by the auxiliaries, but whose results were still pertinent.

14.3 The conditional

The following auxiliary forms (from the verb *byti*) are used with the *l*-participles to express a conditional mood: 1 sg. *bimь*, 2-3 sg. *bi*; 1 pl. *bimъ*, 2 pl. *biste*, 3 pl. *bǫ* or *bišę* . The dual forms are not attested. In Su and Sav these forms are rare; the perfective aorist forms of *byti* (*byxъ*, etc.) are used instead, whereby only *by* (never *bystъ*) serves for 2-3 sg. The conditional of 'to be' is usually *bimь bylъ* (or *byxъ bylъ*), but occasionally the participle is omitted. Very rarely a passive participle is used with *bimь*.

14.31 The forms are used either in conditions or in purpose clauses: ašte *bi věděla* darъ božьi, i kъto estъ glagoljęi ti daždь mi piti, ty *bi prosila* u njego i *dalъ* ti *bi* vodǫ živǫ (J 4:10) "If *thou knewest* the gift of God, and who it is that saith to thee, Give me to drink; *thou wouldest have asked* of him and he would have given thee living water". Ašte otъ sego mira *bi bylo* cěsarjьstvo moe, slugy ubo moę *podviʒaly sę bišę* da ne prědanъ *bimь* ijuděomъ (J 18:26) "If my kingdom *were* of this world, then *would* my servants *fight*, that *I should* not *be* delivered to the Jews." In Sav, аще ... бы было ... подвиглы сѧ бышѧ ... прѣданъ быхъ.

In Su there are five instances of *ašti* and one of *aštišę*, which apparently are contractions of *ašte* ('if') with *bi* and *bišę* (Vaillant 256).

14.4 The future perfect or "futurum exactum"

In seven instances l-participles are used with forms of the future *bǫdǫtъ* to signal an action which is viewed as completed before some future moment and whose results are important for that moment; e.g. ašte ključitъ sę da *bǫdetъ sъgnilo* vъpadъšee, dostoitъ proliěti (Euch 20a25) "If it happens that what has fallen in (i.e. into the wine) *has become rotten*, it (the wine) should be thrown away."

15.1 Verbs with basic stems in -i+

Infinitive		просити 'beg'		поустити 'let go'		
		Present		Imperative		
Sing.	1	прошѫ	поуштѫ	–	–	1
	2	просиши	поустиши	проси	поусти	2
	3	проситъ	поуститъ	проси	поусти	3

Dual	1	просивѣ	поустивѣ	просивѣ	поустивѣ	1
	2	просита	поустита	просита	поустита	2
	3	просите	поустите	–	–	3
Plur.	1	просимъ	поустимъ	просимъ	поустимъ	1
	2	просите	поустите	просите	поустите	2
	3	просѧтъ	поустѧтъ	–	–	3
Pres. act. part. nom. sg.			masc.	neut.	fem.	
			просѧ		просѧшти	
			поустѧ		поустѧшти	
Pres. pass. part. nom. sg.			masc.	neut.	fem.	
			просимъ	просимо	просима	
			поустимъ	поустимо	поустима	

		Imperfect		Aorist		
Sing.	1	прошаахъ	поуштаахъ	просихъ	поустихъ	1
	2-3	прошааше	поуштааше	проси	поусти	2-3
Dual	1	прошааховѣ	поуштааховѣ	просиховѣ	поустиховѣ	1
	2	прошаашета	поуштаашета	просиста	поустиста	2
	3	прошаашете	поуштаашете	просисте	поустисте	3
Plur.	1	прошаахомъ	поуштаахомъ	просихомъ	поустихомъ	1
	2	прошаашете	поуштаашете	просисте	поустисте	2
	3	прошаахѫ	поуштаахѫ	просишѧ	поустишѧ	3
Resultative part. nom. sg.			masc.	neut.	fem.	
			просилъ	просило	просила	
			поустилъ	поустило	поустила	
Past active part. nom. sg.			masc.	neut.	fem.	
			прошь (просивъ)		прошьши	
			поуштьь (поустивъ)		поуштьши	
Past passive part. nom. sg.			masc.	neut.	fem.	
			прошенъ	прошено	прошена	
			поуштенъ	поуштено	поуштена	
Verbal substantive			прошенье	Supine	роситъ	
			поуштенье		поуститъ	

15.11 The stem-final consonant or sequence of consonants undergoes iotation, if possible, in the first person singular present (§6.23), all forms of the imperfect (§9.111), in the past active participle (§11.12), and the past passive participle (§11.34) and the verbal substantive.

15.12 Beside the older, more widely used past active participle in *-ь(š)-* (with truncation and iotation), the younger form with *-vъ(š)-* added to the basic stem is well attested, particularly in the codex Suprasliensis (§11.14).

15.13 This productive class is represented by about 350 verbs (or, counting the derivatives made with different prefixes, over 800 lexical verbs). It includes a large number of verbs which occur only once or twice in the manuscripts, however, and thus will constitute only about 20% of the verbs occurring in a given text.[18]

15.2 Verbs with basic stems in -ě+

Infinitive мьнѣти 'think' трьпѣти 'suffer'

		Present		Imperative		
Sing.	1	мьн̂ѭ	трьпл̂ѭ	–	–	1
	2	мьниши	трьпиши	мьни	трьпи	2
	3	мьнитъ	трьпитъ	мьни	трьпи	3
Dual	1	мьнивѣ	трьпивѣ	мьнивѣ	трьпивѣ	1
	2	мьнита	трьпита	мьнита	трьпита	2
	3	мьнитє	трьпитє	–	–	3
Plur.	1	мьнимъ	трьпимъ	мьнимъ	трьпимъ	1
	2	мьнитє	трьпитє	мьнитє	трьпитє	2
	3	мьнѧтъ	трьпѧтъ	–	–	3

Pres. act. part. nom. sg. masc.	neut.	fem.
мьнѧ		мьнѧшти
трьпѧ		трьпѧшти

Pres. pass. part. nom. sg. masc.	neut.	fem.
мьнимъ	мьнимо	мьнима
трьпимъ	трьпимо	трьпима

		Imperfect		Aorist		
Sing.	1	мьнѣахъ	трьпѣахъ	мьнѣхъ	трьпѣхъ	1
	2-3	мьнѣашє	трьпѣашє	мьнѣ	трьпѣ	2-3
Dual	1	мьнѣаховѣ	трьпѣаховѣ	мьнѣховѣ	трьпѣховѣ	1
	2	мьнѣашета	трьпѣашета	мьнѣста	трьпѣста	2
	3	мьнѣашетє	трьпѣашетє	мьнѣстє	трьпѣстє	3
Plur.	1	мьнѣахомъ	трьпѣахомъ	мьнѣхомъ	трьпѣхомъ	1
	2	мьнѣашетє	трьпѣашетє	мьнѣстє	трьпѣстє	2
	3	мьнѣахѫ	трьпѣахѫ	мьнѣшѧ	трьпѣшѧ	3

[18] The figures here and under the other classes of verbs are intended to show the relative importance of the attested verbs and verbal types in the OCS system. The complete lexicon of OCS contains upwards of 1100 morphological verbs plus about 1400 stems with different prefixes, a total of over 2500 lexical verbs. These numbers are approximate, since there is some disagreement about the derivation of some attested forms, as well as just which manuscripts and fragments are to be used as sources. The general picture, however, is reasonably clear.

Resultative part. nom. sg. masc.		neut.	fem.
	мьнѣлъ	мьнѣло	мьнѣла
	трьпѣлъ	трьпѣло	трьпѣла
Past active part. nom. sg. masc.		neut.	fem.
	мьнѣвъ		мьнѣвъши
	трьпѣвъ		трьпѣвъши
Past passive part. nom. sg. masc.		neut.	fem.
	мьнѣнъ	мьнѣно	мьнѣна
	трьпѣнъ	трьпѣно	трьпѣна
Verbal substantive	мьнѣньє	Supine	мьнѣтъ
	трьпѣньє		трьѣтъ

15.21 This group has the и/ѧ marker in the present forms, like the i-verbs, with the same iotation in 1st person singular. Since the past passive participle has the consonantal *-n-* suffix, no truncation takes place, and the ѣ is retained.

15.22 There are only 27 verbs in this group (about 80 including all possible prefixed stems); most are intransitive and express a state rather than an activity. болѣти 'be sick', бъдѣти 'be awake', велѣти 'order', видѣти 'see' (with derivatives including ненавидѣти 'hate', ꙁавидѣти 'envy', обидѣти 'disrespect, offend, harm'), висѣти 'be hanging', врьтѣти 'revolve, turn', вьрѣти 'bubble, boil', горѣти 'burn' (cf. §8.2), грьмѣти 'thunder', ꙁьрѣти 'see, look at, view' (with derivatives including ꙁаꙁьрѣти 'blame, hold against', прѣꙁьрѣти 'neglect, disdain'), късьнѣти 'be late, slow', кыпѣти 'boil', летѣти 'fly', при-льпѣти 'cling to', мрьꙁѣти 'become abhorrent', мьнѣти 'think, opine' (and сѫмьнѣти сѧ or соумьнѣти сѧ 'be uncertain, doubt'), пльꙁѣти 'be crawling', полѣти 'blaze', свьтѣти 'shine', скрьбѣти 'be grieved, distressed', смрьдѣти 'stink', стыдѣти сѧ 'be ashamed', сѣдѣти 'sit, be sitting', трьпѣти 'suffer, endure', штѧдѣти 'save', -шоумѣти 'sound' and the irregular хотѣти 'wish'.[19]

15.23 *Irregularities*

15.231 The singular imperative of видѣти 'see' is виждь (вижди in Euch), cf. §7.2. (Prefixed stems: не обиди Mk 10:19, не ꙁавиди Ps 37:1.)

---

[19] In Ps Sin's margin by ps. 127:3 is a gloss, гобьꙁѭщиѣ 'yielding rich harvest', presumably to the phrase лоꙁа плодовита 'fruitful vine'. It perhaps is from a dialect verb *гобьꙁ-ѣ+, with {z}. The expected root *gobьʒ* (borrowed from Gothic *gabigs* 'abundant') should have /ž/ before a front vowel, **gobьžęšt-*.

Beside regular pres. passive participle видимъ an archaic form видомъ with the sense 'visible' (and невидомъ 'invisible') is found (Su only).

15.232 Хотѣти 'wish, want; be about to' is irregular in that it has the present-marker *e* (not *i*, the expected correlate of -ę-): {xot-ě+e-} > xotje- (by §6.13 A2), therefore хоштеши, хоштетъ, хоштемъ, хоштете. 1 sing. {xot-ě+Ø-ǫ} > xotjǫ > хоштѫ and 3 pl {xot-ě+ę-tъ} > хотѧтъ as expected. The imperative also has the mutated stem-shape, въсхошти. The present active participle is regular: masc.-neut. хотѧ, fem. хотѧшти, etc.

Twice in Supr and once in Vat (J 5:6) хошти occurs instead of 2 sg. хоштеши (for post-OCS parallels see Vaillant §180). Six times in Su the root vowel is ъ instead of *o*: хътѣти 114.1, pres. act. part. хъта 532.24, and the present forms cited in §6.41.

15.3 Verbs with basic stem in -a+ preceded by a soft consonant other than j.

Infinitive слъшати 'hear' дрьжати 'hold'

		Present		Imperative		
Sing.	1	слъшѫ	дрьжѫ	–	–	1
	2	слъшиши	дрьжиши	слъши	дрьжи	2
	3	слъшитъ	дрьжитъ	слъши	дрьжи	3
Dual	1	слъшивѣ	дрьживѣ	слъшивѣ	дрьживѣ	1
	2	слъшита	дрьжита	слъшита	дрьжита	2
	3	слъшите	дрьжите	–	–	3
Plur.	1	слъшимъ	дрьжимъ	слъшимъ	дрьжимъ	1
	2	слъшите	дрьжите	слъшите	дрьжите	2
	3	слъшѧтъ	дрьжѧтъ	–	–	3

Pres. act. part. nom. sg.	masc.	neut.	fem.
	слъшѧ		слъшѧшти
	дрьжѧ		дрьжѧшти
Pres. pass. part. nom. sg.	masc.	neut.	fem.
	слъшимъ	слъшимо	слъшима
	дрьжимъ	дрьжимо	дрьжима

		Imperfect		Aorist		
Sing.	1	слъшаахъ	дрьжаахъ	слъшахъ	дрьжахъ	1
	2-3	слъшааше	дрьжааше	слъша	дрьжа	2-3
Dual	1	слъшааховѣ	дрьжааховѣ	слъшаховѣ	дрьжаховѣ	1
	2	слъшаашета	дрьжаашета	слъшаста	дрьжаста	2
	3	слъшаашете	дрьжаашете	слъшасте	дрьжасте	3
Plur.	1	слъшаахомъ	дрьжаахомъ	слъшахомъ	дрьжахомъ	1
	2	слъшаашете	дрьжаашете	слъшасте	дрьжасте	2
	3	слъшаахѫ	дрьжаахѫ	слъшашѧ	дрьжашѧ	3

Resultative part. nom. sg. masc.		neut.	fem.
	слъішалъ	слъішало	слъішала
	дрьжалъ	дрьжало	дрьжала
Past active part. nom. sg. masc.		neut.	fem.
	слъішавъ		слъішавъши
	дрьжавъ		дрьжавъши
Past passive part. nom. sg. masc.		neut.	fem.
	слъішанъ	слъішано	слъішана
	дрьжанъ	дрьжано	дрьжана
Verbal substantive	слъішанье	Supine	слъішатъ
	дрьжанье		дрьжатъ

15.31 This type is transparently a variant of the ě-verbs. The classifier {-ě+} regularly becomes *a* after a palatal consonant, see §3.5c1. Two verbs with roots ending in *oj* belong here, {stoj-ě+} and {boj-ě+ sę}, and 13 verbs with stems formerly ending in a velar consonant (with about 40 more forms made with different prefixes): **бльштати сѧ** 'flash', **боꙗти сѧ** 'fear', **бѣжати** 'flee', **движати** 'move', **дрьжати** 'hold', **клѧчати** 'kneel', **кричати** 'shout', **лежати** 'lie, be in a lying position', **льштати сѧ** 'shine', **мльчати** 'be silent', **мъчати** 'push', **слъішати** 'hear', **стоꙗти** 'stand' (with prefixed stems like **достоꙗти** 'befit', **настоꙗти** 'be present', **състоꙗти сѧ** 'consist') **тъштати сѧ** 'hasten, be zealous', **-тѧжати** (**при-**, **съ-тѧжати** 'acquire').[20]

15.32 Here can be mentioned the uniquely anomalous **съпати** 'sleep', which has a hard consonant preceding the *a*, but nonetheless this type of present: 3 pl. **съпѧтъ**, 1 sg. **съпл҄ѭ**; 2 sg. **съпиши**; imv. **съпи**; pres. act. part. **съпѧ**, **съпѧшти**.

15.4 Verbs with basic stems in -j-a+.

Infinitive **дѣꙗти** 'do' **даꙗти** 'give'

		Present		Imperative		
Sing.	1	дѣѭ	даѭ	–	–	1
	2	дѣеши	даеши	дѣи	даи	2
	3	дѣетъ	даетъ	дѣи	даи	3
Dual	1	дѣевѣ	даевѣ	дѣивѣ	даивѣ	1
	2	дѣета	даета	дѣита	даита	2
	3	дѣете	даете	-	–	3

[20] Historically, the forms were presumably **blьsk-ě, boj-ě, běg-ě, dvig-ě, dьrg-ě, klęk-ě, krik-ě, leg-ě, lьsk-ě, mьlk-ě, mъk-ě, slyx-ě, stoj-ě, tъsk-ě, -tęg-ě.*

Plur.	1	дѣемъ	даемъ	дѣимъ	даимъ	1
	2	дѣете	даете	дѣите	даите	2
	3	дѣѭтъ	даѭтъ	–	–	3
Pres. act. part. nom. sg.		masc.		neut.	fem.	
			дѣѩ		дѣѭшти	
			даѩ		даѭшти	
Pres. pass. part. nom. sg.		masc.		neut.	fem.	
		дѣемъ		дѣемо	дѣема	
		даемъ		даемо	даема	
		Imperfect		Aorist		
Sing.	1	дѣꙗахъ	даꙗахъ	дѣꙗхъ	даꙗахъ	1
	2-3	дѣꙗаше	даꙗаше	дѣꙗ	даꙗ	2-3
Dual	1	дѣꙗаховѣ	даꙗаховѣ	дѣꙗховѣ	даꙗховѣ	1
	2	дѣꙗашета	даꙗашета	дѣꙗста	даꙗста	2
	3	дѣꙗшете	даꙗашете	дѣꙗсте	даꙗсте	3
Plur.	1	дѣꙗахомъ	даꙗахомъ	дѣꙗхомъ	даꙗхомъ	1
	2	дѣꙗашете	даꙗашете	дѣꙗсте	даꙗсте	2
	3	дѣꙗахѫ	даꙗахѫ	дѣꙗшѧ	даꙗшѧ	3
Resultative part. nom. sg.		masc.		neut.	fem.	
		дѣꙗлъ		дѣꙗло	дѣꙗла	
		даꙗлъ		даꙗло	даꙗла	
Past active part. nom. sg.		masc.		neut.	fem.	
			дѣꙗвъ		дѣꙗвъши	
			даꙗвъ		даꙗвъши	
Past passive part. nom. sg.		masc.		neut.	fem.	
		дѣꙗнъ		дѣꙗно	дѣꙗна	
		даꙗнъ		даꙗно	даꙗна	
Verbal substantive		дѣꙗньє		Supine	дѣꙗтъ	
		даꙗньє			даꙗтъ	

15.41 Variant spellings indicate for some verbs a hesitation between basic stems of this class (e.g. sěj-a+, inf. sěja-ti 'sow') and stems with the zero-classifier, effectively therefore consonantal stems (sěj-Ø+, 3pl sěj-ǫtъ, inf. sěti [in this case probably older, historically]). The matter is obscured by a dialectical loss of intervocalic *j*, which may bring about contractions, e.g. s*ěja*ti сѣꙗти > s*ěa*ti сѣати > a new s*ě*ti сѣти.

15.42 For variant spellings in the present tense showing loss of stem-final *j* and subsequent assimilation of the present-marker (*aje* > *aa* > *a*; *ěje* > *ěa*) see §6.5).

15.43 The group includes perhaps thirteen verbs (plus about 35 with different prefixes), some of which have variant forms. Offering fairly certain evidence of *-a-* are: **из-ваꙗти** ‘sculpture’, **вѣꙗти** ‘blow’, **даꙗти** ‘give’. **каꙗти сѧ** ‘rue, repent’, **лаꙗти** ‘bark’, **лаꙗти** ambush’, **на-маꙗти** ‘indicate’, **-стаꙗти** ‘stand’, **сѣꙗти** ‘sift’, **таꙗти** ‘melt, thaw’, **чаꙗти** ‘expect’.

15.431 The form **ıсходатаєтъ** ‘obtains through mediation’ (Cloz) does not fit neatly into this group. The underlying segmentation is unclear; cf. *isxodataj-ь* ‘mediator, conciliator’.

15.44 The prefixed forms of **дѣꙗти** ‘do’ (e.g. **съ-дѣꙗти** ‘do’, **одѣꙗти** ‘dress’) function both as imperfective and perfective.

15.441 Certain archaic present forms with the stem *-děžd-* are explicitly perfective (e.g. **одеждемъ** ‘we will dress’, **въздеждѫ** ‘I shall raise’). cf. §16.8.

15.45 Five poorly-attested verbs are usually listed with *-a-* although no forms in *-aja-* or *-ěja-* are to be found in the canonical mss: *grěj*-ǫtъ ‘warm’, *rěj*-ǫtъ ‘push’, *spěj*-ǫtъ ‘prosper’, *sъměj*-ǫtъ ‘dare’, and *vъlaj*-ǫtъ sę ‘be tossed [by waves]’.[21] See §15.92.

15.46 Three verbs (plus 14 prefixed stems) in -ъj-a+ (alternating with -ij-a+, cf. §2.61) have -ěj- in the present system: **лыꙗти/лиꙗти** “pour”, pres. **лѣѭтъ**, imv. **лѣи**, pres. p. part. **лѣемъ**; **смыꙗти/смиꙗти сѧ** “laugh” **смѣѭтъ сѧ** etc., and presumably **zъjati/*zijati* “yawn”, for which only the pres. parts. **ꙁѣѧ**, **ꙁѣѭщи** are attested.

NB: *lъj-a+* (*lъjati/lijati lějǫtъ*) does not differ in meaning from *lъj-Ø+* (*lъjǫtъ*), cf. §15.93.

15.5 Verbs with basic stems in -ova+ or -eva+.

Infinitive		**миловати** ‘pity’		**непьштевати** ‘suppose’		
		Present		Imperative		
Sing.	1	**милоуѭ**	**непьштоуѭ**	–	–	1
	2	**милоуеши**	**непьштоуеши**	**милоуи**	**непьштоуи**	2
	3	**милоуетъ**	**непьштоуетъ**	**милоуи**	**непьштоуи**	3
Dual	1	**милоуевѣ**	**непьштоуевѣ**	**милоуивѣ**	**непьштоуивѣ**	1
	2	**милоуета**	**непьштоуета**	**милоуита**	**непьштоуита**	2
	3	**милоуете**	**непьштоуете**	-	–	3
Plur.	1	**милоуемъ**	**непьштоуемъ**	**милоуимъ**	**непьштоуимъ**	1
	2	**милоуете**	**непьштоуете**	**милоуите**	**непьштоуите**	2
	3	**милоуѭтъ**	**непьштоуѭтъ**	–	–	3

---

[21] Infinitives like **вълаꙗти**, **грѣꙗти**, and **рѣꙗти** occur in dictionaries, but they are unjustified for OCS.

	masc.	neut.	fem.
Pres. act. part. nom. sg.			
	милоуѧ		милоуѭшти
	непьштоуѧ		непьштоуѭшти
Pres. pass. part. nom. sg.	masc.	neut.	fem.
	милоуемъ	милоуемо	милоуема
	непьштоуемъ	непьштоуемо	непьштоуема

	Imperfect		Aorist		
Sg. 1	миловаахъ	непьштеваахъ	миловахъ	непьштевахъ	1
2-3	миловааше	непьштевааше	милова	непьштева	2-3
Du 1	миловааховѣ	непьштевааховѣ	миловаховѣ	непьштеваховѣ	1
2	миловаашета	непьштеваашета	миловаста	непьштеваста	2
3	миловаашете	непьштеваашете	миловасте	непьштевасте	3
Pl. 1	миловаахомъ	непьштеваахомъ	миловахомъ	непьштевахомъ	1
2	миловаашете	непьштеваашете	миловасте	непьштевасте	2
3	миловаахѫ	непьштеваахѫ	миловашѧ	непьштевашѧ	3

	masc.	neut.	fem.
Resultative part. nom. sg.			
	миловалъ	миловало	миловала
	непьштевалъ	непьштевало	непьштевала
Past active part. nom. sg.	masc.	neut.	fem.
	миловавъ		миловавъши
	непьштевавъ		непьштевавъши
Past passive part. nom. sg.	masc.	neut.	fem.
	милованъ	миловано	милована
	непьштеванъ	непьштевано	непьштевана
Verbal substantive	милованье	Supine	миловатъ
	непьштеванье		непьштеватъ

15.501 The classifier **-ova+/-eva+** truncates to *-uj* before vocalic desinences (but see §9.5 for the imperfect).

15.502 In Mar there are cases where the *-uje-* of the present is written *-uu-*, e.g. трѣбоуоутъ for трѣбоуетъ 'needs', радоуоутъ сѧ for радоуетъ сѧ 'rejoices'; cf. §6.5.

15.51 Ova-verbs are a productive class of about a hundred stems (plus another fifty derived with various prefixes). Many of them are rare, so that this class ranks very low in frequency (ca. 2%) in a given sample of text. Without exception, the verbs are derivatives of other OCS words. For example: даровати 'give gifts' (*darъ* 'gift'), польѕевати 'profit, use' (*polьʒa* 'use, profit'), вѣровати 'believe' (*věra* 'belief'), хоуловати 'blaspheme' (*xula* 'blasphemy'), оувраловати or врачевати 'treat' (*balii* or *vračь* 'doctor'), радовати сѧ 'rejoice' (*radъ*), миловати 'have mercy' (*milъ* 'deserving of mercy'), милосрьдовати 'have pity' (*milosrьdъ* 'merciful'), сверѣповати 'be wild' (*sverěpъ* 'wild'), чрьмьновати 'redden' (*črъmьnъ* 'red'), коуповати (I) 'buy' (*kup-i+ti,* P). Many obvious neologisms are formed with an intervening substantival suffix -*ьstv*-: e.g. апостольствовати 'be an apostle' (*apostolьstvo* 'apostolate'), пророчьствовати 'prophesy' (*prorokъ* 'prophet', *proročьstvo* 'prophesy'), послоушьствовати or съвѣдѣтельствовати 'witness' (*posluxъ* or *sъvědětelјь* 'a witness'), четврьтовластьствовати 'be a tetrarch', оржженосьствовати 'guard' (**orǫženosьcь* 'weapon-carrier, guard'), плодоносьствовати 'be fruitful' (*plodonosьnъ* 'fruit-bearing, fruitful'). Most of this last type are efforts to render one Greek word by one Slavonic word; the number of doublets attested and the clumsy ad-hoc character of some of the more complex examples are clear indications of the productivity of this suffix and therefore of this verbal class.

15.52 The two verbs in -*ьv-a+* (~ -*uj-*) may be listed here: пльвати 'spit' and бльвати 'vomit', with 3 pl. pres. forms плюжтъ and блюжтъ.

15.53 The verbs *o-snov-a+ti* 'found' and *kov-a+ti* 'forge' are treated in §15.642.

15.6 Verbs with basic stems in -a+ preceded by a hard consonant other than v

		Infinitive глаголати 'speak'	вѧзати 'tie'			
		Present		Imperative		
Sing.	1	глаголѭ	важѫ	–	–	1
	2	глаголѥши	важеши	глаголи	важи	2
	3	глаголѥтъ	важетъ	глаголи	важи	3
Dual	1	глаголѥвѣ	важевѣ	глаголивѣ	важивѣ	1
	2	глаголѥта	важета	глаголита	важита	2
	3	глаголѥте	важете	-	–	3
Plur.	1	глаголѥмъ	важемъ	глаголимъ	важимъ	1
	2	глаголѥте	важете	глаголите	важите	2
	3	глаголѭтъ	важѫтъ	–	–	3

Pres. act. part. nom. sg. masc.	neut.	fem.
глаголѩ		глаголѭшти
важѧ		важѫшти

Pres. pass. part. nom. sg. masc.	neut.	fem.
глаголѥмъ	глаголѥмо	глаголѥма
важемъ	важемо	важема

		Imperfect		Aorist		
Sing.	1	глаголаахъ	вѧжаахъ	глаголахъ	вѧꙁахъ	1
	2-3	глаголааше	вѧжааше	глагола	вѧꙁа	2-3
Dual	1	глаголааховѣ	вѧжааховѣ	глаголаховѣ	вѧꙁаховѣ	1
	2	глаголаашета	вѧжаашета	глаголаста	вѧꙁаста	2
	3	глаголаашете	вѧжаашете	глаголасте	вѧꙁасте	3
Plur.	1	глаголаахомъ	вѧжаахомъ	глаголахомъ	вѧꙁахомъ	1
	2	глаголаашете	вѧжаашете	глаголасте	вѧꙁасте	2
	3	глаголаахѫ	вѧжаахѫ	глаголашѧ	вѧꙁашѧ	3
Resultative part. nom. sg. masc.				neut.	fem.	
			глаголалъ	глаголало	глаголала	
			вѧꙁалъ	вѧꙁало	вѧꙁала	
Past active part. nom. sg. masc.				neut.	fem.	
			глаголавъ		глаголавъши	
			вѧꙁавъ		вѧꙁавъши	
Past passive part. nom. sg. masc.				neut.	fem.	
			глаголанъ	глаголано	глаголана	
			вѧꙁанъ	вѧꙁано	вѧꙁана	
Verbal substantive			глаголанье	Supine	глаголатъ	
			вѧꙁанье		вѧꙁатъ	

15.61 The classifier *a* becomes *j* before the vocalic desinences of the present system, effecting iotation of the stem-final consonant. (§6.22).

15.62 The expected *-i-* of the imperative plural is sometimes replaced by *ě* (sometimes so written, contrary to normal spelling rules) or *a*: глагол̂ꙗте, глагол̂ѣте for глагол̂ите 'speak!', покажѣте, покажате for покажите (*po-kaz-a*-ti 'show'). See §7.21.

15.63 This class contains about fifty verbs (plus over 60 prefixed stems), some of them very common. Post-OCS evidence indicates that it was still somewhat productive.

алкати алчѫтъ / лакати лачѫтъ	hunger	ꙁыбати ꙁыбл̂ѭтъ	toss, agitate
		каꙁати кажѫтъ	show
вѧꙁати вѧжѫтъ	tie	капати капл̂ѭтъ	drip
глаголати глагол̂ѭтъ	speak	клепати клепл̂ѭтъ	indicate
двиѕати движѫтъ	move	клицати кличѫтъ	call, cry out
въꙁ-дрѣмати -дрѣмл̂ѭтъ	doze	колѣбати колѣбл̂ѭтъ	rock
дъіхати дъішѫтъ	blow	кѫпати кѫпл̂ѭтъ	bathe
жѧдати жѧждѫтъ	thirst	лиꙁати лижѫтъ	lick
ꙁобати ꙁобл̂ѭтъ	eat (with beak)	лѣгати лѣжѫтъ	lie, recline

лѧцати лѧчѫтъ	set trap	-сыпати -сыпл̂ѭтъ	pour, strew
лобъꙃати лобъжѫтъ	kiss	-сѧѕати -сѧжѫтъ	touch
лъгати лъжѫтъ	lie, say untruth	тесати тешѫтъ	hew
маꙃати мажѫтъ	anoint	тратати траштѫтъ	pursue
измрьмьрати -ьр̂ѭтъ	nibble	тѧѕати тѧжѫтъ	question, test
орати ор̂ѭтъ	plow	хапати хапл̂ѭтъ	bite
пискати пиштѫтъ	pipe	чесати чешѫтъ	comb
плакати плачѫтъ	weep	кл̂еветати кл̂евештѫтъ	slander
плакати плачѫтъ	rinse, wash	клокотати клокочѫтъ	bubble, gurgle
плескати плештѫтъ	clap, slap		
поꙗсати поꙗшѫтъ	gird	кльчьтати кльчьштѫтъ	cause (teeth) to chatter
ристати риштѫтъ	run		
на-рицати -ричѫтъ	name, call	ръпътати ръпъштѫтъ	murmur
ръꙃати ръжѫтъ	whinny	скрьжьтати скрьжьштѫтъ	gnash (teeth)
рѣꙃати рѣжѫтъ	cut	скръгътати скръгъштѫтъ	gnash (teeth)
стенати стен̂ѭтъ	groan	трепетати трепештѫтъ	tremble
страдати страждѫтъ	suffer	шьпьтати шьпьштѫтъ	whisper
стрѣкати стрѣчѫтъ	goad	по-штьбьтати поштьбьштѫтъ	twitter
сълати съл̂ѭтъ	send		

15.641 The chief deviations from these patterns imply stems that base competing forms on *-a+* vs. *-Ø+* vs. *-aj+*, chiefly in the present system.

жѧдати 'thirst' has pres. жѧдаетъ in Ps, жѧдаемъ in KF, жѧдаѧ in Su beside regular forms with truncated жѧжде- жѧждѫшт-.

искати 'seek', regularly иштѫтъ (reflecting *isk-j-* and predictable from *isk-a+*) but fairly often 1 sg. искѫ, 3 pl. искѫтъ, pres. act. part. искѫште (as though from *isk-Ø+*). The other forms always show mutation (either *isk-j-e-* and iotation, or *isk-e-* and KI palatalization), иште-.

метати 'throw', regularly мештѫтъ etc. but also метѫтъ etc., along with метаѭште Ps 125:6, and the like. The imperfect has метаахѫ As, and мештаахѫ Su. See Vaillant 308; Koch §67.

15.642 Three verbs have *-a-* before C-desinences and *-Ø+* before vocalic desinences: ковати ковѫтъ 'forge' (impf. *kovaaxǫ* Ps 128:3); съсати съсѫтъ 'suck'; тъкати тъкѫтъ 'push, weave'. Presumably основати 'found' and -ръвати 'tear, pull' belong here, although the presents **osnovǫtъ* and **rъvǫtъ* do not happen to be attested in OCS.

15.643 Eight verbs (plus a dozen prefixed stems) have, or may have, an unpredictable alternation of the root vowel in the present system:

стьлати стєлѭтъ 'spread out'. The participle стєлѧшта Su 332.30 perhaps reflects a late dialect change of nasal vowel after a palatal consonant; cf. reg. стєлѩштє Su 341.12.

имати ємлѭтъ {j-ьm-a+ ~ j-em-j-} 'take, get' may have *-ьmati* after prefixes ending in a consonant: въньмати 'hear', обьмати 'gather'. The prefixed forms are in competition with derivatives of *im-aj+*: въꙁимаѭтъ 'raise', вънимаѭтъ, обимаѭтъ. Imperfect Mar сънъмаахѫ L 5:15 ~ Zo сънимаахѫ.

The vowel of the present stem is found also in infinitive and other forms (principally in Sav): ємати, приємати, подъємати. In Su отънємьꙑи 331.25, отънємьѫштъ 294.4 the root has an epenthetic н (cf. §3.3101).

ꙁьдати ꙁиждѫтъ 'build'. Su 204.7 съжиждєтъ shows dialect assimilation of root-initial *z* to the following *žd* (affirmed by post-OCS examples).

пьсати пишѫтъ 'write'. Forms with *pьsa-* are well attested, but regularized forms from newer *pis-a+* are also found, e.g. написати L 2:1 Zo Mar As ~ напсати Sav.

плѣжѫшт- 'crawling, slithering'; чрѣпѩштє 'drawing (water)'; and въслѣпѩшт- 'gushing, spurting up' perhaps imply **plьz-a+, *čгьp-a+,* and **vъ(z)-slьp-a+*

трѣжєтъ 'tears, rends' may correspond to **trьʒ-a+*; attested forms with тръꙁа- (only in Su) may represent **trьʒ-aj+*.

Note. The patterning of vowels in these verbs is less irregular if we allow the underlying representations {pьlz pelz, čьrp čerp, sьlp selp, tьrz terz} with the same alternation of ь ~ *e* as in {stьl stel}, etc. Since no syllable-final *r* or *l* may occur in surface forms, we may state that before consonant {ьr ьl} metathesize to *rь lь*, and that {er el} become *rě lě*. Cf. §3.912.

стръгати строужѫтъ 'scrape, flay'. However Su 392.5 остроуга indicates a regular (or regularized) **strug-a+*.

15.644 Five verbs (plus 17 prefixed stems) have *-a-* (indicating -a+) before consonantal desinences, but no iotation in pre-vocalic forms (as though based on -Ø+), and unpredictable changes in stem vowel.

бьрати бєрѫтъ 'collect, take'; дьрати дєрѫтъ 'flay, rip', and -пьрати -пєрѫтъ 'trample' happen not to have imperfects attested.

жьдати жидѫтъ 'wait, await' has (in Su) imperfects based on *žьd-a+*, *žid-*, and *žьd-* (жъдааше, жідѣахѫ, жьдѣахѫ).

гънати женѫтъ (prefixed with *iz, raz* > иꙁгънати раꙁгънати ~ иждєнѫтъ раждєнѫтъ, §3.311) has imperfect жєнѣахѫ Su 17.21, 196.15.

15.645 ꙁъвати (with 5 prefixed stems) has the present tense ꙁовѫтъ. Imperfects ꙁъвааше Su 473.16 and ꙁовѣашє Su 516.6.

15.7 Verbs with the classifier -nǫ.

Infinitive ринѫти 'push' двигнѫти 'move'

		Present		Imperative		
Sing.	1	ринѫ	двигнѫ	–	–	1
	2	ринеши	двигнеши	рини	двигни	2
	3	ринетъ	двигнетъ	рини	двигни	3
Dual	1	риневѣ	двигневѣ	ринѣвѣ	двигѣвѣ	1
	2	ринета	двигнета	ринѣта	двигнѣта	2
	3	ринете	двигнете	–	–	3
Plur.	1	ринемъ	двигнемъ	ринѣмъ	двигнѣмъ	1
	2	ринете	двигнете	ринѣте	двигнѣте	2
	3	ринѫтъ	двигнѫтъ	–	–	3

	masc.	neut.	fem.
Pres. act. part. nom. sg.	ринꙑ		ринѫшти
	двигнꙑ		двигнѫшти
Pres. pass. part. nom. sg.	риномъ	риномо	ринома
	двигномъ	двигномо	двигнома

		Imperfect		Aorist		
Sing.	1	ринѣахъ	двигнѣахъ	ринѫхъ	двигохъ	1
	2-3	ринѣаше	двигнѣаше	ринѫ	движе	2-3
Dual	1	ринѣаховѣ	двигнѣаховѣ	ринѫховѣ	двигоховѣ	1
	2	ринѣашета	двигнѣашета	ринѫста	двигоста	2
	3	ринѣашете	двигнѣашете	ринѫсте	двигосте	3
Plur.	1	ринѣахомъ	двигнѣахомъ	ринѫхомъ	двигохомъ	1
	2	ринѣашете	двигнѣашете	ринѫсте	двигосте	2
	3	ринѣахѫ	двигнѣахѫ	ринѫшѧ	двигошѧ	3

	masc.	neut.	fem.
Resultative part. nom. sg.	ринѫлъ	ринѫло	ринѫла
	двиглъ	двигло	двигла
Past active part. nom. sg.	ринѫвъ		ринѫвъши
	двигъ		двигъши
Past passive part. nom. sg.	риновенъ	риновено	риновена
	движенъ	движено	движена

Verbal substantive	риновенье	Supine	ринѫтъ
	движенье		двигнѫтъ

15.71 This group has two major subdivisions: stems with a vowel preceding the classifier *-nǫ*, and stems with a root-final consonant preceding. However, there are some intermediate cases, where the consonant appears in some forms and not in others. Some verbs are poorly attested, so that their classification is not always certain. Although there are only about 60 verbs (plus about 80 prefixed stems) in the class, it is clear that it was productive and used to make new perfective verbs. Some of the older verbs were imperfective.

15.711 The morpheme {nǫ} usually remains intact before consonantal desinences and is truncated to *-n-* before vocalic desinences. Before the *-en-* formant of the past passive participle (and especially its derivative, the verbal substantive), *-nǫ-* is replaced by *-nov-*: *rinǫti, rinǫvъ; rinetъ,* but *otъrinoveni* 'pushed away' past pass. part. nom. pl. masc. (Ps 87:6).

15.712 The common verb **станѫтъ стати** 'stand up, take a stand, stop' (with eight prefixed stems, including **останѫтъ остати** 'leave, cease', **прѣстанѫтъ прѣстати** 'cease') has *n* only in the present system. It is perfective (as opposed to *-staj-a+*), and may be regarded as {staj-(nǫ)}, the classifier being dropped in infinitive and past.

15.72 The following 11 verbs (plus 8 prefixed stems) definitely have a vowel before the -nǫ of the basic stem and always retain the classifier: **-винѫти** (**повинѫти сѧ** 'be obedient', **не обинѫти сѧ** 'be frank, straightforward'), **доунѫти** 'blow', **ȥинѫти** 'gape, yawn', **на-кынѫти** 'nod to', **поманѫти** 'beckon', **минѫти** 'pass', **помѧнѫти** and **помѣнѫти** 'call to mind', **въспланѫти** 'flare up', **плинѫти** and **плюнѫти** 'spit', **ринѫти** 'push', and **и(ȥ)-соунѫти** 'draw out'.

15.73 **въȥ-бънѫти** 'waken', **оу-вѧнѫти** 'wilt' (see §15.773), **гънѫти** 'bend, fold', **канѫти** 'drip', and **вьс-прѧнѫти** 'get up' are attested only with a vowel before *nǫ*, but there is good reason to posit underlying forms with a consonant (and to expect non-present forms without *nǫ*), viz. the roots *bъd, vęd, kap,* and *pręd*. Compare the next paragraph.

15.74 Underlying {u-sъp-(nǫ+)} 'fall asleep' predicts the infinitive **оусънѫти** and past forms like **оусънѫхъ, оусънѫвъ**, where *-pn- > -n-* (§3.3131), and the forms without *nǫ* retain the *p*: **оусъпе, оусъпъшиихъ**.

{top-(nǫ+)} 'submerge' underlies Su **истопнѫшѧ, истопошѧ** as well as **истопѫ** Mt 8:32 Sav ~ **оутопѫ** Mar As ~ **оутопошѧ** Zo.

15.75 The aorist **присвѧде, присвѧдѫ** 'was/were scorched' probably had inf. **prisvęnǫti,* while the past passive part. **оу-дѣв-ена** 'take by surprise, ambush' and the aorists **ȥа-клепе** 'closed' and **оу-трьпоста** '(the two) became numb' may have had *nǫ* forms without the labial stop (*ꙁаклєнѫти, *оутрьнѫти) like оусънѫти, or with it (*ꙁаклєпнѫти, *оутрьпнѫти) like осльпнѫти and загъıбнѫти, see below.

15.76 Most verbs with a consonant before the classifier *nǫ* keep *-n-* in the present system and *-nǫ-* in the infinitive, but allow variants with or without the *n*/*nǫ* in past forms. When the *-nǫ-* or *-n-* disappears, the resultant C-stem behaves like the root-verbs with zero classifier, discussed below in §15.8. For the specific aorist forms, see §10.812. The few verbs attested without *n*-forms beside C-stem forms most probably would be found to have doublets if we had more old manuscripts.

This group comprises 34 verbs (plus over 40 prefixed stems):

-бѣгнѫти 'flee'	-крьснѫти 'be resurrected' (§15.773)
влъснѫти 'stammer'	-къıснѫти 'sour'
от-врьгнѫти 'throw away'	-млькнѫти 'fall silent'
въıкнѫти 'learn'	оу-мѧкнѫти 'become soft'
оу-вѧꙁнѫти 'be ensnared'	-мъкнѫти 'push, move'
гаснѫти 'go out' (§15.773)	-никнѫти 'come up'
гонєꙁнѫти 'be rid of'	отъ-ригнѫти 'eject'
по-грѧꙁнѫти 'sink, be submerged'	по-сагнѫти 'marry'
гъıбнѫти 'perish' (see §15.772)	по-стигнѫти 'attain'
двигнѫти 'move, lift'	съхнѫти 'dry up' (see §15.773)
дрьꙁнѫти 'dare'	оу-сѣкнѫти 'behead' (see §15.771)
-дъхнѫти 'breathe'	и(ꙁ)-сѧкнѫти 'dry up' (see §15.773)
оу-жаснѫти 'be terrified'	тлькнѫти 'knock'
про-ꙁѧбнѫти 'sprout, grow'	-тъкнѫти 'hit, bump'
коснѫти 'touch'	-трьгнѫти 'tear'
въс-кликнѫти 'shout'	-тѧгнѫти 'pull'
кръкнѫти 'grunt'	и(ꙁ)ѵєꙁнѫти (§3.311) 'disappear'

Further, the past active participle поплъꙁъ сѧ 'having slipped' (Su) suggests *попльꙁнѫти.

15.771 Certain fluctuations within the present system and in the infinitive indicate that the classifier *-nǫ+* was replacing (a) the zero-classifier in infinitive and some past forms on the one hand, and/or (b) the underlying *j* of present forms that is regularly correlated with the -a+ classifier. The verb оусѣкнѫти 'behead' (оусѣкнѫть [Su], оусѣкнѫхъ [Ev, Ps], cf. оусѣкновєниє 'beheading' [As]) is attested with the past passive part. оусѣѵєнъ. This participle, and the infinitive прѣсѣшти 'cut through' (Su) and the few attested present forms (посѣѵєши, сѣѵєтє, посѣци imv., сѣкъı nom sg. masc. pres act part.), correspond to {-sěk-Ø+}, cf. §15.85. Su also has doublet infinitives при-сѧгнѫти and присѧшти, but otherwise OCS has only eight forms from {pri-sęg} and осѧгъшии.[22] Attested imv. sg. въньѕи 'sheath!' J 18:11, 3 sg. aor. воньѕє 'pierce' Ps 31:4 presumably represent {-nьz-} and belong with the infinitive вънъѕнѫти (Su 2.23); other prefixes are attested—the root aorist оуньѕѫ Ps 37:3.(= Eu 76a4), and past act. part. въѕньѕъ 'impaling' Mt 27:48, Mk 15:36, J 19:29.[23] The isolated 3 pl. aor. охръмѫ 'they went lame' Ps 17:46 is usually cited under the phonologically improbable infinitive *охръмнѫти (which violates §2.522; cf. §29.813 n. 23).

15.772 The presents formed by underlying *j* (coordinated paradigmatically with the classifier *-a+*) alternate in some verbs with *n*-presents. Particularly well attested are forms from {gyb} 'perish': eg. погыблєтъ J 6:12 Mar ~ гыбнєтъ Zo As; гыблѭштєє J 6:27 Mar Zo гыбнѫштєє As.[24]

15.773 Other examples of the *j*-presents—simply irregularities in OCS—are rare:

оу-вѧнѫти 'wilt' Su 389.14; pres. act. part. нє оувѧждѧ 'unfading' Su 352.23 ~ 3 pl. aor. оувѧношѧ Su 164.19.

гаснѫти 'go out [fire]': нє гашѫштии 'not quenched' (e.g. Mk 9:43).

въскрьснѫти 'be resurrected' has beside many regular forms the isolated 3 sg. imv. въскрьшı Ps 73:22.

исъхнѫти 'be dried up': исъхнєтъ J 15:6 As ~ исъшєтъ Zo Mar Sav; cf. їсъшѫтъ Ps 36:2.

исѧкнѫти 'dry up' has исѧкнєтъ Mt 24:12 (Zo Mar As, Sav 87r) but исѧчєтъ Sav 47r in a repetition of the verse.

Isolated forms that probably belong here: **uglьbnǫti* 'be stuck' 1 sg. pres. оуглъбѭ (for **uglьbljǫ*); Ps 68:15 ~ aor. 3 pl. оугльбѫ Ps 9:16, 1 sg. оуглєбъ Ps 68:3; **prilь(p)nǫti* 'cling, cleave to', 3 sg. imv. прıльплї Ps 136:6 ~ aor. 3 sg. прıльпє Ps 118:25 etc.; unprefixed **niknǫti* 'grow, sprout' 3 sg. pres. нıчєтъ Cloz 12a2.

---

22 It is unfortunate that lexicographers often feel compelled to invent an infinitive. SJS rightly has both присѧгнѫти and присѧщи but cites осѧгъшии sub theoretical осѧгнѫти.

23 The root-shape *niz* is improbable and in any case not in OCS or closely related texts; въѕнисти, вънисти and оунисти are ghosts from scholarly tradition. It is regrettable that SJS repeats them.

24 There is no evidence for an infinitive гыбати, and погыбати is derived from *-gyb-aj+* and should be in a separate lemma from citations of погыблєтъ and the like. See Vaillant §205-207.

15.8 Verbs with zero classifier, stems ending in a consonant other than j

		Infinitive несті 'carry'	вести 'lead'			
		Present		Imperative		
Sing.	1	несѫ	ведѫ	–	–	1
	2	несеши	ведеши	неси	веди	2
	3	несетъ	ведетъ	неси	веди	3
Dual	1	несевѣ	ведевѣ	несѣвѣ	ведѣвѣ	1
	2	несета	ведета	несѣта	ведѣта	2
	3	несете	ведете	–	–	3
Plur.	1	несемъ	ведемъ	несѣмъ	ведѣмъ	1
	2	несете	ведете	несѣте	ведѣте	2
	3	несѫтъ	ведѫтъ	–	–	3

Pres. act. part. nom. sg.	masc.	neut.	fem.
	несы		несѫшти
	веды		ведѫшти

Pres. pass. part. nom. sg.	masc.	neut.	fem.
	несомъ	несомо	несома
	ведомъ	ведомо	ведома

		Imperfect		Aorist		
Sing.	1	несѣахъ	ведѣахъ	несохъ	ведохъ	1
	2-3	несѣаше	ведѣаше	несе	веде	2-3
Dual	1	несѣаховѣ	ведѣаховѣ	несоховѣ	ведоховѣ	1
	2	несѣашета	ведѣашета	несоста	ведоста	2
	3	несѣашете	ведѣашете	несосте	ведосте	3
Plur.	1	несѣахомъ	ведѣахомъ	несохомъ	ведохомъ	1
	2	несѣашете	ведѣашете	несосте	ведосте	2
	3	несѣахѫ	ведѣахѫ	несошѧ	ведошѧ	3

Resultative part. nom. sg.	masc.	neut.	fem.
	неслъ	несло	несла
	велъ	вело	вела

Past active part. nom. sg.	masc.	neut.	fem.
	несъ		несъши
	ведъ		ведъши

Past passive part. nom. sg.	masc.	neut.	fem.
	несенъ	несено	несена
	веденъ	ведено	ведена

Verbal substantive	несенье	Supine	нестъ
	веденье		вестъ

15.81 This is an unproductive class, but its 56 verbs (plus over 175 prefixed stems) express for the most part everyday activities and are therefore relatively frequent in any sample of text. Eight more verbs (plus nearly 35 prefixed stems), which are irregular or partly so, will be treated here.

It is this class which accounts for the majority of the non-productive aorist forms, including the 3 sing. aor. in *-tъ* and the past passive participles in *-t-*. These forms are given in detail in the subdivisions of §10.8 and in §11.321–2; they will not be repeated here.

15.82 The stem-final consonants may be affected by consonantal desinences:

15.821 Stem-final *s* remains unchanged: несѫтъ 'carry', пасѫтъ 'pasture', съпасѫтъ 'save', трѧсѫтъ 'shake, tremble'.

15.822 *z* > *s* before *t*; веꙁѫтъ ~ inf. вести, supine вестъ. Here belong веꙁѫтъ 'convey', оу-вѧꙁѫтъ 'crown' (past pass. part in *t*, §11.32), -лѣꙁѫтъ 'go', -ньꙁѫтъ 'pierce' (*nǫ*-variant §15.771), and **gryz-* 'gnaw' (represented only by гриꙁетъ, for **gryzetъ*, L 12:33 Sav).

15.823 *t d* > *s* before *t*; *t d* are deleted before *l*: ведѫтъ ~ вести, велъ. Here belong: блюдѫтъ 'watch', блѧдѫтъ 'talk nonsense', бодѫтъ 'stab', ведѫтъ 'lead', владѫтъ 'rule', гнетѫтъ 'press', кладѫтъ 'put', крадѫтъ 'steal', -метѫтъ 'sweep' (for метѫтъ 'throw', see §15.641), мѧтѫтъ 'stir, confuse', падѫтъ 'fall', плетѫтъ 'braid, weave', прѧдѫтъ 'spin', растѫтъ (inf. расти) 'grow', and the defective грѧдѫтъ 'come, go', which has no past forms (inf. грѧсти, pres. act. part. грѧдꙑ, грѧдѫшти).

15.824 *p b* are deleted before *t*: тепѫтъ 'beat' ~ inf. тети; гребѫтъ 'bury' ~ грети; and the isolated pres. pass. part. ꙁебоми 'being torn' Su 397.27.

15.83 ь + *nasal* is replaced by *ę* before a consonantal desinence, including the aorist: кльнѫтъ 'curse' ~ infinitive клѧти, l-part. клѧлъ, past passive part. клѧтъ (§11.32), aor. клѧхъ (and клѧсъ §10.82), 2–3 sg. клѧтъ or клѧ (§10.52). Here also: съ-жьмѫтъ '(*squeeze) oppress', жьнѭтъ 'reap', -пьнѫтъ 'stretch; crucify', -тьнѫтъ 'kill', and -чьнѫтъ 'begin'.

The common verb {ьm-Ø+} 'take' preposes *j* if not preceded by a consonant (§3.24); *jь* is written *i*. Thus имѫтъ, prefixed forms иꙁьмѫтъ 'take out', сънимѫтъ, въꙁьмѫтъ 'take' ~ приимѫтъ 'receive', подъимѫтъ 'lift', and others. The truncated stem is *ę*: inf. ѧти (приѧти, въꙁѧти), l-part. ѧлъ (приѧлъ, въꙁѧлъ), aorist ѧхъ/ѧсъ (приѧхъ, въꙁѧхъ), past passive participle ѧтъ (приѧтъ, въꙁѧтъ).

Note that the past active participle is имъ (for **jьmъ*; cf. въѕьмъ). In mss reflecting the replacement of strong *ь* by *e* (§2.622), this participle may be spelled ємъ. Similarly with prefixes: приимъ/приємъ.

15.841 The four (poorly attested) verbs in *-ov* replace this sequence by *u*: плов-ѫтъ 'travel (by boat)' ~ inf. плоути, l-part. плоулъ, aor. плоухъ. Also словѫтъ 'be reputed', на-тровѫтъ 'feed', and ровѫтъ 'bellow, roar'.

The pres. act. part. ревы (Hil) and post-OCS evidence imply an alternative verb *ревѫтъ *рюти.

15.842 Two other verbs end in *-v*. Живѫтъ 'live' (with 6 prefixed stems, including иждивѫтъ {iz-živ} 'spend') loses the *v* before a consonantal desinence (inf. жити, l-part. жилъ, aor. жихъ), except that the 3 sg aor is живе (beside expected житъ and жи). The rare плѣвѫтъ 'weed' is attested only in present forms.

15.85 Stems in *-k* or *-g* undergo (1) automatic KI-mutation before *e* and *ě*, (2) grammatically specific KAI-mutation before the i^2 and e^2 of the imperative-marker, and (3) a special process (in infinitive and supine) whereby stem-final velar combines with desinential *t* in *št*:[25] Thus сѣк-ѫтъ 'cut', мог-ѫтъ 'be able' ~ 3 sg. сѣчетъ, можетъ ~ imv. сѣци сѣцѣте, мѕи мѕѣте ~ inf. сѣщи мощи. In the imperfect, *ěa* effects KI-mutation and shifts to *aa*: сѣчааше, можааше. In the imperative, a root-vowel *e* is replaced by *ь*: рекѫтъ 'say', жегѫтъ 'burn' ~ рьци, жьѕи. Some stems have further idiosyncracies.

Here belong: влѣкѫтъ 'drag' (§15.873), жегѫтъ 'burn' (§15.875), ѕвѧг- 'sound', -лѧкѫтъ 'bend', могѫтъ 'be able', небрѣгѫтъ 'not care, disdain', пекѫтъ сѧ 'worry', -прѧгѫтъ 'join', рекѫтъ 'say', стрѣгѫтъ 'guard', сѣкѫтъ 'cut' (nǫ-variant §15.771), -сѧгнѫтъ 'touch' (nǫ-variant §15.771), and текѫтъ 'run'.

15.86 Verbs in *-ьr* have two possible truncated shapes (exceptions in §16.511-12): Before the consonant of the l-participle and the *t* past passive participle *ьr* becomes *rь*: in the aorist, infinitive and supine *ьr* becomes *rě*: про-стьр-ѫтъ 'spread' ~ прострьлъ, прострьтъ ~ прострѣхъ, прострѣти.

Note: This may be analyzed as underlying {ьr} > *rь* before C in the participles, while a second stem {er} is used before the other consonantal suffixes and yields surface *rě* (see note in §15.643).

---

[25] This surface *št* is identical with the щ resulting from iotation of underlying *t* or *st* or *sk*: (*plati-ti* 'pay', *pusti-ti* 'let', *iska-ti* 'seek' ~ 1 sg pres. плащѫ, поущѫ, ищѫ). The traditional formula is **tj*.

These verbs are -вьрѫтъ 'slide', -жьрѫтъ, 'swallow', мьрѫтъ 'die', по-ньрѫтъ 'submerge', о-пьрѫтъ сѧ 'lean, support self', ра(ꙁ)-скврьрѫтъ 'besmirch', and -стьрѫтъ 'spread'.

Spelling note: scribes seem to have been uncertain as how to write the (probably silent) jers in these verbs. They probably pronounced both оумьрѫтъ and оумрѣхъ with a cluster *-mr-*; they could write or omit the ь in either shape, e.g. оумрѫтъ, оумьрѣхъ. Forms with *-rь-* were usually spelled -ръ-, as were other instances of *-rь-* between consonants (§2.53).

15.861 Exceptionally, the past participial suffix *-vъ(š)* is used in простръвъ, Su 311.6, for usual *prostьrъ*.

Synopsis of forms:

	'say' §15.85	'throw' §15.874	'curse' §15.83	'spread' §15.86
3 pl. pres.	рекѫтъ	врьгѫтъ	кльнѫтъ	простьрѫтъ
3 sg. pres.	речетъ	врьжетъ	кльнетъ	простьретъ
2 sg. imv.	рьци	врьѕи	кльни	простьри
pres. act. part.	рекы	врьгы	кльны	простьры
pres. pass. part.	рекомъ	врьгомъ	кльномъ	простьромъ
3 sg. impf.	речааше	врьжааше	кльнѣаше	простьрѣаше
1 sg. aor.	рекохъ	врьгохъ	клѧхъ	прострѣхъ
(1 sg. aor.)	(рѣхъ)	(врьгъ)	(клѧсъ)	–
2–3 sg. aor.	рече	врьже	клѧ(тъ)	прострѣ(тъ)
l-part.	реклъ	врьглъ	клѧлъ	прострьлъ
past act. part.	рекъ	врьгъ	кльнъ	простьръ
past passive part.	реченъ	врьженъ	клѧтъ	прострьтъ
substantive	реченье	врьженье	клѧтье	(оумрьтье)
infinitive	решти	врѣшти	клѧти	прострѣти
supine	решть	врѣшть	клѧтъ	прострѣтъ

15.87 There are unpredictable vowel (or vowel + sonorant) alternations in some roots. In some verbs the alternation is consistent; in others irregular forms occur, usually beside the normal shapes.

15.871 чьтѫтъ 'count' forms inf., supine, and non-productive aorists from the stem *čit-*: чисти, чистъ, 3 pl. aor. чисѧ and чишѧ (2–3 sg. чьте, 3 pl. regular aorist чьтошѧ; l-part. чьлъ), see §10.82.

цвьтѫтъ 'bloom' has infinitive процвисти Su 300.6, *s*-aor. процвисѧ Cloz 13b4 (~ процвьтошѧ Su 450.12).

15.872 -врьꙁѫтъ 'tie' has inf. -врѣсти and *s*-aorist -врѣсъ (§10.82), with alternating underlying {vьrz/verz}.

почрьпѫтъ 'draw (water)' {čьrp} has the infinitive and supine from *-črěp-* {čerp}: почрѣти Su 551.4, почрѣтъ J 4:7.

15.873 вλѣкѫтъ 'drag' {velk} has l-participle regularly from *-vlьk-* {vъlk} and other past participles from either stem-shape: e.g. обλьклъ 'dressed' (Su); изволькъ 'having pulled out' Mk 14:47, обλькъ 'having dressed' L 23:11, обλьчена 'dressed' Mt 11:8 (~ e.g. съвλѣкъше Su 103.2; облѣчен-, въвлѣчен- Su).

небрѣгѫтъ 'neglect, disdain' {berg} has небрьгъше Su 98.8, небрьг'ша Su 40.14 {bъrg} ~ небрѣгъш- Su 212.16, 354.24.

15.874 тльк ѫтъ 'knock' {tъlk} has inf. from {telk}, тлѣшти L 13:25.

врьгѫтъ 'throw' {vъrg} ~ inf. {verg} -врѣшти, supine вьврѣшть Mar L 12:49.

стригѫтъ 'shear, tonsure' has inf. пострѣшти (Euch), with an isolated alternation *i* ~ *ě*.

15.875 жегѫтъ 'burn' has ь not only in the imperative (жьѕи, жьѕѣте §7.111), but occasionally in other forms: aor. зажьже Mt 22:7, past pass. part. сьжьжена (бѫди 'let [it] be burned' Su 19:7), съжъжетъ Sav L 3:17, pres. pass. part. жъгомъıимъ Su 476.17. (Details, Koch 347f.)

15.876 жладе 3 sg. aor. 'repay, compensate' (Su 494.9), inf. жласти Su 494.4, 5, contrasts with жлѣдетъ Su 360.13. The verb may have been obsolete even for the scribe of Su. The shape *žlěd* is probably historically older. (For discussion, see Koch 583–5.)

15.9 Verbs with basic stems in -aj+, -ěj+, or -j-Ø+

Infinitive дѣлати {děl-aj+} 'do' бити {bъj-Ø+} 'strike'

		Present			Imperative			
Sing.	1	дѣлаѭ	бьѭ	(биѭ)	–	–	–	1
	2	дѣлаеши	бьеши	(биеши)	дѣлаи	бии	(бьи)	2
	3	дѣлаетъ	бьетъ	(биетъ)	дѣлаи	бии	(бьи)	3
Dual	1	дѣлаевѣ	бьевѣ	(биевѣ)	дѣлаивѣ	биивѣ	(бьивѣ)	1
	2	дѣлаета	бьета	(биета)	дѣлаита	биита	(бьита)	2
	3	дѣлаете	бьете	(биете)	–	–	–	3
Plur.	1	дѣлаемъ	бьемъ	(биемъ)	дѣлаимъ	биимъ	(бьимъ)	1
	2	дѣлаете	бьете	(биете)	дѣлаите	бiите	(бьите)	2
	3	дѣлаѭтъ	бьѭтъ	(биѭтъ)	–		–	3

	masc.	neut.	fem.
Pres. act. part. nom. sg.	дѣлаѧ		дѣлаѭшти
	бьѧ		бьѭшти
Pres. pass. part. nom. sg.	masc.	neut.	fem.
	дѣемъ	дѣемо	дѣема
	бьемъ	бьемо	бьема

			Imperfect		Aorist		
Sing.	1	дѣлаахъ	бьꙗахъ	(биꙗахъ)	дѣлахъ	бихъ	1
	2-3	дѣлааше	бьꙗаше	(биꙗаше)	дѣла	би	2-3
Dual	1	дѣлааховѣ	бьꙗааховѣ	(биꙗаховѣ)	дѣлаховѣ	биховѣ	1
	2	дѣлаашета	бьꙗашета	(биꙗашета)	дѣласта	биста	2
	3	дѣлаашете	бьꙗашете	(биꙗашете)	дѣласте	бисте	3
Plur.	1	дѣлаахомъ	бьꙗахомъ	(биꙗахомъ)	дѣлахомъ	бихомъ	1
	2	дѣлаашете	бьꙗашете	(биꙗашете)	дѣласте	бисте	2
	3	дѣлаахѫ	бьꙗахѫ	(биꙗахѫ)	дѣлашѧ	бишѧ	3
Resultative part. nom. sg.			masc.	neut.	fem.		
			дѣлалъ	дѣлало	дѣлала		
			билъ	било	била		
Past active part. nom. sg.			masc.	neut.	fem.		
			дѣлавъ		дѣлавъши		
			бивъ		бивъши		
Past passive part. nom. sg.			masc.	neut.	fem.		
			дѣланъ	дѣлано	дѣлана		
			бьенъ (биенъ)	бьено (биено)	бьена (биена)		
Verbal substantive			дѣланье	Supine	дѣлатъ		
			бьенье (биенье)		битъ		

15.91 This class contains two productive subgroups with the classifiers *-aj+* (about 360, plus some 320 prefixed stems) and *-ěj+* (about 35, with some 20 prefixed derivatives). Their conjugation is entirely regular. For verbs like *um-ěj+* 'to know', the forms have *ě* everywhere *-aj+* forms have *a*: оумѣти, оумѣѭ, оумѣѩ, оумѣахъ, оумѣхъ, оумѣлъ, оумѣвъ, оумѣнье.

There is also an unproductive subgroup of eighteen root-verbs with zero classifier (plus 35 compounds); some of their forms call for special comment.

15.92 The verb *znaj-Ø+* 'know', is entirely regular: ꙁнаѭтъ ꙁнати.

Four poorly attested verbs are to be set up with **ěj-Ø+**, *grěj*-ǫtъ 'warm', *rěj*-ǫtъ 'push', *spěj*-ǫtъ 'prosper', and *sъměj*-ǫtъ 'dare', and one with **-aj-Ø+**, vъlaj-Ø+ sę 'be tossed [by waves]', cf. §15.45.

15.93 Eight verbs have basic stems in *-ьj-Ø+*. The ь is tense (§2.61) and usually is spelled *i*. Before consonant, *ьj > i*: e.g. *bьj*-ǫtъ бьѭтъ or *bij*-ǫtъ биѭтъ ~ *bьj*-ti, *bьj*-x-ъ > бити, бихъ. The imperative plural is *biite* and *biěte* биꙗте; see §7.21.

бьѭтъ/биѭтъ 'beat, strike', въпьѭтъ/въпиѭтъ 'call, cry out' (§3.25), -вьѭтъ/-виѭтъ 'wind', съ-гньѭтъ/-гниѭтъ 'rot', льѭтъ/лиѭтъ 'pour', пьѭтъ/пиѭтъ 'drink', поуьѭтъ/поуиѭтъ 'rest', and шьѭтъ/шиѭтъ 'sew'.

пьѭтъ and -вьѭтъ have 3 sg. aor. in *-tъ* (§10.52), and they and льѭтъ have past pass. part. in *-t-* (§11.32); шьѭтъ has the past pass. part. шьвенъ.

15.94 The five verbs in *-ъj/-yj-Ø+*[26] and the two in *-uj-Ø+* have a special replacement of root-final *j* by *v* before the past passive participial suffix *-en-* (§11.341). The imperative plural is *kryite* and *kryěte*: see §7.21.

крыѭтъ 'cover, hide' (ppp -кръвенъ), мыѭтъ 'wash' (ppp -мъвенъ), оу-ныѭтъ 'be downcast' (subst. оуныньє 'weariness'), рыѭтъ 'dig', оу-тыѭтъ 'grow fat', об-оуѭтъ 'put on footwear' (ppp обоувенъ 'shod'), уоуѭтъ 'sense, feel'.

16. Irregular verbs

Here are included verbs whose conjugations do not fit easily into any of the categories already described. Although the number of verbs is small (20, plus about 80 prefixed stems), most of them are extremely common in any sort of text.

16.1 By far the most frequent and the most irregular verb is 'to be', whose forms are built on three imperfective stems, *bě-*, *jes-*, and *s-*, and two stems which function in both aspects: *bǫd-* and *by-*. The perfective forms usually mean 'come into being, come to be, become'.

Infinitive быти Substantive бытьє 'being, genesis'

		Imperfective			Pfctv/Impfctv		Perfective	
		pres.	imperf.	aorist	future	imperat.	aorist	
Sg.	1	єсмь	–	бѣхъ	бѫдѫ	–	быхъ	1
	2	єси	–	бѣ	бѫдєши	бѫди	бысть (бы)	2
	3	єсть	бѣашє	бѣ	бѫдєть	бѫди	бысть (бы)	3
Du.	1	єсвѣ	–	*бѣховѣ	бѫдєвѣ	бѫдѣвѣ	быховѣ	1
	2	єста	–	*бѣста	бѫдєта	бѫдѣта	быста	2
	3	єстє	бѣашєтє	бѣстє	бѫдєтє	–	бычтє	3
Pl.	1	єсмъ	–	бѣхомъ	бѫдємъ	бѫдѣмъ	быхомъ	1
	2	єстє	–	*бѣстє	бѫдєтє	бѫдѣтє	быстє	2
	3	сѫть	бѣахѫ	бѣшѧ	бѫдѫть	бѫдѫ	быша	3

[26] The alternant *-ъj-* is theoretical; these verbs are always spelled with *y* in OCS (cf. §2.61) except in the truncated stem of past passive participle.

Pres. act. part. nom. sg.: masc. neut. сы; fem. сѫшти
Resultative part. nom. sg.: masc. бꙑлъ, neut. бꙑло, fem. бꙑла
Past active part. nom. sg.: masc. neut. бꙑвъ; fem.. бꙑвъши

16.101 The negative present has special forms: нѣсмь, нѣси, нѣстъ; нѣсвѣ, нѣста, нѣсте; нѣсмъ, нѣсте, but normal negation in не сѫтъ.

16.1011 Third person forms without desinence are rare: е, нѣ, сѫ (§6.61).

16.102 The imperfect forms may contract *ěa* to *ě*; e.g. бѣше. There is some degree of confusion between the closely related imperfect and imperfective aorist. For meaning and use, see §21.21.

16.103 The perfective aorist бꙑхъ, 2-3 sg. бꙑ (not бꙑстъ!) sometimes replaces the conditional бимь, би, etc., cf. §14.3.

16.104 The participle бѫдꙑ, бѫдѫшти, etc., means 'future'.

16.11 The stems *by-* and *bǫd-* are used with prefixes to form perfective stems: *by-* appears before C-desinences, and *bǫd-* usually before vowel. The 2-3 sg. aorist desinence *-stъ* may be omitted (e.g. прѣбꙑстъ/прѣбꙑ 'stayed, remained', събꙑстъ сѧ/ събꙑ сѧ 'took place, happened'), though ȥабꙑти 'forget' has only ȥабꙑ. The only attested past passive participle is ȥабъвенъ. The substantive ȥабъвенье 'oblivion' is exceptional beside ȥабꙑтье; cf. иȥбꙑтье 'riddance' (иȥбꙑти 'be superfluous; be rid of').

16.2 Four other verbs have the same type of present-tense desinences (§5.9, §6.71), with further complications.

16.21 дати дадѧтъ 'give' is irregular in the present tense, imperative, and 2-3 sg. aorist. Present: дамь, даси, дастъ; *давѣ, даста, дасте; дамъ, дасте, дадѧтъ. Imv. sg. даждь (Euch дажди), 1 pl дадимъ, 2 pl. дадите. Aor. 3 sg. дастъ (beside rarer да). Present act. part. дадꙑ, дадѫшти; imperfect дадѣахъ. Other forms are from *da-*: aor. дахъ; past participles далъ, давъ, данъ; substantive данье.

16.22 ѣсти ѣдѧтъ 'eat' is irregular in the present tense, imperative, 2-3 aorist, and it has both an s-aorist and a regular aorist built on the stem *ě-*, see §10.84. Pres.: ѣмь, ѣси, ѣстъ; *ѣвѣ, ѣста, ѣсте; ѣмъ, ѣсте, ѣдѧтъ. Imv. sg. ѣждь, 1 pl. ѣдимъ, 2 pl. ѣдите. Aor. ѣсъ/ѣхъ, ѣстъ, etc. The *-stъ* of 2-3 aorist is omitted only in иȥѣ 'ate up' (Su 138.27, 300.25). Other forms are regular from *ěd*: imperfect ѣдѣахъ, present act. part. ѣдꙑ, ѣдѫшти; past participles ѣлъ (§3.3131b), ѣдъ ѣдъши, ѣденъ; subst. ѣденье.

16.23 **вѣдѣти вѣдѧтъ** 'know' is irregular in the present system. Pres.: **вѣмь** or **вѣдѣ, вѣси, вѣстъ; вѣвѣ, вѣста, вѣсте; вѣмъ, вѣсте, вѣдѧтъ.** Imv. sg. **вѣждь** (Euch **вѣжди**), 1 pl. **вѣдимъ**, 2 pl. **вѣдите**. The *-stъ* of 2-3 aor. is omitted only twice (**не вѣ** Su 382.7, **проповѣ** L 12:3 As). Pres. act. part. **вѣдꙑ** (stem *věd-*),[27] pass. **вѣдомъ**. Aorist and past participles regular from *vědě-*: **вѣдѣхъ, вѣдѣ** etc.; **вѣдѣлъ, вѣдѣвъ, -вѣдѣнъ.**

16.24 The verb 'to have' is made from the root **ьm* with the suffixes *-ěj, -a* and zero. The present is: **имамь, имаши, иматъ; имавѣ, имата, имате; имамъ, имате, имѫтъ** *or* **имѣѭтъ**. Pres. act. part **имꙑ имѫшти** *or* **имѣѧ имѣѭшти**. The *iměj*-alternatives are chiefly from Supr. Other forms are regular from **ьměj-*: imv. **имѣи, имѣимъ, имѣите**; inf. **имѣти**; imperfect **имѣахъ**; resultative part. **имѣлъ**, etc.

Note that **имѫтъ** is also 'they will take' {ьm-Ø+ǫ-tъ}. Forms like **имати, ималъ** are from the imperfective a-derivative, see §15.643.

16.3 **идѫтъ** 'go' has three root-shapes: *i-* (possibly *ji-*), *id-* (?*jid-*), and *šьd-*. Infinitive **ити** {i+ti}. Imperfect **идѣахъ**; aor. **идохъ/идъ** (§10.811). Past active participles: **шьдъ** (f. **шьдъши**); **шьлъ** ({sьd-l-ъ}, §3.3131), f. **шьла**. Subst. **шьстье** and **шьствье**, but prefixed **сънитье** 'descent'.

With prefixes **вън-ид- въ-шъд-** 'enter', **сън-ид- съ-шьд-** 'descend', **възид- въшьд-** 'ascend' {vъz-šьd-}, etc. See §3.3101, 3.311. Note that the *ь* of the past active participle is always strong (šьd-ъ[š-]), but in the l-participle it is usually weak (f. šьla, m. pl. šьli ~ m.sg. šьlъ, cf. §2.622).

The present passive part. underlies the adjective *nepréidomъ* 'impassable'.

16.4 **ѣдѫтъ** 'go, ride' forms a root aorist, **-ѣдѫ** (3 pl., cf. §10.811). Alternative stems are *ě-* and *ěxaj-* and their distribution apparently differed by dialect. Attested are past act. participles **-ѣвъ** and **-ѣхавъ** and an imperative **ѣхаи** beside **ѣди**. The infinitive was presumably ***ѣхати** and/or ***ѣти**.

Mt 14:34 Mar Zo **прѣѣвъше**~ As **прѣѣхавъше** 'having crossed [the lake in a boat]';[28] Mk 6:53 Zo **приѣхавъше** ~ Mar **прѣѣвъше. ѣхаи** Zo L 5:4 (~ Mar **вьзѣди**, As **въѣди**).

16.5 Verbs with *vowel + sonorant* in present forms but *sonorant + vowel* in others include several subgroups. Unless otherwise noted, the 3 p. present furnishes the stem for the present system while the infinitive shows the stem for all other forms. Imperfects will be noted when they are attested.

16.511 **млѣти мелѭтъ** 'grind, mill'. Impf. **мелꙗаше** Su 565.10.[29]

---

27 The **вѣдѫ си** of Su 305.3 is probably an error for **вѣдъи**, as in line 5.

28 Note that Sav Mt 14:34 has **прѣплꙋвъше**, cf. §15.841.

29 Positing underlying {mel-ti mel-j-ǫtъ} and the metathesis rule suggested in §15.643, {mel} predictably will yield *mlě* (before C other than *j*). An extension of

16.512 брати борѭтъ 'fight'. Impf. борѣахѫ сѧ Ps 119.7.
Spellings with бъра- or бьра- are doubtless purely graphic, reflecting scribes' uncertainty about where to use a jer-letter. Attested substantives are бранье (A sg. бьраниѥ Su 86.13, G sg. бьранита 86.14 'contest, agony') and боренье (G pl. борении Su 486.27 'wars').

16.513 клати колѭтъ 'slaughter'. Imv. заколѣте L 15:23 Zo Sav (§7.21) ~ regular заколите Mar As. Past pass. part ꙁаколенъ (*-len-*, opposed to *-lje-* of pres.) and ꙁакланъ.

16.521 жрьти жьрѫтъ 'sacrifice' shows traces of a present stem *žьrjǫtъ*: 1 sg. pres. пожьрѭ Ps 53.8, 115:8, pres. participles жьрѧ Su 115.29, жьремо Su 91.26. The attested substantive is жрьтье (G sg жрътиꙗ Su 148.30). This verb is easily confused with *-žьrǫtъ -žrěti* 'swallow' (§15.86).[30]

16.522 трьти търѫтъ 'rub' implies *-rj-* in 1 pl. imv. сътьримъ Euch 98a9 (~ сътьрѣмъ Su 353.5) 2–3 sg. aor. *-trь* (сътрь Ps 104:16, отръ J 12:3 Zo Mar As) competes with *-tьre* (отьре J 12:3 Sav; сътьре Su 11:29, 311:16).

16.53 пѣти поѭтъ 'sing', imperf. поꙗахъ; 3 sg. aor. пѣтъ, past pass. part. пѣтъ; substantive пѣтье and пѣнье.

16.61 сѣсти {sěd-ti} сѧдѫтъ 'sit down' . For root-aorist see §10.811.
The imv. сѣдѣте (for сѧдѣте) Mar Mt 26:36, L 24:49, if not a mechanical spelling error, may show either a Macedonian dialectal denasalization or an innovative suppression of the traditional but anomalous alternation.

16.62 лешти {leg-ti} лѧгѫтъ {lęg-ǫtъ} 'lie down'. Root-aorist, §10.811.

16.7 -рѣсти {rět-ti} -рѧштѫтъ {-ręt-j-ǫtъ} occurs only with prefixes: сърѣсти 'meet', обрѣсти and приобрѣсти 'find'. For root-aorist see §10.811. Imperative сърѧштате Su. Imperfect обрѧштаахъ.

Forms like обрѣтаахѫ Mk 14:35 are from the regular imperfective verb *-rět-aj*. Vat обрѣщетъ Mt 7:8 ~ обрѧщетъ Sav (~ обрѣтаетъ Zo Mar As).

16.8 -дѣти -деждѫтъ {ded-j-} 'put' occurs only with prefixes, especially одѣти 'dress, clothe' and въздѣти 'lift, raise'; cf. §15.441.

16.91 The *s*-aorist расоусѧ сѧ 'were scattered' Ps 149:7 (2/N) can be analyzed on the basis of post-OCS data as {raz-sup-Ø+}, with present *-sъp-e-*.

---

this rule converts {or ol} to *ra la*, and underlying {bor-ti bor-j-ǫtъ} and {kol-ti kol-j-ǫtъ} will yield the attested forms.

30 We may posit underlying {žьr-ti žьr-ǫ-tъ} versus {žer-ti žьr-ǫ-tъ}and {tьr-ti tьr-(j-)ǫ-tъ}.

16.92 дьмѣ́ше сѧ 'swelled up' Su 239.27, and надъменъ 'puffed up' Su 117.18 may belong in one paradigm with надоувъши сѧ Su 422.35 'puffed up'.

16.93 The verbs доушѫтъ 'blow' and перѫтъ 'fly' (Su 390.10) are attested only with present forms; their infinitive stems are unknown.

CHAPTER FIVE

NOTES ON SYNTAX

17.0 On adjectives

The use of the long and short forms of the adjectives does not have any exact equivalent in English. The juxtaposition of a short-form adjective and a substantive denotes that the combination is presented as a new one: *vъ peštь ognjьnǫ* (Mt 13:50) "into a furnace, a fiery one', i.e. 'a fiery furnace'. The long-form adjective presents the quality as one already known and specifically known to belong to the particular substantive which it modifies: *vъ geonǫ ognjьnǫjǫ* (Mk 9:47) 'into hell the fiery', i.e. 'the fiery hell'.

Adjectives used as substantives contrast the indefinite short-form with the long-form, which specifies that the substantive has previously been mentioned or is generally known: e.g. Mk 8:22–3 privěsę kъ njemu *slěpa* … i imъ slěpaego za rǫkǫ 'they brought *a blind man* to him, and taking *the blind man* by the hand'; compare J 9:32 otъ věka něstъ slyšano jako kъto otvrъze oči *slěpu roždenu* 'since the world began it was not heard of that any man opened the eyes of *one born blind*', and J 11:37 ne možaaše li sь otvrъzyi oči *slěpuemu* sъtvoriti da i sь ne umьretъ 'could not this man, which opened the eyes of *the blind man,* have caused that even this man should not have died?'

17.1 An adjective in vocative function normally has the long form (**бѣсьнъıи пьсє, кръвопивъı ꙁмию** Su 115.27 'o mad dog, blood-thirsty serpent!') unless it follows a substantive in the vocative or is itself used as a substantive: fariseju *slěpe* (Mt 23:25) 'o blind Pharisee!'; *bezumьne* (L 12:20) 'senseless one!'

17.2 In a series of coordinated substantivized participles (rarely other adjectives also) the long form usually occurs for the first only: (L 6:47, 49) *slyšęi* slovesa moja i *tvorę* ja … *slyšavyi* i ne *tvorjь* 'he who hears my words and does them … he who has been hearing and has not been doing'.

18.0 On the use of the cases (not with prepositions)[1]

18.1 The *nominative* is a "zero-case", specifying only that the speaker's attention is directed to the thing or person represented by it. It is used in naming: both absolute (e.g. in headings; *evanǵelie otъ luky* 'the Gospel of Luke'; or in exclamations: *o velezьloba neprijaznina* 'oh the great wickedness of the devil!') and with verbs of naming, *sь* velii *narečetъ sę* (Mt 5:19) 'he shall be called *great*'; as the subject of the sentence; and sometimes in the predicate after verbs signifying being or becoming, e.g. běašete bo *rybarja* (Mt 4:18) 'for they [two] were fishermen'; **григории поставьѥнъ бъıстъ патриархъ** (Su 119.17) 'Gregory was appointed *patriarch*; vьsěkъ iže sę tvoritъ *cěsarjь* protivitъ sę kesarevi (J 19:12) 'whosoever maketh himself a *king* speaketh against Caesar'. See also §18.6d, below.

18.11 The *vocative* specifies direct address. For example: rabe lǫkavyi (Mt 18:32) 'O thou wicked servant'; iosife synu davydovъ (Mt 1:20) 'Joseph, son of David!'; rekǫ emu otьče sъgrěšixъ (L 15:18) 'I will say to him, father, I have sinned'; ne ostavi mene bože sъpasitelju moi (Ps 26:9) 'do not leave me, o God, my saviour!'; izidi duše nečistyi otъ člověka (Mk 5:8) 'come out of the man, thou unclean spirit!'; idi za mъnojǫ, sotono 'Get thee behind me, Satan!'; ženo, se synъ tvoi! (J 19:26) 'woman, behold thy son!'; ne boi sę Marie (L 1:30) 'Fear not, Mary!'. See also §17.1.

The vocative form is explicit only in singular masculine and feminine nouns; otherwise the nominative form is used. OCS nominative forms in places where a vocative is possible are by no means rare.

18.2 The *accusative* functions as the direct object of transitive verbs (unless negated, see §18.3b). Some verbs may take a double accusative ("make, believe, perceive someone [as] something"); e.g. sъtvorjǫ *va lovьca* člověkomъ (Mt 4:19) 'I will make you [two] fishers of men'; simona *egože* imenova *petra* (L 6:14) 'Simon, whom he named Peter'; obrěte *otrokovicǫ ležęštǫ* na odrě i *běsъ išьdъšь* (Mk 7:30) '(she) found the girl lying on the bed and the devil gone out'; mъněvъša že *i* vъ družině *sǫštь* (L 2:44) 'supposing him to be in the company'.

Verbal substantives formed from transitive verbs sometimes may govern an accusative: **по приꙗтии ми отъ ... бога великъıи даръ** (Su 525.15) 'after my receiving the great gift from God'.

---

[1] More detail in *Исследования по синтаксису старославянского языка*, (ed. J. Kurz), Prague, 1963.

The accusative may express extent of time or space: e.g. bě iona vъ črěvě kitově *tri dьni* i *tri nošti* (Mt 12:40) 'Jonah was in the whale's belly for three days and three nights'; aštc kъto poimetъ tę po sile... *poprište edino,* idi sъ njimь *dъvě* (Mt 5:41) 'if anyone compels thee to go a mile, go with him twain'. In a few expressions it denotes a point in time: ubьjǫtъ i, i *tretьi dьnь* vъstanetъ (Mt 7:23) 'they shall kill him, and the third day he shall rise again'; пришьдъшоу кмоу вечер' (Su 275.29) 'when he came [cf. §18.5e] in the evening'.

The accusative is sometimes used with oaths: тако ми великѫ богынѭ артемѫ (Su 231.1) '[I swear it] by the great goddess Artemis'.

18.21 The use of the genitive form for an expected accusative with masculine substantives referring to male persons was mentioned in §4.13. The texts are not uniform in their usage, and it is clear that during the OCS period the tendency to develop a new "personal" accusative was spreading even to animals and thus to form an "animate" category. Isolated examples have the regular accusative even for male humans (e.g. prizovi *mǫžь tvoi* J 4:16 Mar [~ mož*a* tvo*ego* Zo, As] 'call your husband'), and others where normally inanimate nouns are presented as personified (e.g. сего хлѣба марига роди Su 396.3 'Mary bore this Bread [= Christ]).' Personal names tend to keep the accusative form.[2]

Pronouns, adjectives, and participles referring to male persons regularly (but with numerous exceptions) use the genitive form in accusative function. The personal pronouns *mę, tę, sę* and *i* (**jь*), however, are normal accusatives, with *mene, tebe, sebe,* and *ego* used for emphasis.

In most cases, however, no clear distinction can be drawn between the older emphatic use and the newer animate reference (cf. §4.64). Examples: člověče, kъto *mę* postavi sǫdijǫ li dělitelja nadъ vami (L 12:14) 'man, who made me a judge or a divider over you?'; *mene* edinogo ostaviste (J 16:32) 'you left me alone'; ne prostьrěste [§9.3] rǫkъ na *mę* (L 22:53) 'ye stretched forth no hands against me'; tъgda prizъvavъ *i* [Mar ~ Sav *ego*] gospodь ego, glagola...azъ *tę* [Mar ~ Sav *tebe*] pomilovaxъ (Mt 18:32) 'then having called him, his master said ... I had pity on thee.'

In Sav and Su, anomalous feminines (§4.413) also use gen. forms for accusative (*matere* 'mother', *dъštere* 'daughter', *neplodъve* 'barren woman'); exceptionally, non-animates appear in this form (*ljubъve* 'love', *crьkъve* 'church, temple').

The genitive form for accusative in the masculine plural is exceptional, but examples are found, pronouns and adjectives as well as substantives, chiefly in Sav and Su. E.g., Mt 8:16 Sav и вьсѣхъ болѧщихъ ицѣли (~ Zo Mar As *vьsę nedǫžьnyę*) 'and he healed all that were sick'; вѣдѣ та сынъ имѫща (Su 235.17) 'I know that you have *sons*'.

---

[2] Textual disagreement hampers attempts to define usage; e.g., J 16:33, azъ pobědixъ *mira* M (~ ZoAs *vьsego mira*) but миръ Sav. The verb otherwise takes only accusative.

18.3 The *genitive* case has a wide range of functions.

a. It is used as the complement of a number of verbs.

1. Verbs of perception: *bljudǫtъ* 'observe', *zьrěti* 'see', *slušajǫtъ* and *poslušajǫtъ* 'hear', and *sъmotriti* 'look at, see'. *Viděti* 'see' may take either acc. or gen.; *slyšati* 'listen' normally takes acc., rarely gen. *Razuměti* 'understand' normally takes acc., rarely gen. or dat.

2. Verbs denoting striving or attainment: *alkati* 'hunger for', *želějǫtъ* 'desire', *žьdati* 'await', *žędati* 'thirst for', *iskati* 'seek, look for', *prositi* and *vъsprositi* 'ask, beg', *pytajǫtъ* 'question, examine', *posětiti* and *prisětiti* 'visit', *trěbovati* 'demand', *čajati* 'expect', and verbs with the prefix *do—doiti doidǫtъ* 'reach', dotekǫtъ 'run up to', *dovedǫtъ* 'lead up to', *dozьrěti* 'perceive', and *dožьdati* 'achieve'. *Xotěti* 'want' may take either genitive or dative (or, rarely, acc.). *Vъprositi* 'ask' takes the acc. of person asked and genitive of thing asked for.

3. Verbs denoting sufficiency: *isplьniti* and *naplьniti* 'fill (with)', *napoiti* 'give to drink', *naséjati* 'sow', *nasytiti* 'satisfy, satiate', *natruti natrovǫtъ* 'feed'.

4. Certain verbs that normally take the accusative are occasionally found with a genitive that perhaps denotes "part of, some of": e.g. *vъkusiti* 'taste' jako že vъkusi arxitriklinъ *vina byvъšaego* otъ vody (J 2:9) 'when the ruler of the feast tasted the wine made from water'. Attestation is far from uniform for *iměti* 'have', **jьmǫtъ* 'take, receive' (cf. group 2 above): priętъ *xlěba* Mar (J 21:13) 'he took (?some) bread' (but Zo As acc. *xlěbъ*; Greek '*the* bread'); da *života* imate Zo As (J 5:40; Mar *životъ*) 'that you might have life'; imatъ *života věčьnaego* Zo Mar (J 6:47; As *životъ věčnyi*) '(he) has everlasting life'.

5. Verbs denoting deprivation and the like: *bojati sę* 'be afraid of', *izbaviti* and *izbavljati* 'rid', *izbyti izbǫdǫtъ* 'escape, be freed of', *lišiti* 'deprive', *svoboditi* 'free', *stradati* 'suffer loss of', *plakati* (*sę*) 'mourn (loss of)', *sramljajǫtъ sę* and *postyděti sę* 'be ashamed of'; *běžati* and *běgajǫtъ* 'flee from' and the compounds *izběžati, izběgnǫti, otъběžati* and *otъběgnǫti*; and several other verbs with the prefix *otъ*: *otъlǫčiti* 'separate', *otъvrьgǫtъ sę* 'throw off', *otъmětajǫtъ sę* 'reject', *ostanǫtъ ostati* 'leave, let', *oslušajǫtъ sę* 'disobey'. *Otъrekǫtъ sę* 'renounce, disclaim' takes gen. or dat. Some verbs take either a genitive or the preposition *otъ* + gen.: *otъpadǫtъ* 'fall away from', *o*(*tъ*)*stǫpiti* and *o*(*tъ*)*stǫpajǫtъ* 'retreat', *otъstojati* 'be distant from', *otьmǫtъ* 'take away from'. *Razlǫčiti*

'separate' takes acc. of things separated and gen. or *otъ* + gen. or *na* + acc. to express 'from'. *Prostiti* and *praštajǫtъ 'forgive'* take acc. of person and gen. of thing. *Prěobiděti* 'insult' takes gen. or acc. *Mьstiti* 'avenge' takes a genitive to express cause and a dative to express the object of vengeance.

6. With impersonal *ne byti* the genitive is normal: e.g. *boga* něstъ (ps 13:1; 52:2) 'there is no god'; zanje ne bě ima *města* vъ obiteli (L 2:7) 'for there was no room for [the two of] them in the inn'. (Contrast L 14:22: i ešte města estъ 'and there is still room'). See also §23.11.

b. The genitive normally serves as the complement of a negated transitive verb, corresponding to the accusative direct object of a positive verb. For example (see also §23.22):

Nikъtože ne vъlivaet *vina nova* vъ měxy vetъxy (L 5:37) 'no one pours new wine into old skins'; ne umyeši *nogu moeju* vъ věkъ (J 13:8) 'you shall never wash my feet'; blǫdite ne vědǫšte *kъnigъ* ni *sily božię* (Mt 22:21) 'ye do err, not knowing the scriptures nor the power of God'.

With a dependent infinitive: Něsmь dostoinъ otъrěšiti *remene* sapogu ego (L 3:16) 'I am not worthy to unloose the strap of his shoes'; bъdělъ ubo bi i ne dalъ bi podъkopati *domu svoego* (L 12:39) 'he would have watched and would not have let his house be broken into'.

Replacing a double accusative: Ne tvorite *domu* otьca moego *domu kupljьnaego* (J 2:16) 'make not my father's house a house of trading'; jako ne možeši *vlasa edinogo běla* li *črьna* sъtvoriti (Mt 5:36) 'for you cannot make one hair white or black.'

c. It is regularly the complement of a supine (cf. §21.5); pride … vidětъ groba (Mt 28:1) "(she) came to see the tomb'; izide sěęi sějatъ *sěmene svoego* (L 8:5) 'a sower went out to sow his seed'. In Su, the acc. is sometimes found in this function.

d. The genitive is often the complement to a substantive, usually indicating possession, quality, or quantity: duxъ *otьca vašego*; 'the spirit of your father'; godpodinъ *xrama* 'the master of the house'; člověkъ eterъ *dobra roda* 'a man of good family'; sedmь *košьnicь* 'seven baskets' (cf. §20); dъšti *dъvoju* na desęte *lětu* 'a daughter 12 years old', десѧторо братиѩ (Su 279.15) '10 brothers'; mъnožьstvo *rybъ* 'a great quantity of fish', čašejǫ *studeny vody* 'with a cup of cold water'. Observe that the possessive genitive is replaced by possessive adjectives if the possessor is represented by a substantive which denotes a person or animal and which is not otherwise modified: *tektonovъ* synъ 'son of the carpenter' (tektonъ); učenici *ioanovi* 'the disciples of John' (ioanъ). In J 1.11 otъ gradьca *mariina* i *marty* sestry eę 'from the city of Mary and (of) her sister Martha', the adjective for 'Mary's' is used as is normal, but since *Martha* is further defined, the adjective cannot be used and the substantival genitive remains. Compare силоѭ христосовоѭ и архаггела рафаила (Su 231.7) 'by the power of Christ (adj.) and the archangel Raphael (gen.)'.

The dative is in competition with the genitive in this usage, e.g. šlěmъ *sъpasenьja* 'the helmet of salvation' (Eu 97a5) vs. *sъpasenьju* (Eu 94a9, 99a10); see also §18.5h.

e. As complement to pronominal and adverbial expressions denoting or implying quantity or number: kъto *ixъ* 'who of them', kъžьdo *vasъ* 'each one of you', koliko *xlěbъ* 'how many loaves of bread', vьsi elikože *ixъ* pride 'all of them who came', malo *ixъ* estъ 'there are few of them'. Isolated examples like dъva *učenikъ svoixъ* 'two *of* his disciples' are found for the more usual type with *otъ* + genitive.

f. As complement to the adjectives *plьnъ* and *isplьnъ* (indecl.) 'full': sъsǫdъ … plьnъ *ocьta* (J 19:29) 'a vessel full of vinegar', гнѣва испльнь (Su 566.13) 'full of anger'. *Dostoinъ* 'worthy (of)' takes the genitive (dostoinъ … *mьzdy svoeę* Mt 10:10 'worthy of his pay') or dative (dostoiny *pokaaniju* L 3:8 Zo Mar Sav [~ *pokaaniě* As] 'worthy of repentance').

g. With certain expressions of time: събрашѧ же сѧ мѣсѧца маиа (Su 201.22) 'they met in May'; единоѭ лѣта (Su 227.29) 'once a year'; sedmь kraty *dьne* (PsSin 118.164; Sluck дньмь) 'seven times a day'.

h. With comparatives: este lučьši *pъticь* (L 12:24) 'you are better than birds'; boljьša *sixъ* uzьriši (J 1:51) 'thou shalt see greater things than these'; teče skorěe *petra* (J 20:4) '(he) ran faster than Peter'.

i. The genitive is normal in exclamations: ѡ беды (Su 56.25) 'Oh misfortune!'; ѡ беззаконьнааго възбѣшениꙗ (Su 217.7) 'Oh lawless frenzy!'

18.4 The *locative* without preposition is very limited.[3] A few expressions of time or place may be interpreted as independent locatives, though they may also be classed as fixed adverbial expressions, for example, *zimě* 'in winter', *polu dьne* 'at noon', and *polu nošti* 'at midnight', *tomь časě* 'at that moment' (e.g. Mt 17:18).

The locative regularly serves as complement to the verbs *kosnǫti sę* and *prikosnǫti sę* touch' (e.g. kъto prikosnǫ sę *rizaxъ moixъ* Mk 5:31 'who touched my garments?');[4] to several other verbs with the prefix *pri-*: *priložiti* 'add'(also takes dat. or *na* + acc.), *priležati* 'take care of' *pristanǫti pristati* 'take part in', and perhaps others; to *naležati* 'press

[3] Early East Slavic regularly used place-names in the locative case without preposition, and it is highly probable that all 9th-century Slavic shared this usage. OCS offers only a couple of uncertain examples.

[4] Under Greek influence, the gen. appears for loc. with *prikosnǫti sę* twice, while the loc. after *kosnǫti sę* is less common than acc.

upon' (also takes dat. or *na* + acc.), *napadajǫtъ* 'attack' (more often takes *na* + acc), and perhaps a few others.

18.5 The *dative* case signifies the goal towards which something is directed either in a literal sense or in the more abstract meanings of "intended for" or "for the benefit of", or even "with relation to".

a. Specifically directional examples: se cěsarjь tvoi grędetъ *tebě* (Mt 21:5) 'behold thy King cometh unto thee'; i nese *materi svoei* (Mt 14:11) 'she took (it) to her mother'. The directional meaning is more often expressed by using *kъ* plus dative.

b. Less specifically directional verbs taking a dative complement are numerous. They include various verbs of giving, saying, promising, commanding, scolding, rebuking, annoying, pleasing, liking, believing, serving, helping. A partial list: *oběštajǫtъ* 'promise', (*po*)*velěti* 'command', *sǫditi* 'judge', *odolějǫtъ/udolějǫtъ/udelějǫtъ* 'conquer', (*vъz*)*braniti* 'forbid, hinder', *prětiti* 'warn, threaten, rebuke', *prěrekǫtъ* 'rebuke', *ponositi* 'upbraid', *dosaditi* 'annoy', (*po*)*rǫgajǫtъ sę* 'make fun of', *zaviděti* 'envy', *rьvьnovati* 'be jealous', *vražьdovati* 'hate', (*u*)*podobiti* 'compare', *ugoditi* 'please' (and *godě byti* 'be pleasing'), *prijajǫtъ* 'be friendly', v*ъnьmǫtъ* 'heed', *věrovati* (and *věrǫ ęti*) 'believe', *poslědovati* 'follow', *pomagajǫtъ/pomogǫtъ* 'help', (*po*)*služiti* 'serve', *rabotajǫtъ* 'work for', *diviti sę* and *čuditi sę* 'wonder at', *povinovati sę* 'obey', *radovati sę* 'rejoice at', *smijati sę* 'laugh at'. (*Xotěti* 'wish', cf. §18.3a2.)

c. Two verbs are found only with the reflexive short dative *si*: *sъžaliti si* 'pity' and *požaliti si* 'be displeased' (не разгнѣва сѧ, не пожали си Su 364.2 'he did not become angry, he did not become displeased'). *Sъtǫžajǫtъ/sъtǫžiti* 'afflict' may take *si* in the meaning 'despair, be discouraged' (podobaatъ vъsegda moliti sę i ne *sъtǫžati si* L 18:1 [Zo has *sę*] 'one ought always to pray and not be discouraged').

d. Dative with infinitive (cf. 21.4): dastъ imъ vlastь *čędomь božiemь* byti (L 1:12) 'to them he gave power to become the children of God'; чаѭште ѥмоу живоу быти (Su 80.14) 'thinking him to be alive'; glagoljǫšte *vъskrěšenьju* ne byti (L 20:27) 'denying that there is any resurrection'; мьнѣлъ ли ѥси страхы оубоꙗти сѧ намъ (Su 176.16) 'did you think that we would become afraid because of threats?'; azъ že glagoljǫ vamъ ne klęti sę *vamъ* (Mt 5:34) 'but I say unto you, swear not at all (you are not to swear)'; сътвори ми хъіжинѫ сѣсти ми вь ѥи (Su 204.2) 'he will make a hut for me to sit in (it)'; молитвѫ ѥмоу сътвори приѩтоу быти отъ ѥго (Su 547.20) 'he begged him to be received by him'.

e. The "*dative absolute*"—a participial subordinate clause expressing various types of attendant circumstance. For example: *mьnogu sǫštu narodu i ne imǫštemъ* česo ěsti … isusъ glagola … (Mk 8:1) 'the multitude being very great, and having nothing to eat, Jesus said …'; *učęštu emu ljudi* vъ crъkъve … sъstašę sę arxierei (L 20:1) 'as he taught the people in the temple … the chief priests gathered'; po vьsę dьni *sǫštu* sъ vami vъ crъkъve ne prostьrěste rǫkъ na mę (L 22:53) 'when I was daily with you in the temple, ye stretched forth no hands against me'; i abьe ešte *glagoljǫštu emu* vъzglasi kurъ (L 22:60) 'and immediately, while he yet spake, the cock crew'; more že *větru veliju dyxajǫštu* vъstaaše (J 6:18) 'And the sea, since a great wind was blowing, was rising.' Normally the dative participle does not refer to the same person or thing as the subject of the main verb, but this rule is occasionally violated.

f. The dative denoting "for the benefit of, with respect to" occasionally presents difficulties in translating into English, for it sometimes verges on the idea of possession and sometimes is so weak as to be superfluous in English. For example, *člověku eteru bogatu* ugobьʒi sę njiva (L 12:16) 'the field of (lit. for) a rich man brought forth rich harvest'; **съмотри же ми ʒълодѣиство ихъ** (Su 443.7) 'consider [for me] their crime!'; **къде си нынѣ кси** (Su 242.9) 'where are you now [for yourself]?' Cf. the idiom *čьto mьně i tebě* (Mk 5:7) 'what is for me and thee' (i.e., what do we have in common?).

g. The dative serves as the complement of certain adjectives: *podobьnъ* and *tъčьnъ* 'similar', *ravьnъ* 'equal', *ugodьnъ* 'pleasing', *povinьnъ* 'guilty', *dostoinъ* 'worthy of' (also with gen.).

h. The dative complement of substantives is semantically close to the adnominal genitive (§18.3d); dьnье *mъštenьju* (L 21:22) 'the days of vengeance', xramъ *molitvě* … vrьtъpъ *razboinikomъ* (Mt 21:13) 'house of prayer … den of thieves', starěišiny *ljudьmъ* (L 19:47) 'elders of the people'; otъpuštenie *grěxomъ* (L 3:3 MarVat ~ grěx*ovъ* Zo) 'the forgiveness of sins'; syni *světu* (J 12:36 Zo ~ **сынове свѣта** Sav) 'the sons of light'. The possessive meaning is particularly common with the short dative personal pronouns *mi, ti* and *si*: e.g. drugъ *mi* pride (L 6:6) 'my friend has come', **лице отьцю ми** (Mt 18:10 Sav ~ otьc*a* mo*ego* Mar).

Adjectives compete with the genitive or dative adnominal complement. For usual *skrьžьtъ zǫbomъ* 'gnashing of teeth', Su has **скрьжетъ ʒѫбьнъıи**. In Mt 8:28, Sav has **въ ʒемлѫ герьгесиномъ** 'into the land of the Gergesenes' vs. As *ǵerǵesinьskǫ*. (Cf. *domu kupljenaago*, §18.3b, above.)

i. The dative of price: ne pętъ li pъticь věnitъ sę *pěnęʒema dъvěma* (L 12:6) 'are not five sparrows sold for two farthings?'

18.6 The *instrumental* case signifies tool, agent, means, and manner—various types of attendant circumstance.

a. Some examples: idǫ … *korabljemь* (Mk 6:32) 'they went by boat', **бити и жилами соуровамі** (Su 100.30) 'to beat him with raw thongs'; **влъшъбами одолѣвакши** (Su 159.20) 'you will conquer by magic'; bǫdete nenavidimi *vьsěmi* (Mt 10:22) 'you will be hated by all'; iskušaemъ *sotonojǫ* (Mk 1:13) 'being tempted by Satan'; *pritъčami* glagolati (Mk 12:1) 'to speak by parables'; i *tacěmi pritъčami mъnoʒěmi* glagolaaše imъ slovo (Mk 5:33) 'and with many such parables he spake the word unto them'; javi sę *iněmь obrazomь* (Mk 16:12) 'he appeared in another form'; *neumъvenama rǫkama* ědętъ (Mk 7:5) 'they eat with unwashed hands'; vъzъpi *velьemь glasomь* (L 1:42) 'he cried out in a loud voice'; sii ljudie *ustьnami* čьtętъ mę (Mk 7:6) 'these people honor me with their lips'' **кръвь теүааше рѣками** (Su 103.27) 'blood flowed in rivers'; bě poganynji … *rodomь* (Mt 7:25) 'she was a pagan by birth'; **славенъ сы племенемь, высокъ же саномъ** (Su 63.8) 'being famous by descent and high in rank'; sъxoždaaše *pǫtemь těmь* (L 10:31) 'came down (by) that road'; vъniděte *ǫʒъkymi vraty* (Mt 7:13) 'enter ye in at the strait gate'; *četyrьmi desęty* i *šestijǫ* lětъ sъzьdana crьky si (J 2:20) 'forty and six years was this temple in building'.

The adnominal instrumental člověkъ *nečistomь duxomь* (Mk 1:23, Zo Mar) 'a man with an unclean spirit' seems out of place. Similarly, **мѫжоу правьдивоу и добромъ житиимъ** (Su 294.11) '(to) a man [who is] just and virtuous, ἐναρέτῳ' seems to function, incongrously, as an adjective in the dative case.

b. The adjectives *dovolьnъ* (*dovьlьnъ*) 'satisfied with' and *dlъžьnъ* 'owing, in debt' regularly take the instrumental.

c. A number of verbs normally take the instrumental: *vladǫtъ* 'rule' (and others with similar meaning) ty vladeši *drьžavojǫ morьskojǫ* (Ps 88:10) 'Thou rulest the power of the sea'; ti obladajǫtъ *zemljejǫ* (Ps 36:9) 'they rule the earth' (cf. **имѫштааго власть … доушеѭ и тѣломъ** Su 157.11 'having power over soul and body'); *pekǫtъ sę* 'worry about' ne pьcěte sę *dušejǫ vašejǫ* (Mt 6:25) 'take no thought for your soul'; *klęti sę* (and *zaklinajǫtъ sę*) 'swear' ni *glavojǫ svoejǫ* klьni sę (Mt 5:36) 'neither' shalt thou swear by thy head'; *ženiti* 'marry' ženęi sę *puštenojǫ* (L 16:18) 'he who marries a divorced woman'; *isplьniti* 'fill' (usually takes gen.) isplьni sę duxomь svętyimь (L 1:14) 'she was filled with the Holy Spirit'; (*u*)*pъvajǫtъ* 'trust' (also takes *na* + acc.; or dat., sometimes with *kъ*); **воинъ**

пъваꙗ своеѭ силоѭ (Su 105.11) 'a soldier trusting in his own strength'; *pokyvajǫtъ* 'shake' pokyvašę *glavami svoimi* (Ps 108:25) 'they shook their heads'; *skrьžьtati zǫby* 'gnash one's teeth' (e.g. Mk 9:18).

d. The instrumental sometimes occurs in the predicate with verbs denoting being or becoming. Beside normal nominatives such as ědъ že ego bě *akridi* i *medъ* (Mt 3:4) 'his food was locusts and honey', ледъ бъістъ вода топла (Su 78.1) 'the ice became warm water', we find дѣвоѭ бо бѣ еѵа (Su 489.9) 'for Eve was a virgin'; не бѫди никтоже июдоѭ (Su 420.10) 'let no one be a Judas'.

19.0 On the use of the prepositions.

19.11 Prepositions taking the accusative only are *vъz* 'in exchange for' (cf. vъskǫjǫ 'why?', vъskrai 'on the edge [of]'), *skvozě* or *skozě* 'through', and the compound *podlьgъ* 'along'.

19.12 With the genitive only: *bez* 'without' (cf. §3.311), *do* 'to, till', *iz* 'from, out of' (cf. §3.311), *otъ* 'of, from, since, by' (may express agent; e.g. porǫganъ bystъ *otъ* vlъxvъ (Mt 2:16) 'he was mocked by the wise men'), *u* 'near, by, from' (*u groba* 'near the tomb'; prositi česo *u*/*otъ* kogo 'ask for something [gen.] from someone'). Words which function both as adverbs and as prepositions with genitive are: *blizъ* 'near', *vrьxu* 'on top (of)', *kromě* 'outside', *okrьstъ* 'around', *prěžde* 'before, prior to', *razvě* 'except for', *svěnje* 'outside of', and *ędě* 'near'.

The words *radi*/*radьma* and *dělja*/*děljьma* 'on account of, for the sake of' are postpositions: *sego radi* 'for this reason', мене дѣлꙗ 'for my sake'.

The expression *vъ* ... *město* 'instead of' includes the genitive between its members: *vъ iroda město* 'instead of Herod'.

19.13 With the locative only: *pri* 'near, in the time of'.

19.14 With the dative only: *kъ* 'to, toward', and the adverbs *protivǫ* (*protivo*/*protivu*) 'opposite, according to' and *prěmo* 'opposite'.[5]

---

[5] The use of *kъ* + dat. after verbs of saying is a clear case of Greek influence: almost invariably when the Greek has the dative alone, so does OCS, but when Greek has πρός + acc. (a normal construction), OCS has *kъ* + dat. There is no evidence that this usage was ever part of a spoken Slavic dialect.

Greek interference is obvious or probable in a number of case-usages and in selection of prepositions as well; often the evidence is too slim to allow a clear decision as to what native usage OCS might have preferred. The precise choice and use of prepositions varies with time and place; it is not surprising that OCS manuscripts constantly disagree in details.

19.15 With the instrumental only: *meždu* 'between'.

19.21 With the accusative and locative cases:

19.211 *Vъ + accusative* means 'into, to', *vъ + locative* means 'in, inside'. *Vъ* is used with the accusative in many time expressions and fixed locutions of varying meaning.

19.212 *Na + locative* means 'on', also 'concerning'. *Na + accusative* means 'onto, to, toward, against' (iže něstъ sъ mъnojǫ *na mę* estъ Mt 12:30 'he who is not with me is against me'); it occurs in a number of fixed expressions.

19.213 *O* (*ob*) with locative normally means 'around, about, concerning', but the relationship it expresses is often tenuous and can be rendered by various other English prepositions, e.g. sily dějǫtъ sę *o njemь* (Mt 14:2) 'mighty works do show forth themselves *in* him'. *O* (*ob*) + accusative means 'against', but also 'concerning'. Note the fixed expressions *o desnǫjǫ* 'at the right (hand)', *o šujǫjǫ* 'at the left', *ob on polъ* 'on the other side (of)', *ob noštь* 'during the night', *o sebě* 'of oneself, by oneself'.

19.22 With the accusative and instrumental case—the preposition defines a position; the accusative case signals motion directed to the position, while the instrumental case implies rest: *nadъ* 'above, over'; *podъ* 'under, beneath'; *prědъ* 'in front of' or 'prior to'.

19.23 *Sъ* takes either genitive or instrumental. *Sъ* + genitive means 'from, down from, from the surface of' and 'since'; *sъ* + instrumental means 'with, accompanying'.

19.31 *Za* takes accusative, genitive, or instrumental. *Za* + instrumental means 'behind, after' (no motion implied), while *za* + accusative specifies motion to a position behind. *Za* + acc. frequently means 'because of'; but it has other meanings too, e.g., oko *za* oko 'an eye for an eye'; ętъ jǫ *za rǫkǫ* (Mt 9:25) 'he took her by the hand'. In expressions meaning 'strike on the cheek' *za lanitǫ* is found beside *vъ lanitǫ* and *po lanitama*. With the genitive, *za* expresses cause: **раꙁбѣгоша сѧ ꙁа страха июдеиска** Su 483.11 'they scattered for fear of the Jews.'

19.32 *Po* takes the accusative, locative, or dative. It is rare with the accusative: *po čьto* 'why?' (cf. *ponje*[*že*] 'because'); *po města* 'in divers places', *po vьsę dьni* 'daily', *po vьsě lěta* 'every year'; *po imena* 'by their names' (Euch 67b14). *Po + locative* means 'after': *po tomь* 'after this, afterward, then' (cf. also **плака по ѩнихъ** Su 38:5 'he wept for them', i.e. at losing them); and occasionally 'in favor of, for', e.g. iže bo něstъ na vy *po vasъ* estъ (L 9:50) 'for he that is not against you is for you.' *Po + dative* has varied meanings: *po zemlji, po morju, po aeru* 'over the/by land, on the/by sea, by air', *po vьsemu gradu* L 8:39 'throughout the whole city', *po pǫti* 'on the road', *po srědě* 'in the middle; amid, among'; *po dělomъ* 'according to deeds', *po vině* 'according to guilt', *po prědanьju* 'according to tradition', *po silě* 'by force', *po rędu* 'in order'.

20 On the syntax of the numerals

Edinъ edino edina (§4.321) 'one' is a pronoun, and agrees with its singular headword in case and gender. (In Su the stem is also кдьн-.)

Dъva dъvě 'two' and *oba obě* 'both, the two' are likewise pronouns (cf. §4.201) and agree with their dual headwords in gender and case.

Trьe tri 'three' (§4.402) and *četyre četyri* 'four' (§4.4114) are plurals, and agree with their plural headwords in gender and case.

The numerals from five to ten (§4.4) as well as *sъto* 'hundred' and *tysǫšti/tysęšti* 'thousand' are substantives which are followed by the genitive plural (cf. §18.3d).

The teens are expressed by the units + *na desęte*: *edinъ na desęte* '11', *dъva (dъvě) na desęte* '12', etc. (Note *oba* na desęte '*the* twelve'.) The tens are expressed by the units followed by the proper form of *desętь*: *dъva desęti* (dual), *trьe desęte* (nom. pl.), *pętь desętъ* (gen. pl.), etc. The hundreds similarly use units plus the proper form of *sъto*: *dъvě sъtě, tri sъta, pętь sъtъ,* etc.

In principle, the *na desęte* of the teens and the *desęt-* of the tens do not affect the counted substantive: *oběma* zě na desęte *apostoloma* (§18.5h) imena sǫtъ si (Mt 10:2) 'and the names of the twelve apostles are these'. In a number of examples, however, the whole numeral behaves as a substantive requiring the genitive plural: L 9:7 '12 baskets' Zo *koša dъva* na desęte ~ Mar *košъ*; да ... сьцѣнатъ трьмъ десатемь (§18.5i) мѣдьницъ (Su 331.29) 'so they might appraise [him] at thirty coins'.

Units are added by means of *i* (or ти in Su); *sъto i pętь desętъ* i *tri* (sc. *rybъ*, J 21:11); instr. *četyrьmi desęty* i *šestьjǫ lětъ* (J 2:20) 'in the course of 46 years'. For further details, see Vaillant 157ff.

21.0 On the use of the verbal forms

21.1 *The present tense,* as opposed to aorist and imperfect, does not specify time. Imperfective presents most usually denote an action viewed as simultaneous with the moment of speech or with a moment in past or future which is defined by the context; they may also denote actions which are repeated or of general validity. Since the perfective aspect specifies that the completion of the action is envisaged, the present perfective forms cannot denote action in progress. They signify rather action viewed as completed in the future or at any other moment defined by the context. In statements of general validity, the perfective present shows that the action is viewed as completed whenever the situation is suitable. For example, **сльньцоу въсходаштоу съкрыѥтъ са стѣ҃нь** (Su 417.28) 'when the sun rises (cf. §18.5e), the shadow *hides itself*'; ašte k'to bědojǫ ukradetъ sъnědьno čьto, 40 denъ da *pokaetъ sę* (Euch 103b1) 'if anyone *steals* something to eat because of need, *let him do penance* for 40 days (cf. §22.11); ašte li vědělъ … vъ kyi časъ tatь *pridetъ* (Mt 24:43) 'if [he] had known in what watch the thief *would come*'; žena egda raždaetъ pečalь imatъ …, egda že *roditъ* otročę kъtomu ne pomьnitъ skrъbi (J 16:21) 'a woman when she is in travail [= is giving birth] hath sorrow … but as soon as she is delivered of [= *has given birth* to] the child she remembereth no more the anguish'.

21.11 *On the expression of future time.*[6] There is no specific set of forms denoting the future. The most frequent means of expressing future action is the present tense (especially of perfective verbs). The future of 'to be' is expressed by *bǫdǫtъ*. Often the present forms of the verb *xotěti* 'want' (§15.233)—and rarely the presents of *načьnǫtъ* and *vъčьnǫtъ* 'begin'—are used with an infinitive in a sense close to the English future. Rather more common are quasi-futures consisting of the present of *imamь* (§16.24). This construction occasionally means literally "have to", but normally indicates "is to, is destined to"; e.g. azъ brašьno imamь ěsti egože vy ne věste (J 4:32) 'I have meat to eat that ye know not of'; uže ne imamь piti otъ ploda lozьnaego (Mk 14:25) 'I will drink no more of the fruit of the vine'; iže ašte ne priimetъ cěsarьstvьja božьja jako otročę ne imatъ vъniti vъ nje (L 18:17) 'whosoever shall not receive the kingdom of God as a little child shall in no wise enter therein'; koe bǫdetъ znamenьe egda imǫtъ sъkonьčati sę vьsě si (Mk 13:4) 'what shall be the sign when all these things shall be fulfilled?'

Past-tense forms of *xotěti* and *imati* express a relative future—an event regarded as future from the point of view of a past moment: e.g. se že

---

6 More examples and discussion in Radoslav Večerka, *Altkirlchensl. Syntax,* II 174-185 (= Monumenta linguae slavicae dialecti veteris, Tom XXIV [XXVII, 2], Freilburg i. Br., 1993).

glagolaše kleplję koejǫ sъmrьtьjǫ xotěaše umrěti (J 12:33) ‘This he said, signifying what death he would die.’

21.2 The past tenses

While the present tense is indifferent as to time, the aorist and imperfect both specify action presented as taking place prior to the moment of utterance. The *imperfect* specifies an action coordinated with a fact or act in the past: this point of reference may or may not be present in the context. The *aorist* has no such specification – it is merely an event in the past. The aorist thus functions as the story-telling device which presents a chain of events, while the imperfect gives the background events or stops to concentrate on an action being performed at a certain moment.

The majority of aorists are of perfective aspect, but imperfective aorists are not uncommon: the action is presented as past, but there is no specification that it was completed. Imperfects are nearly always of imperfective aspect, but perfective imperfects appear when the need arises; a coordinated yet completed action is specified, and this usually means a repeated action.[7] For example… аште сѧ сълоучаааше не имѣти ѥмоу ничьсоже дати ѥмоу, то котыгѫ…дадѣаше ништоуоумоу (Su 207.14) ‘if it happened that he had nothing to give him, he would…give his (own) dress to the poor man.’

A few examples of aorist-imperfect usage:

Mk 5:24 … ide (1) sъ njimь i, po njemь iděaše (2) narodъ mъnogъ i ugnětaaxǫ i (3) ‘[Jesus] went with him and after him went a great crowd and they pressed on him’. The determined aorist (1) defines a past moment to which further actions (imperfects, 2, 3) are coordinated.

Mt 26:57ff. (in the story of the arrest and trial of Jesus) poimъše isusa věšę i (1) … petrъ že iděaše (2) po njemь izdaleče i sěděaše (3) sъ slugami viděti konьčinǫ … [arxierei]

---

[7] Dostál (*Studie*, pp. 599-600) notes that over 40% of the attested OCS aorists are imperfective, while the 23 perfective imperfects constitute only about 1% of attested imperfects. It is worth emphasizing these figures, for many investigators have assumed that any verb which has an aorist is necessarily perfective, and similarly that an imperfect tense form is proof of the imperfective aspect of the verb in question. It is now clear that in OCS—as well as in Russian (Early East Slavic) and Old Czech and modern Serbian, Macedonian and Bulgarian—tense and aspect are two independent systems. One should not lose sight of the fact that certain forms (like perfective imperfects) are statistically infrequent because the situations requiring them are uncommon. It is only in a narration of complex events in the past that one can expect to find the full range of the possible past tense forms, including the various combinations of participles; virtually no passages of this type happen to be attested in OCS.

iskaaxǫ (4) lъža sъvědětelja na isusa … i ne obrětǫ (5) … isusъ že mlьčaaše (6) … petrъ že vъně sěděaše (7) … i pristǫpi (8) kъ njemu edina rabynji. 'Having seized Jesus, they led him … And Peter followed at a distance and sat with the servants to see the end… [the chief priests etc.] sought false witness … but found none … [they ask questions] … but Jesus was silent … [The trial goes on, and the scene shifts:] Now Peter was sitting outside … and a slave-woman came up to him.' The narration has started with a series of aorists, of which (1) is the last. Two imperfects (2, 3) show the actions of Peter, coordinated to the main flow of action which is centered around Jesus. The third imperfect (4) refocuses on the court and the officials' non-coordinated, unfinished act of searching; the lack of success is summed up by a negated perfective aorist (5). More aorists (not cited) carry on the narration, but through these completed acts by others Jesus, in a coordinated negative action (specified by the imperfect, 6), remains silent. Peter, in the meanwhile, is sitting (coordinated act, imperfect; 7), when another actor appears and completes an action (P aor. 8)

L 1:80 otročę že rastěaše (1) i krěpljaaše sę (2) duxomь, i bě (3) vъ pustynji do dьne avljenьja svoego kъ izdrailju 'And the child grew, and waxed strong in spirit, and was in the desert till the day of his showing unto Israel'. The two imperfects (1, 2) denote actions coordinated with the imperfective aorist (3) which states a fact rather than an event.

21.21 The perfective aorist *bystъ* in principle denotes an event, the appearance of something not present before. The imperfective *bě* ordinarily reports a new fact, without specifically coordinating it to other events. The imperfect *běaše* specifies coordination to some point in past time. The three-way distinction is sometimes blurred, however. Some examples:

I *bystъ* burja větrьna velija (Mk 4:37) 'and a great wind-storm came up'; egda *bystъ* dьnь, priglasi učeniky svoę (L 6:12) 'when day broke, he called his disciples'. On že slyšavъ se priskrьbьnъ *bystъ, bě* bo bogatъ ʒělo (L 18:23) 'and when he heard this he *became* very sorrowful, for he *was* very rich.'

Vъlězъ že vъ edinъ otъ korabljicu, iže *bě* simonovъ, moli i otъ zemlję otъstǫpiti malo, i sědъ učaaše is korablja narody (L 5:3) 'and having entered into one of the ships, which *was* [as a general fact not yet mentioned] Simon's, he prayed (aor.) him that he would thrust out a little from the land, and having sat down, he taught the crowds out of the ship.'

I pomanošę pričęstьnikomъ iže *běaxǫ* vъ druʒěemь korablji (L 5:7) 'and they beckoned to their partners, which *were* [precisely at that time; impf.] in the other boat'.

21.211 Incidents in the Gospels are frequently introduced by a redundant *bystъ* that corresponds to the typically biblical phrase "it came to pass that". The construction is originally Hebrew, literally translated in the Greek Bible. For example:

Bystъ že idǫštemъ po pǫti, reče edinъ kъ njemu, idǫ po tebě jamože koližьdo ideši, gospodi (L 9:57) 'and it came to pass, that, as they went (§18.5e) along the way, a certain man said to him, I will follow thee wheresoever thou goest, Lord'; i *bystъ* egda vъnide isusъ vъ domъ edinogo kъnęʒa fariseiska vъ sǫbotǫ xlěba ěstъ (§21.5) … (L 14:1) 'and it came to pass, when Jesus went into the house of one of the chief Pharisees to eat bread on the sabbath day …'

21.3 On participles

The present and past active participles (of both aspects) are freely used in all cases and numbers.[8] In cases other than nominative and accusative, the long-forms are found more often than the short-forms. The present and past passive participles (of both aspects) are used mostly in the nominative short-forms, but other cases occur as well. True participles are clearly verbal in character; they denote an action which is subordinate to another action that is expressed by a finite verb in the context. Often, however, the participial form functions purely as an adjective.

There are instances where variant readings of the same passage have participial constructions equivalent to relative clauses, e.g. Mt 10:40 Sav **приємлѧи васъ мєнє приємлєтъ** ~ Zo *iže vy primetъ* mę priemljetъ 'he who receives you, receives me'. In translating into English, the participles are often best rendered by finite verbs in dependent clauses of various types.

21.31 The present participles, like the present tense, are unmarked as to time, denoting either general verbal action or (most frequently) action coordinated with the time expressed by the context. For example, active participles: mъnoʒi bo pridǫtъ vъ moe imę *glagoljǫšte* … (Mk 13:6) 'for many shall come in my name, saying …'; běaxǫ že edini … *glagoljǫšte* … (Mk 14:4) 'and there were some that said …'; passive participles: se estъ tělo moe *davaemoe* za vy (L 22:19) 'this is my body which is given for you'; isusъ že slyšavъ slovo *glagoljemoe* (Mk 5:36) 'Jesus, having heard the word which was spoken, said …'; **єгда владъікѫ си видѣ чтома** (Su 425.17) 'when he saw his Lord being honored'. If the present participle is perfective, it signifies a completed subordinate action; the completion most usually is repeated, or else is in the relative future, but the possibility of a relative past is not excluded. For example: **нє бѫдѣмъ оубо нє похвалѧште такого благодѣтєлꙗ** (Su 494.14) 'let us not fail to praise such

---

8 These remarks do not apply to the resultative participles, which are found only in the nominative short-forms either (regularly) accompanied by a form of *byti* in the compound tenses defined in §14, or else with omission of the auxiliary in forms of the perfect (§14.1).

In a single passage (Su 386.5–8) the l-participles occur with **єша** and **ꙗроу** 'would that!; if only!', which also take the conditional (usually with *da*). Non-OCS evidence seems to indicate that the omission of the auxiliary was normal after these conjunctions.

For a detailed and illuminating discussion of the active participles, see Rudolf Růžička, *Das syntaktische System der altslavischen Partizipien und sein Verhältnis zum Griechischen*, Berlin, 1963.

a benefactor (lit. 'let us not be [repeatedly] not praising'); **и єже агг҃єлы похвалимъ дръжитъ сѧ скврънавъıима рѫкама** (Su 506.19; cf. §22.4) 'and he whom the angels praise [who is praised by the angels] is held by dirty hands'.

The present passive participles, particularly if perfective, may denote the possibility of an act: e.g. *vidimъ* 'being seen; visible'; *měrimъ* 'being measured; measurable'; especially common with negation, *nepobědimъ* 'invincible', *nerazorimъ* 'indestructable', and others.

21.321 The past active participles present an action which started (and usually is completed) before the action of the main verb to which the participle is subordinated. For example, sęděte sьde donьdeže *šьdъ* pomoljǫ sę (Mk 14:23) 'Sit ye here while I go (lit. having gone) pray'; *šьdъ* pokaži sę iereovi (L 5:14) 'go (lit. having gone) show yourself to the priest'; *šьdъše* vъ gradъ vъzvěstišę vьsě (Mt 8:33) 'they went into the city and told of everything'.

An example contrasting present and past active participles: (L 6:47–49) *slyšęi* (1) slovesa moja i *tvorę* (2) ja … podobьnъ estъ člověku *ziždǫštu* (3) xraminǫ … na kamene; …*slyšavyi* (4) i ne *tvorjь* (5) podobьnъ estъ človeku *sъzьdavъšu* (6) xraminǫ bez osnovanьja … 'He who heareth my sayings and doeth them … is like a man who builds a house … on a rock; … and he that heareth (=has been hearing) and doeth not (= has not been doing) is like a man that without a foundation built a house'. Here 1 and 2 are present actions, contemporaneous with the moment of utterance, while 3 is a statement of general validity. 4 and 5 show uncompleted (imperfective) actions which started before the principle action, while 6 not only started before, but has been completed.

21.322 The past passive participle denotes a state produced by an outside agent whose action started prior to the moment denoted by the context. In the vast majority of cases the short nominative forms are used with some form of the verb *byti*; e.g. *zъvanъ že bystъ* i isus (J 2:2) 'and Jesus was also invited'; věruęi vъ njь ne *bǫdetъ osǫždenъ,* a ne věruęi juže *osǫždenъ estъ* (J 3:18) 'he that believeth on him will not be condemned, but he that believeth not is condemned already'; možaaše bo si xrizma *prodana byti* (Mk 14:5) 'for this ointment might have been sold'; ně u bo *bě vъsaždenъ* vъ tьmьnicǫ ioanъ (J 3:24) 'for John was not yet cast into prison'. The other cases and also the long forms do occur, however, particularly in the dative absolute construction (§18.5e) *obrǫčeně byvъši* materi ego (Mt 1:18) 'when his mother was espoused …'; rači … prizьrěti na raba tvoego sego padъša grěxy, *poražena* boleznijǫ (Euch 30a22) 'deign to look on this Thy servant (who has) fallen because of sins, (who has been) struck down by disease'; ꙁа приѩтѫѭ отъ ребръ адамовъ женѫ (Su 482.15) 'for woman, taken from the ribs of Adam'; не срамьꙗкши ли сѧ … сътвореньныихъ тобоѭ ꙁълии (Su 161.22) 'aren't you ashamed of the evils done by you (or, which you have done)?'

A number of words which are formally past passive participles are used as non-verbal adjectives, e.g. *prokaženъ* 'leprous', *oslabljenъ* 'paralytic', *sъměrjenъ* 'humble', *učenъ* 'learned', *izbьranъ* 'elect, select'.

21.33 *On verbal adverbs*. It has been suggested that certain forms spelled *-šte* represent verbal adverbs (or *gerunds*), e.g. neže dъvě noꙁě *imǫšte* vъvrъženu byti vъ ǵeonǫ (Mk 9:45) '[it is better for thee to enter halt into life] than having two feet to be cast into hell'; сладъка ти ꙗестъ въкоушаѭште нъ горька по въкоуса (Su 350.29) '[beware the pleasure of sin,] it is sweet for you as you are tasting (it) but bitter after the tasting'. The examples are better explained as scribal errors, for dative *-štu*.[9]

21.4 The *infinitive* is used as the complement of a number of verbs denoting command, desire, will, ability, or various expressions of purpose. The connotation of possibility or duty appears with *estъ*: отъ сего … видѣти ꙗестъ силѫ христосовѫ (Su 413.16) 'from this is to be seen the power of Christ'; нѣстъ намъ оубити (Su 433.12) 'we are (ought) not to kill'; bystъ že (§21.211) umrěti ništuemu i nesenu byti anǵely na lono avraamlje (L 16:22) 'and it came to pass that the beggar died and was carried by the angels into Abraham's bosom'. (Compare the use of infinitive with *imamь,* §21.11.)

Occasionally an infinitive with the conjunction *jako* (cf. §22.3) expresses result: e.g. i ne otъvěšta emu ni kъ edinomu glagolu *jako diviti sę igemonu* ꙁělo (Mt 27:14) 'and he answered him to never a word, *so that the governor marvelled* greatly'; isplьnišę oba korablja *jako pogrǫžati sę ima* (L 5:7) 'they filled both the ships *so that they began to sink*'.[10] Notice the dative as "subject" of the infinitive (cf. §18.5d).

21.5 The *supine* is used after verbs of motion to specify purpose; e.g. idǫ *lovitъ* rybъ (J 21:3) 'I am going (in order) to fish'; česo *vidětъ* izidete (Mt 11:7) 'What did you come out to see?'; i vъsta čistъ (L 4:16) 'and he stood up to read'. However, the use of the specifically purposeful supine was apparently not obligatory, and the semantically neutral infinitive could convey the same meaning in the proper context. Thus in Mt 26:55, As

---

9 For other examples see Vaillant §169, and Jacques Lépissier, in *Studie palaeoslovenica* (Prague, 1971) 215-20.

10 The OCS infinitive is imperfective; the act of sinking is not presented as completed, and the context of the whole passage implies that it was never completed.

izidoste sъ orǫžiemь … *ętъ* mene 'are ye come out … to take me?' is equivalent to Mar Zo Sav *ęti* mę—with genitive object of the supine, accusative with infinitive. Cf. идѫ ꙋготоватъ мѣста вамъ (J 14:2 Sav) ~ *ugotovati* město (Zo Mar As Vat) 'I go to prepare a place for you'.

It is possible that the supine was not part of the dialect of some scribes, and that some infinitives replace an older supine. Thus Mar da ne vъzvratitъ sę vъspętь *vьzętъ* rizъ svoixъ (Mk 13:16) 'let him not go back to get his garments' is "correct", but Zo's phrase *vьzęti rizъ svoixъ* lacks clear motivation for the genitive.

21.6 On *sę* and "reflexive" verbs.

The form **sę** has two functions; the two often overlap.

21.61 *Sę* may be the accusative of the reflexive pronoun (§4.6): javljǫ *sę* emu samъ (J 15:21) 'I [myself] will manifest myself to him'; sъpasi *sę* samъ i ny (L 23:55) 'save thyself and us [two].' In the presence of negation (§18.3b), this accusative *sę* is replaced by the genitive *sebe*: iny sъpase, ali *sebe* ne možetъ sъpasti (Mk 15:31) 'he saved others, but he cannot save himself.'

This true reflexive *sę* may be replaced by the emphatic or "personal accusative" *sebe*: compare, onъ že xotę opravьditi *sę* sam' reče … (L 10:29) 'he, wanting to justify himself, said …'; vy este opravьdajǫštei *sebe* prědъ člověky (L 16:15) 'ye are they which justify yourselves before man'; vъzljubiši iskrьnjaego svoego jako samъ *sebe* (Mar ~ *sę* Zo As) Mk 12:31 'thou shalt love thy neighbor as thyself'; sego obrětomъ … glagoljǫšta *sebe* xrista cěsarja byti (L 23:2) 'we found this man … saying himself to be Christ the King.'

21.62 Much more frequent is the *sę* which has lost the clear meaning and case of the reflexive pronoun and functions more like a particle which imparts some general meaning of intransitivity to the verb. *Sę* may be enclitic and follow the first accented word in the clause, but it usually follows the verb immediately.[11] The *sę* remains unchanged even in the presence of negation: ašte *sę* bi ne rodilъ (Mt 26:24 Zo Mar Sav; ~ As ašte bi ne rodilъ *sę*) 'if he had not been born'; ne divi *sę* (J 3:6) 'do not be surprised'; uněe estъ ne ženiti *sę* (Mt 19:10) 'it is better not to marry'. This fact perhaps allows us to perceive simply intransitivity (and not specific

---

[11] In East Slavic the particle ся is written as part of the verb, and lexicographers treat ся-verbs as separate entries (родить 'bear, give birth (to)' ~ родиться 'be born'). Following this pattern, Russian and Ukrainian scholarly lists of OCS lexical items usually provide two entries. Other Slavs (as well as non-Slavs) include sę-verbs with non-sę verbs; thus SJS puts родити сѧ and рожденъ быти under родити.

reflexivity) in: vъ rizǫ ne oblačaaše *sę* (L 8:27) 'he did not get dressed in clothing.'

In many verbs, the presence or absence of *sę* indicates intransitivity versus transitivity: azъ umyxъ vaši noʒě (J 13:14) 'I washed your feet', but umyxъ *sę* (J 9:15) 'I washed' (with the context supplying 'my eyes'; this could be taken as reflexive). Some verbs acquire a different meaning with *sę*: klьnǫtъ 'curse' but klьnǫtъ sę 'swear, take an oath'. Sometimes a semantic difference is not clear from the available evidence, e.g. plakati ~ plakati sę 'weep; (+ gen. or *o* + loc.) mourn', although here perhaps the *sę* adds a note 'for one's own benefit' similar to the dative *si* (§18.5c). Several verbs never occur without *sę*: e.g. bojati sę 'fear', postiti sę 'fast', rǫgajǫtъ sę 'mock'.

Sometimes it is difficult to distinguish an active reflexive from a passive meaning; in some passages different manuscripts show variants. For example, synъ člověčьskъi *prědastъ sę* (Mt 26:2, Zo) but Mar and As explicitly passive *prědanъ bǫdetъ* 'the Son of Man will be betrayed'; ašte tъkъmo prikosnǫ sę rizě ego *sъpasena bǫdǫ* (Mt 9:21, Mar As) but Sav *sъpasǫ sę* 'if only I touch his garment, I will be saved'.

22.1 The conjunction *da* plus present (of either aspect) means 'in order to', or simply 'to, that': e.g. izide sěęi *da sěetъ* (Mt 13:3) 'a sower went forth to sow'; priněsę ... děti *da* rǫcě vъzložitъ na nję (Mt 19:13) 'they brought children, that he should put his hands on them'; něsmь bo dostoinъ *da* podъ krovъ moi *vъnideši* (L 7:8) 'I am not worthy that you should come under my roof'. The meaning of purpose is made more specific by adding *jako,* see below. The negative may be *da ne* or *eda* (or *da ne kako, eda kako*) 'in order not to, lest'; e.g. moljaaxǫ i *da ne povělitъ* imъ vъ bezdъnǫ iti (L 8:31) 'they besought him that he should not command them to go out into the deep'; bljudi ubo *eda* světъ iže vъ tebě tьma *estъ* (L 11:35) 'take heed therefore that the light which is in thee be not darkness'. The conditional may be used instead of the present: molišę i *da bi prěšьlъ* otъ prědělъ ixъ (Mt 8:4; Sav has ꙗко да прѣидетъ) 'they besought him that he would depart out of their coasts'; i drъžaaxǫ i, *da ne bi otъšьlъ otъ njixъ* (L 4:42) 'and they stayed him, that he should not depart from them'.[12]

---

[12] Complete data, with a historical and comparative study, in Herbert Bräuer, *Untersuchungen zum Konjunktiv im Altkirchenslavischen und Altrussischen. I. Die Final- und abhängigen Heischesätze* (= Veröffentlichungen d. Abteilung f. slav. Spr. u. Lit. des Osteuropa-Inst. a. d. Freien Universität Berlin, Vol. 11), Wiesbaden, 1957.

22.11 In an independent clause, *da* plus 3rd person present (rarely 1st sg./pl.) may represent an exhortation: *da pridetъ* (J 7:37)'let him come'; *da svętitъ sę* imę tvoe (Mt 6:9) 'hallowed be Thy name'; samъ o sebě *da glagoljetъ* (J 9:21) 'let him speak for himself'; *da ne postyždǫ sę* vъ věkъ (Ps 30:2) 'let me never be ashamed'.

22.12 With past tenses, and occasionally with a present, *da* means 'and, and then'.

22.2 *Eda* (§22.1) serves also to introduce a question which expects a negative answer: e.g. *eda* možetъ slěpьcь slěpьca voditi (L 6:39) 'can a blind man lead a blind man?'; *eda* imatъ xvalǫ rabu tomu, jako sъtvori povelěnaja? ne mьnjǫ (L 17:9) 'Doth he thank that servant because he did the things that were commanded him? I trow not.'

22.3 The conjunction *jako* has a very wide range of meaning—'that, so that, for, as, like, since, because'. It is used to introduce both direct and indirect quotations, and sometimes it is difficult to see which is meant. For example: vy glagoljete *jako* vlasvimljaeši zanje rěxъ *jako* synъ božьi esmь (J 10:36) 'Ye say, Thou blasphemest, because I said, I am the Son of God.' Here the 2nd sg. form shows clearly that the first *jako* introduces a direct quotation, but the statement after the second *jako* could be indirect: 'I said *that I was* …' Or: Otъvěšta žena i reče emu, ne imamь mǫža. Glagola ei Isusъ, dobrě reče *jako* mǫža ne imamь (J 4:17) 'The woman answered and said to him, I have no husband. Jesus said to her, Thou hast well said, I have no husband.'

22.4 Beside the normal use of the relative pronoun *iže* in an explanatory phrase with a form of *byti* 'to be' (e.g. iže estъ otъ boga, glagolъ božьi poslušaetъ J 8:47 'he that is of God heareth God's words'), there are cases where the verb is omitted: e.g. světъ iže vъ tebě (Mk 6:23) 'the light within you'; **ѡ їѡсифѣ иже отъ аримаѳеꙗ** (Su 447.28) 'about Joseph of Arimathea'; glavy evanǵelija eže otъ luky 'chapters of the Gospel [which is] of Luke'.[13]

The neuter *eže* may be used with an infinitive; e.g. čьto estъ *eže* iz mrьtvyixъ vъskrьsnǫti (Mk 9:10) 'what is [the] rising from the dead?'; *eže* neumъvenami rǫkami ěsti ne skvrьnitъ člověka (Mt 15:20) 'to eat (i.e. the fact of eating) with unwashed hands defileth not a man' **нъ ѕъло єже сътворити ѕъло** (Su 406.8) 'but doing evil [is] evil'.

---

13 Josef Kurz cites all the examples, *Byzantinoslavica* 7: 336ff.

Eže is also found as a conjunction'because, inasmuch as'. Occasionally *iže* is found for *eže,* and vice versa.

23. On negation

23.1 Two morphemes express negation: *ne* and *ni*. *Ne* 'not' stands immediately before the verb or other syntactical unit that it negates. *Ni* expresses denial (the antonym of *ei* 'yes'), or—usually in conjunction with *ne*—'neither, nor, and not, not even'. *Ne* ordinarily occurs only once in a major clause; *ni* may be repeated. A clause containing a negative pronoun or adverb (such as *nikъtože* 'no one', *ničьtože* 'nothing', *nikyiže* 'no sort of', *niedinъže* 'no, none', *nikoliže* 'never', *nikъdeže* 'nowhere', *nikakože* 'in no way') usually has *ne* before the verb; the double negation is presumably normal Slavic syntax. The *ne* is often omitted, however, if *ni* (*ni-*) stands earlier in the clause: this imitates Greek (where, as in English, two negatives signify a positive).[14] Thus *i niktože daěaše emu* (L 15:16, As) 'and no one gave him [anything], Mar *i niktože* ne *daěše emu.* Some examples:

Ne moja volja nъ tvoja da bǫdetъ (L 22:42) '*not my will,* but thine, be done.' Obače *ne* jakože azъ xoštǫ, nъ jakože ty (Mt 26:39) 'nevertheless, *not as* I wish but as you [wish].' Vy čisti este nъ *ne* vьsi (J 13:10) 'You are clean, but *not all.*' *Ne* o vьsěxъ vasъ glagoljǫ (J 13:18) 'I speak *not of you all.*' vrěmę moe *ne* u pride (J 7:5) "My time is *not yet* come.'

On že reče, *ni* (Mt 13:29) 'And he said, "*No.*"' *Ni* bratrьja bo ego věrovaaxǫ vъ njь (J 7:5) 'for *not even his brothers* believed in him.' *Ni* azъ tebe osǫždajǫ; idi i otъselě *ne* sъgrěšai kъ tomu (J 8:11) '*Neither* do I condemn thee; go and sin *no more.*' Pride Ioanъ *ni* pię *ni* jady (Mt 11:18 Zo ~ *ne... ni* Mar) 'John came, *neither* eating *nor* drinking.' *Něsmь* azъ xristosъ (J 1:27; §16.101) 'I *am not* the Christ.' *Něstъ* umrьla děvica (L 8:52) 'the maiden has not died.' Da *ne* vidętъ očima *ni* razumějǫtъ srьdьcemь (J 12:40) 'that they should *not see* with their eyes *nor understand* with their heart.' Položi e [tělo] vъ grobě isěčeně vъ nemьže *ne* bě *nikъtože nikogdaže* položenъ (L 23:53) '[he] laid it in a hewn tomb where *no one* had *ever* been laid.' *Nikomuže ne* rabotaxomъ *nikoliže* (J 8:33) 'we have *never* been in bondage to *anyone.*'*Ni otъ edinogože ne* može iscěl̂ěti

[14] Variations in usage are extreme, and many examples are hard to interpret (see note 16 below). Some of the fluctuation must be attributed to dialect variants, both in time and in region. Here only the most general statements are possible. For fuller treatment, see R. Večerka, *Altkirchensl. (altbulgarische) Syntax* I (1989) 33-41, III (1996) 128-140.

(L 8:43 ZoMarSav; As omits *ne*) 'she could *not* be healed by *any* [one of the doctors].'

23.2 Negation affects case-usage in two types of construction: existential, and transitive (cf. §18.3a6, 18.3b).

23.211 Existential negation combines the impersonal *něstъ* (*ne bǫdetъ, ne bě*) 'there is no[t] (will not be, was not)' with the genitive: *něstъ inogo boga razvě mene* (Su 264.2) 'there is no other god except for me'; otъ plъti *něstъ polьzę nikakoęže* (J 6:63) 'from the flesh there is no profit whatsoever'; *něstъ člověka* iže živъ bǫdetъ i ne sъgrěšaetъ (Eu 57a10) 'there is no man who will live and not sin'; **не бѣ никогоже** (Su 241.27) 'there was no one there.' *Něstъ* with the nominative expresses a negative definition: e.g. **нѣстъ велико чоудо** (Su 33.24) 'the miracle is not great'; this construction is normally distinct from *něstъ* with genitive, existential negation: e.g. sьde tebě *něstъ těsta* (Eu 37a24) 'here for you *there is no* place.'

23.212 The distinction is sometimes blurred. E.g. i *něstъ svętъ* razvě tebe gospodi (1Ki 2:2, Sin 2/N) 'there is none holy besides thee, Lord'; *něstъ* bo *ničьtože* taino eže ne avitъ sę (Mk 4:22) 'for there is nothing hid which shall not be manifested'; **нѣстъ кто милоуѩ, и нѣстъ кто милосръдоуѩ** (Su 57.9-10) 'there is no one who pities and there is no one who shows mercy'; **нѣстъ никтоже противѧи сѧ тебѣ** (Su 232.5) 'there is no one resisting you.' *Nikъtože* estъ otъ roždenija tvoego iže naricaetъ sę imenemь těmь (L 1:61) 'there is no one of your kin who is called by this name.'—The fig-tree which has no fruit because it is not yet the season (cf. Mt 21:18-19) is cursed by Jesus, **не бѫди къ семоу плодъ отъ тебе** (Su 346.19) 'may there be henceforth no fruit from you'; *plodъ* could be Gp, but normally it is collective in meaning, and it may be Ns here. Compare Su 350.12 **зане смокы плода не сътвори** 'because the fig-tree has not produced fruit.' Su 345.26 has an unexpected genitive in **не бѣ юи врѣмене** 'it was not its time,' but 351.24 has nominative, **не бѣ юи врѣмѧ плодъ сътворити съмрьтьнъ** 'it was not its time to produce deadly fruit.'

23.22 Transitive negation involves a transitive verb that normally takes an accusative direct object; when the verb is negated (or is subordinate to a negated verb) the object is in the genitive:[15]

---

15 Indirect objects are not affected by negation; e.g. *sǫdi+* takes dative, whether positive (po zakonu vašemu sǫdite *emu*, J 18:31, 'judge him according to your law') or negative (otьcь bo *ne* sǫditъ *nikomuže*, J 5:22, 'for the father doesn't judge anyone').

Ne ěstъ *ničesože* (L 4:2) 'he did not eat anything.' Jako *ne* věste dьne *ni* časa (Mt 25:13) 'for you don't know the day or hour.' *Ne* prěrečetъ *ni* vъzъpietъ; *ne* uslyšitъ *nikъtože* na raspǫtiixъ glasa ego (Mt 12:19) 'He shall *not wrangle nor cry, neither* shall any man hear his voice in the streets.' I prěgrěšixomъ o vьsemь i zapovědei tvoixъ *ne* poslušaxomъ, *ni* sъbljusomъ *ni* sъtvorixomъ ěkože zapovědě namъ (Daniel 3:29–30, Sin 2/N 26a) 'and we have sinned in everything and *not* obeyed your commandments *and not* observed *and not* done as you commanded us.'[16] *Ničьtože* ixъ *ne* vrěditъ (Mk 16:18) 'nothing will harm them.' I *nikomuže ničesože ne* rěšę (Mk 16:8) 'and they said *nothing* to *anyone*.'[17] *Nikogože* obidite *ni* okljevetaite (L 3:14 ZoMar ~ *ne* obidite AsSav) '*Do not* disrespect *or* slander *anyone*.'

Ne mogǫ azъ o sebě tvoriti *ničesože* (J 5:30) 'I can of myself do *nothing*.' *Ne* dostoitъ tebě vъzęti *odra svoego* (J 5:10) 'It is not proper for you to pick up your bed.' I *ne* imǫtъ česo ěsti, i otъpustiti ixъ *ne* ědъšь *ne* xoštǫ (Mt 15:32) 'and they *do not have anything* to eat, and I will not send them away hungry (lit. *not having eaten*).'[18]

23.3 In rhetorical questions, *ne* serves to mark the item that is emphasized: *Ne* azъ li vasъ dъva na desęte izbьraxъ (J 5:70) 'Was it not I who chose you twelve?' *Ne* sь li estъ tektonovъ synъ (Mt 13:55) 'Is not this the carpenter's son?' *Ne* samъ li sь otьcь tvoi sъtęža tę (Deuteronomy 32:6, Sin 2/N 14b) 'did *not he himself* thy father purchase thee?' *Ne* i mytare li tako tvorętъ (Mt 5:47) 'do not even the publicans do so?'

23.4 *Ne* serves as a lexical prefix in about 300 stems, *bez* in about 100. Editors and lexicographers often differ on when to write a space after *ne*.

---

16 There are ambiguous or contradictory phrases, e.g. *ne* sъkryvaite sebě sъkrovištь na zemlji (Mt 6:19 AsSav ~ sъkrovišta ZoMar) 'Do not hide for yourselves treasures on earth'. The form *sъkrovišta* can be taken as Gs 'a treasure' and explained as a conscious or unconscious change of meaning, or else as an Ap that (probably intentionally) imitates the Greek.

17 The nom. or acc. *ničьtože* occasionally appears where gen. *ničesože* is to be expected: Zo *nikomuže ničьtože ne* rьci (~ Mar ni*česože*; Mk 1:44) 'say *nothing* to *anyone*.'

18 Note that *ixъ* is genitive because the infinitive *otъpustiti* is governed by the negated auxiliary (§21.11). Compare: i ne obrětъša *ego* ... vъziskajǫšta *ego* ... obrětete *jь* sědęštь ... iskaaxově *tebe* (L 2:45-46, 48) 'and not having found *him* [G with negation] ... looking for *him* [G required by verb] the two of them found *him sitting* [A, direct obj.] ... we [two] sought *you* [G required by verb].' In L 23:2, *sego* obrětomъ *razvraštajǫšta* ęzykъ našь 'we found *this* [*man*] *perverting* our nation', the genitive form is dictated by the personal reference (§18.21), cf. obrěte *filipa* (J 1:42) 'he found Philip.'

23.41 The imperfective *nenaviděti* 'hate' usually takes genitive, while the perfective *vъznenaviděti* takes accusative.

23.42 Some examples: něstъ *nepravьdy* vъ njemь (ps 91:16) 'there is no *unrighteousness* in him'; ne bǫdi *nevěrьnъ* nъ věrьnъ (J 20:27) 'Do not be *without belief* but believing'; rabi *nedostoini* esmъ (L 17:10) 'We are *unworthy* servants.' (Compare *něsmь* dostoinъ, Mt 8:8, 'I am *not worthy*.') Su 483.12 нъ не не имѣ ӏ҃с водъı 'but Jesus did not not-have water' is a comprehensible translation of a negated Greek verb 'be in want of, lack for'.

23.5 Idiomatic phraseology using *ne*:

The negated imperative of *mog-* 'be able' + infinitive occasionally appears in the Supraslienisis as a periphrastic prohibition: *ne mozi* mene ostaviti (Su 539.8) '*Do not* leave me' (~ *ne* ostavi mne, ps 37:22 [§4.61]).[19]

The imperative *ne dě(te)* means 'permit': *ne děite* sixъ iti (J 18:8) 'let these go their way'; не дѣı да видимъ Sav (Mt 27:49: *ostani* da vidimъ ZoMarAs) 'let us see.'

Prěžde daže ne 'before [a particular moment comes]': sъnidi prěžde daže *ne* umьretъ otročę moe (J 4:49) 'Come down ere my child die.'

Uže ne 'no longer': Těmže *uže něsta* dъva nъ plъtь edina (Mk 10:7) 'then they *are no more* twain, but one flesh.'

Da ne 'in order that not, lest' (cf. §22.1): bljuděte sę vraga, *da ne* nagy sъtvoritъ vy ěko Adama (Eu 97b9) 'watch out for the enemy, lest he make you naked as Adam.'

Ašte ne 'unless': *Nikъtože ne* možetъ sъsǫdъ krěpъkaago, vъšedъ vъ domъ ego, rasxytiti *ašte ne* prěžde [prьvěe Zo] krěpъkaago sъvęžetъ (Mk 3:27 ZoMar) '*No one* can steal the vessels of a strong man, having entered his house, *unless* beforehand he binds the strong man.'

24. Vocabulary and the structure of words

24.1 The vocabulary of the canonical OCS manuscripts approaches 10,000 lexical items.[20] Some 1500 lexemes are non-Slavic personal or geographic names or derivatives. Foreign stems are adapted to fit OCS inflectional patterns.

---

[19] Su 239.3 не мози не вѣровати 'do not disbelieve'.

[20] Scholars disagree on just how to write many items, and lexicographers then argue about how to normalize. Thus no one doubts that *vъ* and *na* and *sui* 'empty, meaningless' and *tъštь* 'empty' are separate, but are there three more "words", *vъsue* and *nasue* and *vъtъšte* 'in vain'? SJS allows the first two but "вътъщє" is merely a cross-reference to "тъщь". Is *mimo* an independent adverb 'past, by', or is it a prefix to seven independent verb-stems meaning 'go (carry, run) past'? A different kind of problem is *xlǫbaję* 'begging' (Mk 10:46) in Mar but *xlǫpaję* in Z ~ *xlǫpati* (L 16:3) in both Zo and Mar. Are there two similar stems, or is one merely a spelling error? The rough statistics I provide can only be approximations.

24.11 The exact list is determined by the texts which happen to have survived. The gospels contain short narratives, mostly straightforward, but with cryptic sayings and occult allusions whose meaning depends on traditional religious exegesis. The psalms are poetry, much of it esoteric; the Greek is often obscure, the OCS translation was not particularly good, and the scribes were careless. The prayer-book (Euchologium) is intended for monastic use. The homilies in the Clozianus and Suprasliensis are mostly concerned with explicating details of Christian doctrine, and the saints' lives are placed in societies and geographical locations quite remote from the Slavic world of the ninth century. The OCS translators struggled to reproduce the often elaborate Greek and its richly varied lexicon, but their success was limited—and subsequent copyists failed to transmit the texts accurately.

24.12 The words we know from this meager set of sources provide a fair sample of basic lexemes and many special terms. Certain everyday items are missing: e.g. *nose, daughter-in-law, short, to cough* (though post-OCS information guarantees **nosъ, *snъxa, *kratъkъ, *kašьljaj+*). Some are not attested in their primary sense, e.g. *skovrada* 'grill, frying-pan' refers only to instruments of torture (18x). Others are merely implied by derivatives: e.g. *govęždina žila* 'steer-tendon' (a kind of whip that is contrasted to *bičь, voštaga,* and *xrъzanъ*) must be based on **govędo* 'steer'. Frequency of individual stems reflects subject-matter: *bogъ* 'god' occurs over 2100 times, *božьjь* 'god's, divine' more than 800x, *svętъ* 'holy' well over 1000x, *moli+* 'pray' 500+, *molitva* 'prayer' 400+—and *grěxъ* 'sin' 300+, *běsъ* 'demon' 200+ and *dijavolъ* 'devil' 100+.

24.13 In order to distinguish between words actually attested in canonical OCS (as I define it, §0.32) and those I believe can safely be attributed to OCS because they are found in specific later copies of certain texts, I will write ***OCS** (with the asterisk on the label, not the word): *OCS *nosъ*.

24.2 Meaning is deduced in part from the texts (chiefly Greek) on which the OCS translation is based, and in part from our knowledge of more recent Slavic vocabulary. Problems of interpretation appear at every step.

24.21 Not infrequently a Slavic word apparently has a connotation that the Greek original lacks. Thus the bowl or dish shared by Jesus and his betrayer (Mt 26:23, Mk 14:20) is *solilo,* surely 'salt-container', cf. *solь* 'salt'.

24.22 Occasionally the meaning that seems obvious for an OCS word or phrase does not fit the Greek text from which it was apparently translated.

A passage in Su, for example, retells an Old Testament parable (Greek II Kingdoms [Hebrew II Samuel] 12:1ff.) about a poor man whose pet ewe-lamb (ἀμνάς) is slaughtered by a rich man to make a feast for a visitor. The 'lamb' consistently becomes телица (Su 259.29, 260.5, 13), unquestionably the feminine counterpart of тельць 'calf'. We may speculate as to why the translator (or an editor) chose to change the species of the animal, but surely lexicographers err if they define *telica* as 'lamb'.[21]

24.23 Sometimes we are faced with a flat error: a translator or scribe has mistakenly omitted, added, or transposed letters or syllables. We must deal with what the scribes wrote, but we should explicitly label any emendation that we have made.

24.24 A pervasive difficulty is alternate words in the "same" context. Most examples are from the gospels, but parallel texts in the Clozianus and Suprasliensis offer many instructive variants. Some differences surely are stylistic, some are regional, some are historical, and many probably combine these features. Similar variants occur in the translation of the same Greek phrase in different passages. Proper treatment of the OCS material should be in some sort of explanatory dictionary. Here there is room only to sketch general principles.

24.25 Sometimes a Greek borrowing—usually taken as a sign of antiquity—is contrasted with one or more Slavic equivalents. Thus *blasphemy* (βλασφημία) may be власвимиꙗ or хоула or хоулѥние and the corresponding verb may be *vlasvimis-a+* or *vlasvimlj-aj+* or translated *xul-i+, xul-ova+*, or *vъsxuljaj+*. "Our *daily* bread" of the Lord's Prayer (Mt 6:11), with the controversial adjective ἐπιοῦσιος, remains хлѣбъ нашь епиоусии in Vat, but is interpreted as наставъшаго дне in MarSav, насѫщьнъи in A (and Sin 2/N), and a phrase beginning настоꙗшт- that was erased and overwritten by a later cyrillic scribe in Zo.

24.26 Often the contrast is a matter of Slavic derivation; e.g. *pastyrjь* 'shepherd' MarAsVat ~ *pastuxъ* Sav (Zo uses both); *životъ* 'life' ~ *žiznь, kъnižьnikъ* 'scribe' (usual) ~ *kъnigъčijь* (rare); *raspьnǫtъ* 'crucify' ~ *propьnǫtъ*. Different roots may supply semantically equivalent forms, e.g. *rasxyti+* 'to plunder' ~ *razgrabi+, xyštenьje* 'plundering' ~ *grablenьje, xyštьnikъ* 'robber' ~ *grabiteljь*.

24.261 Sometimes a word whose origin is obscure competes with a transparent lexeme; e.g. 'fence' is *xalǫga* in L 14:23, but *oplotъ* in Mk 12:1 (easily associated with *o* 'around' + *plet-* 'weave' and the type of

---

21 SJS and SS do just that. SS often, but not always, alerts readers to discrepancies by "!" after the Greek word provided as the source.

fence made by weaving together young branches); *odrъ* 'bed, litter' (widespread) ~ *lože* (of more restricted usage; cf. *ložiti sę* 'lie down').

24.262 Frequently, the competing words are built from native Slavic morphemes, and often we can perceive differing semantic nuances. Thus the 'lawyer' of Mk 22:35 is *zakonьnikъ* in AsSav, but 'teacher of law' *zakono-učiteljь* in Mar. The general verb 'will stand up' *vъstajetъ* of Mt 17:23 in MarSav corresponds to the explicit 'will be resurrected' *vъskrьsnetъ* in As. In both of these case there are explanations based on Greek words, but it is important to note that within OCS many near-synonyms change meanings slightly and are redistributed in ways that are not easy to predict. In the dramatic context of Mt 27:23, 'persuaded' is rendered *naučišę* 'instructed' in As, *naustišę* 'urged, goaded' in ZoMarVat, and *navadišę* 'lured, enticed' in Sav. The 'flood' of Mt 24:38 and 39 is *potopъ* both times in As, but merely *voda* 'water' in v. 39 in ZoMarSav. Yet different formations with apparently identical meanings are not unusual. The noun *věra* 'faith' is opposed to *nevěrьje, nevěrьstvo, nevěrьstvьje* and *bezvěrьje* 'lack of faith'. Religious concepts do not always have stable definitions; 'sin' is always *grěx-* (*grěxъ* 'sin', *grěšьnikъ, grěšьnica* 'sinner [m, f]', *grěšьnъ* 'sinful', *bezgrěšьnъ* 'sinless', *grěxovьnъ* 'pertaining to sin'), but the distinctions between the verbs *pogrěšiti* and *prěgrěšiti* 'to sin, err' are hard to discern. The 'forgiveness (remission) of sins' varies: in MarSavVat Mt 26:28 *vъ otъdanьje grěxomъ* [Vat **грѣховъ**] ~ *vъ otъpuštenьje grěxomъ* Zo ~*vъ ostavljenьje grěxomъ* As.[22]

24.3 The external history of OCS presumes ninth-century beginnings that involve possible eastern Bulgarian Slavic dialects near Constantinople (perhaps also in Bythinia, in Asia Minor), the Macedonian dialects near Saloniki, and western dialects (Morava and Pannonia), followed by developments more specifically tied to the Macedono-Bulgarian lands in the tenth and eleventh centuries. In the process, some dialect words or forms became normal or even obligatory (e.g. *abьje* 'at once'; *azъ* 'I'

---

22 In Mk 4:1, L 1:77, 3:3, 24:47 *otъpuštenie* and *ostavljenie* appear with different distributions. The scribe of Zo put both in L 1:77, *vъ ostavljenьe vъ otъpuštenьe grěxъ našixъ*. We may speculate that *otъdanьe* (which otherwise signifies 'repayment, retribution') in this expression is a reminiscence of Old High German *vergebnis,* while the other two imply *sending away* or *leaving alone,* both possible for ἄφεσις. This Gk noun occurs twice in L 4:18, "preach *deliverance* to the captives" and "set at *liberty* them that are bruised"—OCS *otъpuštenьe,* but otъpustitъ sъkrušenyę vъ *otъradǫ*. *Otъrada* is possibly a Moravism, but any classification has to be guesswork.

[probably a local eastern Bulgarian shape, although *jazъ* was surely universal elsewhere]), while others were gradually replaced (e.g. *ašutъ* 'in vain' ~ *vъsuje, vъtъšte; balьji* 'doctor' ~ *vračь*), and still others survived in specific contexts. Thus *rěsnota* 'truth' is well attested in the Psalter, along with its synonym, *istina,* but only the latter appears in gospels (although evidence from post-OCS gospel mss allows us to suspect that *rěsnota* was present in early copies and eliminated by conscious scribal intervention).

24.31 Readers and scribes easily tolerated alternate expressions. Thus "Lo, the hour is coming" of J 16:32 in Sav is both **се грѧдетъ часъ** (in the lection for the 7th Thursday after Easter, ed. p. 5) and **се идетъ година** (for the Thursday before Easter, ed. p. 98). ZoMarAs have *se grędetъ godina.* We can confidently surmise that **грѧдетъ** represented a familiar everyday verb for Slavs from what is now western Croatia and Slovenia or from Macedonia, but a bookish equivalent of **идетъ** in eastern Bulgaria. The nouns **часъ** and **година** (and also **годъ**), on the other hand, probably had varying meanings in different regions.

24.32 The shifting distribution of competing lexemes shows that no single manuscript embodies a consistent redaction. The general usage seems to be Macedonian, partly—it is assumed—reflecting the original translation of most of the texts, and partly reflecting the normalizing influences presumably exercised by scribes and editors throughout the tenth century. Yet the major manuscripts have words deemed by modern scholars to be typical of eastern Bulgarian usage, the effect of a standard assumed to have been developed in Preslav and perhaps other cultural centers. It is important to keep in mind that there is no OCS manuscript that exemplifies the hypothetical eastern or Preslav redaction of OCS. The chief works that supposedly were translated in this Bulgarian cultural zone have survived only in post-OCS manuscripts, and to retrieve their original wording is a complex task fraught with difficulties.[23] Much of the scholarship in this field is fragmentary and the assumptions and premises of individual investigators are often so different that results cannot be compared. Here there is space only to remark that there are OCS words generally agreed to be ancient and/or "western" (from the Moravan Mis-

---

[23] Parts of the Suprasliensis are believed to represent Preslav translations. Other probable examples are the *izborniki* of 1073 and 1076 (both copied in Rus') and the *Hexameron* (Шестоднев) by John the Exarch, known from a Serbian ms of 1263 and later ESl copies.

sion), and others characterized as "eastern" or Preslavian. The majority of OCS lexemes, including most synonyms, are neutral.

-*-

24.4 Most OCS words are complex (§3): stem + desinence. The stem must contain a root; it may contain one or more affixes.

Stems with more than one root are called *compounds*.

Canonical OCS includes about 2000 roots (some of which surely were felt as foreign) and a store of affixes that can be called native Slavic.

To the prefixes listed in §5.31 may be added *ne* 'not, un-', *bez* 'without', *meždu* 'between', and *protivъ* 'against'. Suffixes are more varied; here we will deal chiefly with morphemes—numbering about 60—that seem to form relatively new words.

24.41 A stem must be verbal, substantival or adjectival. The meaning is arbitrary, although usually it is partly predictable from the sense of the root as supplemented and/or limited by each affix. When a root serves as a stem, we may posit zero-affixes to specify gender and declension. Thus, the root in *sъl-a+* 'send' serves as a substantive-stem *sъl-ъ* 'envoy', which presumably is lexically marked as masculine, animate, and personal. The root *ljub* in *ljubi+* 'love' functions as an adjective stem, *ljubъ ljubo ljuba* 'dear'. The root *zъl* 'bad' can serve as an adjective (*zъlъ zъlo zъla*) or, with a change of declensional marking, a substantive, *zъlь* (i-stem fem., 'wickedness, evil'). The root *čęd* underlies the neuter substantive *čędo* 'child' and the feminine collective *čędь* 'servants, companions, household members, retinue'.[24]

24.42 Some 620 stems are compounds: e.g. *čęd-o-ljub-ъ* 'child-loving' is an adjective—the root *čęd* joined by {o/e} to *ljub*.[25] *Vodonosъ* (m) and *vodonosь* (f., i-stem) 'water-pot, vessel for carrying water'; cf. the verbal root in *nos-i+* 'carry' and the substantive *vod-a* 'water'. Zero-affixes are

---

24 It is important to keep in mind the practical results of differing decisions about analysis. Adjectives, including passive participles, may function as substantives (*slěpъ* 'blind; a blind man'; *zъlo* 'bad [neut.]; evil, a wicked act or intention'; *posъlanъ* 'sent; one sent, envoy'). Are such items to be entered in a dictionary as separate entries, or as subheadings, or can they be assumed to be predictable from the Nsm or basic-stem information? Negated passive participles easily are interpreted as having a sense of potentiality: e.g. *ukrot-i+* 'to tame' ~ *ukroštenъ* 'tamed, domesticated' ~ *neukroštenъ* [or *ne ukroštenъ*] 'untamed; untamable, uncontrollable'. Two words or one? Is a theoretical stem *cěsar-ova+* sufficient to identify Npm *necěsarujemi* as 'ungoverned, free from rule' (a sense obtained from the Greek text)?

25 If the first member is a numeral, it may itself consist of two roots: ***dъvoj**-e-na-**desęt**-e-luč-ьn-oje* slъnьce 'the 12-rayed sun' Su 231.2 (cf. *luča* 'ray'; §20).

assumed to specify that the compound stem is adjectival or substantival (and provides the declension type). Either root, or both, may be affixed, e.g. *čędoljubivъ* 'child-loving', *(za-kon)-o-(uč-itelj)-ь* 'law-teacher; lawyer', cf. *zakonъ* 'law' and *učiteljь* 'teacher' (*uč-i+* 'to teach').[26] As a rule, the first root is semantically subordinate to the second.[27]

24.431 Most substantives and adjectives are stems that must be listed in the lexicon even though many are made up of recognizable elements. For instance, *danь* 'tax, tribute' and *darъ* 'gift' obviously share meaning with the anomalous verb *dati* 'to give' and suggest a segmentation *da-n-ь* (whereby the *-n-* is lexically marked for feminine gender and i-stem inflection), and *da-r-ъ* (masculine o-stem). Within OCS, however, the morphemes must be *dan-* (simple decl., fem.) and *dar-* (hard masc. twofold decl.) and the verbal root {da[d]} (see §16.21); they are part of the knowledge that was, so to speak, recorded in the memory of speakers of OCS. In terms of stem analysis, *dar* and *dan* are OCS roots.

24.432 The substantive *darovanьje* 'donation, donating', on the other hand, is {(dar-ova+n)-ьj+e}: the root *dar* is converted into a verb by the *ova* classifier (§15.5), made a past passive participle by the suffix *n*, and a verbal substantive by the formant *ьj* (cf. §12). This process of formation is productive, given the basic morpheme *dar*; the meaning 'act(s) of donating' is expected for the formation. In grammatical terms, this verbal substantive is part of the morphology of the verb *dar-ova+*, and it is predictable in terms of normal suffixes and productive rules. This kind of derivative easily acquires a new meaning—here 'thing(s) donated'—and lexicographers must decide whether it deserves a separate entry in a dictionary.

24.44 Analysis of words rests on a knowledge of prefixes, desinences, and the major derivational suffixes. By removing the desinence, one finds the stem. The premise that the root must be of the shape (C)VC (less often CVCVC), makes segmentation of morphemes easier. For example, *na vъzglavьnici* 'on a pillow' (Mk 4:38, Mar) obviously is Ls of *vъz<u>glav</u>ьnic-a*, made up of a prefix *vъz-*, a suffixal sequence *-ьnic-* and a root *glav*,

---

[26] The term *compound* here does not include prefixed stems like *za-kon-*, although it is obviously a lexical unit that enters into other complex stems, e.g. *vъzakoni+* 'establish as law', *bezakonova+* 'behave lawlessly'. Another kind of complex stem consists of root plus suffix, e.g. *kon-ьc-ь* 'end'; *beskonьčьnъ* 'endless', *nedokonьčaj+*.'fail to complete'.

[27] See also §24.4422 on calques.

approximately "(alongside-head-substantive)-desinence"—a transparent parallel to the Gk (προσ- κεφάλ- αι)- ον. In contrast, Zo has *na doxъtorě*, surely Ls, but of indeterminable gender. We might take *do* as a prefix, but *xъtor* remains isolated; *doxъtor-* is synchronically an indivisible unit.[28]

24.441 In Su both *štuždekrъmьnica* and *jatъxulьnica* stand for ξενοδοχεῖον 'hospice, guest-house; guest refectory'. The first is transparently *štužd-* 'alien' + *krъm-* 'feed'+ *ьnic* (suffix) + *a* (desinence), similar to Gk *ksen* 'alien/guest' + *dox* 'receive' + *ei* (suffix) + *on* (desinence). The second clearly has suffixal *-ьnic-*, but *jatъxul* is a sequence that fits no Slavic patterns. It may include two roots, or it may parallel another OCS word, *gostinica* 'inn', where the root *gost* 'guest' is followed by *-in-ic*, a complex suffix.[29]

24.4421 Many OCS compounds are simplistic calques of Greek words. Roman Palestine had regional officials called "quarter-rulers" in charge of one fourth of a larger region. The title *tetrarch* (τετραάρχης) and the verb *rule as tetrarch* (in Gs participial form, τετραρχοῦντος) occur in the gospels. The adapted loan *tetraarxъ* (Zo; *tetrarxъ* Mar) remains in Mt 14:1, but is replaced by *četvrьtovlastьcь* in L 9:7 and *četvrьtovlastьnikъ* in L 3:19; cf. *cetvrьt-ь* '1/4' and *vlast-ь* 'power, dominion'. The verb is *četvrьtovlastьstv-ujǫštu*. Mt 23:23 has the verb "you tithe" ἀπο- δεκατ- οῦτε, rendered in Mar accurately as *otъ-desęt-ьstv-uete*. (A more natural equivalent appears in L 11:42, *desętinǫ daete*, lit. 'you give a tenth'.)

24.4422 Calques are usually subject to native constraints. Thus *ljuboništь* 'loving the poor' is a calque of φιλό- πτωχ- ος, but has the dominant root first and is therefore peculiar; *ništeljubьje* converts φιλο- πτωχ- ία to the Slavic pattern. Gk *miso-* 'hate' has no single equivalent; it caused trouble: *nenavidęi člověka dьjavolъ* 'the devil who hates man' for ὁ μισάνθρωπος διάβολος, *nenavistьnikъ člověkomъ* 'misanthrope'. *nenavistije bratьnje* 'brotherly hate' and *bratoljubьstvije nenavistьnoe* 'hateful brotherly-love' and *bratiję neljubьstvo* 'brothers' not-loving' for μισαδελφία.

24.5 The list of clearly productive nominal and adjectival formants is modest. The dominant shape is VC. Front-vowel formants entail KI-palatalization of stem-final velars and *c/ʒ*. Some important suffixes begin with *j* and therefore trigger iotation (§3.6). A few begin with *t* and interact with a preceding obstruent (§3.3131).

---

[28] SS imprudently lists it sub дъхъторъ, guessing at gender and phonology.

[29] Space precludes discussion of the hierarchies of cohesion or closeness of the morphemes in various structures. Questions of the immediate constituents of stems and affixes can only be hinted at. I suggest that *gostin* is base for *gostin-ic-ǫ* (ZM L 10:34) and *gostin-ьnic-ǫ* (As); the *gospod-ǫ* of Sav represents a different lexeme, *gospoda*. The *-in-* is presumably possessive, as in *zvěrinъ* 'beast's', cf. 24.84. In L 10:35, 'host, inkeeper' is Ds *gostin-ьnik-u* in ZMA and *gost-ьnik-u* in Sav. Semantically apart is another derivative, *gostin-ьc-ь* 'highway, main street'. There is also a verb, *gost-i+* 'be host, receive guests'.

24.501 Many stems combine adjectival and substantival suffixes: thus *tьm* 'dark' underlies *tьma* 'darkness', the adjective *tьm-ьn-ъ* 'dark', *tьmьnica* 'prison', *tьm-ьnič-ьn-ъ* 'pertaining to prison', *tьmьnьničьnik-ъ* 'prisoner'. The adjective in **въ оубитєльничьскѫ пєштєрѫ** 'into the killers' cave' is an extreme example. The base is *u-bьj-* 'kill' (§15.93), with agentive *-telj-* and a seemingly redundant *-ьnik-* (§24.524 below), plus the stem-defining adjectival suffix *-ьsk-*.[30]

24.51 Suffixes may be simply a lexical component of the stems; they seem to contribute nothing to the meaning: *ot-ьc-ь* 'father', *slъn-ьc-e* 'sun', *ov-ьc-a* 'sheep', *pěs-ъk-ъ* 'sand', *braš-ьn-o* 'food'.

24.52 Stems denoting humans, male and female, often lack any marking, but many contain special suffixes. *Rabъ* m. and *raba* f. 'servant, slave' (and *sluga* m. 'servant'), for example, are minimal stems, while *rab-ynj-i* (§4.18) has a suffix that, with a root indicating person, specifies female. Female reference is often supplied by a suffix that is absent from the masculine equivalent: e.g. *prorokъ* 'prophet' ~ *proroč-**ic**-a* 'prophetess', *sǫsěd-ъ* m. ~ *sǫsěd**ynji*** 'neighbor', *vladyka* m. 'lord' ~ *vladyč**ica*** 'lady, female ruler', *otrokъ* 'boy, child, servant' ~ *otrok**ovica*** 'girl', *vratarjь* m. ~ *vratarj**ica*** f. 'gate-keeper' (cf. *vrat-a* [n. pl] 'gate, gateway'). Sometimes a masculine suffix is replaced by a feminine one: e.g. *star-**ьc**-ь* 'old man; monk' ~ *star-**ic**-a* 'old woman'; *dvьr**ьnik**ъ* m. ~ *dvьr**ьnica*** f. 'door-keeper' (cf. *dvьri* [f. i-stem pl.] 'door'), *mǫč**enik**ъ* m. ~ *mǫč**enica*** f. 'martyr'.

24.52 Many words denoting male agents are made with five suffixes: *-telj-*, *-arj-*, *-čьj-*, *-ьnik-*, and *-ьc-*.

24.521 The suffix *-telj-* signifies *human* (or divine) *actor* (about 50 examples). It is added directly to a basic verbal stem: *vlad-Ø+* 'rule' > *vlasteljь* 'ruler, lord'; *prij-aj+* 'favor' > *prijateljь* 'friend'; *sъvěd-ě+* 'witness' > *sъvěděteljь* 'witness'; *služ-i+* 'serve' > *služiteljь* 'server, servant' (*idoloslužiteljь* 'servant of idols, one who serves idols').

An extended form *-itelj-* is used with some exceptional stems: *sъpas-Ø+* 'save' ~ *sъpasiteljь* 'savior'; *zьd-a+* (§15.643) 'build' ~ *zižditeljь* 'creator'; *po-da(d)-* (§16.28) 'give' > *podateljь* and *podaditeljь* 'giver'.

---

[30] The Gk has simply Gp 'of murderers'. The translator chose not to use either of the available nouns, *ubьjьca* or *ubojьca* 'murderer' m., a-stem. *Peštera* 'cave' is nearly synonymous with *peštь* (f., i-stem), but *peštь* also means 'stove'. The suffix *-er-* is peculiar to *peštera*; it therefore makes the sense of the stem more precise; see §24.51.

Two feminine equivalents are attested: *služiteljьnica* 'servant' (cf. *raba, rabynji*) and *roditeljьnica* 'parent' (~ *rod-i+* 'beget, bear', *roditeljь* 'parent').[31]

24.522 The suffix *-arj-* (8 stems) also denotes a human actor: e.g. *rybarjь* 'fisherman' ~ *ryba* 'fish'; *grъnьčarjь* 'potter' ~ **grъnьcь* 'pot'. (The loanwords *cěsarjь* 'king' (L *caesar* 'Caesar') and *oltarjь* 'altar' are simple stems in OCS; *cěsarjica* 'queen' is obviously a new word.)

24.523 Masculine a-stems with the suffix *-čьj-* (§4.16) denote male persons (and contain non-native roots): e.g. *kъnjigъčiji* 'scribe' (= *kъnjižьnikъ,* cf. *kъnjigy* [pl tant] 'book'), *šarъčiji* 'painter' (= *šaropisateljь,* cf. *šarъ* 'color').

24.524 The suffix *-enik-ъ* or *-ьnik-ъ* is found with over 165 stems denoting male persons (and about ten with other meanings, see 24.7 below).[32]

-enik- is generally associated with a past passive participial stem (§11.23), e.g. *krъmljenikъ* 'nurseling' (cf. *krъmi+* 'feed, nurture'), *blaženikъ* 'happy man' (cf. *blaži+* 'deem happy'), *kaženikъ* 'eunuch' (cf. *kazi+* 'spoil'). Note that *ljubljenikъ* 'lover, admirer' has an active sense, while *vъzljubljenikъ* 'beloved [man]' fits the typical pattern (cf. *vъz-ljubi+* 'love').

-ьnik- generally occurs with stems that are nominal rather than verbal, but the meaning often implies actor. Thus *pobědьnikъ* 'victor' is based on *poběda* 'victory', while its synonym *poběditeljь* is associated with the verb *pobědi+* 'conquer, prevail' (cf. §24.52 above). A *pěnęžьnikъ* 'money-changer' deals with *pěnęʒь* 'money'; a *praštьnikъ* 'slinger' is presumably proficient with a **prašta* 'sling'.

24.525 The suffix *-ьc-ь* in about 25 stems based on verbal roots refers to persons: e.g. *kupьcь* 'merchant' (*kupi+* 'buy'), *tvorьcь* 'maker' (*tvori+* 'make, do'), *žьrьcь* 'priest' (*žьr-Ø-* 'sacrifice'), *skopьcь* 'eunuch' (*skopi+* [sę] 'castrate [self]'); *čьtьcь* 'reader', *bogočьtьcь* 'pious, god-honoring man' (*čьt-Ø+* 'read; honor'); *pri-šьl-ьc-ь* 'immigrant; convert' (cf. participle *prišьl-* 'arrived', §11.222). A-stems with *-ьc-a* (e.g. *sěčьca* 'executioner', cf. *u-sěk-(nǫ)+*, §15.771) may well have been feminine as well as

---

31 Some synonyms: *vladyka ~ vlasteljь, sъpasъ ~ sъpasiteljь, zьdateljь ~ sъzьdateljь ~ zižditeljь, davьcь ~ dateljь, samodrьžьcь ~ samodrьžiteljь.* There were surely differences in meaning, but we can only speculate what they were.

32 The only evidence for an independent suffix *-ik-* is Adu *zlatika* '[two] gold-pieces' (Su 145.25). It is vitiated by the fact that *zlatica* occurs 11 times in the same meaning in the same text. Compare *sьrebrьnikъ* '(silver) coin, money' and *mědьnica* '(bronze) coin'.

masculine; some of them may have had a pejorative sense (as they do today).

24.5251 Compounds are not always felicitous: *Rod-o-tvor-ьc-ь* 'creator [of generation, origin]' in Wisdom 13:5 (Su 534.4) mimics γενεσιουργός; English translators overlook the first root. *Samodrьžьcь* (and *samodrьžiteljь*) 'autocrat' (cf. *drьž-ě+* 'hold, rule'—calques involving the Greek root *krat*) fit OCS patterns well, but *samo-vlast-ьc-ь* (like *četvrьtovlastьcь*) contains the substantive-stem *vlast-ь* 'dominion'.

24.526 Stems with the suffix *-ěn-* or *-jan-* (usually in plural, Np *-e*) signify a group of human beings, see §4.53. The singulative *-in-* emphasizes the individual: e.g. *krьstьjaninъ* = *krьstьjanъ* 'Christian': e.g. *vojinъ* 'soldier' ~ *voji* pl (rarely *vojini*) 'army'.

24.53 Female persons (or divinities) may be designated by suffixes that also occur with non-personal senses:

-ynj-i (§4.18): e.g. *bogynji* 'goddess' (cf. *bogъ* 'god'), *solunjanynji* 'Thessalonian' (*solunъ* 'Saloniki', cf. *solunjane* 'Thessalonians'); *magdalynji* 'Magdalene, woman of Magdala'.

-ic-a occurs in about 100 stems, only 24 of which denote female humans. Eight in *-n-ic-* have corresponding masculines, e.g. *učenica* 'pupil, disciple' ~ *učenikъ*; *plěnьnica* 'captive' ~ *plěnьnikъ*. But while *starica* means 'old woman' (cf. above), *junica* means 'heifer, young cow' (cf. *junъ* 'young', *junьcь* 'young bull') and *črьnica*—transparently based on the adjectival root *črьn-* 'black'—is (1) 'monastery' or (2) 'mulberry tree'. See also §24.7 below.

24.6 Young males may be indicated by *-išt-ь*, : e.g. *mladeništь* 'baby boy' (~ *mladenьcь* ~ *mladętьce* neut.), *kozьlištь* 'kid' (= *kozьlę*, cf. *kozьlъ* 'goat'), *pъtištь* 'baby bird' (cf. *pъtica* 'bird' [apparently without differentiation of sex]).[33] Less specific is *-ęt-*, e.g. *agnę* 'lamb' (~ *agnьcь* or *jagnьcь*), see §4.414–415.

24.7 The chief suffixes in nouns that denote objects, acts, and abstractions are: with masculine gender, *-ьnik-*, *-ьc-* (15), *-ъk-ъ* (17); with feminine gender, *-ynj-i, -ic-a, -ьnic-a*; *-ost/-est-ь* (45), *-ot/et-a, -ьb-a* (14), *-tv-a* (10), *-in-a* (30); with neuter gender, *-ьc-e* (8), *-ьj-e* (45 + 730 *-nьj-e*), *-ьstv-o, -išt-e* (30), *-l-o* (25). The suffix *-j-* (which entails KI or iotation, §3.6) is used in a few masculines and neuters and more than 30 feminines. Some examples:

-ьnik-: *svěštьnikъ* 'candle-holder' (= *svěštilo*), cf. *světъ* 'light'; *vъtorьnikъ* 'Tuesday' (*vъtorъ* 'second'); *sъrebrьnikъ* 'coin' (*sъrebro* 'silver')

---

[33] Su 513.2 младеньци ıако и птишти corresponds to the Gk 'the young of sparrows'.

-ьc-ь: diminutive/hypocoristic: *odrьcь* (*odrъ* 'bed, pallet'), *kovьčežьcь* (*kovьčegъ* 'box, ark'); other: *studenьcь* 'spring, source' (*stud-en-ъ* 'cold').

-ъk-: *pribytъkъ* 'profit, gain' (*pri-by-ti* 'arrive, be successful')

-ynj-i *pustynji* 'desert' (*pustъ* 'empty'), *grъdynji* 'arrogance' (*grъdъ* 'proud')

-ic-a: *šujica* 'left hand' (*šujь* 'left'), *mantijica* 'cloak' (**mantija* 'mantle')

-ьnic-a: *košьnica* 'basket' (= *košь* m.); *dvьrьnicę* [plur tantum] 'door'

-ost-ь: *jarostь* 'fury' (*jarъ* 'furious'), *dobrostь* 'goodness' (= *dobrota*, cf. *dobrъ* 'good'), *bujestь* 'stupidity' (= *bujьstvo*, cf. *bujь* 'foolish'),

-ot-a: *pravota* 'justness, justice' (= *pravostь* = *pravynji* = *pravьda*), *sujeta* 'emptiness, vanity' (*sujь* 'vain')

-ьb-a: *svętьba* 'consecration' (*svęti+* 'consecrate'), *alčьba* 'hunger, fasting' (*alk-a+* 'hunger'), *tatьba* 'theft' (= *tatьbina*, cf. *tatь* m. 'thief')

-tv-a: *žętva* 'harvest' (*žьnj-Ø+* 'harvest' §15.83), *molitva* 'prayer' (cf. *molьba* 'petition'; *moli+* 'pray, request')

-in-a: *desętina* '1/10' (*desętь* 'ten'), *konьčina* 'end' (= *konьcь*, *konьčanьje*, *sъkonьčanьje*), *maslina* 'olive' (*maslo* '[olive] oil'), *xramina* 'house, building, dwelling' (=*xramъ*), *udavljenina* 'meat of strangled animal' (*u-dav-i+* 'strangle')[34]

-ьc-e: diminutive/hypocoristic, e.g. *čędьce* ~ *čędo* 'child', *iměnijьce* ~ *iměnьe* 'property'; shifted meaning, *plesno* 'sole' ~ *plesnьce* 'sandal'

-ьj-e: abstracts; *veselьje* 'joy' (*veselъ* 'joyful'), *obilьje* 'abundance' (*obilъ* 'abundant'), *mil-o-srьd-ъ* 'merciful' (*milosrьdьje* 'mercy'); noun from phrase, *podъgorьje* 'foothills' (cf. *podъ gorami* 'below the mountains'), *bezumьje* 'foolishness' (cf. *bez uma* 'without mind'); collectives *trupьje* 'corpses' (*trupъ*, see §4.1022).

-ьstv-ьj-e is semantically equivalent to -*ьstv-o*, e.g. *veličьstvo* = *veličьstvьje* 'greatness' (=*veličьje*, cf. *velikъ* 'great'), *cěsarьstvo* = *cěsarьstvьje* 'kingdom' (*cěsarjь* 'king'), *otьčьstvo* 'fatherland' = *otьčьstvьje* (= *otьčina*, cf. *otьcь* 'father').

---

34 This word is part of the religious code inherited from the Old Testament. Although OCS has no other example, we can be certain that -*ina* 'meat of' could be used with the name of any animal, e.g. *telętina* 'veal', *konjina* 'horse meat'; it is a productive suffix in most modern Slavic dialects. The *Izbornik* of 1073 has *kъlpina* probably 'swan meat'.

-*ьstv-o*: *světьlьstvo* 'brightness' = *světьlostъ* = *světьlota* (*světьlъ* 'bright'; *světъ* 'light'); *besъmrьtьstvo* 'immortality' (= *besъmrьtьje*, cf. *bez* without', *sъmrьtь* 'death'); *episkupьstvo* 'bishopric, office of bishop' (*episkupъ* 'bishop')

-*išt-e*: place, *sъnьmište* 'synagogue, sanhedrin' (*sъn-ьm-Ø+* 'gather together'), *pristanište* 'harbor, haven' (*pri-sta*[*n*]- 'arrive' §15.712), *blǫdilište* 'brothel' (cf. *blǫdьnica* 'prostitute')

-*j-ь*: *voždь* 'leader, guide' (= *vod-i-* 'lead'), *plačь* 'weeping' (*plak-a-* 'weep'),

-*j-e*: *ǫže* 'rope, bond' (*ǫza* 'bond, fetter'; *ǫz-ъk-ъ* 'tighty, narrow')

-*j-a*: *volja* 'wish' (*vol-i+* 'wish'; vel-*ě*+ 'command', *lъža* 'lie' (*lъga+* 'lie'), *duša* 'soul' (*duxъ* 'spirit, breath'), *svěšta* 'candle, lamp', *mežda* 'boundary' (see §26.21, n. 8).
prědъteča 'forerunner' (tek-Ø+ 'run')

-*l-o*: *počrьpalo* 'dipper' (= *počrьpalьnikъ*; {čьrp} §15.643); *svętilo* 'sanctuary' (= *svętilište*; *svętъ* 'holy'); *světilo* 'lamp, light' (*světi+* 'illuminate'); *kadilo* 'incense' (*kadi+* 'burn incense')

24.8 Adjectival root-stems (e.g. *pustъ* 'empty', *šujь* 'left', *veselъ* 'glad') number about 130. Most stems end in one of ten suffixes: -*ьn*- (about 750), -*ьsk*- (80+), -*ěn*- (about 12), -*iv*- (170+), -*it*- (about 15), -*av*- (5); -*ьnj*- (with adverbial bases, 35+); and possessives with -*in*- (about 12), -*j*-, -*ov*- (25+) and -*ьnj*- (with proper names).

24.81 The suffix -*ьsk*- in principle means 'characteristic of' as opposed to the very general -*ьn*- 'pertaining to': *gradьscii mǫži* 'the men of/from the town' ~ *gradьnyę stěny* 'the walls [that are part] of the town'. In practice, the two may become synonymous. Thus *nebesьskъ*, referring to *nebesa* 'heavens', is exclusive in Zo and Mar, but only *nebesьnъ* is in As, while Sav has both.[35] Both formants are used with borrowed stems, e.g. *aerъ* ~ *aerьnъ* 'air' (cf. *vъzduxъ* ~ *vъzdušьnъ* 'air), *mъnixъ* 'monk' ~ *mъnišьskъ* (cf. *črьnьcь* 'monk' ~ *črьnьčskъ*).[36] A compound suffix -*ovьn*-/ -*evьn*- seems to have about the same meaning, e.g. *duša* 'soul' ~ *duševьnъ*, *duxъ* 'spirit' ~ *duxovьnъ*, *věra* 'faith' ~ *věrovьnъ* 'of faith' and *věrьnъ* 'faithful'. Similarly, *adovьskъ*, *adovьnъ*, and *adьskъ* all mean 'of hell' (cf. *adъ* 'hell, Hades'). In many instances, ьsk-forms function as possessives.

---

35 SS defines both OCS words as "небесный, nebeský", that is -*ьn*- has survived in R., -*sk*- in Cz.

36 *Mъnixъ* must represent an adaptation of a Germanic form **munīx*-, cf. mod. *Mönch*.

24.82 The suffix *-ěn-* means 'made of' the material denoted by the base; *-it-* usually signifies 'characterized by'; *-iv-* and *-av-* may be somewhat emphatic. Some examples:

-ěn-: *lьněnъ* 'linen' (**lьnъ* 'linen'); *měděnъ* 'bronze' (= *mědьnъ*; *mědь* 'bronze'); *trьněnъ* 'of thorns' (= *trьnovъ*; *trьnъ* 'thorn'); *moždanъ* 'of marrow' (**mozgъ* 'marrow; brain')

-it-: *mъnogoočitъ* 'many-eyed' (*mъnog-* 'many', *ok-o* 'eye'), *znamenitъ, imenitъ* 'famous' (*znamenьje* 'mark, sign, signal'; **jьmę* 'name'); *plodovitъ* 'fruitful' (*plodъ* 'fruit'; cf. also *mъnogoplodьnъ*)

-iv-: *nedǫživъ* 'unwell, sick' = *nedǫžьnъ* (cf. *nedǫgъ* 'ailment') *pravьdivъ* 'just' = *pravьdьnъ* (cf. *pravъ* 'straight, authentic, just')

-liv-: *mlьčalivъ* 'silent, quiet' (= *mlьčalьnъ*, cf. *mlьk-ě+* 'be silent')

-ьliv-: *nerazumьlivъ* 'unintelligent' (= *nerazumivъ, nerazumičьnъ, nerazumьničьnъ*; cf. *razumъ* 'understanding')

-av-: *lǫkavъ* 'crooked, foul, deceitful' (= *lǫkavьnъ*, cf. *lǫka* 'deceit, trickery'); *sědinavъ* 'grey-haired' (= *sědъ*, cf. *sědiny* f pl 'grey hair')

24.83 The formant *-(šь)nj-* makes adverbs into adjectives; there are often variants, presumably from regional dialects: *iskrьnjьjь* or *bližьnjьjь* 'nearby, closest (one's neighbor)' (*iskrь* 'close'; *bliže* 'closer'), *domašьnjьjь* and *domaštьnjьjь* 'domestic' (*doma* 'at home'), *nynjašьnjьjь* and *nynjaštьnjьjь* 'contemporary' (*nynja* 'now'). These adjectives are usually definite in form.

24.84 Possessive suffixes are widely used: *-j-* (*-ij-* with monosyllabic stems) and *-ov-* go with twofold o-stems, *-in-* with most other stems, and *-nj-* largely with kinship terms:

-ov- *jugovъ* 'of the south wind'(*jugъ* 'south, south wind'; *južьskъ* 'of the south'), *kitovъ* (*kitъ* 'whale'), *ženixovъ* (*ženixъ* 'bridegroom'), *sъpasovъ* and *sъpasiteljevъ* (*sъpasъ, sъpasitelјь* 'savior'), *zmьjevъ* (*zmьjь* 'dragon'); *cěsarjevъ* 'royal, of kings; imperial, of emperors' = *cěsarjь* = *cěsarjьskъ*; *pilatovъ* and *pilaštь* (*pilaštaja* 'Pilate's wife';[37] *pilatъ* 'Pilate')

-ij- *lьvijь* 'of the lions', *lьvovъ* 'of the lion', *lьvьskъ* 'leonine'; *kravьjь* (**krava* 'cow'); *rabijь* 'slavish, servile' (= *rabьskъ, rabъ* 'slave')

---

[37] The long femine possive adjective from a man's name denotes his wife; this is the only example in OCS, but the usage is securely attested in early Rus'.

-j-: *ovьnjь* (*ovьnъ* 'ram'), *ovьčь* (*ovьca* 'sheep'), *aveljь*(*avelъ* 'Abel'), *igumenjь* (*igumenъ* 'hegumen, abbot'), *inorožь* (*inorogъ* 'unicorn'), *solomonjь* = *solomonovъ* (solomonъ 'Solomon')

-nj-: *gospodьnjь, vladyčьnjь* (*gospodь, vladyka* 'lord'), *družьnjьjь* (*drugъ* 'friend'), *větrьnjь* (*větrъ* 'wind')

-in-: *julijaninъ* (*julijana* 'Juliana'), *bogorodičinъ* (*bogorodica* 'theotokos, mother of god'), *zmьjinъ* (*zmьja* 'serpent'), *igъlinъ* (*igъla* 'needle'), *neprijazninъ* (*neprijaznь* 'enemy'), *sotoninъ* devil's (*sotoninьskъ* 'devilish'; *sotona* 'Satan'); *osьlętinъ* (*osьlę* 'kid')

24.9 A number of important nouns contain the unproductive suffix *-t-ь* (fem. i-stem): *vlastь* 'rule, domain' (~ *oblastь*; *vlad-Ø+* 'rule'); *slastь* 'pleasure, luxury' (*sladъkъ* 'sweet'); *věstь* 'news' (*věd-ě-ti* 'know'); *pověstь* 'story, tale' (*pověd-ě-ti* 'recount'); *sъmrьtь* 'death' (*mьr-ǫtъ* 'die')[38], *nenavistь* 'hate' (= *nenavistьje, nenaviděnьje*; *nenaviDě+* 'to hate'), *zavistь* 'envy' (= *zavida, zavistь*; *zavidě+* 'envy'), *čьstь* 'honor' (*čьt-* 'to regard, honor'); *peštь* 'stove; cave'; *noštь* 'night'; *pomoštь* 'help' (*pomog-Ø+* 'to help'); *zabytь* 'oblivion (= *zabytьje*; *zaby-ti* 'forget').

[38] The prefix *sъ* here is not 'with; down from' (IE **sun*, §29.815) but IE h_1*su-* 'good' (cf. Gk **esu-* > *eu-* εὐ, e.g. in εὐαγγέλιον 'good message, gospel'). It survives in a few Sl stems, including **sъ-dorw-* 'healthy', OCS *sъdravъ*; **sъ-ręt-j-a* 'encounter; fate', OCS *sъręšta* 'meeting' (cf. §16.7, 45.11), **sъ-čęst-* 'good part', *OCS *sъčęstьje* 'happiness'.

CHAPTER SIX

A SKETCH HISTORY: FROM LATE INDO-EUROPEAN TO LATE COMMON SLAVIC

INDO-EUROPEAN AND SLAVIC

25.0 Indo-European is the name given to a large genetic family that includes most of the languages of Europe and extends across Iran and Afghanistan to the northern half of the Indian subcontinent. The earliest documentation is for Anatolian, in central Turkey, where Hittite writings of perhaps 1700–1200 BCE have survived. Indo-Iranian is known from Sanskrit texts (the oldest probably composed from c1500 BCE but written down much later), and from Avestan and Old Persian of somewhat later date. Armenian has been written since the fifth century CE. The oldest surviving Greek, from Crete and the Mycenean mainland, dates to about 1200 BCE, and from about 800 there is a continuous record. Old Latin, with some closely related dialects, is datable to the sixth century BCE. Celtic was widely spoken in Europe during the first millennium BCE, while Germanic is not known before about 250 CE.[1] The common ancestral language must be assigned a date no later than 3500 BCE—more likely considerably earlier.

25.1 Slavic is not documented before the activities of Cyril and Methodius (cf. §0.1), starting after 860. At that time, Slavic groups were surely in contact with speakers of varieties of several IE subdivisions: Baltic in the northwest, Germanic in the west (roughly in a broad frontier zone that

---

[1] For an authoritative sketch, see Calvert Watkins, "Proto-Indo-European", in Ramat, Anna Giacalone, and Paolo Ramat, *The Indo-European Languages*, London-NY, 1998, pp. 25-73. In that same volume (pp. 415–53) Henning Andersen provides a more traditional account of Slavic. See also Baldur Panzer, *Die slavischen Sprachen in Gegenwart und Geschichte; Sprachstrukturen und Verwandtschaft*. (= Heidelberger Publikationen zur Slavistik A. Linguistische Reihe, Band 3.) Frankfurt-Bern-NY-Paris 1991.

extended from the Danish peninsula nearly to the Adriatic), Romance along the Adriatic littoral and in many internal regions (probably in mountains from Croatia through Bosnia into Serbia and Macedonia eastward through Bulgaria to Rumania), Albanian (in the extreme southwest—present-day Montenegro, Macedonia and Albania), and Greek. Information about the inhabitants of most of the Balkans and eastern Europe from 600 until about 1100 is far too skimpy to provide a history of the movements of groups speaking these different language-types.[2]

25.2 The hypothetical homeland of the Indo-Europeans, in the current view of many specialists, was north of the Black and Caspian Seas, in an area from which it was easy to move eastward over the steppes, westward into central Europe, or southward to Greece. Roughly the same general area, perhaps extending westward from the middle Dniepr to the headwaters of the Bug and Dniestr, is favored by many scholars as the "cradle" of the Slavs. There is no tangible evidence whatsoever for these theories, attractive and plausible as they may seem; they are working hypotheses, based on complex assumptions and corollaries that must be accepted on faith.

25.3 The very existence of Slavs is uncertain until near 600 CE, when a new wave of invaders appeared from the east and north and devastated southeastern and central Europe. Contemporary observers call some of these hitherto unknown intruders Slavs—a wholly new designation. This fits the linguistic evidence; the sixth-century Slavs are a nascent ethnos with a newly consolidated language.

25.4 OCS permits us to posit a **Late Common Slavic** dialect continuum that existed c800–c1100 (*LCoS*). As we shall see, internal reconstruction and outside comparisons (chiefly with Baltic) imply a **Middle Common Slavic** system that is virtually without dialects (*MCoS*), and an **Early Common Slavic**, whose origin can be no earlier than about 300 C.E. (*ECoS*). A Pre-Slavic and a Pre-Baltic *état de langue* may be posited as subdivisions of a variegated dialect continuum of late Indo-European that

---

[2] The oldest recorded (very brief) texts of Albanian date from the mid-fifteenth century; its connection with remnants of earlier Balkan languages such as Illyrian to the northwest or Dacian and/or Mysian to the east must remain in the realm of speculation. In any case, Albanian must be deemed a special branch of IE. The division of continental Balkan Romance into western Arumanian (still spoken in parts of Macedonia and Greece) and eastern (Daco-)Rumanian, the dialects underlying standard Rumanian, appears to be no older than the tenth century. Dalmatian, on the Adriatic coast, survived till the 1890s.

might be called **Pre-Balto-Slavic** (*PBS*). This leaves us with some 4000 years between the epoch when a community spoke Indo-European and the demonstrable appearance of Slavic. This is the temporal distance between the oldest Latin and the variegated dialects of contemporary Rumanian, Portuguese, French, and the other Romance languages. Surely the linguistic systems that eventually evolved into Slavic underwent many metamorphoses, but we must admit that we lack the evidence to validate any theories. What is clear is that the reconstructible Slavic of the mid-ninth century indeed is Indo-European, distinct from its nearest cousins, the Baltic dialects of Lithuanian and Latvian.[3]

25.5 For the last nine or ten centuries the Slavs have been settled in the same general areas they now occupy (discounting the eastward expansion of Russia). The western frontiers with Germans have moved repeatedly, so that the Sorbs have been isolated from their Slavic neighbors to the south and east, and the northwesternmost group, the Polabians, have disappeared. The Pomeranians of the Baltic coast for the most part became Germanized, and the surviving communities speak highly Polonized dialects called Kashubian. Today's West Slavs have five standard languages: Upper and Lower Sorbian, Polish, Czech, and Slovak. The East Slavs have three standard languages: Ukrainian, Belarusian and Russian, which are fairly closely related. From the 11th to 14th centuries, the northern rim dialects (Pskov-Novgorod) were notably deviant in many features from their more southerly neighbors, but these communities were dispersed in the 15th century. The North Slavs (West and East) have long been separated from their southern Slavic kin by a broad zone occupied by speakers of German (in Austria), Hungarian, and Rumanian (including the Moldavians who now have abandoned attempts at maintaining a separate standard language).

25.6 The Eastern South Slavs have two standard languages, Bulgarian and Macedonian. The Western South Slavs recently had two standards, Slovenian and Serbo-Croatian. On purely linguistic grounds (phonology, morphology, syntax, derivational processes) the dialects of Croatia, Bosnia, Montenegro, and Serbia can be viewed as one—I will do so and will use the term Serbo-Croatian, with apologies to anyone who might

---

[3] Apart from isolated words and a few sentences, Baltic is not documented before c1550. Old Prussian is known essentially from Protestant catechisms translated from German; it died out not long after 1600. Lithuanian and Latvian represent two branches of a dialect continuum called East Baltic.

consider it inappropriate. As of early 2001 there are certainly two standards, Croatian and Serbian, and strenuous efforts to establish a third, Bosnian. The geographical positions are approximately as in the chart (non-Slavic neighbors printed in italics).

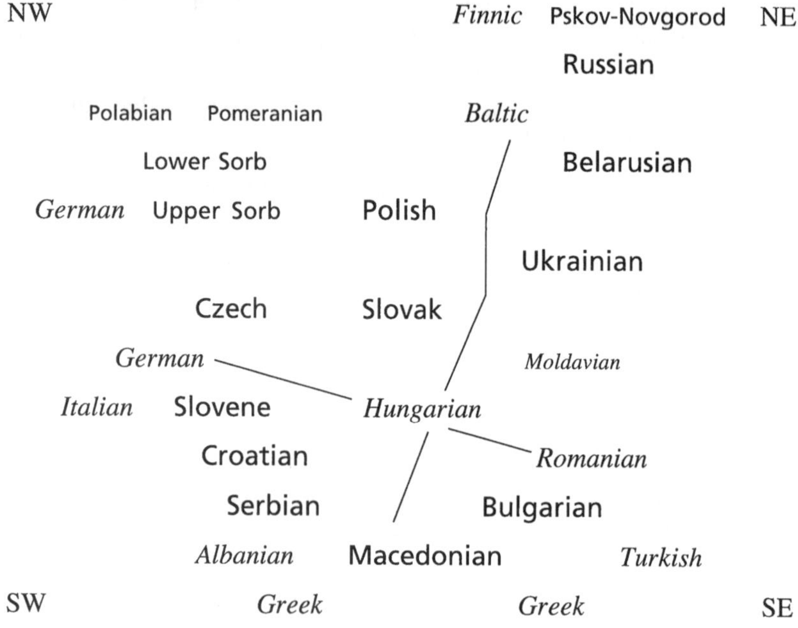

25.7 I hold that the Late Common Slavic of c1000 CE had four regional variants or macrodialects: NorthWest, SouthWest, SouthEast, NorthEast. Rapid local differentiation took place as social conditions changed radically. In the NorthWest, change was particularly significant; by c1150 important features of the Polish and Czech-Slovak regional dialects were clearly different from each other and both were sharply set apart from East Slavic, which was still a single language, with the weakest of local variations. I call the common (North-) East Slavic language (up to the first half of the 14th century) Rusian. Despite its physical distance from the SouthEast or Bulgarian dialects, it still had much in common with them. The boundaries separating the SE and SW (eventually Macedonian vs. Serbian) were relatively weak. The differentiation into regional dialects and then standard languages is extremely complex; this table is a grossly simplified outline:

1000	NW	SW	SE	NE
1100	Cz-Slk ~ Pol	kaj~ča~ čto	west ~ east	Rusian
1200	Cz-Slk ~ Pol	west kaj ~ east kaj ~ ča~ čto	west ~ east	Rusian
1500	Cz ~ Slk ~ Pol	Sln ~ SC	Mac ~ Bg	R/BR ~ Ukr
1700	Cz ~ Slk ~ Pol	Sln ~ SC	Mac ~ Bg	R ~ BR ~ Ukr

Documentation is uneven. For Rus', a standard based on OCS was used until after 1600; despite regional and temporal variants that indicate some local developments, the standard spelling systems obscure important details. Texts in Czech have survived from before 1300; by 1400 there was a flourishing literature. Polish texts begin from the mid-14th century, and show heavy Czech influence. Slovak writing is uncommon until about 1450, when long documents begin to appear. The earliest datable written Slavic, the Freising texts, represent Alpine dialects (cf. §1.04), yet Slovene is essentially unwritten until the Protestant movement; from about 1550 on there is a steady stream of translations and original works. Slovenia and northern Croatia shared many important features, constituting what may be called the "kaj-dialect"; later on, the kaj-zone in Croatia was attracted more to its eastern neighbor, the "što-dialect". The northeastern Adriatic coast and adjacent islands developed a "ča-dialect" that was the basis of inscriptions and documents from the late 12th century on. Documents from Bosnia and the nearby Adriatic coast of the same early period, as well as from Serbia, provide fundamental (if incomplete) information about the što-dialect. (The names of SC dialects are based on variant reflexes of IE *k^{w}id* 'what?' [OCS *čьto*], see §38.21.)

*

26.0 A comprehensive history of a language compares a particular linguistic system with one or more prior stages of the same system and attempts to account for the differences. Morphophonemic alternations play an important role in OCS, and their genesis and evolution are part of the history of the phonology. Synchronic alternations may imply historical phonetic changes. Observing that *klьnǫtъ* 'they swear' has an infinitive *klęti,* and that the genitive *sěmene* 'of a seed' goes with a NA *sěmę,* we formulate a generalization that a sequence *front vowel* + *nasal* before vowel is replaced by *ę* before consonant (cf. §3.313, 4.415). The background knowledge that a nasal consonant between a vowel and a consonant often (in languages all over the world) becomes non-consonantal and merges with the vowel allows us to hypothesize that at an older stage of the language the forms **klьnti* and **sěmen* could have existed. This latter form looks startlingly like the Latin word for 'seed': *sēmen*. This *internal reconstruction* of a hypothetical earlier form is confirmed by *external comparison* with the Latin cognate (and patterns of relationship established by many other examples): **sēmen* (with a zero NA desinence) 'seed' is indeed to be posited for early Slavic as well as for some earlier stages of Indo-European. A root **klin* is thoroughly plausible for early Slavic, but its exact meaning and its affinities with words in other languages is not so clear.

26.01 Internal reconstruction and careful comparisons of thousands of words with all sorts of Indo-European sources, most importantly Baltic, have established rules that allow us to convert attested OCS words to earlier shapes—first of all Middle Common Slavic.

26.1 Let us define some phonological terms. The dialects we need to consider have consonant systems determined by four points of articulation: labial, dental, palatal, and velar.[4] *Labial* means "articulated with the lips (or upper lip and lower front teeth)" or, in terms of distinctive features, /+labial/ (*p b f v m*). *Velar* is "articulated with the back of the tongue" /-labial -coronal/ (*k g x γ*). *Dental* is "articulated with the tip of the tongue" /+coronal + anterior/ (*t d s z n l r*). *Palatal* is "articulated with the middle part of the tongue" /+coronal -anterior/ (*ḱ ǵ ś ź ń ĺ ŕ*). The sibilants may further be "hushing" /+high +back/ (*š ž*) as opposed to the "hissing" dentals and palatals (*s z* ; *ś ź*). In addition, we distinguish three sets of affricates, hissing dental *c ʒ* ~ hushing *č ǯ* ~ (hissing) palatal *ć ʒ́*.[5]

26.11 Note that this inventory involves *simple segments*. OCS provides no reason for assuming *compound segments* of the type well known from Russian "palatalized consonants" which are produced by means of two simultaneous articulations (see *IJSLP* 41: 52). The appearance of this sort of "palatalization" surely developed as the jer-shift ran its course; it belongs to the nascent regional dialects of North Late Common Slavic (and perhaps eastern Bulgaria).

26.12 The term *palatalization* is used in confusing ways by Slavists.[6] Here we attempt to use it (1) as a synonym of the synchronic descriptive term *substitutive softening*, and (2) as the historical process (or processes) whereby a consonant changed articulation from non-palatal (velar or dental) to palatal, e.g. *t* or *k* is replaced by *ḱ* or *č*. It may also include a further step whereby the palatal articulation shifts to non-palatal (usually dental); thus the historical development "*k* > *c*" may be referred to as palatalization. This kind of shift of articulation from non-palatal to palatal usually takes place in the environment of a front vowel, particularly a high front vowel, or the front glide *j*.

Evidence from languages of many types demonstrates that palatalization of non-labial stops starts with a shift of articulation from velar (*k/g*)

---

4 The retroflex or domal consonants of the Indian subcontinent, the glottalized consonants of the Caucasus, and the uvulars or pharyngeals of Semitic are irrelevant to our discussion.

5 Labial and velar affricates (*pf kx*) are foreign to most Slavic, and the distinction between tongue-tip dental versus alveolar articulation is phonologically irrevelant.

6 Terms like "distinctive feature of palatality" or "palatal correlation" are meaningless without explicit definition in articulatory and/or acoustic terms.

or tongue-tip (*t/d*) to mid-dorsal (i.e. palatal) position, *k/t* > *ḱ*, *g/d* > *ǵ*. Palatal stops are prone to develop a sibilant offglide, thereby becoming affricates; the articulation may shift either toward "hissing" *s* or toward "hushing" *š*, so the affricates are *c* [t^{s}] or *č* [$t^{š}$] (voiced *z ž ʒ ǯ*). The affricates may then lose the initial closure and become sibilants, *s* or *š*, *z* or *ž*. A sibilant that precedes the stop adapts to the articulation of the stop; an affricate may become a simple stop after a sibilant.

	c > s			sc > st
k/t > **ḱ** >	ć > ś		sk/st > **śḱ** > ść >	śś > ś
	č > š			šč > sḱ/št
	ʒ > z			zʒ > zd
g/d > **ǵ** >	ʒ́ > ź		zg/zd > **źǵ** > źʒ́ >	źź > ź
	ǯ > ž			žǯ > žǵ/žd

The intermediate stages may last for generations, but observations of change in progress have shown that *k* and *č* or *c* (or even *š* or *s*) may be variants in the speech of individuals—in effect the whole process takes place at once. The voiced affricates ʒ, ʒ́, and ǯ readily become continuants (*z*, *ź*, *ž*), while their voiceless counterparts tend to remain (*c*, *ć*, *č*). The three-way contrast *c* ~ *ć* ~ *č* may persist, but it seems to be unstable, and *ć* easily merges with *č*.

26.13 In *iotation,* triggered by a post-consonantal *j*, the iod ordinarily fuses immediately with the palatal consonant: *kj/tj* > *ḱ* (which may immediately become *c* or *č*). This process too is found in diverse languages all over the world.[7] A less common but nonetheless widespread alternate is a geminate stop, *ḱḱ/ǵǵ*. Depending on the language, the geminate may simplify and participate in the processes outlined above, or it may remain. A final possibility is that the *j* becomes a spirant *ś* or *š* and fuses with the stop as an affricate.

26.21 Iotation in OCS is productive; it operates in conjugation and word-formation. The underlying *j* is a theoretical morphophoneme that never appears in surface forms; its presence is deduced from consonantal alternations. Thus, for example, infinitive and past passive participial stems contrast according to formulas CV ~ CjV: *nositi* ~ *nošenъ* 'carry', *svętiti* ~ *svęštenъ* 'sanctify', *čistiti* ~ *čištenъ* 'cleanse', *sǫditi* ~ *sǫždenъ* 'judge', *prigvozditi* ~ *prigvoždenъ* 'nail'. The participial stems correspond

---

[7] Compare the informal and/or rapid pronunciation of English *can't you, won't you, did you, would you*; trisyllabic *Indian* versus disyllabic "Injun".

to underlying {nos-j-en-, swęt-j-en-, čist-j-en-, -gwozd-j-en-}—in traditional notation **sj, *tj, *stj,* and **zdj*. The standard examples for **tj/*dj* are the derived nouns {swět-j-a} 'light, candle, lamp' and {med-j-a} 'median, frontier, boundary-marker': OCS **свѣща, межда.**[8]

26.22 A minor morphophonemic rule of OCS converts {gt kt} to *št*, §15.85. The historical sequence was approximately **kt* (> **k̑t*) > **jt* followed by the same assimilative processes that took place with the more frequent **tj* combination. See §26.13.

26.23 The two-unit *št* and *žd* that represent **tj/*dj* are distinctive for SE LCoS. It is only in Bulgaria and Macedonia that the *j* did not fuse with the preceding *t/d*, but produced geminates **k̑k̑/*ǵǵ* that became **śk̑/*źǵ* and (to fit the constraint that the first of two obstruents must be a sibilant, §2.522) presumably **šč/žǯ*. For other MCoS dialects we may posit **k̑/*ǵ*. Only SE LCoS, therefore, has the same reflexes for **tj, *stj,* and **skj* (which always = **sk* before front vowel).

26.3 The consonant inventory of MCoS is nearly identical with that of OCS (§2.12); the cover symbols "**tj *dj*" mean SE dialect **k̑k̑/*ǵǵ* versus **k̑/*ǵ* in other regions.

p	b	t	d	c	ʒ	č	ǯ	**tj*	**dj*	k	g	m	n	l	r	w	j
		s	z			š	ž			x			nj	lj	rj		

26.4 Rusian surely had *č/ž* for **tj/*dj,* but the written language retained the OCS spellings in most instances, so that citable ER examples are rare. Early Western South Slavic (= SouthWestern LCoS), the ancestor of Slovene and Serbo-Croatian, had palatal stops **k̑/*ǵ,* except that in the west **ǵ* > **j* (cf. Sln and Cr. dial. *meja* < **medja*). Early Czech seems to have had **ć/*ź*. Polish and Slovak presumably had **ć/*ʒ́*.

The majority of examples are from inflection or word-formation:

OCS	svę**št**enъ	ro**žd**enъ	lju**št**e	xu**žd**e	gra**žd**aninъ
MCoS	*swę**tj**enъ	*ro**dj**enъ	*lju**tj**e	*xu**dj**e	*gor**dj**aninъ
ER	*svę**č**enъ	ro**ž**enъ	*lju**č**e	xu**ž**e	*goro**ž**aninъ

---

[8] These two words are to be found in nearly all of the hundreds of Slavic dialects that have been even partially described, but formal etymological identity does not guarantee that the meaning will be the same. OCS *mežda* occurs only once in the canonical mss, Su 397.12, where it renders a Greek word meaning 'lane, side-street'. The preposition *meždu* 'between' is etymologically **medju,* a dual locative "on the two boundaries". It (or an alternate Ls **medji*) is often attested in dialects where the base noun is unknown.

EWSS	*svę**ḱ**enъ	*ro**ǵ**enъ	*lju**ḱ**e	*xu**ǵ**e	*gra**ǵ**aninъ
ECz	*sve**ć**enъ	*ro**ź**enъ	*lju**ć**e	*xu**ź**e	*gra**ź**aninъ
	'sanctified'	'born'	'fiercer'	'worse'	'townsman'

Compare *svęt-i+* 'sanctify', *rod-i+* 'bear', *ljutъ* 'fierce', *xudъ* 'thin, poor', **gordъ* 'town'.

26.41 MCoS **tj* is also posited where **kt* is indicated by morphological or comparative evidence: **petji* 'to bake' {pek-ti} > OCS *peštь,* ER *pečь*; **motji* 'to be able' {mog-ti} > *mošti/moči*; **notjь* 'night' [Latin Gs *noctis*] > *noštь/nočь*; **dъtji* 'daughter' [< **dukti* < **dugtēr*] > OCS *dъšti,* ER *dъči.*

26.51 A salient difference between hypothetical Middle Common Slavic and attested OCS and Rusian (SE and NE LCoS) lies not in the phonological inventory, but in the distribution of units—in particular the liquids (*l, r*) in contact with the lax vowels (*ь ъ e o*) and the tense low vowels *ě* and *a*. Rusian consistently writes "neutral" jers before *r* and *l* (v**ьr**xъ 'crest', g**ъr**dъ 'proud', x**ъl**mъ 'hill', and v**ъlk**ъ [for MCoS *w**ьlk**ъ] 'wolf'), cf. §2.631. This direct evidence for four *liquid diphthongs* with jers as the first member is supplemented by indirect evidence for four more with *e* or *o*. If "t" stands for any consonant, MCoS **tert, *telt, *tort, *tolt* > OCS *trět, tlět, trat, tlat.* The lax vowel has become tense, and the order of elements has been reversed. In Rusian, there is neither tensing nor metathesis. Instead, the vowel is repeated after the liquid: *teret, torot,* and *tolot* (for **el* **ьl* had previously backed to **ol* **ъl*). This East Sl process is called *pleophony* or *polnoglasie*. For example:

	'bank'	'booty'	'city'	'hunger'	'crest'	'proud'	'wolf'	'hill'
OCS/LCoS	b**rě**gъ	p**lě**nъ	g**ra**dъ	g**la**dъ	v**rь**xъ	g**rъ**dъ	v**lь**kъ	x**lъ**mъ
Middle CoS	*b**er**gъ	*p**el**nъ	*g**or**dъ	*g**ol**dъ	*w**ьr**xъ	*g**ъr**dъ	*w**ьlk**ъ	*x**ъl**mъ
LCoS/Rusian	b**ere**gъ	p**olo**nъ	g**oro**dъ	g**olo**dъ	v**ьr**xъ	g**ъr**dъ	v**ъlk**ъ	x**ъl**mъ

The Czech-Slovak reflexes of the **tert* diphthongs agree with those of OCS and all South Slavic (although there are complications with word-initial diphthongs, see §30.35).

26.511 LCoS initial clusters with *tl, dl, vl, vr, ml, mr, smr, sr, zr, čl, čr, žl, žr,* and *šl* reflect the metathesis of MCoS liquid diphthongs: e.g.,

	'interpreter'	'palm'	'rule'	'rope'	'milk'	'dark'	'stink'
OCS	tlъkъ	dlanь	vlastь	vrъvь	mlěko	mrakъ	smradъ
MCoS	*tъlkъ	*dolnь	*wolstь	*wьrwь	*melko	*morkъ	*smordъ
	'member'	'worm'	'through'	'yellow'	'staff'	'foal'	'helmet'
OCS	*člěnъ	črьvь	črěsъ	*žlьtъ	žrьdь	žrěbę	šlěmъ
MCoS	*čelnъ	*čьrvь	*čersъ	*žьltъ	*žьrdь	žerbę	*šelmъ

26.52 A second pervasive difference is that Rusian has lost the nasal vowels that are so well attested in OCS. The earliest mss, obviously copied from OCS models, generally reproduce the proper nasal-vowel letters correctly, but numerous errors demonstrate that *ǫ had been replaced by *u*, and *ę by a newly distinctive low front *ä*. In spelling, ѫ = ѹ and ѭ = ю, while ѧ (or ѩ in blocked position) stands for older *ę and for *a (after *j č š ž c*):

MCoS/OCS	rǫkǫ	mojǫ	męso	tę	moję	moja	otročę
EarlyRusian	ruku	moju	mäso	tä	mojä	mojä	otročä
written	рѫкѫ	моѭ	мѧсо	тѧ	моѩ,	моꙗ	отроуѧ, отроуа
	'hand [As]'	'my [Asf]'	'meat'	'thee [As]'	'my [Ap]'	'my [Nsf]'	'boy [NAs'

NB: Ap *moję* was South Slavic, in principle different from North Slavic *mojě* (§29.814, 36.52), but Rusian scribes resolutely tried to adhere to the SSl norm, and spellings like моѣ are extremely rare.

From Indo-European to Common Slavic

27.1 The early Indo-European phonological system may be assumed to have had 17 obstruents, 4 sonorants, 5 vowels (occuring both long and short), and 3 consonants called *laryngeals* (conventionally symbolized as h_1, h_2, h_3). Stops could be voiceless, voiced, or voiced aspirated, with 5 kinds of articulation (labial, dental, palatal, velar, and labio-velar).[9] The short high vowels *i* and *u* could follow other vowels to form diphthongs, while between vowels they could function as glides (*j* and *w*).[10] The sonorants could function as syllabic (*m̥ n̥ l̥ r̥*).

obstruents	sonorant	laryngeal	vowels
p b t d ḱ ǵ k g kʷ gʷ s **bh dh ǵh gh gʷh**	**m n l r**	**h_1 h_2 h_3**	**ī i ē e ā a ō o ū u**

27.2 Baltic and Slavic do not reflect all these distinctions. In terms of Slavic evidence, the IE labio-velar consonants have fallen together with the velars, and the aspirated stops with the unaspirated voiced stops. We posit, therefore, a post-IE system where eight stops stand for the original fifteen. The four-position series (labial, dental, palatal, velar) is posited

---

9 Specialists wrangle about almost every item in this statement, in particular the phonological nature of the three-way opposition in stops and the number and definition of /–anterior/ or dorsal articulations formerly called *gutturals* and recently dubbed *tectals* ("prevelar, velar, postvelar"—among other terms). I generally rely on the works of Helmut Rix and Manfred Mayrhofer, moderated by advice from my Harvard colleagues Jay Jasanoff and Calvert Watkins.

10 Indo-Europeanists often write the labial glide (or *semi-vowel*) "u̯" and the iod "i̯" or "y". Since the symbol "y" in Slavic studies refers to the high mid to back [ɨ]—written "ы" in Russian and "ꙑ" in OCS, I follow Slavistic tradition and write *j* for the glide: OCS вꙑꙗ 'neck' is transliterated *vyja*, but its hypothetical MCoS equivalent is **wyja*. Similarly, OCS оумꙑвъ 'having washed' = *umyvъ*, older **umywъ*.

also for Indo-Iranian (as opposed to Germanic, Greek and Latin, where reflexes of labio-velars remain distinct, but those of palatals and velars are indistinguishable).[11] The laryngeals had played a significant role in many early dialects, affecting the quality and quantity of vowels in many morphemes. They were gradually lost in most regions; their effects had become lexicalized (and perhaps sometimes morphologized) long before a distinctively Slavic system emerged.

27.3 Baltic and Slavic reflect an innovation that is shared by Indo-Aryan and Iranian: *s* after *r, k, i* or *u* became dorsal *š*. This variant eventually resulted in a new phoneme. IE *s* was non-labial but unspecified as to place of articulation. In the new system, /+anterior/ *s* became distinctively opposed to /-anterior/ *š*. The "ruki-rule" operated under somewhat differing conditions in various regions; in Pre-Slavic it does not affect *s* before consonant. In Slavic, *š* replaced every desinential *s* (unless a consonant followed); in Baltic, desinential *š* reverted to *s*.

27.31 Since the timing of the replacement of desinential *s* by *š* is unknown and the *š* disappeared before Slavic writing began, the hypothetical *š* will not be indicated in the derivations offered in the rest of this book.

27.41 The simpler late Indo-European system that is reflected by Baltic and Slavic therefore has the following phonemes:

obstruents	sonorants	vowels
p b t d ḱ ǵ k g s š	**m n l r j w**	**ī i ē e ā a ō o ū u**

Long and short diphthongs are assumed (*ei ēi eu ēu ai āi au āu*). Further, short high vowels were inserted before the syllabic liquids and nasals: *m̥ n̥ l̥ r̥* > *im um in un il ul ir ur*. Scholars have not discovered the conditions that determined whether *i* or *u* was selected. What is important is that these combinations still serve as diphthongs (called liquid or nasal diphthongs) in Lithuanian.[12] It is assumed that early Slavic had parallel series of diphthongs (cf. §26.51).

---

[11] The traditional label for dialects that had this palatal series is *satem*, recalling the sibilant reflex of **ḱ* in **ḱm̥t-om* '100' in Avestan (early Iranian) *satəm*, as opposed to the Latin reflex *kentum* (confusingly spelled with *c* and, as a result of very late Latin or post-Latin regressive palatalizations, pronounced [s], [t^{s}], [t$^{\check{s}}$], [θ] in various modern Romance dialects). Germanic, Latin, and Greek are *kentum*-languages. Luvian (and presumably Common Anatolian) preserved the five-position series.

[12] The liquid or nasal functions as the second member of the syllabic nucleus (as do *o* or *e*), and the accent may fall on either member, e.g. *úoga* 'berry' ~ *sesuõ* 'sister'; *píenas* 'milk' ~ *miẽstas* 'city'; *várna* 'raven', *var̃das* 'name'; *gìnti* 'to defend' ~ *giñti* 'to chase'.

27.42 Pre-Balto-Slavic words could begin in any vowel or consonant (except *š*), or consonant clusters limited to *s* + *stop* + *sonorant*. Closed syllables were common, and word-internal consonant clusters of considerably more variety occured.

Words could end in *t* or *d*, in *n, s, ns, nts* and rarely in *r*. The final syllable is ordinarily a desinence—a grammatically meaningful morpheme—or part of a desinence; sometimes a change in the phonemes of a desinence is to be interpreted as morphological substitution rather than phonetic evolution. Yet we must also assume special developments that can be defined in phonetic terms (including the word boundary, symbolized #).

Middle Common Slavic is—in contrast to PBS—a language of open syllables; except for the liquid and nasal diphthongs (*ьr ъr er el, īn ūn ēn ān*), the tonality (or sonority) was lower at the onset than at the coda.

28. The Slavic vowel system evolved in steps that are not always easy to correlate with the changes in the consonantal system.

28.1 The IE non-high back vowels *a/ā* and *o/ō* merged completely in a vowel-pair I will write *a/ā*. The resulting Early Common Slavic system is fully defined by the features ±*high,* ±*back,* and ±*long*:[13]

	+long	-long	-long	+long		oral diphthongs			
+high	**ī**			**ū**					
+high		**i**	**u**		+	**ei**	**ai**	**eu**	**au**
-high		**e**	**a**						
-high	**ē**			**ā**					
	-back	-back	+back	+back					

Also nasal and liquid diphthongs: *im in um un il ir ul ur*
em en am an el er al ar

(In Pre-Baltic, short *o* > *a,* but long *ō* remained generally distinct from *ā*.)

Contrast the Middle Common Slavic system which eventually resulted:

tense	**i**		**y**	**u**					**īn**	**ūn**
lax		**ь**	**ъ**		+	**ьr**	**ьl**	**ъr ъl**		
lax		**e**	**o**			**er**	**el**	**or ol**		
tense	**ě**		**a**						**ēn**	**ān**
+nasal	**ę**		**ǫ**							
	-back		+back							

[13] Let me stress that the presence or absence of *rounding* is not distinctive for this system, nor was it distinctive for the /+high -low/ *ū/u* or the /-high -low/ *ō/o* of the older system. See *IJSLP* 41: 19.

Only *u* is distinctively /+round/; **i** and **y** are distinctively /minus-round/.

It appears that the first element of a diphthong could be long or short in ECoS, and the possibility remains for MCoS. Since it seems that the first member of the nasal diphthongs usually lengthened, the table shows this notation. The final emergence of unitary nasal vowels, **ę* < **īn/*in, *ēn/*en* and **ǫ* < **ān/*an,* may well have occurred after the **y* and **u* were fully established, cf. §29.8202.

28.2 Late Common Slavic had, in principle, only open syllables. Its Pre-Balto-Slavic predecessor, however, allowed syllables that ended in a non-syllabic high vowel or resonant (i.e. diphthongs like *ei au en er*) or obstruents (including word-boundary #). The syllable is a surface unit of phonotactic organization: underlying morphemes are affected by the rules of syllabic structure. A morpheme like **sup* 'sleep' or **poi* 'sing' would automatically (so to speak) admit a syllabic boundary before its final unit if followed by a vowel (**sup-ā-tei* 'to sleep' = **su.pā.tei*; **poi-e-te* 'you sing' = *po.je.te*) but remained intact before a consonant (**sup-no-s* = **sup.nos* [noun, Nsm], **poi-tei* 'to sing [inf.]' = *poi.tei*). See §29.8.

29. The first crucial steps that set Slavic irrevocably apart from its Baltic cousins involve the /-anterior/ consonants, i.e. the palatals (/+coronal/ *ḱ ǵ*) and velars (/-coronal/ *k g*).

29.1 The IE palatal stops (*ḱ ǵ*) became hissing affricates, *c ʒ*, then *s* and *z*.[14] There are now three continuants: *s, z,* and *š*. This process is surely very old.

29.2 New palatals split off from the velars and became hissing affricates (*c ʒ*), attested in OCS. The environment was very specific: the conditioning factor stood before the *k g*, so the process is progressive. A velar after a non-diphthongal high front vowel (*i ī*) [optionally followed by a nasal (*n*)], and before a low back *a* or *ā*, became palatal. This *progressive palatalization* is called BdC:

k g > ḱ ǵ | /+ syllabic -high -back/ (/+cons +nasal/) __ /+syl -high +back/

---

[14] Pre-Baltic *ḱ ǵ* > hushing *č ǯ*, then *š* and *ž* – which survive in modern Lithuanian. The system from which modern Baltic dialects are derived has these two obstruents and unchanged *t/d p/b k/g s m n l r j w*, along with *ī/i ē/e ā/a ō ū/u*. Unlike Slavic, it does not, in its early stages, undergo mutative palatalization of velars. Iod-palatalization of dentals is far in the future, and quite without connection to phonetically comparable Slavic processes. The distance from the PBS phonological system to modern Lithuanian dialect systems is remarkably short.

That is, *ika inka* (etc.) > *iḱa inḱa* (etc.). The diphthongs *ai* and *ei* (etc.) do not trigger palatalization; see §29.921.

29.3 Results of the ruki-rule (§27.3), the affrication of IE *ḱ ǵ*, and BdC:[15]

IE *s either remains or shifts to *š* (which later becomes *x* before back vowel):
**sūnus* > OCS *synъ*, Li *sūnùs*
**rosa* 'dew' > OCS *rosa*, Li *rasà*
**wetusos* 'old' > OCS *vetъxъ*, > Li *vẽtušas*;
**moisos* 'bladder'(?) > OCS *měxъ* 'wineskin', > Li *maĩšas* 'sack'
**wirsus* 'top, crest' > **wiršuš* > OCS *vьrxъ*; Li *viršùs* (with reversion of desinential *š* to *s*).

The IE palatals **ḱ* **ǵ* diverged at the outset (§29.1):
**ḱoino-* 'hay' > OCS *sěno*, Li *šiẽnas*;
**proḱ-* 'ask' > OCS *prositi*, Li *prašýti*
**ǵeim-* 'winter' > OCS *zima*, Li *žiemà*
**weǵh-* 'convey, go' > OCS *vezǫ* 'I convey', Li *vežù*.

IE velar **k* **g* remain except in the BdC environment :
**kou-* 'hew, strike' > OCS *kovati* 'beat, forge', Li *káuti* 'beat'
**tek-* 'run' > OCS *tekǫ* 'I run', Li *tekiù*
**nogutis* '(finger)nail' > OCS *nogъtь*, Li *nagùtis*
<u>in contrast to</u> **woinikos* 'wreath, crown' > OCS *věnьcь*, Li *vainìkas*
Germanic **kuningaz* 'king' > OCS *kъnęʒь*, Li *kùnigas* 'priest'.

29.4 Still another pair of palatals began to appear when a front vowel (*ē e ī i*) or *j* followed *k g*; the velars became hushing affricates, attested in OCS as the voiceless *č* but voiced *ǯ*. This is the *First Regressive Palatalization* (KI):[16]

k g > ḱ ǵ | __ /-back -consonantal/.

That is, *ki gi ke ge kj gj* etc. > *ḱi ǵi ḱe ǵe ḱj ǵj* etc. > *či ǯi* (*ži*) *če ǯe* (*že*) etc.

---

15 Word-final *-*us* and *-*os* yield -ъ (or -ь) by later rules: see §29.7.

16 The First Regressive Palatalization is called KI in this book, while the Second Regressive Palatalization is KAI (a much later process that affected most of Slavdom by c1000, but did not reach the peripheral dialects of Pskov-Novgorod). The Progressive Palatalization (BdC) is assumed by many Slavists to be a late process and therefore called the Third or Second Palatalization. ("BdC" recalls the Polish scholar who first pointed out some of the difficulties of explaining the data, Jan Baudouin de Courtenay). The sequence I propose here is BdC–KI–KAI. Most recent handbooks assume either KI–BdC–KAI or KI–KAI–BdC, often remarking that BdC and KAI are two phases of a single process.

29.41 The BdC and KI environments for the palatals are mutually exclusive, and theoretically the affrication could be viewed as immediate:

ḱ/ǵ > c/ʒ *before* /-high +back/ OR > č/ǯ *before* /-back -cons/
> č/ǯ *otherwise* > c/ʒ *otherwise*

29.5 It is probably at this time that sibilants + *j* underwent iotation: *sj* and *šj* both yielded *š*, and *zj* > *ž*. We assume further that *š* before back vowels became *x*—a new phoneme.

29.51 Post-consonantal *j* disappears in the process of iotation. We therefore assume it as part of KI and sibilant-iotation. Iotation of *n l r* produced unit palatals that will be written here with digraphs, *nj lj rj* (cf. §1.22). There is no evidence to locate the appearance of new palatal sonorants in chronological sequence. They surely were in place in MCoS. Iod after labial and dental stops (*pj bj mj*; *tj dj*) remains until late MCoS.

29.6 The way these early rules interact is important. Here are stages of the history of OCS **pьsati* 'to write', **pьxati* 'to pound', **sьcati* 'to piss', **pьšeno* 'millet', and **sьčitъ* 'pisses [3s pres]':

IE satem	ruki	c ʒ > s z	BdC	KI	> OCS
si**k**ātei >	–	–	si**ḱ**ātei >	si**c**atei >	*sь**c**ati
pi**ḱ**ātei >	pi**c**ātei >	pi**s**ātei >	–	–	*pь**s**ati
pi**s**ātei >	pi**š**ātei >	–	–	pi**x**ātei >	*pь**x**ati
piseno >	pi**š**eno >	–	–	pi**š**ena >	*pь**š**eno
si**k**-ī-(?)- >	–	–	si**ḱ**-ī-t- >	si**č**īt- >	*sь**č**itъ

The ruki-rule must operate before the deaffrication of the satem *c/ʒ* produces an *s* that can stand after *i*, so that the three-way contrast *ik* ~ *iḱ* ~ *is* or *ik* ~ *ic* ~ *is* is maintained as it becomes *iḱ* ~ *is* ~ *iš* and later **ьc* ~ **ьs* ~ **ьš*/**ьx*.[17]

29.7 Two vowel processes interacted to produce a new morphophonemic situation: Vowel Raising (VR) changed the shape of many desinences, and Vowel Adjustment (VA) imposed new constraints on possible CV sequences. A preliminary condition is that a vowel is long before **nC*, see §29.814.

---

[17] No form of the verb **sьcati* is written, as far as I know, in any Slavic text before c1650, but the comparative evidence suffices to establish it as a parallel to *sъp-a+* 'sleep', §15.32. See Vaillant 1966 405. The i/ę present is assured, but the shape of the 3s desinence for this early period is uncertain.

NOTE: Vowel Raising concerns syllables that are grammatical morphemes and therefore subject to morphological influences; see §36, esp. 36.41-42.

29.71 Vowel Raising was limited to final closed syllables; it shifted the low vowels **a* and **ā* (and possibly **e*) to **u* and **ū* (**i*). The final syllable could end in a nasal, a sibilant, or both. In present active participles, **nts* is posited.

VR¹	a low short vowel raises before *n#* or *s#*:	*-an# -as#* > *-un -us*
NØ¹	**n* is lost after a high vowel and before (*s*)#:[18]	*-īns# -ūns#* > *-īs -ūs*
VR²	a long vowel raises before *ns#*:	*-āns* > *-ūns*

Final **ān* is not raised, and therefore contrasts with **ūn(s)* and **īn(s)* at this stage. Then the nasal in **ūn* is lost and **ū* yields *y*, while **ān* and **īn* become unit nasal vowels, *ǫ* and *ę*. See examples in §32.

29.72 Vowel Adjustment is neutralization of the back ~ front opposition. It applies to a vowel in position after the glide **j* or the stops **ḱ *ǵ* resulting from BdC (*or the affricates that replaced them*). VA had two phases, probably separated in time. In the first, both the /+back/ high vowels (*ū u*) and the short /+back/ low vowel (*a*) fronted (to *ī i e*); in the second, the long front low vowel (*ē*) backed to *ā*:

after *ḱ ǵ j*	VA¹	**ū u a** >	**ī i e**	: VA²	**ē**	>	**ā**
/+coronal -back/		/+back/	/-back/	/-back -high +long/			/+back/

VA¹ in effect is a progressive assimilation, while VA² is dissimilation. VA² applies to the output of KI, so that **ḱē* > **čē* > **čā*, yielding OCS *ča*. VA¹ applies to diphthongs (**ai *au* > **ei *eu*).

29.73 The syllables *kū ku gū gu* resisted palatalization in all environments. The syllables *kā ka gā ga* became *ćā ća ʒ́ā ʒ́a* only if they were preceded by *ī(n) i(n)*. But VR produced *ćū ću ʒ́ū ʒ́u*. These syllables then became *ćī ći ʒ́ī ʒ́i* by VA¹ (as *ća ʒ́a* became *će ʒ́e*). For example: *atrak-as ~ atik-as* Ns 'boy' ~ 'father'; BdC > *atrakas ~ ati**ḱ**as*; VR > *atrak**us** ~ atiḱ**us***, VA > *atrakus ~ atiḱ**i**s*, eventually OCS *otrok**ъ** ~ otьc**ь***.

	earliest Sl	BdC	VR	VA	OCS
Ns 'boy'	*atrak-as*	> *atrakas*	> *atrak**us***	> *atrakus*	> *otrok**ъ***
Ns 'father'	*atik-as*	> *ati**ḱ**as*	> *atiḱ**us***	> *atiḱ**i**s*	> *otьc**ь***

[18] This rule is required for Ap of *i*-stems, e.g. PBS **gostins* 'guests' > **gasťīns* > OCS *gosti*, see §38.51.

In this way certain desinence-initial vowels at an early date became variables defined by the stem-final consonant. BdC, VR and VA established the morphophonemic basis for the twofold declensions of LCoS.

*

29.8 In early Slavic times, syllable-final obstruents disappeared or adapted to function as the onset of the next syllable; **sup-n-as* (with reinterpretation of morphemic boundaries) > OCS *sъn-ъ,* not obviously related to the infinitive *sъp-a+*. A PBS diphthong in a closed syllable becomes a LCoS monophthong, but before a vowel it becomes vowel plus heterosyllabic glide; **poi-tei* > *pěti* 'to sing', **poi-e-te* > *pojete* 'you sing'. (Cf. §28.2.)

Some of the processes survived as generative rules in OCS. The infinitives **grebtei* 'dig' and **pāk̂tei* 'herd, pasture', for example, have become *greti* (gre.ti) and *pasti* (pa.sti)—in underlying form {greb-Ø+ti}, {pas-Ø+ti}. See §§3.31, esp. 3.3131.

The phonetic deletion of syllable-final obstruents is assumed to be an early process, but there is no decisive evidence.

29.81 Syllable-final nasals before C/# were part of a nasal diphthong, **klintī* 'to swear' ~ *klinānt-*. Before a vowel or **j,* the nasal was consonantal and the syllabic boundary was adjusted: {klon-i+ti} > *klo.ni.ti* 'to incline' but past passive participle **klon-i-en-* > **klon.je.nъ* > *klo.nje.nъ* (where *nj* is a unit palatal); {lom-i+} **lo.mi.ti* 'break' ~ **lo.mje.nъ* > *lo.mlje.nъ* (§3.521).

29.811 Nasal diphthongs became unit nasal vowels (**in *en *im *em* > **ę*; **un *on *um *om* > **ǫ*), e.g. *klęti klьnǫtъ*. The front nasal of LCoS seems to have been phonetically a tense non-low vowel [ę̣] or [į], the back nasal a tense non-low [ų, ǫ̣] or else low [ą].[19]

29.812 Stem-final alternations of nasal vowel before C/# but vowel + heterosyllabic nasal before V became normal by the end of MCoS: **wer-men-Ø* 'time' Gs **wer-men-es* > OCS *vrě.mę vrě.me.ne* (§4.414).[20]

---

19 In terms of patterning, **ǫ* behaves like **u* (cf. §2.11), but in terms of later development, **ǫ* became unrounded nasal *schwa* in Poland (later front *ę* if short, *ą* if long), non-nasal *schwa* in Bulgaria, but rounded [u ǫ] elsewhere.

20 The IE neuter nominative of this suffix surely was **-mēn* or zero-grade **-mn̥*. This does not guarantee that the same shape survived into early Slavic; for my purposes **-men#* > *-mę* suffices.

29.813 Nasal diphthong before nasal consonant apparently varied by dialect. OCS has both *pomęnǫti* and *poměnǫti* 'call to mind, remember' (cf. *po-mьn-ě+* and *po-min-aj+* 'remember, have in mind' and *pamętь* 'memory'), **-min-n-* or **-men-n-*.[21] OCS adjectives like *drěvěnъ* 'wooden' and *měděnъ* 'of brass' are regularly spelled -ѧн- in Rusian texts, as are ethnic or regional designations like OCS *Izmailitěne,* Rus' Измаилитѧне 'Ishmaelites'. Clearly these two suffixes originally had **-en-n-*;[22] South Slavic regularly developed **-ěn-* while North Slavic had a nasal vowel: **-ęn-* (which became open front **än* by 1000).[23]

29.8131 OCS *imę* 'name' surely was **jьmę* in some dialects, < older **in-men* < **n̥-men* < IE **h₁nh₃-men,* zero-grade of the root **h₁neh₃* (cf. Gk ὄνομα, La *nōmen*). The **n* of the root disappeared before the nasal **m.*

29.814 The hypothetical early distinction of short vs. long initial elements of nasal diphthongs is hard to reconstruct; it seems safe to assume that all ECoS vowels are long before **nC* or **nC#,* but may be short before **n#*. The regular relationships of IE final closed syllables and OCS are these:

PBS	in#	un#	on#	ōns# āns#	īns#	ūns#
LCoS	ь	ъ	ъ/ь	y/ę	i	y

The first two represent As i-stems and u-stems, e.g. *gostь* 'guest' and *synъ* 'son'; the last two are Ap of the same (*gosti, syny*). The middle two illustrate Asm and Apmf of the twofold declension (e.g. *stolъ, strojь*: *stoly, stroję*: *ženy, struję* ~ Ns *stolъ* 'seat', *strojь* 'order', *žena* 'woman', *struja* 'stream').

In the first two and last two, the consonants are simply lost. The third requires a near-final stage with **-u/*-i*. The contrasting back nasal versus front oral vowel of the fourth implies earlier **-ūn/*-īn*.

Loss of the original nasal consonants took place in stages: VR¹ raises *on#* to *un#*; NØ¹ deletes the nasal after a high vowel in a word-final syl-

---

[21] Cloz and Sav have only *ě*, Zo and Mar strongly prefer it. Euch has only *ę* (17x), Su has 24 *ę* ~ 1 *ě*. Ps Sin varies by scribe: B 4 *ě*, 2 *ę*; A 12 *ę*; G 18 *ě*: E 1 *ě*, 8 *ę*. The evidence of modern dialects is conflicting; in all probability the stems have been re-formed.

[22] *Kaměnъ* 'of stone' (cf. *kamenь* 'stone', §4.412) is an inherited word, derived from the stem **kamen-* (§4.412) by the archaic formant **n*: *kamen-n-*. OCS has a competing lexeme with the productive suffix **ьn*: *kamenьnъ*.

[23] Ps 17:46 *oxrъmǫ* 'they became lame' surely represents the reduced grade of *xrom-* 'lame' but there is no guarantee that the verb had forms with *-nǫ*.

lable: *in# īns# > i# īs#, un# ūns# > u# ū*. Then VR² converts *āns#* to *ūns#*, which is split by VA¹ into *īns#* and *ūns#*, whereupon NØ² deletes the nasal after the high back vowel, leaving nasal **-īn(s)* opposed to **-ū(s)*,[24] i.e. the morpheme {y/ę}. In effect, NØ¹ applies only to i-stem and u-stem Ap (e.g. *gosti, syny*); NØ² accounts for the oral/nasal contrast in {y/ę}.

Exceptions seem to be determined by morphological analogy, e.g. the twofold NAs neuter {o/e} ~ IE **-om*, see §38.42.

OCS *-ę* in these {y/ę} desinences represents the South Slavic forms; North Slavic had *-ě* (although Rus' scribes resolutely continued to spell in the OCS fashion). The northern "soft" variant {y/ě} is called *ě tertium* or *ě³* as opposed to *ě primum* (= *ě¹* < **ē*) and *ě secundum* (= *ě²* < **ai* < IE **oi*, **ai*). See §38.52.

29.8141 Final **ān* is to be posited for three important desinences reflected in OCS by non-alternating {ǫ}: accusative singular feminine twofold (e.g. *šujǫ rǫkǫ* 'left hand'), first person singular and third person plural present (e.g. *pojǫ, pojǫtъ* 'I/they sing'; *nesǫ, nesǫtъ* 'I/they carry').

Asf was **-ān* in PBS, from somewhat older **-ā-m*. It was not subject to Vowel Raising or Vowel Adjustment; the evolution to *ǫ* is straightforward.

The OCS *-ǫ* of 1st person singular present goes back to PBS **-ō*, which became ECoS **-ā*. Later on, a nasal (probably **m*) was added. Thus 'I sing' was **poi-ō*, yielding ECoS **pajā*, then **pajām*, OCS *pojǫ*.

The IE third person plural was **-onti*,[25] from which we derive ECoS **-ānti* (e.g. **nek̑-onti, *poi-onti > *nesānti, pajānti* > OCS *nesǫtъ, pojǫtъ*).[26]

Desinential *-ę* in Nsm *poję* (Gs *pojǫšta*) 'singing', on the other hand, is the "soft" variant of the morphophoneme {y/ę} and goes back to **poi-on-t-s*. ECoS **pajānts > *pajūnts > *pajīn > poję* vs. **pajāntjā > *pojǫšta* (cf. §29.814, §30 C ##40-45). North LCoS had {a/ě}, see §39.421.

29.8142 The *-ǫ* of 3p root-aorist (*padǫ* 'they fell'; *mogǫ* 'they were able') never occurs after palatal C. We posit PBS **-ont*, ECoS **-ānt*. (This same desinence serves in the imper-

---

24 Hypothetical **ūn* is extremely rare except in these desinences; it may well be that it always lost nasality and yielded LCoS *y*.

25 For most LCoS dialects, the third person terminal desinence was **-tь*; OCS *-tъ* is exceptional. See §43.13.

26 Without the assumption that **onC* > ECoS *ānC*, **nek̑onti* (and most stems) would yield desinential *-ǫt-*, but **poionti* would be subject to VR and yield **pajenti* and †*pajęt-*. One might hypothesize that the less frequent "soft" variant of this alternating desinence was eliminated in favor of non-alternating *-ǫt-*.

fect 3p *-ěa-x-ǫ*.) The alternative 3p aorist *-ę* (*jęsę* or *jęšę* 'they took', *rěšę* or *rekošę* 'they said') seems to reflect IE **-n̥t*.

29.8143 The OCS verbal classifier **nǫ* derives from IE **nou*: in tautosyllabic position, **nowC* > **noNC*, whereby the whole syllable became nasal. Thus **ri-now-ti* > **rinoNti* > *rinǫti* (inf, 'to push') but the past passive participle **ri-now-en-* > *rinovenъ* (§15.711).

In similar fashion, nasalization sporadically appeared in roots with initial nasal, but not in all dialects: e.g. *nud-/nǫd-* 'annoy', *mud-/mǫd-* 'delay, be slow', see §2.71.

29.815 The preposition *kъ* 'to' and the prefix-prepositions *sъ* 'with, from' and *wъ* 'in' represent older **kun*, **sun*, and **un*. When followed by the third person pronominal stem **j-*, the **nj* becomes a unit palatal. From forms like *kъ njemu* 'to him' and *sъ njimi* 'with them', the *nj* eventually was abstracted as a suppletive form of the root to be used with most or all other prepositions (§4.25). As a prefix, **sun* before a consonant could become *sǫ-*: *sǫsědъ* 'neighbor' (*sěd* 'sit, settle'), *sǫpьrjь* 'disputant, adversary' (*pьr-ě+* 'dispute');[27] *sǫmьněnьje* ~ *sumьněnьje* 'doubt'. Before a vowel—chiefly the roots **i/*id* 'go', **im/*em* 'take', and **ēd* 'eat'—the nasal remains: *sъniti* 'descend', *vъniti* 'enter', *sъněsti* 'eat up'. Lexemes with these variant prefixes belong to a list of inherited words; these formations are no longer productive.

29.8151 Early **un* (< IE **n̥*, §27.41) 'in' retained nasality and back quality in *ǫtrь* 'within' and *ǫtroba* 'entrails', while **en* or **in* survives in **jętra* neut. pl. 'innards' (not OCS, but clearly CoS; sg. *jętro* usually means 'liver'). The nouns *ǫdolь* and *ǫdolьje* 'valley' imply **un-dol-* (with **dhel* 'hollow'). The denasalized form **wъ* is to be seen in *vъtorъ* 'second' (dial. **wъterъ*, §41.82).

Similarly, the zero-grade of the negational particle **ne* occurs in *ǫrodъ* 'fool' (**n̥-rod-* > **un-rod-*, meaning approximately "degenerate"; *rod* means both 'kin' and 'generate'), *ǫtьlъ* 'leaky' (of a vessel; *tьlo* 'bottom').

29.8152 The IE root **h₂enh₁* 'breathe, breath' (cf. ἄνεμος 'wind', La *animus* 'spirit') in o-grade underlies LCoS **w-on-j-a* 'fragrance' and *ǫ-x-aj+* 'to smell'. The prothetic *w* is unexpected, and the suffix *x* is isolated; see §35.13 (g).

---

27 Attested **sъsědъ*, and **sъpьrjь* are *OCS; they occur in post-OCS copies of surely OCS texts.

29.8201 The evolution of the oral diphthongs brings about an essential restructuring of the vowel system and inaugurates Middle Common Slavic. The diphthong **ei* > **ī* (or **ьj*, see §29.92), and **ai* > **ē* (written *ě* in the new system). This amounts on the surface to a redistribution of extant phonemes, but in terms of underlying morphophonemes, the new *ě* is distinct: it has special distributional restrictions (§3.5c2). Therefore we distinguish *ě*^{2} (< **ai*) from *ě*^{1} (< **ē*) in Middle and Late Common Slavic.

29.8202 Tautosyllabic **ou* and **eu* became a high back round monophthong **ū* that remained distinct from the inherited long high back vowel that up to now we have written **ū*. The opposition we now write **y* vs. **u* (< **ū* vs. **au*/**eu*) requires reevaluation of distinctive-feature marking, cf. §28.1. For examples, see §29.95.

29.821 Early CoS **ū* was defined /+high +back/, distinct from /+high -back/ *ī*; the phonetic degree of rounding was irrelevant. Middle Common Slavic is defined by the new three-way opposition **i* ~ **y* ~ **u* (< ECoS **ī* ~ **ū* ~ **au*). Rounding has become distinctive for the new high long back vowel, if not for the inherited short back vowels. The inherited long vowels had presumably been redundantly tense; in MCoS they retain their articulation but the defining feature is now /+tense/.

The nasal diphthongs of ECoS are tentatively symbolized *iN* and *āN* here: the development to late MCoS is not altogether clear.

ECoS	ī ei	i	ū	u	eu au	ai ē	e	ā	a	iN	āN
{MCoS}	i	ь	y	ъ	u	ě^{2} ě^{1}	e	a	o	ę	ǫ
/MCoS/	i	ь	y	ъ	u	ě	e	a	o	ę	ǫ
high	+	+	+	+	+	–	–	–	–		
back	–	–	+	+	+	–	–	+	+	–	+
round	–	–	–	(–)	+	–	–	–	(+)		
tense	+	–		+	+	+	–	+	–	+	+

The writing systems of OCS and most early Slavic do not mark accent (or length or possible rising or falling pitch or intonations). Evidence from modern dialects (often bolstered by comparative data from Baltic and even more remote IE dialects) guarantees that the tense vowels could be long or short; it is probable that the new lax vowels occasionally lengthened.

It is notable that Common Slavic (and Baltic) segmental phonology—in sharp contrast to early Indo-European, Germanic, and Latin and its Romance daughter-languages—shows little or no effect from accentual factors.

29.822 This slightly asymmetrical 11-vowel array (cf. the display on p. 192, above) is a system from which we can derive all subsequent Slavic dialects. It is documented (except for the liquid diphthongs) by Old Church Slavonic.[28] It is a new and significant stage, deserving a special label; we call it Middle Common Slavic.

*

29.91 The diphthongs became monophthongs before C or # but remained, with a modified syllabic boundary, before a vowel. Thus **-auC* > **uC, *auV* > **owV*; **aiC* > **ěC, *aiV* > **ojV*. OCS reflects this in part by systematic morphophonemic alternations (esp. nontruncated *-ov-a* ~ truncated *-uj-*: *milovati* ~ *milujǫtъ* §15.501, 29.951 below, and in part by isolated relics (*pěti* ~ *pojǫtъ* 'sing' §16.53).

29.92 The diphthong **ei* before vowel yields OCS *ьj*, e.g. IE *treies* 'three [masc. nom.]' > *trьje* (which is spelled *trьe* and *trie*, §2.61). This implies raising, **e* > **i*.

29.921 The progressive palatalization (BdC, §29.2) is triggered by a high front vowel before the velar stop that shifts articulation, yet the diphthongs **ei* and **ai* apparently block the rule. We assume a slight lowering of the **i* in **ai* (as in Latin, Avestan, and mod. German) > [ae], but a metathesis of elements in **ei*, [ie]. Therefore the masculine derivational suffix **-ineik-* with Gs desinence would be **-iniek-ā*, yielding OCS *-ьnika*. The corresponding feminine **-inīk-ā* (with Ns desinence) would undergo BdC, yielding *-ьnica*.

29.93 Long **ū* followed by a vowel functions like **uw* (short V + glide). Thus **leub-ū* 'love [Ns]' but **leub-uw-i* '[As]' > *ljuby* ~ *ljubъwь*. This is reinterpreted in OCS morphophonemic terms as {ljub-ъw-Ø} ~ {ljub-ъw-ь}, cf. §4.413. For complications in verbal stems, see §44.35.

29.94 Long **ī* before vowel yields OCS **ьj* and its functional equivalent **ij*. The distinctive feature /tense/ is neutralized before **j* (§2.61). Later morphophonemic adjustments were made in different regions. Separating older **ej* from **ij* or ** ī* is difficult.

29.95 Heterosyllabic **eu* (**ew*) merged with **au* (**aw*); e.g. **neu-ā* 'new [Nsf]' > **nawā* > *nova*. Tautosyllabic **eu* early became **jau*, then MCoS **(j)u*; tautosyllabic **au* > *u*. E.g. **seuj-ā* 'left [Nsf]' > **sjaujā* > *šuja*.

---

[28] While seven of the vowels imply a certain immediate ancestor, four are somewhat opaque: *i* may go back to *ei* or *ī*; *ě* < *ai* or *ї*; *ę* < any front vowel + *n/m*, and *ǫ* < any back vowel + *m/n*.

29.951 By LCoS, the monophthongization of **ow* before **j* was completed; the alternation of full-stem {-ova-} and truncated {u-je} is a fact of the lexicon. Although the forms do not happen to occur in OCS, we confidently assume that *lovi+* 'to hunt' generated 1s pres **lovljǫ*, past passive participle **lovljenъ*, and substantive **lovljenьje*. The borrowed name 'Jacob' is **ijakovъ*, and the usual possessive adjective is **ijakovljь* 'belonging to Jacob'.

30.1 OCS words may begin with a vowel, but there are severe constraints (§2.51). Initial *o*, *u* and *ǫ* offer only isolated problems (see §36.5). Initial *a* is limited to

(1) the conjunctions *a* 'and, but' (and derivatives like *acě* 'though' and *ali* 'but, whether') and *ašte* 'if';

(2) recent borrowings (e.g. *apostolъ* 'apostle'), and

(3) words that are also attested (sometimes within OCS, more often in post-OCS or modern dialects) with *ja* (e.g. *aviti/javiti* 'reveal, make plain'). It appears that all Slavdom but eastern Bulgaria has *ja* in morphemes of this last group; the variants with *a-* are LCoS dialect forms. (See §36.2)

30.2 Initial high back *y* and *ъ* do not occur. Instead, the glide *w* is preposed as a syllabic onset. The process survives in unprefixed *vъpiti* ~ prefixed *vъz-ъpiti* 'cry out' (§3.25). The prefix *vy-* (typical of Northern and westernmost SW LCoS; marginal in OCS), corresponds to Germanic **ūt-*, Eng. *out* (< IE **ūd*): **ū-* > **y-* > **wy-*.[29] The exact shape underlying *wъ* 'in' is uncertain; we posit ECoS **un* > **wъn-* > *wъ*. See §29.8151.

30.21 The sequence **bw* (only at the boundary joining the prefix *ob-* with root-initial **w*) either did not develop or was simplified, cf. *oblakъ* 'cloud' {ob-wolk-} vs. *vlač-i+* 'drag'; *obyknǫ+* 'become accustomed' vs. *navyknǫ+* 'learn' < MCoS **ūk-* (root **ouk*: *nauči+* 'teach'). See §3.312. Alternate forms probably coexisted for a long time.

30.31 Initial **i* seems certain for the ubiquitous conjunction and particle *i* 'and, even, indeed', but otherwise front vowels preposed a iod: **ji*, **jь*, *je*, *ję* and **jě* (automatically > **ja* by the phonotactic constraint that originated with VA², cf. §3.5c).

30.311 It is possible that OCS *ese* 'lo, see!', perhaps *ei* 'yes', and *eda* 'lest' had initial [e]. Common loanwords such as *episkopъ* (or *episkupъ*) 'bishop' and *evanǵelije* (and derivatives) very probably were pronounced with an initial glide by many or most early Slavic Christians. Unfortunately the glagolitic alphabet has no device for specifying *j* and cyrillic orthographies are inconsistent.

---

29 In OCS the name David is rigorously spelled *Davydъ*, which does not correspond to Gk Δαβίδ. The Muslim equivalent is *Daūd*. If we assume a borrowing of this form, *ū* > *wy* explains the attested spelling.

30.312 The negated present *něsmь* 'I am not' (§16.101) implies that contraction occurred before prothesis: **ne esmi* > **nēsmi*; later on **es-* > **jes-*.

30.32 Prothesis of iod before front vowel is late. It appears only to mark the beginning of a syllable in forms like **ѧти ~ имѫтъ** 'take' (§3.24) and **ꙁаѧти ꙁаимѫтъ** 'hire' as opposed to **вꙁъѧти ~ вꙁьмѫтъ, вꙁъемлѭтъ** or the suppletive stems in **ити идѫтъ** 'go' ~ **иꙁити иꙁидѫтъ** 'go out'. If *j* had been part of the underlying stems, **zj* should have yielded **ž*.

30.33 Only one stem appears to combine prefix-final consonant with root-initial *j*: *oštut-i+* 'sense, feel, perceive' (Rusian *očut-i+*) < **ot-jut-* < **at-jaut-*, cf. Li *atjausti* 'to sympathize' (*jaut-* 'feel'). Some words clearly reflect an inherited iod: *igo* 'yoke' goes back to IE **jugom* (> **jьgo* by VA[1], cf. Cz *jho*).

Su **вꙁъꙗривъ** and **вꙁьꙗривъ** 'becoming enraged', have a jer to separate prefix from root {vъz-jar-}; implying restructuring at this boundary after the jer-shift. See §3.3111.

30.34 The exact provenance of certain other stems is obscure, in part surely because of different late dialect developments. OCS **igъla* 'needle' could represent **jьgъl-* with a strong jer in the initial syllable (therefore Cz. *jehla*, Gp *jehel*) or **igъl-* with a jer only in the pre-desinential syllable (like R. иглá, Gp и́гол, SC *ìgla*, Gp ~ *igálā*).

The verb 'have' is persistently *ima-* in South Slavic, but *jma-* or *ma-* in Czech-Slovak. Similarly, East and SSl имя, *ime* 'name' but OCz *jmě*, mod. *jméno* (cf. §4.414).

The suppletive stems *i-ti* ~ *id-ǫtъ* 'go' perhaps contrasted **ei-* to **id-*; these stems shifted about in manifold ways in later dialects. SC, for example, has *ići* ~ *idu* (as though from **ij-ti *id-u*) but *poći* ~ *pôđu* (as though from **po-j-ti *po-jd-u*).

The prefix *iz* 'from' retains *i-* in South Slavic, but in Czech-Slovak and Polish older **jьz* > **jz-* > *z* (alternating with *s*).[30]

The stem *igr-aj+* 'to leap, play' (and *igra* 'amusement, entertainment; game', by chance not OCS) also have *i-* in SSl, but **jь-* in the northwest, including Ukrainian.

ECoS **irg-āj-e-* can plausibly be interpreted as containing a metathesized zero-grade of IE **h₁ergh* 'be sexually excited, mount' (Av *r̥ghāyāte* 'be sexually excited', Gk ὀρχέομαι 'dance, mime'). [Lunt, 1977.]

---

30 Moreover, the merger includes the preposition **sъ* 'with; down from'—not only in West Slavic but also in most Ukrainian and Belarusian dialects.

30.35 Word-initial liquid diphthongs were eliminated by metathesis (#VRT > *#RVT*), but with Late CoS local variation. The modern isoglosses generally divide North Slavic (including Rusian and Czech) from South Slavic. For internal liquid diphthongs, Czech agrees with SSl in that *ToRT* > *TRaT* (cf. §26.51). In initial position, certain morphemes need special marking. We posit *#aRT* (as opposed to *#oRT*) as ancestor of *ra-* in all dialects: **ar-dl-o* > OCS/Rusian *ralo* 'plow', Cz *rádlo* (cf. *orati* 'to plow'), Gk ἄροτρον (< IE **arə-tron* < **$h_2$erh$_3$-tr-*; **arm-* > OCS *ramo* 'shoulder', Cz *rámě* (arch., now *rameno*), IE **arəm-* (cf. Engl *arm*).[31] The more common formula **oRT* corresponds to North Slavic *roT-*: OCS *rab-* 'slave' ~ Rusian, Cz *rob-* (IE **$h_3$orbho-* 'bereft', Gk ὄρφανος 'orphan'); prefix *raz-* ~ Cz, Rusian *roz-*.[32]

30.351 OCS has *rob-* once in Zo and, with other derivatives, more than 30 times in Su. It survives in modern SC. It probably represents an old borrowing from a northern dialect, but perhaps the 9th-century isoglosses were more complex than those of modern times.

30.36 Similarly for marked *#alT*, **alk-om-* > OCS, Rusian *lakomъ* 'hungry, greedy', Cz *lakomý* 'miserly'; unmarked *#olT*, **olkъtь* 'elbow' (cf. Li *alkūnė*) > OCS *lakъtь* ~ Rusian *lokъtь*, Cz *loket*.

30.361 Yet the root *alk-* (cf. Li *álkti* 'be hungry') is attested in OCS, *alkati* beside *lakati* (and *vъzalkati vъzlakati*) 'hunger; fast'. Both shapes continue to be used in post-OCS manuscripts. A second OCS doublet is *aldii* 'boat' and *ladii*. Rusian has *lodьja*, Cz *lod'*.[33]

31. When **ai* became *ě*, the sequences **kě*, **gě*, and **xě* were created, but they did not last. OCS and most early recordings of other regional speech affirm that the velars had mutated, by a process known as the Second Regressive Palatalization (here called KAI). Only the region of Pskov and Novgorod was not affected by KAI, and *kě*, *gě*, and *xě* persisted.

OCS has *cě*, *ʒě* and *sě*: e.g. Ls *otrocě*, *boʒě*, *dusě* from *otrok-ъ* 'boy', *bog-ъ* 'god', *dux-ъ* 'spirit'. The written *s* in *sě* (< *xě*) presumably was a hissing palatal for a time, but it soon fell together with the *s* of other

---

31 The precise nature of the marking of such syllables (ancient laryngeal? "acute" intonation?) is hotly debated.

32 Rusian scribes generally held to SSl spelling in such words. Раб, работа and many other words are simply loans that have displaced congruent East Slavic forms.

33 Su 232.30 ѥдина отъ мьнии implies альнии for expected лании (< **alnьjь*) 'one of the roes', cf. R ланъ.

origins in South Slavic and most of Rusian; NorthWest LCoS normally has *šě* (*dušě*), although there are exceptions and morphological complications we will not deal with.[34]

Foreign words with *k* before front vowel were adapted by shifting *k* to *c*, e.g. *ocьtъ* 'vinegar', cf. La *acetum*; *cęta* 'cent [a coin]'. KAI does not affect Greek loans.

*

32. Here are examples of typical relationships between OCS words (or rather their presumed late MCoS equivalents) and their hypothetical Early Common Slavic shapes. Some mutually exclusive processes have been lumped together in this compressed scheme.

Line ***1*** : the effect of the progressive palatalization, BdC (§29.2).
Line ***2*** : (***a***) VA^1 (*ū u a* > *ī i e* after *j, ć, ʒ́*) and
(***b***) an unrelated special process—"breaking" of *eu* to *jeu* (§29.95).
Line ***3*** : (***a***) KI (*k g* > *č ǯ*), (***b***) iotation of sibilants (*sj* and *śj* > *š*), (***c***) the appearance of *x* < *š* before back vowels, and (***d***) the loss of *j* after palatal.
Line ***4*** : VA^2 (*ē* > *ā* after *j č ǯ š*).
Line ***5*** : *ei* > *ī* and *ai* > *ē*.
Line ***6*** : (***a***) *ū* > distinctively /-round +tense/ *y*; (***b***) *au eu* > *ū*; and
(***c***) new symbolization of 9 oral vowels (*i y u, ь ъ, e o, ě a*).
Line ***7*** : KAI (*k g x* > *ć ʒ́ ś*).

Examples 1-16 illustrate the velar stops, while 17-31 deal with *s ś š* and *x*. 8, 16, 29 and 30 (Nsm *-as*) are subject to Vowel Raising between ***1*** and ***2***; the *s* drops, and the final result is -*ъ* for the first three. 30 is subject to VA^1, so *-u* > *-i*, and the final result is -*ь*. These steps are included in 37-39.

1. *atrak-ā* > OCS *otroka* 'boy' [Gs]'
1b. *kunīng-ā* > OCS *kъnęʒa* 'prince [Gs]'
2. *ak-a* > OCS *oko* 'eye'
2a. *līk-a* > *lice* 'face [Nsn]'
3. *awik-a* > *owьce* 'sheep [Vs]'
4. *awik-ai* > *owьci* '[DLs]'
5. *atrak-ai* > *otrocě* '[Ds]'
5a. *raik-ai* > *rěcě* 'river [DLs]'
6. *awik-ā* > *owьca* '[Nsf]''
6a. *raik-ā* > *rěka* '[Nsf]'
7. *atik-e* > *otьče* 'father [Vs]'
7a. *kunīng-e* > *kъnęže* 'prince [Vs]'
8. *kēs-as* > *časъ* 'time, hour'
8a. *gēb-ā* > *žaba* 'frog'

---

[34] The only roots affected are **xoid-* 'gray-haired' (OCS *sědъ*) and its near-synonym **xoir-* 'gray', which is absent from OCS, barely attested in pre-modern East Slavic, and rare in medieval Bulgarian/Macedonian, while *šěr-* is well documented in Old Czech. Fourteenth-c. Novgorod merchants used the term хѣрь 'coarse undyed cloth'. See §35.11.

9. *keist-as* > *čistъ* ‘pure [Nsm]’
10. *atrak-j-a* > *otroče* ‘boy’s [poss. aj. NAsn]’
11. *atik-j-a* > *otьče* ‘father's [poss. aj. NAsn]’
12. *lauk-j-ā* > *luča* ‘beam, ray’
13. *atik-j-ai* > *otьči* ‘[poss. aj. DLfs]
14. *keud-es-a* > *čudesa* ‘miracles [NAp]’
15. *atik-j-au* > *otьču* ‘[poss. aj. Dsmn]’
16. *kaup-as* > *kupъ* ‘heap’
17. *sauš-a* > *suxъ* ‘dry [NAsn]
18. *dauš-ai* > *dusě* ‘spirit [Lsm]’
19. *dauš-e* > *duše* ‘spirit [Vsm]’
20. *dauš-ā* > *duxa* ‘spirit [Gs]’
21. *slūš-ē -tei* > *slyšati* ‘to hear’’
22. *dauš-j-ā* > *duša* ‘soul [Nsf]’
23. *dauš-j-a* > *duše* ‘soul [Vsf]’
24. *bas-ā* > *bosa* ‘barefoot [Nsf]’
25. *bas-e* > *bose* ‘barefoot [Vsm]’
26. *nās-j-a* > *naše* ‘our [NAsn]’
27. *kes-j-e-te* > *češete* ‘comb [2p pres]
28. *nās-j-ā* > *naša* ‘our [Nsf]’
29. *sauš-as* > *suxъ* ‘dry [Nsm]’
30. *seuj-a* > *šujь* ‘left [Nsm]’
31. *kos-j-ou* > *košu* ‘basket [Dsm]’

(A)	**1**	**2**	**3**	**4**	**5**	**6**	**7**	**8**	**9**	**10**	**11**	**12**	**13**	**14**	**15**	**16**	
	kā	ka	ika	ikai	kai	ikā	ke	kē	kei	kje	kja	kjā	kjai	keu	kjau	kau	
1	.	.	ć	ć	.	ć	.	.	.	.	.	.	.	.	.	.	*1*
2	.	.	će	ćei	.	.	.	.	.	.	kje	.	kjei	.	kjeu	.	*2*
3	.	.	.	.	.	.	č	č	č	č	č	č	č	č	č	.	*3*
4	.	.	.	.	.	.	.	čā	.	.	.	.	.	.	.	.	*4*
5	.	.	.	.	ē	.	.	.	ī	če	če	čā	či	.	.	.	*5*
6	.	.	.	i	ě	.	.	a	i	.	.	a	.	u	u	u	*6*
7	.	.	.	.	ćě	.	.	.	.	.	.	.	.	.	.	.	*7*
	ka	**ko**	**ьce**	**ьci**	**cě**	**ьca**	**če**	**ča**	**či**	**če**	**če**	**ča**	**či**	**ču**	**ču**	**ku**	
	1	**2**	**3**	**4**	**5**	**6**	**7**	**8**	**9**	**10**	**11**	**12**	**13**	**14**	**15**	**16**	

(B)	**17**	**18**	**19**	**20**	**21**	**22**	**23**	**24**	**25**	**26**	**27**	**30**	**29**	**30**	**31**	
	ša	šai	še	šā	šē	šjā	šja	sa	se	sja	sje	sā	sau	seu	sjau	
2	.	.	.	.	.	.	šje	.	.	sje	.	.	.	sjeu	e	*2*
3	xa	xai	.	xā	.	.	še	.	.	š	š	.	.	š	e	*3*
4	.	.	.	.	šā	.	.	.	.	.	.	.	.	.	.	*4*
5	.	ē	.	.	.	.	.	.	.	še	.	.	.	.	.	*5*
6	o	ě	.	a	a	a	.	o	.	.	.	a	u	u	u	*6*
7	.	śě	.	.	.	.	.	.	.	.	.	.	.	.	.	*7*
	xo	**śě**	**še**	**xa**	**ša**	**ša**	**še**	**so**	**se**	**še**	**še**	**sa**	**su**	**šu**	**šu**	
	17	**18**	**19**	**20**	**21**	**22**	**23**	**24**	**25**	**26**	**27**	**30**	**29**	**30**	**31**	

Here are illustrations of the chief complications in final closed syllables.

32. *rānk-ān* > *rǫkǫ* ‘hand [Asf]’
33. *awik-ān* > *owьcǫ* ‘sheep [Asf]’
33a. *stig-ān* > *stьʒǫ* ‘path [Asf]’
34. *atrak-an* > *otrokъ* ‘boy [Asm]’
35. *atik-an* > *otьcь* ‘father [Asm]’
36. *mēsīnk-an* > *měsęcь* ‘month [Asm]’
37. *atrak-as* > *otrokъ* ‘boy [Nsm]’
38. *atik-as* > *otьcь* ‘father [Nsm]’
39. *mēsīnk-as* > *měsęcь* ‘month [Nsm]’
39a. *kunīng-as* > *kъnęʒь* ‘prince [Nsm]’
40. *plāk-j-ant-s* > *plačę* ‘weeping [Nsm]’
41. *rek-ant-s* > *reky* ‘saying [Nsm]’
42. *dauš-j-ān* > *dušǫ* ‘soul [Asf]’
43. *dauš-j-āns* > *dušę* ‘souls [Apf]’
44. *dauš-āns* > *duxy* ‘spirits [Apm]’
45. *slūš-ī-nt-s* > *slyšę* ‘hearing [Nsm]’

VR^1	a low short vowel raises before *n#* or *s/š*	*-an# -as# > -un -us*
NØ	word-final *n* or *s/š* drops after *i* or *u*	*(in# iš#) un# uš/us#> (i) u*
VL	short vowel lengthens before *n(t)s#*	*onts ons > āns*
VR^2	long vowel raises before *n(t)s#*	*āns > ūns*
UN	*n* drops after *ū*	*ūn > ū*
ṽ	front vowel + *n* > *ę*; back vowel + *n* > *ǫ*	

Loss of final *s/š* takes place after VR^2: it is not specified in the table.

(C)	**32**	**33**	**34**	**35**	**36**	**37**	**38**	**39**	**40**	**41**	**42**	**43**	**44**	**45**	
	kān	ikān	kan	ikan	inkan	kas	ikas	īnkas	kjants	kānts	šjān	sjāns	šāns	šīnts	
VR1	.	.	un	un	un	us	us	us	.	.	.	.	.	.	*VR1*
VL	.	.	.	.	.	.	.	.	ā	ā	.	.	.	.	*VL*
NØ	.	.	u	u	u	u	u	u	.	.	.	.	.	.	*NØ*
VR2	.	.	.	.	.	.	.	.	ū	ū	.	ū	ū	.	*VR2*
BdC	.	ć	.	ć	ć	.	ć	ć	.	.	.	.	.	.	*BdC*
VA	.	.	.	i	i	.	i	i	ī	.	.	ī	.	.	*VA*
=	kān	icān	ku	icu	īnci	ku	ici	īnci	kjīn	kūn	šjān	šjīn	šūn	šjīn	=
KI	.	.	.	.	.	.	.	.	č	.	š	š	x	š	*KI*
UN	.	.	.	.	.	.	.	.	.	kū	.	.	ū	.	*UN*
ṽ	kǫ	ьcǫ	kъ	ьcь	ęcь	kъ	ьcь	ęcь	čę	ky	šǫ	šę	xy	šę	*ṽ*
	32	**33**	**34**	**35**	**36**	**37**	**38**	**39**	**40**	**41**	**42**	**43**	**44**	**45**	

(**D**) Here are the same examples, rearranged to show how the OCS syllables correspond to their ancestral bases.

OCS	**ka**	**ko**	**ьca**	**ьce**	**cě**	**ьci**	**če**	**či**	**ča**	**ču**	**ku**
ECoS	kā	ka	ikā	ika	kai	ikai	ke kje kja	kei kjai	kjā kē	keu kjau	au
	1	2	6	4	5	3	7, 10, 11	9, 13	12, 8	14, 15	16

OCS	**xo**	**xa**	**śě**	**še**	**ša**	**so**	**se**	**sa**	**su**	**šu**
ECoS	ša	šā	sai	še šja sja sje	šē sjā	sa	se	sā	sau	seu sjau
	17	20	18	19, 23, 26, 27	21, 22	24	25	28	29	30, 31

OCS	**kǫ#**	**cǫ#**	**kъ#**	**cь#**	**čę#**	**ky#**	**šǫ#**	**xy#**	**šę#**
ECoS	kān	ikān	kan kas	ikan=īnkan, ikas=īnkas	kjānts	kānts	šjān	šāns	sjāns šīnts
	32	33	34, 37	35=36, 38=39	40	41	42	44	43, 45

The voiced velar *g* of PBS becomes MCoS *ʒ* where *k* > *c*, and *ž* where *k* > *č*, cf. examples 1b, 7b, 8a, 33a, 39a.

33. OCS words on the whole allow us to reconstruct earlier shapes if we follow certain procedures. The word needs to be analyzed in terms of stem and desinence, root and affixes; and possible morphophonemic clues are required. Morphophonemic and phonotactic characteristics of theoretical

Pre-BaltoSlavic must also be considered. Chief among them is the assumption that most roots have the shape (C)VC, where V is normally **e* but may be any vowel or diphthong. In conformity with the processes called *ablaut* or *apophony* (cf. §3.9), the **e* in some formations becomes **o,* and in still others **ē* or **ō*. In earliest Slavic terms, after **ō *o* have merged with **ā *a,* these variations involve the specifications *front* or *back* and *short* or *long*. The theoretical zero-grade, with no *e* or *o* at all, is represented in Slavic by a "reduced" grade, with *i* or *u* before nasal or liquid.

	obstruents	sonorants	vowels
Pre-Balto-Sl	**p b t d ḱ ǵ k g s š**	**m n l r j w**	**ī i ē e ā a ō o ū u**
Earliest CoS	**p b t d** (s) **z k g s š**	**m n l r j w**	**ī i ē e ā a ū u**

Diphthongs	e-grade	o-grade	zero / reduced grade
oral	**ei eu**	**ai au**	**i u**
nasal	**en em**	**an am**	**in im un um**
liquid	**er el**	**ar al**	**ir il ur ul**

ECoS **s* is ambiguous; it could go back to satem-IE **ḱ,* or to ancient **s*.

34. The evolution of early Indo-European to the late dialect continuum we dub PBS depends on data from many languages with extremely different histories. Here only a few examples will be cited in order to hint at the striking correspondences that establish the plausibility of a common linguistic ancestor of English, Latin, Greek, and Slavic.

34.1 Let us start with a small store of standard etymologies of MCoS words as examples of the usual relationships back to early Indo-European. Although our focus is generally on the simplified array of Pre-Balto-Slavic, these examples include some of the evidence for the earlier voiced aspirates (*bh* etc.), the labiovelar stops (k^w g^w g^wh), and the laryngeals (h_1 h_2 h_3 [or *H,* in unclear cases]). Greek, Latin, and Germanic have undergone consonant changes that must be taken into account; here are the chief equivalents:

IE	*p*	*b*	*bh*	*t*	*d*	*dh*	*ḱ*	*ǵ*	*ǵh*	*k*	*g*	*gh*	k^w	g^w	g^wh
Gk	p	b	ph	t	d	th	k	g	kh	k	g	kh	p/t	b/d	ph/th
Lat	p	b	f/b	t	d	f/d	c	g	h	c	g	h	qu	u/gu	f/u
Gm	f/b	f/b	b	þ/d	t	d	h/g	g	h/g	h	g	g	hw	kw	w
San	p	b	bh	t	d	dh	ś	j	h	k	g	gh	k/c	g/j	gh/h
Slav	**p**	**b**	**b**	**t**	**d**	**d**	**s**	**z**	**z**	**k**$^+$	**g**$^+$	**g**$^+$	**k**$^+$	**g**$^+$	**g**$^+$

The symbols **k**$^+$ and **g**$^+$ in the last line are intended to include *c ʒ* and *č ž,* see the summary tables in §32D, page 208 above.

34.2 The Slavic in the alphabetical list below is OCS except that asterisks mark unchanged MCoS liquid diphthongs, _*tj,_ or words not attested in canonical OCS. The Pre-Balto-Slavic etymon is given first, followed by the early IE form (usually only the root, marked by √), with parallels from other languages. The symbol "H" indicates a laryngeal whose exact definition remains uncertain.

> Abbreviations: Av(estan), ER - Early Rusian, Gmc - Germanic, Go(thic), G(ree)k, La(tin), Li(thuanian), ME - Middle English, OE - Old English, OHG - Old High German, Sa(nskrit)

berǫ 'I take' < _*ber-,_ √bher 'carry': Sa _bhárāmi,_ La _ferō,_ Gk φέρω, Go _baira_

*berza 'birch' (R _berëza,_ Cz _březa_) < _*berz-,_ √bherHǵ-: Li _béržas,_ Gm _*birkjōn-,_ OHG _birihha,_ Sa _bhūrjás_

*běgǫ 'I run, flee' < _*běg-,_ √bheg^w: Li _bègu,_ Gk φέβομαι 'I flee, fear', φόβος 'fear'

bljudǫ 'I observe' < _*beud-,_ √bheudh: Sa _bódhāmi_ 'I notice', Homeric πεύθομαι 'learn (by enquiry)'

*blъxa 'flea'< _*blu-s-ā_: Li _blusà_; cf. _*plou+k-_ in Gmc _*flauhaz,_ G _Floh_; _*plus-/pusl-_ La _*puslex_ > _pūlex,_ Gk _*psul-ya_ > ψύλλα

boljьjь 'bigger, better' < *bol-, √bel: Sa _bálīyān_ 'stronger', Gk βέλτερος 'better', La _dēbilis_ 'deprived of strength, weak'

*boršьno (OCS _brašьno_ 'food', SC _brȁšno_ 'flour') < _*bors-in-_ √bhars 'barley': cf. La _farīna_ < _*bhars-īn-_

bratrъ 'brother' < _*brātr-_ < _*bhréh$_2$ter-_: Sa _bhrā́tā,_ Gk φράτηρ, La _frāter,_ Go _brōþar_

byxъ, bysta, byšę < _*bū-s-om, -tā, -n̥t_ 'I was, you two were, they were'; √bhuH

cěna 'price' < _*kainā_ < _*k^{w}oi-neh$_2$-_ : Li _kainà_ 'price', Gk ποινή 'fine, penalty'

-cěstiti 'cleanse < _*kaist-_:
čistъ 'pure, clean' < _*keist-_: | ? Sa _ketús_ 'brightness', German _heiter_ 'gay, clear'; Li _skaistùs_ 'bright; fresh; untouched, innocent'

desętь 'ten' < _*dek̂m̥t-_ : Li _dẽšimt,_ Sa _daśā́t_ '[quantity of] ten', La _decem,_ Gk δέκας, δέκα

_dě-l-o_ 'deed' < _*dē-_ √dheh$_1$
_dě-ti_ 'to do' | Li _déti_ 'to do, put', Sa _ádhām_ 'I put', Gk ἔθηκα 'I (have) put', La _faciō, fēcī_ 'put, have put', OE _dōn_ 'to do'

domъ 'house' < _*domus_ : Sa _dámas,_ Gk δόμος, La _domus_

dymъ 'smoke' < _*dhūmas_ < _*dhuh$_2$-mó-,_ √dhweh$_2$: Sa _dhūmás,_ La _fūmus,_ cf. Gk θυμός '(onrush of) courage'

**dъtji* 'daughter' (OCS *dъšti*, ER *dъči*) < **duktēr* < **dhugh$_2$tér-* : Li *duktẽ*, Sa *duhitā́*, Gk θυγάτηρ

ěd-ętъ 'eat' < **ēd-*, √h$_1$ed: Li *édmi*; Sa *ádmi*, La *edō*, Gk ἔδομαι 'I will eat'

**gojь* (SC *goj* 'health, peace', OCz *hoj* 'abundance') < **g^{w}oj-*, √*g^{w}eih$_3$ 'live' [compare *žіwъ*]

gorěti 'burn' < **gor-* √g^{w}her : cf. Sa *ghr̥nóti* 'burns', *háras* 'flame'; cf. also *požarъ*, *žeravъ*

gostь 'guest' < **ghostis* 'stranger' : Go *gasts* 'guest', La *hostis* 'enemy'

**govędo* 'steer' < **gou-en-d-*; √g^{w}ou-/g^{w}ōu : cf. Latv *gùovs* 'cow', Sa *gáus*, La *bōs bovis*, Gk βοῦς [Gs βοῒῦς], OE cū

goniti gъnati 'drive' < **gen-/gan-/-gun-* √g^{w}hen, cf. Li *ganýti* 'to herd'; Sa *hánti* 'strikes' 3p *ghnánti*; Gk θείνω 'strike' < **t^{h}en̯iō*, φόνος 'murder' < **p^{h}onos*;
ženǫtъ

jesmь 'I am' < **esmi* √h$_1$es: Sa *ásmi*, Li *esmì*, Gk εἶμι (< **esmi*)

junъ 'young' < **jaun-* √h$_2$i̯eu-H(o)n- : Li *jáunas*; Sa *yúvan-* 'young; youth'; La *juvenis; jūnior*, Go *juggs* [spelled gg = phonetic ŋg]

kolo 'wheel' < **kal-* √k^{w}el- : OPrussian *kelan*, ONorse *huel*, Gk πόλος 'axis of sphere, pole'

kowati kowǫ 'forge' < **kau-* : Li *káuju káuti*; OHG *houwan*; La *cūdō*

**kry* 'blood' < **krū* √kreuh$_2$: Sa *kravíṣ-* 'raw meat', Gk κρέας 'meat', La *cruor* 'meat', *crūdus* 'raw'; Gmc **hrawa-* > E. *raw*

lajǫ 'bark' < **lā-* √*leh$_2$: Li *lóju* 'I bark', Sa *rā́yati* 'barks'; La *lā-mentum* 'lament'

lěwъ 'left' < **laiwas* : La *laevus*, Gk λαιός < λαιϊός

ljubъ 'pleasing' < **leub-*, √leubh- : Sa *lúbhyati* 'desires'

luna 'moon' < **lauk-s-nā*, √leuk: OPrussian *louxnos* (pl) 'stars', La *lūna* 'moon'

lъgati 'lie' < **lug-* √leugh: cf. Go *liugan*, OE *lēogan*

medъ 'honey' < **médhu-* : Li *medùs*, Sa *mádhu*, Gk μέθυ 'intoxicating drink' (cf. E *mead*)

měxъ 'skin, bag' < **maisas* : Li *maĩšas* 'big sack', Sa *meṣa-* 'ram, hide'

mьzda 'reward, just due' < **mizd-*, **misdhó-*: Go *mizdo*, Av *miždəm*, Gk μισθός 'pay'

měsęcь 'month, moon' < **mēs-n̥-k-* : Sa *mā̐s* (Gs *mā́sas*), OPers *māhyā* (Loc sg)

męso 'meat' < **mems-* √*mēmso- 'flesh': OPrussian *mensā*, Sa *mā̃ṃsám*, Go *mimz*

mętǫ 'I disturb, mix' < **menth$_2$-* : Sa *mánthati* 'mixes, disturbs'

**mozgъ* < **mazg-* : Sa *majján-* 'marrow', Av *mazgəm* 'marrow, brain', OHG *marg*, OE *mearg* > E *marrow*

mъxъ 'moss' < **musas* : Li *mūsaĩ* 'mold'] OHG *mos* 'moss', La *muscus*
**myšь* 'mouse' < **mūsi-s* : La, OHG *mūs*, Gk μῦς, Sa *mūṣ-*
nebo 'sky' < **neb-* √nebh: Sa *nábhas* 'mist, cloud', Gk νεφέλη 'cloud', La *nebula* 'cloud', Hittite *nepiš* 'heaven'
**nosъ* 'nose' < **nasas* : *nās-* > La *nāsus* 'nose'
oči '[two] eyes (Ndu)' < **akī* < *h_3ok^w-ih_1*, √h_3ek^w; Li *akì*
ostrowъ 'island' < *ab-sraṷ- 'flow around' [-sr- > -str-] : compare *struja*
ostrъ 'sharp' **asras* < **aḱros* √h_2eḱ: Gk ἄκρος 'topmost, extreme'
owьca 'sheep' < **owikā*, < *$h_2$ówi-*: La *ovis*, Gk ὄ(ϝ)ις
**pelnъ* 'booty' (OCS *plěnъ*, R *pólon*) Li *pel̃nas*; cf. OHG *fâli* < **fēl-ja-* 'for sale' (?)
pěna 'foam' < **poin-* < **(s)poim-n-*: Sa *phénas*; Li *spáinė* 'foam [on waves]', La *spūma*; OHG *feim*
**pьlnъ* 'full' < **piln-* < *$pl̥h_1$-no-*: Li *pìlnas*, Go *fulls* (< **fulnaz*)
počьjetъ 'rests' < *-*kei-* √k^weiH: La *quies*
pokojь 'rest' < *-*kai-as*
**požarъ* 'conflagration' < **po-žēr-*, √g^wher- (cf. *gorěti, žeravъ*): cf. Sa *gharmás* 'heat, glow'; La *formus* = G θερμός = OHG *warm* 'warm, hot'
pǫtь m. 'road' < **pant-* : Sa *pánthās* 'way', La *pons pontis* 'bridge'
rosa 'dew' < **rasā* : Li *rasà*, Sa *rasā* 'dampness'; La *rōs rōris* 'dew'
sěmę sěmene 'seed' < **sē-men* √seh_1 'sow': La *sēmen*, OHG sāmo
směją sę 'laugh' < **smēj-* √smei-: Latvian *smeju*; Sa *smáyate* '(he) smiles'
**sьrdьce* 'heart' < **ḱrd-i-k-a* √ḱerd: Li *širdìs*, Gk καρδία, La *cor cordis*
sněgъ 'snow' < **snaigas*, √sneig^{w}h: Li *sniẽgas*, Go *snaiws*
solь 'salt' < **sal-i-s*: La *sal*, cf. Go *salt*
sta (3s aor) 'stopped, stood' < **stā*, √$steh_2$: Sa *ásthāt*, Gk ἔστη
stojati 'to stand' < earliest Slavic **staj-ē-tei* < possible earlier **stə-* < *sth_2-* (zero-grade of √$steh_2$)
stignǫti 'arrive, reach' 3s aor *stiže* < **steig-* √steigh: Sa *stighnoti* 'climbs', Go *steiga* 'I climb', Gk στείχω 'I go'
struja 'stream, current' < **straujā* √sreu: East Li *sraujà* 'stream', *sraũjas* 'rapid', cf. Gk ῥέϊω 'flow'
synъ 'son' < **sūnus*, √seuH 'give birth': Li *sūnùs*, Go *sunus*
**šujь* 'left' < **seu-jo-* : Sa *savyás*
topiti 'heat' *teplъ* 'hot' < **top-/*tep-* : Sa *tápati* 'heats', La *tepeō; tepidus* 'warm'
trьje 'three (m)' < **treįes*: Gk τρεῖς, La *trēs*, Li *trỹs*
turъ 'aurochs' < **tauras*: Li *taũras*; Gk ταῦρος, La *taurus* 'bull'
uxo 'ear' (Gs *ušese*, du *uši*) < **ous-* √$h_2$eus-: Li *ausìs*, Go *auso*, La *auris*
wesna 'spring' < **wes-* : Li *vasarà* 'summer', Sa *vasantás* 'spring'

wezǫ 'convey' < **weǵ-* √weǵh-: Li vežù, Sa *váhati* 'goes', La *vehō* 'convey'

**wьlkъ* 'wolf' < **wl̥kos,* *wl̥k^{w}os : Li *vil̃kas,* Sa *vr̥kás*

**wьrxъ* 'top' < *wr̥su- √wer: Li *viršùs* 'top', Sa *várṣiṣṭhas* 'highest', La *verrūca* (< **-rs-*)

wьsь 'village' < **wiḱos* √weiḱ: Sa *viś-* 'tribe'; La *vīcus* 'village', OE *wīc,* ME *wike* 'village'

**wydra* 'otter' < **ūdrā,* √wed 'water': Li *ū́dra*; Gk ὕδρα 'water snake'

zima 'winter' < **ǵeim-ā,* √ǵheim: Li *žiemà*; La *hiems,* Gk χειμών

znati 'to know' < **ǵnō-,* √ǵneh$_3$: Li *žinóti;* La *gnōscō* 'recognize', Gk γιγνώσκω 'know', Go *kunnan* 'know'

zǫbъ 'tooth' < **ǵombos,* √ǵembh: Li *žam̃bas* 'sharp edge', Sa *jámbhas* 'tooth', Gk γόμφος 'nail', E *comb*

ženǫtъ 'they chase': see *goniti*

**žeraw(j)ь* 'crane' (Bg *žérav,* SC *žȅrāv* [cf. R *žurávl'*]) < **ger-āw,* √gerh$_2$: Li *gérvò,* Gk γέρανος, OE *cran,* La *grūs grŭis*

**žerawъ* 'glowing' < **ger-,* √g^{w}her: see *požarъ* and *gorěti*

žiwъ 'living' **gīw-* < *g^{w}ih$_3$-wo-, √g^{w}eih$_3$: Li *gývas,* Sa *jīvás,* Go *qius,* La *vīvus*; Gk βίος 'life'

ʒělo 'very' < **ghoil-* : Li *gailùs* 'strong, bitter'; OHG *geil* 'exuberant'

IE phoneme	-	reflected in Slavic by the following words:
p	-	teplъ, topiti, *pelnъ, pěna, pǫtь
b	-	boljьji
(bh)	-	berǫ, *berza, *-běgǫ, bljudǫ, *boršьno, bratrъ, bysta, byšę, byxъ, ljubъ, nebo
t	-	bratrъ, čistъ, *dъtji, gostь, mętǫ, pǫtь, sta, stignǫ, teplъ, topiti, trьje, turъ
d	-	cěditi, cěstiti, čistъ, desętь, domъ, ědętъ, *sьrdьce, *wydra
(dh)	-	bljudǫ, dělo, děti, dymъ, *dъtji, mьzda
ḱ	-	desętъ, *sьrdьce, wьsь
ǵ	-	*berza, znati, zǫbъ
(ǵh)	-	wezǫ, zima
k	-	cěditi, cěstiti, čistъ, kopati, kowǫ, měsęcь, owьca, *sьrdьce
g	-	*dъtji, *golsъ, polьʒa, lъgati, mozgъ, *žerawъ
(gh)	-	stignǫ, stiže, gostь, ʒělo
(k^w)	-	cěna, kolo, oči, *wьlkъ
(g^w)	-	*-běgǫ, *gojь, gowędo, žiwъ
(g^{w}h)	-	goniti, gorěti, gъnati, požarъ, sněgъ, ženǫ, žerawъ
s	-	*blъxa, *boršьno, bysta, byxъ, byšę, *golsъ, gostь, jesmь, męso, měsecь, měxъ, mъxъ, rosa, solь, sěmę, směјǫ sę, sněgъ, sta, stignǫti, stojati, struja, synъ, šujь, uxo, *wьrxъ
[z]	-	mozgъ, mьzda
m	-	domъ, dymъ, jesmъ, medъ, měsęcь, měxъ, męso, mętǫ, mozgъ, mъxъ, myšь, zima, zǫbъ

n	-	cěna, gъnati, junъ, luna, mętǫ, nebo, *nosъ, ǫzъkъ, pěna, pǫtь, sěmę, sněgъ, synъ, znati
r	-	berǫ, *berza, *boršьno, bratrъ, gorěti, požarъ, rosa, struja, *srьdьce, trьje, turъ, *wьrxъ, wydra, žerawь, žerawъ
l	-	bljudǫ, *golsъ, kolo, lajǫ, lěvъ, ljubъ, luna, polьʒa, lъgati, *pelnъ, solь, *wьlkъ, ʒělo
w	-	lěwъ, owьca, wesna, wezǫ, *wьlkъ, *wьrxъ, wьsь, žiwъ
j	-	počьjetъ, pokojь, smějǫ sę, trьje, junъ
(h_1)	-	dělo, děti, jesmь/sǫt-ъ/ь, *pьlnъ
(h_2)	-	bratrъ, byxъ, *dъtji, dymъ, *kry, ostrъ, [stojati,] uxo
(h_3)	-	*gojь, oči, znati, žiwъ
ą	-	kopati, nosъ, solь
ā	-	bratrъ, lajǫ, owьca, rosa
ai	-	lěwъ, ʒělo
au	-	turъ, kowati, junъ, ostrowъ, struja
ĕ	-	berǫ, *berza, desętь, jesmь, medъ, nebo, *pelnъ, teplъ, wesna, wezǫ, *žerawъ, *žerawь
ē	-	*-běgǫ, dělo, děti, ědętъ, měsęcь, pěna, požarъ, sěmę, smějǫ sę, sněgъ, stojati
ei	-	čistъ, stignǫ, trьje, zima
eu	-	bljudǫ, ljubъ, nowъ, šujь
ĭ	-	jesmь, gostь, mьzda, owьca, *sьrdьce, vьsь
ī	-	oči, žiwъ
ŏ	-	*boršьno, domъ, *golsъ, goniti, gorěti, gostь, kolo, mozgъ, nosъ, oči, owьca, rosa, topiti
oi	-	cěditi, cěna, cěstiti, *gojь [?], měxъ
ou	-	gowędo, junъ, luna, ostrowъ, struja, uxo
ō	-	znati
ų	-	*blъxa, *dъtji, lъgati, mъxъ
ū	-	dymъ, myšь, synъ, wydra
[ə	-	stojati < *sth$_2$- (the laryngeal yields a vowel, **ə**: this "schwa" symbol is widely used in older scholarly literature)

35. The general outlines of phonological development and the morphophonemic structure of inflectional patterns are clear enough, but the individual histories of many morphemes and words are full of puzzles.

35.1 A striking difference between the Indo-European and OCS phonemic inventories is that IE had a single continuant obstruent, *s* (with allophonic [z] before voiced stops), while OCS has two voiced continuants, *z* and *ž*, and at least three voiceless ones (*s*, *š*, and *x*); a possible fourth (*ś*) may be posited for the pronominal stems *sь* 'this' and *wьsь* 'all' and/or in such declensional forms as Ls *dusě* and Np *dusi* (from *duxъ* 'spirit'). Late IE **s* split into *s* vs. *š* by the ruki-rule (§25.3). New and specifically Slavic morpheme-shapes with *s* appeared as the IE palatal stops *ḱ* and *ǵ* became *s* (merging with and indistinguishable from the extant *s*) and *z* (a new phoneme of transparent origin), cf. §27.1. At a later date, *sj* and *šj* merged in *š* which could be followed only by *ī, i, e, ē* (§27.4); *š* in any other position backed to *x* (see examples 17–31 on page 207). By VR² (§27.72), *šē* > *šā* and the contrasts *sā* ~*sē* ~ *šā* ~ *xā* (and the exclusion of *šē* and *xē*) are established in lexical entries and phonotactic rules. Schematically:

s		**s**	**š**		**s**	**ś**	**š**	**x**
[z]	>	**z**		>	**z**		**ž**	

35.11 Initial *x* and *š* are well documented in LCoS. Where did they come from? The ruki-rule has been invoked to explain the variants *xod* and *šьd* 'go'. They reflect the IE root **sed*: the o-grade **sod-o-* (cf. Gk ὁδός 'way, journey', whence E *odometer*) and an anomalous zero-grade **sid,* after prefixes like **per-, *prei-.* Thus **per-sod-os > *peršadas,* which provided the stem for a denominative verb, yielding OCS *prěxodъ* 'crossing, transition' and *prěxod-i+* 'cross'; **prei-sid-us- > *prei-šid-uš-* > OCS *prišьdъ* 'having arrived'.[35] The numeral *šestь* 'six' may reflect **kseks-ti-s > *kšekstiš > *šesti*; in any case, Baltic also has initial *š*. Two roots have *š* from **sj*: **sjū-tei > *sjītei > *šiti* 'to sew' (§15.93), and **seu-j-os > *sjaujas> šujь* 'left' (cf. §29.95). *Šum-* 'sound (of water, wind)' and *šьpъt-* 'whisper' seem to be onomatopoetic.

35.12 Many roots or stems beginning in *x* or *š* are plausibly explained as borrowings. New loans from Greek are clear—including some where *x* is followed by a front vowel (*xerowimъ* 'cherubim'; *xitonъ* 'chiton, tunic, undergarment)'. Germanic contributed *xlěbъ* 'bread' (< **hlaib-,* cf. Go *hlaifs,* G *Laib,* 'loaf'), and *šlěmъ* 'helmet' (< **xelm-,* < Gmc **helmaz*). *Šarъ* 'color' (*šaropisateljь* 'painter') is from Turkic, presumably Proto-Bulgarian, the language of the founders of the Bulgarian state. Iranian origin is called on to explain several roots (e.g. *xwala* 'praise'), but the resemblances between the Slavic and Iranian words, tempting though some of them may be, do not fit into systematic patterns that establish acceptable evidence. Another line of investigation is to posit **ks* as a result of **sk* or **sg,* with "mobile s" (coopted from a desinence-final consonant of a preceding word). Proposals are imaginative but, in my opinion, unconvincing. Most roots with initial *x* remain unexplained—as do some with *š*, e.g. *šir* 'wide, broad' (OCS *širokъ*), *šija* 'neck' (marginal

---

35 Just why these particular allomorphs achieved independent status (while *s*-variants predominated in all other roots) remains unexplained.

in OCS but wide-spread in later dialects), *šęt* ‘rage, behave violently, insolently’. Proposals that appeal to a putative IE **x* or **kh* are no longer taken seriously.[36]

35.13 Stem-final *x* and *š* are often hard to account for.

(a1) An *s* after LCoS *i, y, u,* ь, or ъ may represent IE **k̑* (e.g. *pьsati* ‘to write’ §27.6) or a consonant cluster with a stop other than **k* or **g* (e.g. **k̑s)* **osь* ‘axis’ < ECoS **assis* < IE **ak̑s-i-* [cf. Li *aššìs*]), *wys-ok-ъ* ‘high’ < **ūps-*, cf. Gk ὑψηλός ‘high, tall’). *Kys-nǫ+* ‘ferment’ and *kysělъ* ‘sour’ go back to **kūp-s-*, cf. OCS *kyp-ě+* ‘to boil’.

Thus the stative *wis-ě+* ‘be hanging’ and causative *wěs-i+* ‘hang’ (perfective *ob-ěs-i+,* iterative *ob-ěš-aj+*) suggest *weik̑-/*woik̑-* or else **weiC-s/*woiC-s*; attempts to find suitable cognates in any other language have not been successful.

(a2) Or the stem may be borrowed: e.g. *kusi+* ‘taste, try, tempt’; **kaus-* is from Germanic, cf. Go *kausjan* (< IE **geus-* [> E *choose*]).

(b) Stem-final *-ěs-* may go back to **aiCs*. It has been argued that *běsъ* ‘demon’ and *běda* ‘danger, catastrophe’ and *bojati sę* ‘be afraid’ (cf. Li *baisùs* ‘frightening, scary’, *baidýti* ‘to frighten’) demonstrate a late IE **boid-s-*.

(c) The verbs *wъs-krьs-nǫ+, wъs-krьs-aj+* ‘rise again’ and *wъs-krěs-i+* ‘resurrect’ imply zero-grade **kris* vs. o-grade **krois* (§42.14). The persistent use of this stem in OCS to denote the fundamental Christian conception of rising from the dead (rather than the more literal *wъ(z)-sta-, wъ(z)-staw-aj-, wъ(z)-staw-i* ‘stand up, cause to rise’ that occasionally appear) surely indicates that the earliest translators found it an effective translation. Post-OCS data associate **krěs/*krьs* with the summer solstice and pre-Christian ritual festivities (particularly bonfires); the exact nature of these practices and beliefs remains unknown, but a connection with rebirth and new life seems highly plausible. Li has a formally suitable verbal root *kreip/kraip* ‘turn, change direction’. Some scholars believe that this sense can be accomodated with hypothetical PBS **krips/*kroips* and a meaning involving new life.

(d) The adjective *pěšь* ‘on foot, walking’ (e.g. *po njemь idǫ pěši* ‘they followed him on foot’ Mt 14:13) or ‘walker, pedestrian; foot-soldier’

---

[36] A recalcitrant problem is R *soxá* ‘wooden plow’ ~ Li *šakà*, Sa *śaknā* ‘branch, forked stick’ and many other apparent cognates.

surely is based on IE *ped/pod* 'foot', a root known in most IE languages (cf. La *pēs,* Gs *pedis,* Gk ποῦς ποδός). We can invent a suitable phonetic ancestor, **pēd-s-jo-*, but the *s*-element has no obvious parallel.

Cz *pěchota* 'infantry' is known from 1487. It appears in Polish about 1600, and then in a Ruthenian text in 1609. It seems therefore to be a fairly modern formation, but easily travelled from one Slavic language to others. It was taken into Slovene in the 19th century.

(e) The OCS noun *směxъ* 'laughter' is obviously related to *smьj-a+ směj-ǫtъ* 'laugh' and the IE root **smei*, but it is uncertain whether the *x* represents an old **s* (**smoi-so-*?, **smōi-so-*?) or a newer and independent **x*. An iterative stem **-smis-aj+* 'mock' appears to be a recent formation with the formant **sā*. Similarly, *pospěxъ* 'capability' and *uspěxъ* 'success' go with *spěj-Ø+* (§15.45), IE **speH* 'thrive, prosper' (cf. Gmc **spō-di-z,* E *speed*; La *spēs* 'hope').

(f) *Grěxъ* 'sin' strongly points to *grěj-Ø+* 'to warm', but the Christian sense is apparently adapted from a native meaning 'miss the mark, fail to do correctly'. Perhaps we should posit **groi-so-*, suggested by early *grěza* 'confusion' (early Rus', possible OCS) and Li *graĩžas* 'rim' < **groi-ǵo-*, cf. Latv *greizs* 'oblique, slanting'.

(g) The *x* in *jaxa-* 'ride' (§16.4) and *ob-ǫx-aj+* 'to smell, have sense of smell, perceive by smelling' (a synonym of *ob-(w)onj-aj+*) must be considered new suffixal elements, perhaps no older than LCoS.

(h) Isolated suffixes (e.g. in *ženixъ* 'bridegroom', cf. *žena* 'woman, wife', *ženi+* 'marry'; *pustošь* 'trivial matter, trifle', cf. *pustъ* 'empty; *junoša* 'young man', cf. *junъ* 'young') provide no helpful information. We may surmise that some of them are affective, usually hypocoristic but sometimes pejorative. Later Slavic dialects provide a wealth of affective *x/š* suffixes.

(i) The problematic sibilant in the pronominal stems сь сє си 'this' and вьсь вьсє вьсѣ 'all' is treated in §40.11-40.123.

35.14 Slavic *luna* 'moon' is (like, but entirely independent of, Latin *luna*) derived from **louk-snā-* (cf. *luča* 'ray' < **lauk-j-ā,* IE **leuk* 'light' [> Gmc **leuk-to-* > E *light*]). The sequence **ksn* > **kšn* > *n,* while in OPrussian *ksn* remains: *louxnos* 'stars'. OCS *čьrnъ* 'black' corresponds to Sa *kr̥ṣṇá-* 'black', OPr *kirsnan*. Expected ECoS **kirsna-* > **kiršna-* > MCoS *čьrnъ*. Such etymologies are opaque; they require information not available in the Slavic forms.

36 Constraints on initial vowels belong to dialects of Late Common Slavic. In many regions the constraints changed over time; unfortunately, lack of documentation makes it hard to follow many important details. It appears that LCoS generally disallowed *#a-*, and added prothetic *j* regardless of etymology. Yet certain eastern Bulgarian dialects preferred *#a-* to *#ja-*, and removed etymological *j* at least in some words. The OCS and later medieval texts are inconsistent, and more modern sources present further complications that cannot be discussed here.

36.1 The two ECoS roots that began in **ē* are assumed to have preposed *j-*: then **jē* > **jā* in SE LCoS: OCS *jadь* 'food', *jasti* 'to eat' (§16.22). The spelled "ě" in forms of *ěxati ědǫtъ* 'to ride' (§16.4) is justified as standing for *jě/ja* by modern forms like Uk їхати їдуть. On the other hand, SC and Sln have only *jahati* (with a new j-present *jaše*). The etymology is surely **jā-* (Li *jóju jóti,* Sa *yāti* 'goes').

36.2 (a) For *azъ* and *jazъ* 'I', see §40.311-12.

(b) OCS *avi+/avljaj+* 'reveal, make clear' (*avě* 'openly, in the open, manifestly, clearly') are somewhat less frequent than *javi+, javljaj+,* or *javljenьje,* but no *j* is indicated in *obavi+ obavljaj+* 'show, reveal', *obavljenьje* 'appearance, apparition' (or the rare *obavaj+* 'charm, work magic', *obavьnikъ* 'charmer, magician'). The PBS root **āw-* 'clear, mani–fest, reveal' fits with * Sa *āvís* 'obvious', and, more remotely, La *audēre* 'hear'. The modern Slavic languages have only *jav-*.

(c) Unsuffixed **aje/*jaje* 'egg' is less common in Slavdom than **ajьce* (OCS Ap *aica)/*jajьce*: **aj-e* suggests IE **ōy-on,* a form that is comparable to Gk ᾠόν; speculation about relationships with **awi-* 'bird' remain inconclusive. Czech and Slovak have initial **w*: **waj-* > OCz, Slk *vajce,* mod. Cz *vejce*. Upper Sorbian has *wejo* and *jejo*. The **waj-* probably is the result of late and local dissimilation from **jaj-*.

(d) The root **agn-* 'lamb' (OCS *agnę, agnьcь/jagnьcь*) presupposes long **ā,* with LCoS prothesis of *j*. The initial vowel is short in Lat *agnus,* Gk ἀμνός; evidence from other languages suggests $*g^w$ and $*g^wh$.

(e) The *apple,* though not attested early, surely was **ablъko* in some parts of Bulgaria, and **jablъko* elsewhere in LCoS. Late IE **abel-* or **abl-* (cf. Gmc **apalaz*; Li *óbuolas, obuolỹs* 'apple') became a u-stem, to which a regularizing (diminutive?) *-*ko-* was added. The *j-* is present in all the standard languages, but the gender varies: R *jábloko,* Uk *jábluko,* Mac, Sln *jabolko,* Cz, Slk *jablko,* P *jabłko*; Bg *jabъlka,* SC *jabuka*; BR *jáblyk*.

(f) *Agoda* 'berry; strawberry' (OCS Mt 12:35 Sav 'fruit'), with Li *úoga,* establishes ECoS **āg-ad-ā* and PBS **ōg-*. It goes with IE $*h_3eg$-, which in zero-grade underlies Gmc *ak-ran-*, E. *acorn*. The *ja-* is now in all the Slavic languages.

(g) The phrase дрѣвѣ соусѣ аворовѣ (Ds) translates ἐπί δένδρου πλατάνου ξηροῦ 'to a dry *X* tree'; *avorovъ* is an adjective based on **avorъ,* now represented by forms with initial *ja-* in Sl dialects. It is the sycamore, or maple, or plane-tree; the Greek here has πλάτανος 'plane-tree'. Whatever this passage may have meant, **avorъ* is probably a borrowing from Old Bavarian **āhor* (OHG *ahorn*) 'maple'; the initial *j-* is added in LCoS.

(i) Not mentioned in early texts is **jasenь* 'ash-tree', which has been seen as based on IE **ās-* with an **n* suffix **āsen-* (cf. La *ornus*). Gmc used a **k* suffix: **askiz* > G *Esche*.

(j) The noun *pojasъ* 'belt' and verb *pojasa+* 'gird' retain the **j-* of IE **yōs* (cf. Li *júosta* 'belt'; Gk ζωνή 'girdle' < *yōs-nā*). The adjective *jarъ* 'furious' may come from IE **yōr* (< IE **yeH-r-*), cf. Gk ζωρός 'sheer, undiluted', used of wine; a semantic association of "strong, forceful, heady" and "furious" is assumed.

(k) Other words beginning in *ja-* in many or most Slavic languages have no plausible etymologies. Among them are OCS *jasnъ* 'bright, clear'; *jama* 'ditch, trench, pit'; *jarьmъ* 'yoke' (or neuter **jarьmo,* post-OCS); *jazwa* 'wound' and *jazwina* 'cave, burrow, lair'; along with later-attested **jalъ* and **jalovъ* 'barren, sterile, unable to reproduce'; **jarębь* 'partridge'; **jastrębъ* 'hawk'.

36.3 Prefixed stems or compounds offer some contrasting forms.

(a) *paǫčina* and *pajǫčina* 'spider-web' imply **paǫkъ/*pajǫkъ* 'spider': *-ǫkъ* (cf. R паýк, SC *pȁūk*) is compared to IE **$h_2$onkos* 'hook' (La *uncus* 'hook', Gk ὄγκος 'barbed hook', Sa *añkas* 'hook, bend' and the shape of a spider's legs.[37] The *j* must be an ECoS addition, attested in farflung dialects: e.g. P *pajək,* Sln *pajək,* Mac *pajak,* dial. *pajek*. Uk павýк and Cz *pavouk* illustrate later prothetic *w/v* before *u* in certain regions.

(b) *rǫkowętь* and *rǫkojętь* 'sheaf' are analyzed as "amount one can grasp with both arms"; they seem to show older and newer compounding. The first is ECoS **ronk-au+im-t-i(š),* GL dual (OCS *rǫku*) plus a noun-stem with the root. The second is a normal LCoS compound: *rǫk-o-* is the usual combining form, and *j* is expected as prothesis to older *ьm* or newer *ę*.

---

37 The *pa-* is an old lengthened variant of *po,* used in nominal formations; *paguba* 'ruin, destruction' (cf. *pogubi+* 'destroy'), *pamętь* 'memory, memorial' (<**pā-min-ti-s,* cf *pomьně+* 'remember'), and *pažitь* 'meadow, pasture, feeding-ground' (cf. *živ-* 'live'), see Vasmer sub па-.

36.41 OCS *blagovonjьnъ* and *blagoǫxanьnъ* 'sweet-smelling, fragrant' are synonymous, as are the verbs *obonjaj+* and *obǫxaj+* 'smell, perceive by smelling'. The roots *wonj* and *ǫx* surely go back to ECoS **an* and IE **$h_2$enh$_1$* (Sa *aniti* 'breathes'; Gk ἄνεμος 'wind'; La **anamos > animus* 'spirit'). The reasons for prothetic **w* in one and final **x* in the other are unknown.

36.42 OCS *sъǫzъ* and *sъvǫzъ* share the meaning 'bond, fetter; union'. The root is *ǫz-* < PBS **anǵ* < IE **$h_2$enǵh* 'tight, constricted' (La *angere* 'draw tight' [> E *anxious*], *angustus* 'narrow [> E *anguish*]; Gmc **angaz,* E *anger*). Otherwise *ǫz* appears in *ǫza* 'bond, fetter', *ǫže* {ǫz-j-o} 'chain, rope; snare', *ǫzъkъ* 'narrow, tight' (comp. *ǫže*), *ǫžika* m/f 'relative' (< ECoS *(anz-j-ei*, *ǫžičьstvo* 'kin, relatives'. The phrase *zьrěti podъ obǫzomь* means 'look askance, with suspicion'. Prothesis is unexpected. (Prothetic *j* in R союз, a much later borrowing from Bg Slavonic, is also unexplained.)

36.43 The synonyms *ǫzьnikъ* and *ǫžьnikъ* 'prisoner' (*ǫzilište* 'prison') compete with *tьmьničьnikъ* (*tьmьnica* 'prison'; *tьma* 'darkness') and *sъvęzьnjь* (*sъvęza+* 'tie up'). The root *węz* 'twist, tie, entwine, ensnare; wreathe, crown' (cf. *uvęz-Ø+* 'crown' §15.822, *obęzanьe* 'diadem') suggests ECoS **wenz,* and possibly older **wenǵ*. More remote ties with the ancestor of *-vьj-/-vij-* 'wind' (§15.93) and **wěnъ* 'wreath' (cf. *věnьcь* 'wreath', Li *vainìkas*) seem possible. A connection with *ǫz-* 'narrow, tight' is improbable.

36.44 The word meaning *mustache* (and perhaps *upper lip*) was **ǫsъ* (not OCS), usually used in the plural. If OPrus *wanso* '(beginning) facial hair (on youth)' is a cognate (and not a borrowing from Slavic), initial *w-* was deleted in part of Bulgaria and perhaps Rus', cf. R усы́.

OCS *gǫsěnica* 'caterpillar' seems to have a LCoS parallel **ǫsěnica,* perhaps **ǫsěn-* or **ǫsen-* meaning 'fuzzy, hairy'. The *g* is puzzling.

36.45 *OCS *osa* 'wasp' surely represents PBS **wopsā* (Li *vapsvà*; metathesized form Gmc *wosp-*, La *vespa*); the initial **w* has been lost. Contrast OCS *voskъ* 'wax' (cf. Li *vãškas*; OHG *wahs*).

OCS **językъ* 'tongue', by comparison with OPrus *insuwis,* Go *tuggō,* OLa *dingua,* suggests ECoS **inzū* < PBS **n̥ǵū*. The initial consonant of IE **dn̥ǵū* has been lost, and later prothetic **j-* was added; the complexities of ū-stem declension have been obviated by the addition of stem-final **k-*.[38]

---

[38] Latin changed initial *d* to *l* in several words, possibly indicating borrowing from a related dialect. Li *liežùvis* has modified the first syllable seemingly in accord with the verb *liẽžti* 'lick' (cf. OCS *liza+* < IE **leiǵh-*).

36.46 OCS root-initial *vr* and *vl* imply ECoS syllables with liquid diphthongs (§26.511), e.g. *vlьkъ* < **wьlkъ* 'wolf', *vragъ* < **worgъ* 'enemy'. Older initial **wr-* lost the glide: **wrughyo-* 'rye' > **rugj-a-s* > **rъžь*. It is possible, however, that the early Slavs borrowed Gmc **rugi-* (cf. E. *rye*). There are no plausible examples of initial OCS *l-* from hypothetical PBS **wl-*.

36.5 Where South and West Slavic have initial *je-*, East Slavic often has *o-*: e.g. *jedinъ* ~ *odinъ* 'one', *jedъva* ~ *odъva* 'hardly', *jelenь* ~ *olenь* 'deer', *jesenь* ~ *osenь* 'autumn', *jezero* ~ *ozero* 'lake.

Henning Andersen (1996) has examined the full list of these words in a broad linguistic and geographical framework of Baltic and Slavic. He offers stimulating suggestions as to how language shift (Baltic to Slavic dialect) and eroding dialect boundaries combined over time to produce distributions of these words that could not have resulted from internal development in a settled and homogeneous community.

36.6 South and West Slavic initial *ju-* correspond to Rusian *u-* in three roots: *jun-ъ* 'young', *jug-ъ* 'south', and *juxa* 'broth, soup'– only two of which have solid etymologies. (*Junъ* is cognate with Li *jáunas*, E *young*, and the root in the La comparative *jūnior*. *Juxa* goes with Sa *yuṣ* 'broth', OPr *juse* 'meat broth', La *jūs* 'broth, soup' [whence E *juice*]. No satisfactory source has been found for *jugъ*.) OCS *uže* and *juže* 'already' are interchangeable, while *ne u* 'not yet' is clearly the norm, *ne ju* being rare. OCS *utro* 'morning' (with derivatives) is normal, but *jutro* occurs. In more modern times, *utro* is eastern (ESl, Bg, Mac) and *jutro* (in appropriate phonetic shapes) is western (SC, Sln, WSl). Matters are complicated by OCS *zaustra* 'in the morning, the next morning' (and mod. Mac. dial. *zastra* 'tomorrow morning'), plus OP *justrzenka* 'morning star' and other forms that suggest **ustr-* < **usr-*. The etymology is disputed.

Morphology

37 OCS morphology is unmistakably Indo-European, but the inherited elements have been rearranged. Though the declensional system is conservative (and is relatively close to Baltic) and exhibits familiar patterns, the detailed evidence of the oldest texts shows that a fundamental reorganization is still under way. Post-OCS regional data affirm that our earliest texts illustrate transitional phases of a system undergoing rapid change. Conjugation in OCS has been radically reshaped (and differs substantially from Baltic). The outlines of the verbal system are simplified IE. The materials are for the most part recognizable morphemes or parts of morphemes, yet the combinations are new.

37.1 The basic form classes of the IE nominal system remain in OCS: substantives and adjectives; demonstrative, relative and interrogative pronouns; and personal pronouns. The framework of three genders (masculine, neuter, feminine) and three numbers (singular, dual, plural) is intact, but OCS has lost one IE case—the *ablative,* which has merged with the genitive. (The Baltic system generally agrees with Slavic. Greek very early merged genitive and ablative, while the dative absorbed the old locative and instrumental.)[39] Like IE, Slavic had special vocative forms only for masculine and feminine singular.

37.21 Late Common Slavic declensional stems always end in a consonant. Desinences are vocalic, with the outstanding exception of the nominative (and sometimes accusative) singular zero-marker that characterizes active participles and a list of special stems (including one productive formant {ęt}, §4.414). From the lexical form of a stem, including its inherent gender, the array of desinences is predictable; morphophonemic alternations in the stem-final C (or cluster) are determined by mutation rules (KI, KAI). In the exceptional cases where a terminal zero-desinence is to be posited, alternations may affect the VC that is the end of the inflectional stem. The vowels within a stem otherwise remain constant in all paradigmatic forms.

37.22 Indo-European had a very different system, where a paradigm could include vowel alternations (apophony) in root, derivational suffix, and desinence. There were several types of stems that ended in consonants (C-stems), some consisting only of a root and others with consonantal derivational suffixes. The final C or V of a stem could combine with desinence-initial C or V, often with phonotactic changes. Desinences often ended in a consonant. The details of some of the paradigms are disputed, and citable forms clearly show local modifications in the behavior of individual words.

37.31 Some important nouns were *heteroclitic,* utilizing different stem-suffixes within a paradigm. For example, the "r/n" or "l/n" stems contrasted NAV singular to other forms by a liquid-suffix (*-r-/-er-/-ēr-*; *-l-*) opposed to a nasal-suffix (*-en-/-on-/-n-*), e.g. Hittite 'water', Ns *wat-ar,* Gs *wet-en-as*.

37.311 The hypothetical root **wed* 'wet, water' is represented by a bewildering range of variant forms; it may have had Ns **wed-ōr* (Gk **udōr* ὕδωρ) but Gs **ud-n-és* (Sa *udnás*).

---

[39] Such mergers are called *syncretism*. In Latin, the old locative and instrumental functions were taken over by the ablative.

Greek augmented the n-suffix with *t (and *n̥t > at), ὕδατος. Lithuanian has a root with a nasal diphthong and a stem-suffix *-en-* that is modified before a zero desinence: Ns *vanduõ*, Gs *vandeñs*. English *wet* goes back to **wēd-o-*, *winter* (the wet season) to **we-n-d-*. Latin *unda* 'wave' (cf. E *inundate, undulate*) is from **u-n-d-ā-*. Slavic *vydra* is cognate with E *otter*, and *vědro* 'bucket' presumably has this same ancient root. The noun for 'water' had surely become a regular *a*-stem, *voda*, by MCoS times.[40]

37.312 Hypothetical IE **seh₂wol* 'sun' justifies the shape **sāwel-jo-* as ancestor of older Greek ἠέλιος, classical ἥλιος, and the variants **swōl-* for La *sōl*, **sowl-* for Li *saúlė*, and **swen-*, **sun-* for Gmc **sunnōn* > Ger *Sonne*, E *sun*. Slavic evidence establishes MCoS **sьlnьce*, from which we imply an early **sl̥n* plus a suffix *-*iko-*. The end result is a regular Slavic noun {sьln-ьc-e} which is of little help in establishing IE relationships, but is itself indubitably of IE origin. Similarly *žena* 'woman' (implying ECoS **gen-ā*) is a regularized noun ultimately derived from IE **gʷen*, the root underlying E *queen*, as well as the Gk morpheme *gun* in *gynecology, polygyny* and many other learned words.

37.32 Slavic has adapted its few remaining consonant-stems to the i-stem paradigm (see the table on page 224 for the IE desinences). Moreover, i-stem feminines took on certain distinctive desinences, while i-stem masculines tend to adopt twofold desinences.

These remnants of the IE consonant-stems are therefore called *the anomalous type* of simple declension in this book (§4.1–.414).

For example, the OCS masculine NA *zvěrь* 'wild animal' corresponds to IE As **ǵʰwēr-m̥*: the syllabic nasal had become *-*im*, indistinguishable from the i-stem desinence. Similarly Ap *zvěr-i* could reflect *-*n̥s* or i-stem *-*ins*. The lexeme eventually is redefined as an i-stem. Within OCS, masculine i-stems are being reclassified as regular soft twofold nouns (cf. §4.5).

37.4 The vocalic stems were defined by formants that were subject to ablaut (apophony). The formants *-*i* (with others like *-*ti*, *-*ni*) and *-*u* are zero-grade; e-grade *-*ei* (*-*tei*, *-*nei*) and *-*eu* also appear.

37.5 The major paradigms for masculines and neuters contain the suffix known as the *thematic vowel*, symbolized by $*^{o}/_{e}$: it usually appeared as **o*, but in certain morphemic contexts as **e*. It may mark a root as a noun (e.g. Gk **tok-o-s* 'birth' ~ **tek* 'beget, give birth to' [< IE **tek*]; cf. Sl *tek-Ø+* 'flow, run' [< IE *tekʷ*] ~ PBS **tok-os* 'flow')[41] or it may be the final element of a formant (e.g. **sup-no-* 'sleep'), OCS *tok-ъ, sъn-ъ*. Closely related is the suffix **ā*, which provides the feminine forms of adjectives and, in Slavic, a wide variety of substantives.[42]

---

[40] Heteroclisis was apparently absent from LCoS, but it reappears in new forms in later dialects, e.g. the R type телёнок 'calf' (with -ен plus -к) vs. pl. телята (with ят < ęt).

[41] Some scholars consider the Gk and Slavic to represent a single IE root.

[42] The variable *e* vs. *o* represents IE grades of apophony (ablaut); it also appears in the formant $j^{e}/_{o}$. The Slavic morphophoneme {o/e} is a new entity that is governed

38 Any attempt to trace the history of desinences has to reconcile internal Slavic reconstruction with heterogeneous IE comparative evidence that has serious gaps. The reduction in number of formal paradigms has involved complex processes of analogy. Sometimes the pieces of evidence do not fit together. The behavior of word-final syllables may require special reference to the word-boundary (#), see §24.52.

38.1 The inflection of pronouns in IE differed in certain critical respects from that of substantives. Alternate stems are combined in paradigms that vary considerably from one dialect to another.

This table summarizes evidence that may be pertinent for Slavic. It contains controversial items that cannot be treated here. In any case, many more variants are required to account for all of the early IE languages.

Note that the *-m-* of Instr sg and pl and Dat pl is reflected by Slavic, Baltic and Germanic, as opposed to *-bh-* of all other groups.

The IE ablative was formally like the genitive except in the singular of o-stems; there the ablative desinence took over genitive function in pre-Baltic and Slavic.

<table>
<tr><th></th><th>C-stems</th><th>i-st.</th><th>u-st.</th><th>o-st.</th><th>ā-st.</th><th>pronom.</th></tr>
<tr><td>Ns</td><td>s, Ø</td><td>is</td><td>us</td><td>os (om)</td><td>ā</td><td>o | od id | ā</td></tr>
<tr><td>As</td><td>m̥</td><td>im</td><td>um</td><td>om</td><td>ām</td><td>om | ām</td></tr>
<tr><td>Voc sg</td><td>Ø</td><td>ei</td><td>eu</td><td>e</td><td>ă</td><td>-</td></tr>
<tr><td>Gs | Ab</td><td>es/os/s</td><td>eis, ois</td><td>eus, ous</td><td>os(j)o | ōd</td><td>ās</td><td>osjo | esjās</td></tr>
<tr><td>Ls</td><td>i, Ø</td><td>eyi, ē(i)</td><td>ewi, ēu</td><td>oi</td><td>āi</td><td></td></tr>
<tr><td>Ds</td><td>ei</td><td>eyei (eyai)</td><td>ewei (ewai)</td><td>ōi < o-ei</td><td>āi</td><td>osmōi | esjāi</td></tr>
<tr><td>Is</td><td>mi</td><td>imi</td><td>umi, ū</td><td>ō</td><td>āmi</td><td>ajā</td></tr>
<tr><td>Np</td><td>es</td><td>eyes</td><td>ewes</td><td>ōs</td><td>ās</td><td>oi</td></tr>
<tr><td>Ap</td><td>n̥s</td><td>ins</td><td>uns</td><td>ons</td><td>ās āns?</td><td></td></tr>
<tr><td>Gp</td><td>ōm</td><td>iōm, yōm</td><td>uōm, wōm</td><td>ōm</td><td>?</td><td>oisōm</td></tr>
<tr><td>Lp</td><td>su</td><td>isu</td><td>usu</td><td>oisu</td><td>āsu</td><td>oisu</td></tr>
<tr><td>Dp</td><td>mos</td><td>imos</td><td>umos</td><td>omos</td><td>āmos</td><td>omos</td></tr>
<tr><td>Ip</td><td>mis</td><td>imis</td><td>umis</td><td>ōis</td><td>āmis</td><td>ōis</td></tr>
<tr><td>NAdu</td><td>he_1?</td><td></td><td></td><td>ō</td><td></td><td>ō | oī</td></tr>
</table>

---

by specifically Slavic phonotactic environments. The IE feminine *-*ā* in the older language is *-eh_2, that is, the e-grade of the thematic vowel plus a laryngeal consonant that "colors" the vowel (*e* > *a*) and lengthens it (*a* >*ā*) before disappearing. The formant $j^{e}/_{o}$ had a fem. Ns with the thematic vowel (*jeh_2) and one without it (*-ih_2); the glide becomes *i* and is lengthened, yielding -*ī*. (Cf. §4.18.)

38.2 IE u-stems included neuter nouns, e.g. **medhu-* 'honey' (cf. Sa *madhu*). Early Slavic has only masculine u-stems (including *medъ*).[43] OCS demonstrates that o-stems have adopted some u-desinences, while the u-paradigm has disappeared; its remnants are preserved in the form of certain lexemes marked to take special optional desinences, see §4.145.[44] IE u-stem adjectives have been adapted to the twofold paradigm by adding suffixal **ko*: e.g. **slād-u-ko-* 'sweet', is reinterpreted as **slad-ъk-ъ, sladъko, sladъka*.

38.3 IE desinences utilize very few consonants, see §27.42. It would seem that final stops were eliminated fairly early, while the final **s* remained nearly to the historical period (§25.3). Some nasals disappeared, and some survived into OCS in the form of nasal vowels, cf. §29.814. Their history depends in part on their status in special morphemes.

38.41 IE had separate forms for nominative and accusative (in both singular and plural), except in neuters. IE Ns ~ As of u-stems and i-stems **-us* ~ **-um* and **-is* ~ **-im* became Slavic NA *-ь and -ъ (*synъ* 'son', *gostь* 'guest'). IE thematic **-os* ~ **-om* yields twofold -ъ and -ь (e.g. *stolъ* 'seat' ~ **strojь* 'order') for which a more complicated history must be constructed:. a vowel-raising rule (§27.71) operating before #, followed by the vowel-adjustment or fronting rule (§27.72): **-os* **-om* VR[1] > **-uš* **-um* > **-u* ~ **-i* > -ъ ~ -ь.

IE **-os* > -ъ also in (1) **-mos* of dative plural desinences (*gostьmъ, synъmъ, stolomъ, strojemъ, ženamъ*) and (2) **-mos* of the first person plural verbal desinence -(*nesemъ, nosimъ* 'we carry', *něsomъ* 'we carried', cf. §5.9, 10.602).[45]

IE Lp **-su* > *-šu* by the ruki-rule (§27.3) in **-isu*, **-usu*, and **-oisu*, and by analogy in **āsu*, yielding OCS -ьxъ, -ъxъ, *-ěxъ/-ixъ*, and *-axъ*.[46]

---

43 Li *medùs* 'honey' is also masculine, but Li and Latv have completely eliminated the neuter gender.

44 In many Slavic dialects, u-stem desinences have acquired special distribution and varied significance. These innovations do not provide evidence that allows us to identify lexemes as LCoS "u-stems".

45 Post jer-shift regional developments introduce a new vowel to 1p desinences: *-mo, -me, -my*. They surely are innovations, serving to keep such forms as *damь* 'I give' and *damъ* 'we give' from merging; the plural is marked by adding a distinctive vowel.

46 The vowel *e* in locative plurals like *dьnexъ* (and Dp, *dьnexъ*) is unexpected. Although I have left *-exъ* and *-emъ* in the table in §4.41, I strongly suspect that the 9th century texts regularly had -ьxъ and -ьmъ.

38.42 The twofold NA neuter *-o/-e* (*stado* 'herd, flock', *polje* 'field') corresponds to IE **-om*. Why didn't **-om* yield OCS -ъ? There are two traditional explanations. (1) The IE demonstrative pronoun had **to* for Ns masculine, and **tod* for NAs neuter. The masculine added **s* (from other paradigms) and *-os* > -ъ, while the neuter desinence developed regularly as **-o*: the contrast NAsm **t-ъ* ~ NAsn **t-o* was taken over by o-stem nouns. (2) Neuter s-stems had o-grade **os* before a zero NA desinence, and e-grade **es* elsewhere: NA **neb-os-Ø* vs. Gs **neb-es-es* 'sky'. The final C was lost, yielding **nebo* ~ **nebese*; the NA was reinterpreted as **neb-Ø-o* and this new desinential **-o* was extended to other neuters.[47]

The pronominal forms surely were critical. The influence of the two inherited s-stems (*nebo, slovo* 'report, word') have sufficed to introduce the *es* into some forms of other neuters (§4.55), yet this untypical alternation seems unlikely as a model for the class of neuters as a whole. Thus I posit that NAsn **-om* was early replaced by PBS **-o* or ECoS **-a*, then by VR > OCS {o/e}. IE **yugom* 'yoke'→ **jugo* or **juga* > OCS **jьgo*.

38.43 OCS *kamy* 'stone' and *plamy* 'flame' are archaic Nsm, though they and the forms *kamenь/plamenь* function also as accusative. Descriptively, they contrast *-y* to stem-final *-en-*.. IE consonantal stem in **-en-* could have a Nsm desinence **-s*, or zero with quantitative or qualitative ablaut (**-ēn-Ø*, **-on-Ø*). A hypothetical **kāmons* (**polmons*) for ECoS will produce the desired *kamy* (*plamy*), but the combination of elements is implausible for earlier IE.[48]

38.44 The -i of Ns *mati* 'mother' and *dъšti* 'daughter' (§4.413) descriptively is correlated with *-er*, but historically the ancestor is surely *-ēr*, cf. the Gk cognates μήτηρ, θυγάτηρ (and the masculine πατήρ 'father'). The IE suffix **-ter-* was subject to apophony within the declension: compare the Gk forms Ns μήτηρ As μητέρα, Gs μητρός. Why **-ēr* raised to **-ī(r)* is unexplained. OCS *dъšter-* and Rusian *dъčer-* (with *mater-*) allow us to posit earlier **dukter-* (§26.41)-; forms from other languages establish IE **dhugh₂tér-*.[49]

38.51 The IE Ap of u-stems and i-stems, **-uns* and **-ins*, became **-ūns* **-īns* (§29.814), and deleted the nasal; **-ū* **-ī* > *-y -i* (*syny, gosti*). This denasalization (NØ[1]) affected originally high vowels, and it was chrono-

---

47 The generalization of **š* or **x* to desinences may be called on to mark the genitive **-eš* as different from the formant-final sibilant of NA **slowos*; this does not strengthen the argument.

48 MCoS **kāmen-* 'stone' is cognate with Li *akmuõ*, Gs *akmeñs*. The etymology is disputed. OCS *korenь* 'root' appears as *korę* in a few post-OCS examples; I believe it to be a local innovation. Similarly, R пла́мя (Gs пла́мени) is a borrowing from Slavonic with regularized Ns neuter desinence, like OCS *vrěmę*. The root is **pol*.

49 The parallel IE stem **bréh$_2$ter-* (with zero-grade suffix **tr*) > OCS *bratrъ*, which lost the *r* within the OCS period in SSl. In Czech dialects, *bratr* still exists; *brat* is the Pan-Slavic norm.

logically prior to VR². C-stem Ap *-*n̥s*, behaved like i-stem *-*ins* > -*i* (*dьni, materi*).

38.52 IE Ap o-stem and a-stem *-*ons*/*-*ōns* and *-*āns*, raised to *-*ūns*, split to *-*ūns* ~ *-*īns*. Nasality was lost (by NØ²) in the back variant, *-*ū* ~ *-*īn* > -*y* ~ -*ę*, i.e. {y/ę}. The North Slavic reflex, however, is *ě* (§29.814). We may speculate that the +high nasal diphthong [īN] lowered to [-high -low] *ēN* and nasality was lost in these morphemes (and in *-*en-n*, §29.813), while other front nasal syllabics lowered maximally to [äN] before nasality disappeared. The Rusian *ě* of all origins presumably was lower than /i/ but higher than /e/ and the /ä/ that is the normal reflex of ECoS *ę, e.g. *sē-men-Ø* 'seed' > SSl *sěmę*, NSl *sěmä*; Gs *sē-men-es* > all LCoS *sěmene*.

38.61 The consonantal Np desinence *-*es* survives as OCS -*e* in personal nouns with the suffixes -*tel*-, -*arj*-, or -*ěn*-/-*jan*- (see §4.52-53). It also is usual in the Npm of comparatives and of present and past active participles: e.g. *vęštьše* 'bigger'; *nesǫšte, nosęšte* 'carrying', *nesъše* 'having carried' (see §4.19).

38.62 Twofold masculine Np -*i* (morphophonemically {i²}, §3.5c2) goes back to the IE pronominal *-*oi*. Just why it did not become *ě* (per §29.8201) is unknown.

38.7 OCS relics of u-stems have -*ove* (Np), -*ovi* (Ds), and -*u* (Gs, Ls) contrasting with IE*-*ewes*, *-*ewei*, and *-*eus*. This has been interpreted (contrary to §29.8202) as a regular phonological adaptation of *e to *o before *u/*w, cf. *novъ* 'new' but IE *new-os*. Or perhaps it may be a substitution of o-grade for e-grade vocalism in the desinences (cf. IE Gs *-*ous*). The allomorphs -*ewe* and -*ewi* are Slavic adaptations used with soft twofold stems, such as *zmijeve, zmijevi* 'dragon', *mǫževi* 'man [Ds]', *vračevi* (apparently with historical *j, < *mong-j-, *wrāk-j- [*work-j-?]).

38.8 OCS i-stems have departed farther from the IE shapes that closely parallel IE u-desinences. OCS i-masculines evolved the appropriate phonological Np desinence -*ьje* < *-*ejes* (cf. §29.92), but the feminines have -*i* (*gostьje* 'guests' ~ *kosti* 'bones'). Gs -*i* matches IE *-*eis*, and Ds -*i* may be from IE C-stem *-*ei*. Locative -*i* brings the i-stems into conformity with the pattern that feminine dative and locative singular share the same form.

38.9 Slavic vocatives correspond closely to the IE forms, except that the twofold "hard" -*e* (from the e-grade of the IE thematic vowel [§37.5] is coupled with -*u* (implying *-*ou*, although IE u-stem has *-*eu*).

39.1 Formally distinct nominative and accusative forms were maintained in the singular of a-stems (e.g. *žena* 'woman', *vojevoda* 'general' ~ *ženǫ, vojevodǫ*), in masculine present active participles (Nsm *nesy, nosę* 'carrying' ~ Asm *nesǫštь, nosęštь*), in masculine plurals (e.g. Np *stoli* 'seats', *gostьje* 'guests', *synove* 'sons', *dьne* 'days' ~ Ap *stoly, gosti, syny, dьni*), and in some remnants of C-paradigms (§4.413, e.g. Ns *ljuby* 'love', *mati* 'mother' ~ As *ljubъvь, materь*; for *kamy* 'stone' see above, §38.43)

39.2 OCS a-stems have final *-ǫ* in As and Inst sg *-ojǫ/-ejǫ* (e.g. *ženǫ ženojǫ* 'woman'; *strujǫ strujejǫ* 'stream'; *sǫdьjǫ sǫdьjejǫ* 'judge'~ Ns *žena, struja, sǫdьji* [m]). The IE As was **-ām* and development to LCoS is straightforward. The IE instrumental may reflect the pronominal **-ajā* plus a reduced form of the **-mi* found in other paradigms: **-ajām*.

39.31 IE instrumental singular **-mi* spread from the C-, i-, and u-stems to the o-stems (e.g. *gostьmь 'guest', synъmь* 'son'; *stolomъ* 'seat', *strojemь* 'order'). Feminine i-stems, however, and a-stems have terminal *-jǫ*: *kostьjǫ, ženojǫ, strujejǫ*. This seems to be a blend of the fem. pronominal desinence **-ajā* with the nasal from other instrumental desinences.

39.32 North LCoS and perhaps some regional southern dialects extended Is *-ъmь* and *-ьmь* to twofold stems (*stolъmь, strojьmь*). The evidence is indecisive because the jer-shift eliminated the distinctions in most dialects and later redistribution of individual desinences differed by locality.

39.41 OCS final *-ę* of forms like NAs *vrěmę* 'time' and *otročę* 'boy' represents a truncated stem-final suffix (cf. Gs *vrěm-en-e*, *otroč-ęt-e*), §4.414. Similarly in the Nsm of the present active participle of verbs with *i/ę* presents (§8.11), e.g. *pustę* 'letting go' ~Nsf *pustęšti*; *slyšę* 'hearing' ~ *slyšęšti*. They seem to reflect older non-alternating front nasal diphthongs.

39.42 OCS {y/ę} occurs also as the OCS participial Nsm ending, *nes-y* vs. Nsf *nes-ǫšt-i* 'carrying' and *poj-ę poj-ǫšt-i* 'singing' (verbs that have *-ontъ* in 3p pres., §5.602). The participial stem ends in {-ǫšt-}; and the Nsmn form is anomalous (§8.1). IE morphology suggests a masculine-neuter consonantal stem **-o-nt-*, opposed to a feminine **-o-nt-yā-*: Nsm **-ont-s* would be expected. Slavic has generalized the feminine stem with **j* to all genders, with normal soft twofold desinences except for Nsf *-i* (< IE *-yh*$_2$) and Nsmn **-s*. MCoS {-ontj-} > OCS {-ǫšt-} and Rusian {-uč-}. The environment for the vowel-raising rule (VR) is to be written **-n(t)s#*.

The participial *-nt-* is used also in verbs with i/ę-presents; the front vowel quality may rest on a syllabic **-n̥t-* or an *-ī-* added before the nasal, *-*īnt*-, e.g. OCS Msmn *nosę, stoję* ~ Nsf *nosęšti, stojęšti,* from {nos-i+} 'carry' and {stoj-ě+}, 3s pres *stojitъ,* 3p *stojętъ.*

39.421 The North Slavic Nsm participial ending was *-a* for hard stems (*nesa nesuči* 'carrying'); *-onts#* yields *a*. In theory *-ě*^{3} developed in soft stems (**poję pojuči* 'singing'), as in §38.52, but in fact Rusian spellings are universally of the type поѧ or поꙗ, мажѧ or мажа (§26.52). Scribes do not violate the grammar of OCS. OCz evidence for *-ě*^{3} in this ending is stronger.

39.5 The OCS genitive plural -ъ is often counted a regular development from an IE variant **-on*. The equation is tempting but unfounded, for the argument is essentially circular: the chief "proof" for the IE short-vowel variant is precisely the Slavic -ъ. IE evidence establishes only **-ōm* (or something more complex); we must admit that the uniform Slavic **-u* (or **-i* by VA^1) is unexplained.[50]

Accusative plurals ~ Ns pres. active participles ~ NA i-stems and u-stems							
		VL	NØ^1	VR^2	VA^1	NØ^2	
NApf	strauj-ans#	> strauj-āns	> -	> straujūns	> straujīns	> struję	SSl
NApf	strauj-ans#	> strauj-āns	> -	> -	> straujēns?	> strujě	NSl
NApf	raik-ans#	> raik-āns	> -	> raikūns	> -	> rěky	all
Apm	stroj-ons#	> straj-āns	> -	> strajūns	> strajīns	> stroję	SSl
Apm	stroj-ons#	> straj-āns	> -	> ?	> strajēns?	> strojě	NSl
Apm	stol-ons#	> stal-āns	> -	> stalūns	> -	> stoly	all
Nsm	nes-onts#	> nes-ānts	> -	> nesūns	> -	> nesy	SSl
Nsm	nes-onts#	> nes-ānts	> -	> -	> -	> nesa	NSl
Nsm	poj-onts#	> paj-ānts	> -	> ?	> pajēns?	> pojě?	NSl
Ap	sūn-uns	> sūn-ūns	> sūnūs	> -	> -	> syny	all
Ap	gost-ins	> gast-īns	> gasfīš	> -	> -	> gosti	all
Ns	sūnuš	> -	> -	> -	> -	> synъ	all
Ns	gostiš	> -	> -	> -	> -	> gostь	all

39.61 LCoS instrumental plural **-mi* (*synъmi, gastьmi, kostьmi, ženami, strujami*) implies an older long vowel or diphthong (**-ī* or **-ei*), and Baltic allows us to posit PBS **-mīs*. Yet IE otherwise points to **-mis* (with short **i*). The long vowel we attribute to PBS remains unexplained.

39.62 OCS twofold non-feminine instrumental plurals (*stoly, stroji, městy, polji*) imply ECoS **ū* (or **-ī* by VA^1). IE had **-ōis*, which should

---

[50] The desinential jer in Gp in pre-SC LCoS also requires explanation: despite its eminently "weak" position at the end of a word (§2.621, 2.6241), Gp *-ъ survives into most dialects as *-a* with special accentual properties. In medieval mss it is regularly written "ъь", e.g. женъь, градъь.

yield ECoS *-*āiš*. We may include this with other cases of raising *ā > *ū in a final closed syllable, noting that the unique diphthong *ūi discards *i. It is far better simply to admit that this desinence resists explanation. The twofold non-feminine dative singular *-*u* (*stolu, stroju, městu, polju*) is also unexplained. It implies *-*au* (and IE *-*ou*, *-*au*), but IE offers strong evidence only for *ōi (which—like DLs fem. *a*-stems—should yield LCoS *-*ě* via ECoS *-*āi*).

39.71 The IE comparative suffix was apophonic *(*i*)*yes* *(*i*)*yos* *is. By what was probably a series of adaptations, non-alternating *-*jijiš*- emerged; the feminine had the suffix *-*yā*- (IE *-*ih*$_2$-, §37.5, n. 42), and the *j* was generalized to all forms: **jijiš-j*- > OCS {jьj-ьš}, except for neuter NAs (§4.71). The newer and productive formant began with *ē, *-*ējiьš*- > OCS {ěj-ьš}.

39.72 The past active participle formant {(w)-ъš}, §11.11, goes back to the zero-grade form of a suffix **wes* ~ **us*: **us*- was used for masculilne and neuter, and **us-yā* for feminine. In the pre-history of Slavic, the stem **uš* was generalized, and **w* was added if the stem was vocalic.

40 The OCS pronominal declension (§4.2) has much in common with the twofold nominal declension. Some desinences belonged originally to one or the other type (see table on p. 224 above). The *g* in Gsmn *t-ogo, moj-ego* seems to replace an older *s*, preserved in the interrogative pronoun *česo* 'of which' (§4.24). The two-syllable Dsmn *t-omu, moj-emu* lack the **s* of IE forms, but share the final *-*ōi* that yields OCS Ds -*u* (cf. §39.62). The -*oj*- of feminine singular GLDI and dual GL is perhaps based on IE pronominal Is *-*ajā*.

40.11 The pronoun *sь* 'this' takes the "soft" desinences that otherwise are called for by stems ending in *j* (**mojь* 'my', *našь* [< **nās-j*-] 'our'); it has an optional variant stem **sij*-, §4.22. Its IE equivalent used suppletive stems: **ḱi*- and **ḱjo*-. This would yield ECoSl **siš* for Nsm and **sj*- + "soft" desinence in most forms, then MCoS **si* vs. **šego*.[51] The evolution cannot be reconstructed, but it would seem that the alternation of the root, *s ~ *š, was obviated by substituting **sij*- for **sj* or incipient *š. The end result was a root consisting of a single consonant plus soft desinences; morphophonemically this {s-} requires a mark for this paradigmatic oddity. I am inclined to believe that this is a separate phoneme, *ś. In any case, the same mark is needed for the pronoun *wьsь* 'all', whose origin is obscure.

---

[51] Li Nsm *šis*, Nsf *ši*; most other forms reflect **šj*- (e.g. Gsm *šiõ*, Gsf *šiõs*).

40.121 OCS *wьsь* {wьś} takes soft desinences unless the basic variant begins with *ě* (§4.21), e.g. GLp *wьsěxъ* (like *těxъ*) vs. Nsm *wьsь,* NAsn *wьse,* and *těmь ~ simь*). The stem itself varied by region. South Slavic and most of Rus' had **wьsь*, NorthWest Late Common Slavic had **wьš-* (with the same distribution of desinence allomorphs), while the NorthEast periphery (Novgorod) had **wьxъ,* a regular hard stem like *tъ*. This distribution matches the KAI-reflexes of **xai* (e.g. ECoS **xaid-* 'gray-haired' > **xěd-* > WSl **šěd-*, OCS [and general] *sěd-*, Novg *xěd-* [in place-names], §29).[52]

There are two questions: what is the historical origin of the stem-final consonant? why do desinences beginning with LCoS **ě* appear? By the rules I have suggested, an IE **wisos* would become **wišos* by the ruki-rule and eventually **wьxъ,* i.e. the Novgorod forms, but with **x* mutated to **š* or **ś/*s* before the *ě*-desinences (like **wьsěxъ*) by KAI.[53] An IE **wikos* would yield **wьsъ,* where the **sě* of **wьsěxъ* (etc.) would appear by simple juxtaposition. The former might be related to a root **weis/wais* 'engender, breed, multiply' that is well attested in Lithuanian. The latter perhaps could be the **weik/*woik* 'dwell' that underlies OCS *vьsь* 'village'; cf Sa *viś-* 'settlement, community; *viśva-* 'all, every, whole'.[54] Could the two have been blended?

40.122 *Wьsь* is the sole example traditionally cited to illustrate the progressive palatalization of velar **x* to **ś* (> **s*), while the *sě*-forms arise from KAI. Most accounts are vague about the details and chronology of the processes I call VA (§29.72). My proposals place BdC at a time before the appearance of **x*. Evidence that allows resolution of these questions simply is not available. This word is not solid evidence for any theory.

40.123 This sort of enigma is not surprising in a pronoun. Furthermore, puzzles concerning words denoting 'all' and/or 'whole' have engendered a vast literature because of local variability (e.g., Gk **pant-*, **hol-*; Lat. *omnis, totus*; Gmnc *all-, hail-*) combined with etymological obscurity.[55]

---

52 Note that North Slavic permitted **ě* after **š*. Another word for 'gray' is **sěr-* (not OCS, marginally attested in ESl), WSl *šěr-*; it implies early **xair-*, which is explicable as a loan from Gmc **haira-* (cf. E *hoar, hoary*), < IE **kei-*. IE **koi-r-* would yield *sěr-* but not *šěr-*. See note ### to §31.

53 KAI did not reach the Pskov-Novgorod periphery of Slavdom (§29); the progressive palatalization (BdC), however, had the same effects as in the rest of Rus'.

54 Lithuanian *vìsas* 'all, whole' is no help, because it should have *š* either by the ruki-rule or from **k*. Li *viẽšas* 'public, communal' surely is from IE *weik*.

55 In German, *ganz*—etymology unknown—has spread from the extreme southeast over most of the territory since about 800 (replacing *heil* < IE **kailo-* > OCS *cělъ*).

40.21 IE interrrogative forms $*k^{w}o(s)$ and $*k^{w}id$ lie behind OCS *kъ(to)* 'who' and *čь(to)* 'what'. The personal *kъto* seems to been universal, but *čь* without reinforcement, and *kъjь may be ascribed to LCoS dialects. (The modern reflexes are *ča* and *kaj,* and these words serve as symbols of the *čakavski* dialect of Croatia, and the old macrodialect underlying both Croatian *kajkavski* and Slovenian, §25.7.)

40.22 The IE relative *yo- survived as *j- (see §4.25 and 29.815).

40.23 The IE apophonic suffix *-tero-*, denoting *alternative,* appears in *j-e-ter-ъ 'a certain', *k-o-tor-ъ-jь 'which' (with LCoS variants *koterъjь [OCS, but rare], and *kъterъjь > Cz *který*), *někotorъjь 'a certain', and *nikotorъjь 'no, none'. *Jeterъ* is obsolescent in OCS, but lives on for generations as a bookish archaism.[56]

40.3 The personal pronouns show irregular allomorphy between the nominative (always stressed, syntactically emphatic) and other cases. It is probable that accusative and dative had both tonic and enclitic forms. LCoS forms, though quite different from their equivalents in the older languages, demonstrate complex idiosyncratic rearrangements of old materials. Here we will note only a few details.

40.311 The IE and Slavic 1st sg nominative 'I' is completely distinct from the other declensional forms, whose stem begins in *m-. The OCS form *azъ* was native only to the Slavs of (eastern) Bulgaria; in all the rest of Slavdom the form was *jazъ. It is true that canonical OCS, with about 850 examples spelled "correctly", offers just one example of *ězъ* (Mk 11:29 Mar). Yet this fact must be placed in its cultural context: the name of the first letter in both alphabets was *azъ*, and to write the pronoun with "а" and not "ѣ" or "ꙗ" was a symbol of medieval Slavonic literacy.

When the weak -ъ dropped, the word-final /z/ in all LCoS dialects must have been subject to complex allophonic variation as it adapted to the following word-initial phonemes, indeed approximately the range noted for prefix-final /z/ of OCS (§3.111). The modern shape is *ja* for most regions, but standard Bulgarian has {*az*}, Macedonian *jas* (dial. *jaska, jaze, jazeka*), Slovenian *"jaz"* (usually pronounced [jest]); Old Czech had *jáz*, but the *z* was lost during the 14th century. Rusian documents (as opposed to church texts) use *jaz* freely.

40.312 OCS *azъ* allows us to posit early *āzu < *āǵ- or *ōǵ-. Gk ἐγώ, La *ego,* Sa *aham* suggest IE $*e\acute{g}h_2om$. The final -ъ is compatible with IE

---

56 IE *-tero-* is perhaps in *wъtorъ* 'second', see §41.82.

-*on*, but the initial long back vowel has not been satisfactorily explained. There is no Slavic evidence whatsoever for positing IE **ē-* here, tempting though the supposition might be.

40.32 The accusative *mę* (< IE **mē-m*) could be tonic or enclitic (as could *tę* and *sę*). Gen *mene* corresponds to an IE variant (cf. Av *mana*). The other case-forms, with *mъn-* or *mьn-* and o-stem pronominal desinences, probably are late formations, subject to considerable regional variation.

40.33 The 2s N *ty* continues older **tū* (cf. La *tū*); the stem *teb-/tob-* shows redistribution of inherited materials. The OCS LD *tebě* is SSl; North Sl had *tobě*. So also the parallel reflexive LD *sebě/sobě*.

40.34 IE had forms with **w, *n,* and **y* in 1p and 2p, e.g. La NA *nōs* 'we' and *vōs* 'you'. The **w* was generalized to Sl 1st person Ndu **wě*, but otherwise serves as 2nd person dual and plural marker (*vy vasъ*, etc.). The **n* persisted in dual and plural, except for the nominatives *vě* and *my*, opposed to Acc *na* and *ny*. 1p plural *ny* is found in the Kiev Folia (7x Nom, 35x Acc), and ны begins to replace N мы in Macedonia and Bulgaria after about 1200. Standard Macedonian and Bulgarian now have ние.[57]

40.4 The possessives *našь* 'our' and *vašь* 'your' show old NA **nōs* and **wōs* with thematic **-y$^e/_o$-* and **-yā-* (or in Slavic terms, *-j-*): ECoS **nās-j-as, *wās-j-as*. Reflexive **svojь*, 1s **mojь*, and 2s **tvojь* have the same suffix with old stems **mo-, two-*, and **swo-*.

41.1 The cardinal number 'one' has syntactic gender and forms of the pronominal declension, §4.201: *jedinъ, jedino, jedina*, etc. (In the plural it signifies 'some, only'.) An alternate form *jedьnъ* is attested in Supr and reflected in the modern languages.[58] The *(j)ed-* is of obscure origin (some scholars suggest a deictic particle); *-in-* is supposed to represent **ein-*, the e-grade of the **oi-no-* underlying Germanic **ains* (cf. Gk οἴνη '1 on dice').

41.2 *Two* has dual pronominal forms: NA **dъva* m < IE **dūō*, a variant form, cf. δύω, La *duo*, Go *twai*. *Oba, obě* 'the two, both' is related to Li *abù*, Sa *ubhāu* 'both' (cf. Gk ἄμφω, La *ambō* 'both').

---

57 OCS has a clear formal distinction between nominative and accusative (*azъ ty vě my* vs. *mę tę na ny*); KF's NA *ny* violates that status. It could be an archaism or a regional innovation.

58 ESl has the stem *odin* in Nsm only, otherwise *odn-*: Nsn *odnó*, Nsf *odná*. Bg has *edín ednó edná*. The other languages have {ъ} in Nsm, i.e. the vowel-zero alternation, e.g. SC *jedan jedno jedna*.

41.3 *Three* has plural forms, Nm *trьje* < IE **treies* (Sa *trayas*, Gk τρεῖς), GL *trьxъ* (Sa Loc *trišu*).

41.4 *Four* is also plural: *četyre* Nm implies ECoS **ketūres,* and related forms with *četvor-* or *četver-* in others imply **ketwor-*, **ketwer-*, along with MCoS **četvьrtь* 'quarter' < **ketwirt-* as regularized reflexes of IE **k*ʷ*etwer- *k*ʷ*etwor- *k*ʷ*etwr-ti-* and other shapes.[59] NW monosyllabic stems, e.g. Cz *čtyr- čtver-* (and the like), point to **čьt-*, perhaps a reflex of IE zero-grade **k*ʷ*tūr-*.

41.5 The numerals *pętь* '5', *šestь* '6', *sedmь* (ESl *semь*) '7', *osmь* '8', *devętь* '9', and *desętь* '10' are i-stem nouns (§20), closely related to the o-stem forms that serve as ordinals. The IE cardinals first apparently gave way to stems built with the ordinal suffixes *-to-* or *-h_2o-*, then shifted to i-stems.[60] As in other languages, adjacent numerals seem to have affected each other: the stem-final *m* is expected in '7' but not '8'; initial *d* is original in '10' but not '9'. The voicing of *d* in NW and SSl *sedmь* is unexpected, and *dm* is a unique internal cluster; loss of *d* in Rusian *semь* seems more regular.

	IE cardinal	ordinal	new cardinal	OCS card.	ordinal
5	**penk*ʷ*e*	**penk*ʷ*-to*	**pen(k)-ti-s*	*pętь*	*pętъ*
6	**ksek̑s*	**ksek̑s-to*	**kše(k)s-to-*	*šestь*	*šestъ*
7	**septm*	**septm-h_2o-*	**sebdm-i*	*se(d)mь*	*se(d)mъ*
8	**ok̑teh₃ *ok̑tō*	**ok̑t+mo*	**ok̑(t)-mi-*	*osmь*	*osmъ*
9	**$h_2$newn-*	**newn-to-*	**newn-ti-*	*devętь*	*devętъ*
10	**dek̑m*	**dek̑m-to-*	**dek̑m-ti-*	*desętь*	*desętъ*

41.6 IE **dk̑mtom* '100' (usually shortened to **kmtom,* whence Li *šim̃tas,* Av *satəm*, La *centum*) is replaced by *sъto,* which keeps the neuter gender but has ъ where we expect a nasal vowel.[61]

41.7 OCS *tysęšti* or *tysǫšti* are soft a-stem feminines, analyzed as an ECoS compound, **tū-sint-j-ī* or **tū-sunt-j-ī* (parallel to Gmc **thus-hundi-*, E *thousand*). The first element is from IE **tuh-* (zero-grade of **teuh-* 'swell'), and the second is **k̑m̥t-om* '100', therefore 'swollen hundred'.

---

[59] OCS *četvrědьnevьnъ* '4-day' and *četvrěnogъ* '4-legged [creature]' show MCoS **četver-* as the combining form in compounds, cf. §26.51.

[60] The data of even the ancient dialects shows extreme variability in numerals; the hypothetical IE forms given here are chosen from many possibilities as most compatible with attested Slavic.

[61] Rumanian borrowed the word as *sută,* obviously before the jer-shift, perhaps as early as 1000.

LCoS seems to have had the *ǫ* variant in SW and NW dialects; except for Sln *tisoč,* SSl now uses *hiljada* (in varying form), borrowed from Gk χιλιάδα.[62]

41.81 The ordinal **pьrwъ* 'first' represents **pr-wo-s,* from the IE root **perh*$_2$ that underlies Li *pìrmas,* Gk πρῶτος, Latin *prīmus,* and E *first, foremost.*

41.82 *Vъtorъ* 'second' and *vъtorьnikъ* 'Tuesday' (**wъter-* in pre-Czecho-Slovak) suggest ECoS **uɴtar-,* with the apophonic suffix **-tero-,* denoting *alternative* (as in *jeterъ,* §40.23). Li *añtras* and *añtaras,* Go *anþar* 'other, second' point to **an-,* a deictic particle. Apparently **an-* closed to **un-* (cf. the preposition **un,* §29.815); the loss of nasalization remains puzzling.

41.821 (The numeral survives only in R второ́й; otherwise the reflexes of **drugъ* 'other, another' have taken over as 'second'. 'Tuesday' generally maintains the old root, but often reflects the suffix **-ъkъ* (i.e. a vowel-zero alternation, /-rVk ~ -rkV/: SC *utorak,* Sln *torek* (also *vtorek*), (Cz *úterý* and *úterek*), Slk *utorok,* P *wtorek,* Uk *vivtórok,* BR *awtórak;* R, Bg, Mac *vtornik.* Notice that the *wъ* - lost its weak jer, leaving initial **wt-.* In SC the glide became a vowel *u-* (in all words). In P, R, Bg, and Mac the glide became a voiceless consonant /f/. In Cz and Slk a vowel is exceptional in this root; [ft] is normal for other words. In Sln, the glide persisted and though initial [wt] is common, in this word the glide was lost. In Uk and BR [wt] occurs in many words, the glide was reinforced, [v́iwt] in standard Uk, [awt] in BR. This special treatment seems to be defined by the lack of an underlying boundary; {wtor-Vk-} has a different fate from {wV-t-} where the morpheme is the prefix 'in, into').

41.83 *Tretьjь* (§2.61) 'third' comes from **tr̥-tijo-s* (cf. Sa *tr̥tīyas*), with an unexpected *e.*

41.84 **Četvьrtъjь* 'fourth' corresponds to Li *ketvir̃tas.*
'Thursday' is *četvrьtъkъ* in OCS and, in appropriate form, most mod. Sl languages; *četvьrgъ* is attested very early in Rus' (cf. Li *ketvérgis* '4-year-old').

41.85 'Friday' is OCS *pętъkъ* and its descendants in all but ESl today. **Пѧтьница** is known in ESl from 1056.

Conjugation

42 The Indo-European verb had stems expressing voice (active, middle), state (the perfect), and tense (present, aorist), and desinences ex-

---

62 Cz *tisíc* shows unusual complications: **tyśęc* (with palatalization of *s* before a front vowel) was apparently blended with **tysǫc* to produce **ťuśúc,* and both syllables were fronted, yielding mod. /ťisīc/. This markedly Cz form was borrowed into Slk.

pressing number and person. These stems were essentially independent. Thus, for example, the IE root **bheudh* 'be aware, make aware' provides contrasting autonomous present tenses that can be approximated by Slavic derivatives that constitute elements in the paradigms of different verbs.

**bheud-*$^{e}/_{o}$- 'observe': Sa *bódhati* 'awakes, becomes aware'; πεύθεται 'learns'	**1**	OCS *bljudetъ* 'observes' {bljud-Ø+}
**bhundh-*$^{e}/_{o}$- 'become aware': Li *bundù* 'I wake up' πυνθάνομαι (with a secondary n-suffix) 'ask, enquire, learn'	**2**	**bъdnetъ* 'wake up, become awake' {bъd-nǫ+}
**bhoudh-ey*$^{e}/_{o}$- causative: Sa *bodháyati* 'he wakes [someone]'	**3**	*buditъ* {bud-i+} 'wakes [someone]'
**bhudh-y*$^{e}/_{o}$- 'be awake': Sa *budhyáte* [pass.] 'is awake'	**4**	*bъditъ* 'is awake, vigilant' {bъd-ě+}

The phonetic change of **eu* > **ju* and the shift of **j* to **lj* after a labial (§3.71) in (1) disguises the relationship of the first root-shape (e-grade or basic) to zero-grade **bъd* and o-grade **bud*; in fact *bljud-e-tъ* is the cognate of Sa *bodh-a-ti* except for the final vowel. (2) shows an *infixed n* in IE in contrast to a Slavic *suffixal* nasal that continues the same general meaning of inception (see §45 below). The formation of the causative (3) in Slavic is perhaps a reflection of the IE, while the *i* of the stative (4) is new.

The distance between early IE and OCS verbal systems is too great for us to reconstruct the many intervening stages that would make the genesis of the Slavic clearer. The materials of LCoS conjugation are mostly IE, but there are many shifts in use and significance. The morphological paradigms expressing the middle (or medio-passive) voice disappeared without trace, and categories variously labelled subjunctive, conjunctive, and optative survive only in the Slavic imperative.

43 Reference to present ("the here and now") as opposed to past underlies the formal distinctions of present and preterite in OCS (see §5.6). The origins of the vowel-morphemes *ě*, *a*, and *i* that play a major role as verbal classifiers are not clear. The stative *ě* of *bъd-ě+* 'be awake' recalls IE ē-morphemes associated with stativeness and aorist paradigms. The *a* and the *i* remain without satisfactory explanations; for *ǫ*, see §49.1ff. below.

43.1 Let us look first at the present desinences and then at stem-formation.

IE person-number desinences used with the present indicative ("primary endings") differed somewhat from those used with aorist and imperfect ("secondary endings"). This contrast survives under rather different form in OCS (§5.9). Here are the chief variants pertinent for Slavic:

	1s	2s	3s	1du	2du	3du	1p	2p	3p
Prim.	-mi, -ō (h_2)	-si	-ti	-wes, -wos	-tes	?-tes	-mes, -mos	-te	-nti -enti
Sec.	-m	-s	-t	-we	-tom	-tām	-me (?)	-te	-nt -ent

43.11 All desinences began with a consonant except 1s **-ō*; the original 1s desinence was **-h_2*. The **-o-h_2* of thematic forms > **-ōh_2*, later **-ō*; the resulting Slavic **-ā* was augmented, probably by the primary **-mi*, that then lost its vowel, yielding **-ām* > LCoS *-ǫ*.

43.12 OCS 2s *-si* (*esi, dasi, ěsi, věsi*) implies older **-sī* or **-sei*; no satisfactory explanation has been found. Normal OCS *-ši* requires **-šī* or **-šei*: the consonant surely represents generalization of **š* from the ruki-rule to all prevocalic **s* in desinences (§27.3); the long vowel remains mysterious. The constant presence of *-ši* in OCS surely proves that it existed in the dialect of the original translators and had the full approval of early scribes. It is, then, to be posited for a part of 9th-century Bulgaro-Macedonian regional dialects. Yet the tenacious spelling contradicts all other evidence, which points to **-šь* as LCoS (and its eventual adoption in all of SE Slavic).

43.13 OCS 3 person singular and plural has **-tъ*. This is a regional peculiarity of the standardized language; **-tь* (= inherited **-ti*) is to be posited for most LCoS dialects. The *tъ* may have arisen in part through the influence of the demonstrative *tъ* 'this, that' which in some dialects functioned as subject pronoun of the third person. The dialectal zero-desinence (§6.61) was surely relatively new and arose in different localities in varying environments.

43.1311 The *-t* (несёт, несýт; нóсит, нóсят 'carries/carry') of modern standard Russian is a peculiarity of central Great Russian dialect that appeared after 1350 in Muscovite documents. It spread slowly over the whole Great Russian area. Most Belarusian and Ukrainian dialects retained the palatalized consonant /c′/ or /t′/ that go back to **-tь*; many dialects have zero in some paradigms.

43.14 OCS 1du **-wě* was probably general LCoS, but it is replaced by *-va* (probably under the influence of the numeral *dъva*) in most regions later on. The Slavic dual desinences are not easily explicable from the hypothetical IE.

43.15 OCS 1p _-mъ_ can be derived from *_-mos,_ see §38.41.

43.16 Five verbs have _-mь_ in 1s present (four of which have _-si_ in 2s); they are the remnants of an ancient group of presents consisting of root plus person-number desinence. Their anomalies are typical of irregularities that are tolerated in basic every-day words. At the same time their histories illustrate the complex ways allomorphs influence each other.

43.171 The OCS morphemes {jes} and {s} underlying the present forms *_jesmь,_ *_jesi_ {jes-si}, *_jestъ, sǫtъ_ (§16.1) are unmotivated in the system; they are simply suppletive. They derive from allomorphs _es/s_ that survive elsewhere with different distribution (Sa, with _a_ for *_e_ [and *_o_], _ásmi, ási, ásti_ ~ 1p _smas,_ 2p _stha,_ 3p _sánti_; Latin 1s _sum,_ 1p _sumus,_ 3p _sunt_ ~ 2s _es,_ 3s _est,_ 2p _estis_). The IE root *h_1_es_ and rules governing apophony show that this present was once quite normal: if accented, the root was *h_1_es_ (e-grade); if unaccented, then zero-grade *h_1_s_: *h_1_ésmi,_ *h_1_ésti_ vs. 3p *h_1_sénti_. The expected 3p *_-n̥t-_ *_-int-_ (cf. _dadętъ, vědętъ_) has been replaced in Slavic by the more neutral *_-ont-_: _sǫtъ._

Modern dialects have rearranged these elements in many ways. SC has a set of accented forms, and an enclitic set. Polish retains 3p (without a final _t_) and builds new forms for first and second person with _jest_ as stem.[63]

OCS	_jesmь_	_jesi_	_jestъ, je_	_jesmъ_	_jeste_	_sǫtъ_
SC (stressed)	_jesam_	_jesi_	_jest(e), jȅ_	_jesmo_	_jeste_	_**je**su_
SC (enclitic)	_sam_	_si_	_je_	_smo_	_ste_	_su_
Polish	_jes**tem**_	_jes**teś**_	_jest_	_jes**teś**my_	_jes**teś**cie_	_są_

43.172 OCS _dati_ 'to give', with its present forms, requires two underlying root-shapes, {da} for the infinitive, and {dad} for 3p and the forms with _-st-_:

{da-ti}	{da(d)-mь}	{da(d)-si}	{dad-tъ}	{da(d)-mъ}	{dad-te}	{dad-ętъ}
dati	_damь_	_dasi_	_dastъ_	_damъ_	_daste_	_dadętъ_

Further, the imperfective _dajati_ requires underlying {daj}.[64] Older Slavic had *_dā,_ *_dād_ from *_dō,_ *_dōd_ (cf. Li inf. _dúoti,_ old 1s _dúomi,_ mod. _dúodu_), ultimately based on the IE root *_deh_$_3$. The Gk 1s δίδωμι and its Sa equivalent _dádāmi_ exemplify an IE formative device called reduplication: preposing a syllable made up of the root-initial consonant followed by a short vowel. In Pre-Balto-Slavic the vocalism has changed: *_dōd-mi._

[63] The form _sąchmy_ for 1p is found in a major P writer, P. Skarga, early 1600s.

[64] The substantive _daw-ьcь_ 'giver' requires still another shape, {daw}.

43.173 A second Slavic complex of stems includes a somewhat different reduplication. IE *$d^h eh_1$ 'set, put' underlies the OCS *dě* in a series of words meaning 'do, put' (e.g. *děj-a+* §15.44, *děl-aj+*). There are also prefixed presents with {-ded-j-} (*o-deždǫtъ* 'put on, dress', *vъ-deždǫtъ* 'put in', *vъz-deždǫtъ* 'lift, raise') that seem to be equivalent to forms based on {děj}. The short vowel *e* is unexpected;. perhaps it represents the archaic reduplication syllable, *$d^h e$-$d^h eh_1$. An old alternate not attested in OCS is {dě-nǫ}, e.g. *zadeneš* 'you set, assign' (Freising), mod R. *odénut* 'they will dress'.

43.174 OCS *ěd-/jad-* 'to eat' has an unexpected long vowel (as does Li *ėd-*), IE **ed-*. See also §36.1.

43.175 OCS *věd-ě-ti* 'to know' shows the intersection of perfect—reference to past from point of view of present—and stative; the root **weid* 'see' and a form meaning 'I have seen = I know', comparable to 1s perfect in Gk (ϝοῖδα) and Sa (*veda*). IE *$\bar{e}$ was a morpheme marking perfect; as a non-present marker in Slavic it usually denoted state. The desinence of 1s *vědě* is isolated, historically and synchronically. Though it was generally eliminated from western OCS (including the Gospels and Psalter), where *věmь* is almost exclusive, *vědě* survived in Old Czech and early Rusian.

43.176 OCS *im-ě-ti* 'to have' surely had the root *ьm* with prothetic *j* (**jьm-*, §2.22). The perfect or stative *$\bar{e}$ in non-present forms and the *$\bar{a}$ in the present produce the meaning 'have taken = possess'. The 2s desinence is normal *-ši,* and the 3p *-ǫtъ* probably replaces an older *-*ętъ*. Still newer is **jьmějǫtъ*. The root is IE **em*; Slavic *ьm* represents the zero-grade, IE * $\mathring{m}$.

44 Slavic has two regular types of present, *e/ǫ* and *i/ę* (§6.11). The *e/ǫ* present-marker is descended from IE *$^e/_o$ (called the *thematic vowel,* cf. §37.5). In IE, **o* appeared before sonorant or laryngeal, **e* before obstruent; in 3 pl this meant **o-nt-*, whence OCS *ǫ*. Slavic generalized **e* to all other persons. The present-sign *$\bar{\imath}$ corresponds in part to a short *i* in some Baltic forms, and in part to the IE causative *-$ey^e/_o$-; the history may involve the loss of intervocalic *j*, contraction, and analogical reshapings. The third person plural *-ętъ* presumably goes back to *$\bar{\imath}nt$-.

44.11 The *i/ę* presents are paradigmatically linked in Slavic with non-presents made with non-present suffixes *ě* or *i*.

44.12 OCS ě-verbs (§15.2, 15.3) are generally stative and intransitive. Roots had zero-vocalism in principle, but there are innovations. The class is not productive.[65]

44.13 OCS i-verbs include iteratives (e.g. *nos-i+ti nosętъ* 'carry'), causatives (e.g. *bud-i+ti budętъ* 'wake [someone] up', cf. §42), and denominatives (*gost-i+ti gostętъ* 'be host' cf. *gostь* 'guest'). The last two types were not clearly opposed, and both were productive.

44.14 The various types of IE presents included complex rules for apophony, in particular the distribution of zero-grade and e-grade allomorphs. Remnants of this kind of rule are still visible in OCS stem-formation, but they are fully lexicalized. The details of allomorphy were perturbed by monophthongization, and OCS manifests a strong tendency to re-shape the forms.

e ē	*leg-ě*	*sěd-ě*	ei	-	-	*wis-ě*	eu	-	er	-	-
o ō	*log-i*	*sad-i*	oi	*lěp-i*	*swět-i*	*wěs-i*	ou	*bud-i*	or	*mraz-i*	*wrat-i*
Ø	-	-	i	*lьp-ě*	*swьt-ě*	-	u	*bъd-ě*	r	*mrьz-ě*	*wrьt-ě*

The table illustrates verbs which in late IE did not permit zero-vocalism (*lež-ě+* 'to be lying', *sěd-ě+* 'be sitting') and verbs with diphthongs which allowed zero-grade. Thus *lьp-ě+* 'be clinging' corresponds to *lěp-i+* 'cause to adhere' (older **lip* ~ **loip*) as *swьt-ě+* 'be shining' to *swět-i+* 'cause to shine'; *wis-ě+* 'be hanging', on the other hand is surely new, replacing unattested **wьs-ě+*. Within OCS, *swět-ě+* is found instead of *swьt-ě+* (e.g. J 5:35 ZM *svьtę* ~ As *světę*). For *bъd-ě+* ~ *bud-i+* see §42 above. MCoS **mьrz-ě+* presumably meant 'be freezing, chilly' but OCS *mrьzě+* has only the figurative sense 'be repulsive, revolting'; **morz-i+* is attested as 'congeal, make solid' (while the noun *mrazъ* means 'frost' and 'ice'). MCoS **wьrt-ě+* and *wort-i+* might well have been transitive; the few OCS and early post-OCS examples all have *sę*. The former means 'twirl, go around'; the latter is 'return; turn around'.

44.151 The apophonic alternations are not productive in LCoS, and the meanings of related stems tend to diverge. Older **skend-/*skond-* 'insufficiency' underlies transitive *štęd-ě+* 'be sparing of'; causative *o-skǫd-*

[65] The influence of *vid-ě+* 'see' and *zьr-ě+* 'see, look at, observe' perhaps is responsible for the shift of *sъ-motr-i+* 'look at' to R смотре́ть (about 1350), and *ględ-aj+* 'see, look over' to R глядеть (about 1600).

i+ 'diminish, make lesser' is matched by *(o)skǫd-ěj+* 'become lesser, diminish'.

44.152 Many roots do not change at all, e.g. MCoS **skъrb-ě+* 'be sorrowful' ~ **skъrb-i+* 'afflict' (like *skrъbь* 'affliction').

44.2 The *e/ǫ* presents occur with stems that have no overt verb-forming suffix and with stems that have any suffix but *i* or *ě*. This includes a large number of heterogeneous verbs, many of which require special morphological information in their lexical definition (e.g. §15.64, §15.8). IE $*^{o}/_{e}$ was a component of suffixes used exclusively or primarily in the present. Thus $*d^{o}/_{e}$ appears in the irregular presents *id-ǫtъ* and *jadǫtъ* 'go' (inf. *iti, jaxati*), IE roots **ei/i* and **ja*.

44.21 The traditional classifications of OCS verbs posit *je-stems* and *ne-stems*. Some je-stems go back to IE $*y^{o}/_{e}$ verbs, and the ne-stems are comparable to an IE $*n^{o}/_{e}$ group, but the rearrangement of various kinds of presents into Slavic paradigms that join them with aorist-infinitive stems blurs the historical relationships.

44.31 Early IE roots like $*deh_3$ 'give' and $*d^heh_1$ 'put' conformed to the general constraint that a root should end in a non-syllabic element (including laryngeals, liquids, nasals, and **i/*j* and **u/*w*). They evolved into **dā-* and **dē-*, which do not fit the canonical shape of early Slavic roots. When, in these new circumstances, they were combined with a vocalic suffix, a **j* was affixed, creating root-variants like those underlying the imperfective or iterative *daj-a-ti* and *děj-a-ti*. Presents like *dajetъ* may have originated as $*y^{o}/_{e}$ forms at an early date or as $*^{o}/_{e}$ later on: **dā-je-t-* or **dāj-e-t-*.

44.32 OCS *znajetъ* 'knows' (§15.92) presumably shows **znā* + $*y^{o}/_{e}$, since the non-present has no **ā* (inf. *znati*). The IE root is **ǵnō* < $*ǵneh_3$.

OCS *kaj-a+* 'blame' and *čaj-a+* 'expect' are believed to derive from $*k^w\bar{o}i$ and $*k^w\bar{e}i$, lengthened-grade forms of $*k^wei$ 'pay, compensate'. This implies relatively old $*^{o}/_{e}$ in the present tense.

44.33 Other verbs listed in §15.43 and 15.45 fit these patterns: *laj-a+* 'bark, scold' (<**lā,* cf. La *lāmentum* 'lament'), *laj-a+* 'lie in ambush' (< $*leh_2$, cf. La *latēre* 'to lie hidden' < extended root, zero grade $*lh_2dh\text{-}\bar{e}$), *taj-a+* 'melt' (< $*teh_2$-, cf. Gmc *þaw-*, E *thaw*). *Vaj-a+* 'sculpt' and *maj-a+* 'beckon' have no plausible etymologies. *Sěj-a+* 'sow', *sěj-a+* 'winnow', and **věj-a+* go back to **sē* (a. La *sēmen* 'seed'; b. Gk ἠθέω 'sift, strain'), and **wē* (which is from $*h_2weh_1$, Sa *vāti* 'he blows'; E *weather,* *wind*). *Spěj-* 'ripen, be successful' is from **spē* (**speH*: La *spēs* 'hope'), *rěj-* 'push' is usually associated with **rei-* 'run, flow' (cf. *rinǫ* §45.3). *Sъměj-* 'dare' is obscure. *Vъl-aj-* (possibly **wьl-aj*) 'toss' is surely related to **wьlna* 'wave' and *wal-i+* 'to roll', from **wel-* 'turn, roll' (cf. La *volvere* 'roll', E *revolve*).

Gr-ěj- 'to warm, heat' represents a zero-grade root, *gr-*, < **g^wher*, related to *gor-ě* 'burn' (cf. **žarъ* 'glowing coals; conflagration' < ECoS **gēr-*).

44.34 The root-alternation in OCS *zijǫtъ zějati* 'yawn' (§15.46) shows older **ǵhē(-i)-* (whence **zěj-a+*), with a zero-grade variant **ǵhī*, which may be posited as the base for an *$^o/_e$ present, eventually **zī-e-* > **zьj-e-*. This set of processes is explicable in terms of laryngeals, but the precise environments for each root-shape are disputed. *Lijǫtъ/lьjǫtъ* 'pour' fits an IE root **lei* (for **lei-*$^o/_e$*-nt-* would yield *lьjǫtъ*). While **lēi-* could well be an old lengthened-grade present, the combination with *lěj-a-* seems to be an innovation. The same is true of OCS *směj-a-* with relation to IE **smei*.

44.35 OCS verbs with zero-classifier preceded by *j* (§15.93) show the same set of problems.

OCS *kryjǫtъ* 'cover, hide' probably goes back to **krū-je-*, and *šijǫtъ* 'sew' to **sjū-je-*, while *bijǫtъ* 'strike' is rather **bьj-e-* or **bij-e-* (from older *b^h*eiH-*$^o/_e$*-*), and *pijǫtъ* 'drink' is **pьj-e-* < **pī-e-* (a root-form derived, some will argue, by metathesis from zero-grade **ph*$_3$*i-*, from extended root **peh*$_3$*(-i)-*).

So also *myjǫtъ* 'wash' (cf.. IE **meu* 'damp'), *-nyjǫtъ* 'be despondent' (cf. IE **nāu* 'death; be exhausted'), *ryjǫtъ* 'dig' (cf. IE **reu(H)* 'ruin; knock down; dig up'), *-ujǫtъ* 'put on, take off footwear' (cf. IE **eu* 'wear') *čuj-ǫtъ* 'feel, sense' (cf. IE **keuH* 'pay attention, perceive [preternaturally])'.

In the verbs with a back vowel in the root, the *j* of the present becomes *w* before the past passive participial suffix *-en-*: e.g. *umyvenъ, obuvenъ*. The precise historical sequence of changes is not clear.

44.351 The dissyllabic stem **(w)ъpij-* 'cry out' stands apart. It seems to be based on a noun **(w)ъpъ* that survives as *vep* in OCz. The **ij/ьj*, then, looks like a derivational suffix.

44.36 IE *$y^e/_o$ presents were often associated with **ā* aorist stem (in LCoS terms, non-present). Slavic has two paradigmatic relationships: the verb-formant *j* alternates with *a*, or it is added to *a*. Thus **māz-ā-tei* 'to anoint' > *maz-a-ti* ~ **māz-j-e-te* 'you anoint' > *mažete*, or else **māz-āj-e-te* > *mazajete* 'you (repeatedly) anoint'.

In this book, the paradigmatic relationships *maza-* ~ *maže* and *maza-* ~ *mazaje-* are presented in terms of morphonemic {a} alternating under specific conditions with {j} (§6.22), or else {aj} being truncated to /a/ under other conditions (§13.2c). This type of description has proved to be an effective pedagogical device for students of OCS and other Slavic languages, and it provides useful units for comparative and historical purposes. This is not the place to debate its possible relationship to linguistic models in the brains of individuals who use these languages.

44.361 The **ā* suffix added to a velar stem could trigger BdC (§29.2): **lenk/*ln̥k* 'bend' formed **link-ā-* > **lęc-a-* (§15.63). Similarly, **āj* in iterative formations could establish the BdC formula. By LCoS, the productive rules for iterative or imperfective formation included "mutate root-final C if possible" and the specification *k g* > *c ʒ* (regardless of the vocalism of the root). This process has continued, with numerous local variations, to produce ever new secondary imperfectives. OCS attests *-strig* ~ *striʒaj* 'shave', *-žьg* ~ *žiʒaj* 'burn' and *-wyk* ~ *-wycaj* 'learn' (< **ūk-*), see §5.712ab.

44.371 The **ā* non-present marker exceptionally goes with the *i/ę* present only in *sъp-a-* 'sleep' and **sьc-a-* 'piss' (see note to §29.6).

44.372 OCS *xot-ě-ti* 'wish, want; be about to' (§15.233) is unique and inexplicable. It has a je-present except for the 3p *xotętъ,* which might be an old athematic (like *dadętъ*) with **-n̥t-*. The alternative stem *xъt,* rare in OCS, is normal in the non-present system in SC (inf. *htjeti,* 3s pres *hoće*), and all forms in Cz (inf. *chtít,* 1s pres *chcí* or *chcu,* 3p *chtějí,* past *chtěl*) and Polish (inf. *chcieć,* 1s pres *chcę*).[66] Some scholars have linked the root-forms *xъt* and *xot* to *xyt-i+* and *xvat-aj+* 'rob, grab, steal, carry off', but the origin of the initial *x* and the exact apophonic relationships have so far resisted explanation. Compare *kys/kvas* in *vъkysnǫ+* 'ferment' and *kvasъ* 'yeast', presumably **kūt-s-* **kwāt-s-* < **kwHt-* **kwoHt-* (cf. Sa *kváthati* 'boils, cooks').[67]

44.38 The *a*-paradigm continued to be marginally productive, chiefly with onomatapoetic words for sounds like *gurgle* and *twitter,* which vary extremely from dialect to dialect.[68] Individual verbs may have doublet

---

[66] The formula **xъtj-e-* > **xḱe-* produces a wide variety of phonetic variations in the dialects of several languages; none of this material helps explain the ECoS forms.

[67] It is doubtful that La *cāseus* 'cheese' belongs here. (E *cheese* goes back to the La word.)

[68] SC may nativize a foreign stem with a suffix *-isa-* ~ present *iše-*, e.g. *anatèmisati* 3s pres *anatèmiše* 'anathematize' *infòrmisati infòrmiše* 'inform'. The origin is the modern Gk aorist form of the *-iz-*, e.g. ἀναθεματίζω 'I curse' ~ ἀναθεμάτισα 'I cursed'.

present forms, cf. *žęda+* ~ *žędaj+* 'thirst' §15.64. The anomalous verbs that have apophonic alternations, usually contrasting present to infinitive/aorist stems, will be treated below, §50.1.

44.39 Verbs with *aj* have been continually productive in most dialects, especially for creating secondary imperfectives (see §5.71–.7112).[69] This function corresponds to the IE iterative sense of the suffix. Note that when *-aj-* is added to a stem ending in *j*, the stem-final glide usually becomes *w*: see §5.712e.

44.41 Verbs with *ěj* often denote a change in status, e.g. *blěděj+* I (*oblěděj+* P) 'become pale, fade' (*blědъ* 'pale'), *omrьtvěj+* 'become numb' and *umrьtvěj+* 'mortify'(*mrьtvъ* 'dead'); *zapustěj+* and *opustěj+* 'become deserted' (*pustъ* 'empty'); *raslaběj+* and *oslaběj* 'weaken, become paralyzed' (*slabъ* 'weak'); *vъzběsьněj+* 'become mad, delirious' (*běsъ* 'demon', *běsьnъ* 'possessed, mad'). Some are stative, e.g. *gověj+* 'be respectful, pious'; *goněj+* 'suffice'. *Pitěj+* 'feed' is transitive (and is replaced in innovative OCS by *pit-aj+*); *pitomъ* 'fatted' implies that this was once a C-verb (§8.13).

44.42 The prefixes *o-* and *u-* are particularly common to make perfectives correlated with ě-stems and ěj-stems denoting change; they also serve with i-verbs to specify causation: e.g. *umrьtvi+* 'kill, put to death; mortify'; *opusti+* 'devastate, make empty'; *oslabi+* 'make weak, paralyze'. Occasionally an i-verb may be used with *sę* as an "anticausative"; thus *omrьzěj+* 'be abhorrent' is semantically almost identical with *omrazi+ sę* 'make self abhorrent, become abhorrent'.

45.1 IE had several formations using *n* (**neu, *nou, *nu, *nū*) and generally signifying the beginning or inception of action.

45.11 The **n* could be inserted (infixed) before the final consonant of a root; Slavic provides only four examples, *sęd-ǫtъ* 'sit down' (§16.61), *lęgǫtъ* 'lie down' (§16.62), *-ręštǫtъ* 'encounter' (§16.7), and *bǫdǫtъ* 'will be' (§16.1). On the premise that infixation goes with zero-grade, we posit PBS shapes **sind* (~ **sed,* though the non-present stem in Slavic has lengthened-grade **sēd*), **ling* (~ **leg*), **rint-j* (~ ?**rēt*; the etymology is uncertain), and **bund* (~ **beud* < **bheudh* 'be, grow').

45.12 OCS has partly regularized the distribution by placing *n* in the present system, *nǫ* in infinitive and past forms, and *now* in the past passive

---

[69] In South and West Slavic the *j* of most forms has disappeared as *-aje-* contracted to *-ā-*. These complex developments cannot be discussed here.

participle (§15.7). The nasal vowel in *nǫ* is a relatively recent development, see §21.8143. The distribution of *nǫ* in infinitive and preterite forms varied in LCoS dialects (§15.76).[70]

45.2 OCS *stanetъ* 'will stand, take a stance; come to a halt' goes with non-nasal perfective forms *stati, stalъ,* aor *sta* in contrast to imperfective **stajetъ* 'continues to stand, be' (with inf. **stajati*).[71]

	root	stative		iterative		causative
lie	**leg*	leg-ě i	lęg-e	lěg-a lěže-	lěganьje	lož-i
sit	**sed*	sěd-ě i	sęd-e	sěd-aj-e-	-sědanьje	sad-i
stand	**stā*	stoj-ě i	stan-e	*staj-a -e		staw-i

45.21 An archaism preserved only in Rusian mss is the anomalous **krьnjetъ kriti* 'to buy'; it apparently had a j-present (and imv. крьни, крьните), but otherwise followed the pattern of *bьjǫtъ,* §44.35. It continued in active use in northern Rus', but two forms (past pass part оукрикнаго 'bought [Gsn]'; verbal substantive по критии 'after the purchase, ransom') in 12th-c. copies of originally OCS texts imply it was known in Bulgaria in the 10th c. The Sa cognate *krīṇáti* 'buys' has a nasal infix; the IE root is *k^wreih$_2$-* (Gk πρίαμαι, OIr *cren[a]im* 'I buy').

45.3 The nǫ-verbs with vowels before the suffix represent old diphthongs:

**weiH-* turn, twist' > *wi-nǫ, *dheuH-* 'rise as vapor, smoke', PBS o-grade **dou- > du-nǫ-*; **ǵhē(-i-)-* 'gape' (§44.34 above) > *ẓi-nǫ*;

IE ? *(s)keu* > ECoS **kū(w)* 'beckon' (cf. *nakynǫ, pokywaj* 'nod, wag [head]';

ECoS **māj-* 'gesture' (cf. Li *móju* 'beckon' < IE **mei-* 'go, change'; La *meāre* 'go, pass' [E *permeate*]); *měnǫ/męnǫ* (cf. *mьn-ě+* 'think'; see §29.813;

**pol-n-* > SSl *planǫ-,* cf. *pol-ě+* (o-grade) 'burn', *pal-i+* (ō-grade) seems to be connected with **pel-* 'dust'; *pli-nǫ* 'spit' (cf.*pljьva-* §15.52) is phonetically difficult (cf. Li *spiáuju,* IE **spyeu-*); *rinǫ* 'run' < **rei-* 'flow, run' **rei-wo-* > La *rīvus* 'stream' (> E *rivulet*) ~ *rěj-* 'push'; **sou-sovaat* < **sowajetъ* 'surges [boils over]' Li *šaúju* 'shoot; put, place [bread

[70] Russian retains a vowel alternation but no nasality in сесть сядут 'sit down' and лечь лягут 'lie down'; SC has re-formed the stems with a nasal suffix in the present, *sjesti* 3p *sjednū* and *leći legū*.

[71] Attested OCS "stajati" is an error for the noun *staja* 'stable', but the forms are assured by post-OCS data.

into oven]' (< IE *ḱou* ?). Zero-grade roots are common with *nǫ* but by no means exclusive: **sup-* 'sleep'< *swep* (like *sъp-a+*); **wyk-* < ECoS **ūk-* 'become accustomed, learn' is a Slavic "lengthened reduced grade" replacing **uk-* (cf. IE **euk-* 'become accustomed').

46 The imperative markers *ě* and *i* (§7.1) must go back to an ECoS diphthong, **ai*. Its origins seem to lie in IE optative forms; a detailed history of analogies and restructuring must be speculative. The singular *i* is particularly difficult to explain.[72] The irregular singular forms *daždь ěždь věždь* and *viždь* (§7.2) manifestly reflect **-d-ji* (affirmed by KF *-dazь,* with the Czech reflexes of **dj*): these forms remain enigmatic.

47 The imperfect tense is obscure because the philological evidence is contradictory and the forms and paradigms are remote from imperfects in other languages. The LCoS forms are surely relatively new, and they are already evolving into diverse local forms. It seems plausible that ECoS imperfects were a combination of verbal stem (usually infinitive/aorist) plus an auxiliary based on the root 'to be'—very probably a periphrastic construction by origin. Descriptively, the distinctive suffix has two vowels, *-ěa-*: historically, the segmentation may have been something else. What is apparent is that the formant *x* is followed by the desinences of the root aorist.[73]

	1s	2 sg	3 sg	1 du	2 du	3 du	1 pl	2 pl	3 pl
ECoS	ā-š-u	ā-š-es	ā-š-et	ā-š-awē	ā-š-etā	ā-š-ete	ā-x-anu	ā-š-ete	ā-š-ant
OCS	axъ	aše	aše	axowě	ašeta	ašete	axomъ	ašete	axǫ

48.1 The aorist is relatively faithful to the IE heritage. Except for first person singular *-ъ*, the desinences of the root aorist consist of the thematic vowel $*^{o}/_{e}$ (whereby **e* appears before obstruent, **o* otherwise) plus the past person-number desinences (see §5.9, 10.601).

48.2 The newer paradigms are marked by the IE *s,* with special innovations. The person-number suffixes are preceded by *-e-* before a terminal consonant (or, at a later stage, zero) or *-nt-*; the 3p pl desinence is therefore *-s-ent*. The original **s* remained dental after non-velar consonants, the root-final consonant was deleted, with concomitant length in the root if

---

72 Development of **-ois#* to OCS *-i* is posited also for the twofold Np masc desinence, see §39.62.

73 The imperfects in modern SC, Mac, and Bg (in the south) and Upper Sorbian (in the northwest) vary greatly by region. The imperfect was lost in Czech during the 1400s, and in Rus' probably after about 1250.

possible (§10.6022).[74] After velars, *s* became *š* before front vowel, *x* before back vowel. In both types, the second and third persons singular lack the preterite marker. During the early historical period, the rules change and the x-desinences no longer cause lengthening and truncation of the root, but insert *o* after the root.

48.3 The original s-desinences had shifted to the x-type in i-verbs, and in ECoS surely had spread to all verbs with an overt classifier.

	1 sg	2 sg	3 sg	3 du	1 pl	2 pl	3 pl
IE	-om	-es	-et	-ete	-omos	-ete	-ont
root-aor	-u	-es	-et	-ete	-amu	-ete	-ant
ECoS	pād+u	pād+es	pād+et	pād+ete	pād+amu	pād+ete	pād+ant
OCS	padъ	pade	pade	padete	padomъ	padete	padǫ
s-aor	-su	-es	-et	-ste	-samu	-ste	-s**ent**
ECoS	wēd+su	wed-es	wed-et	wēd-ste	wēd-samu	wēd-ste	wēd-sent
OCS	wěsъ	wede	wede	wěste	wěsomъ	wěste	wěsę
x-aor	-xu	-es	-et	-ste	-xamu	-ste	-š**ent**
ECoS	rēk+xu	rek-es	rek-et	rěk-ste	rēk-xamu	rēk-ste	rēk-sent
OCS	rěxъ	reče	reče	rěste	rěsomъ	rěste	rěšę
ox-aor	rek-xu	rek-s	rek-t	rek-xte	rek-xamu	rek-xte	rek-xent
OCS	rekoxъ	reče	reče	rekoste	rekoxomъ	rekoste	rekošę
	nos-i-xъ	nos-i	nos-i	nos-i-ste	nos-i-xomъ	nos-i-ste	nos-i-šę

49 The infinitive and supine are believed to be frozen case-forms of ancient verbal substantives. The *-ti* of the infinitive probably represents the dative of a **-ti-* derivative, **tēi* or **tei,* while the *-tъ* of the supine is from an accusative of a u-stem **-tum.*

50.1 In IE, apophonic alternations were widely used within the inflection of individual verbs (e.g. the present tense of 'to be', §43.171, above). The LCoS list (probably not much shorter than the MCoS list) is already restricted to something under 40 verbs: the 4 with nasal infix (§45.11) presents, and the little groups with varying distribution of normal-grade in some forms and reduced grade in others. The roots involved are chiefly those with former diphthongs: **ei ~ *i, *eu ~ *u, *er ~ *r̥, *el ~ *l̥, *em ~ *m̥, *en ~ *n̥,* whereby the syllabic sonorants added a short **i* (> **ir, *il, *im, *in*). In theory, a sonorant should not be syllabic between consonant and vowel (*trt* > *tr̥t* but *tra* remains); in fact, the presence of hypothetical reduced-grade roots before vowel implies that the distribution of root-shapes is not original. The infinitive *trьti* < **tьrti* < **tr̥tēi* fulfils expecta-

[74] The long vowel probably reflects an inherited apophonic characteristic, rather than a new compensatory lengthening connected with the loss of the consonant.

tions, although in OCS terms the verb is exceptional (§16.522); infinitives like *bьrati* and *stьlati* imply a complex history.

The tables provide samples of the alternating stems; for details see §15.643-645, §15.86, §15.871-.875, §16.511-.522, §16.91.

inf/aor	*werz*	*keit*	*telk*	*werg*	*straig*	*-soup*	*stil-ā*	*kirp-ā*
pres	*wirz*	*kit*	*tilk*	*wirg*	*streig*	*-sup*	*stelj*	*kerp*
OCS	врѣсти	чисти	тлѣшти	врѣшти	стрѣшти	-*соути	стьлати	чрьпати
	врьꙃѫтъ	чьтѫтъ	тлькѫтъ	врьгѫтъ	стригѫтъ	*-съпѫтъ	стел҄ѭтъ	чрѣпл҄ѭтъ
	open	count	knock	throw	cut hair	strew	spread	dip
inf	*welk*	*berg*	*mer*	*im-ā*	*zid-ā*	*pis-ā*	*slip-ā*	
pres	*wilk*	*birg*	*mir*	*emj*	*zeidj*	*peisj*	*sloipj*	
OCS	влѣшти	брѣшти	мрѣти	имати	ꙃьдати	пьсати	сльпати	
	влькѫтъ	брьгѫтъ	мьрѫтъ	емл҄ѭтъ	зиждѫтъ	пишѫтъ	слѣпл҄ѭтъ	
	drag	care for	die	take	build	write	spurt	
inf	*tirg-ā*	*bir-ā*	*sir-ā*	*strug-ā*	*gid-ā*	*zuw-ā*	*gun-ā*	*gin*
pres	*tergj*	*ber*	*ser*	*strougj*	*geid*	*zow*	*gen*	*ginj*
OCS	тьрѕати	бьрати	*сьрати	стръгати	жьдати	ꙃъвати	гънати	жѧти
	трѣжѫтъ	берѫтъ	*серѫтъ	строужѫтъ	жидѫтъ	ꙃовѫтъ	женѫтъ	жьн҄ѭтъ
	tear off	gather	defecate	scrape	await	call	chase	harvest

50.2 The verb **sьrati *serǫtъ* 'shit' is easily reconstructable from modern dialects; it belongs with *bьra-ti* in §15.644. **Jebati* or **jeti *jebǫtъ* 'fuck' (from IE **yebh-;* cf. Sa *yábhati* 'fucks') has alternate forms that go either in §15.642 (with *sъs-a-ti*) or §15.824.

50.3 The vowel-change in the imperative of *rek-* 'say', *pek-* 'cook', *tek-* 'run', *žeg-* 'burn' (§7.111) is unexplained. The root **geg* (OCS *žeg/žig* §15.875) is unique; it seems to represent a modification of **deg* < **dheg*^{w}*h* cf. Li *degù dègti* 'burn'; Sa *dahati* 'burns'). The root *tek* comes from IE *tek*^{w} 'run, flow' (cf. Li *tekù* 'I run'; Sa *tákti* 'hastens'), *rek* has no clear cognates, and *pek* (the meaning 'cook' is by chance not attested in OCS) goes back to IE **pek*^{w} (cf. Sa *pácati,* Av *pačaiti* 'cooks, bakes'; Li, with metathesis, *kepù* 'I bake'; Latin *coquō* [< **k*^{w}*ek*^{w}*ō*] 'I cook').

On Slavic Accent

51 The Late Common Slavic accentual system must be hypothesized on the basis of fairly modern evidence. Written texts (including modern standard languages) ordinarily fail to note vowel length, pitch, or stress, but a few medieval East and South Slavic manuscripts do have systems of diacritic symbols that indicate prosodic features accurately. This material, together with detailed information from modern dialects, can be compared to data from modern Baltic dialects and from ancient IE languages to reconstruct IE, Baltic, and Slavic systems. The data is enormously complex and scholars disagree on just what constitutes evidence and how questions are to be formulated. Here I can merely sketch some fundamental points.[75]

52 *Accent* is an underlying property of morphemes; *stress* is a phonetic manifestation. Every morpheme is either accented or unaccented.

Root morphemes belong to one of three classes: **A**. accented (on any syllable); **B**. post-accenting (i.e. accent falls on following syllable); **C**. unaccented. Late Common Slavic vowels could be underlyingly long or short; the exact distribution seems to have varied regionally, and even greater diversity was created after the jer-shift. If more than one accented syllable occurs on an underlying word, stress is assigned to the first (leftmost). If there is no accented syllable, stress is assigned to the first syllable.[76]

A (accent fixed on stem)		B (accent follows stem)		C (stem unaccented)	
p'org-ъ	por'og	korlj'-ъ	kor'ol'	gord-ъ	g'orod
p'org-a	por'oga	korlj'-a	korol''a	gord-a	g'oroda
w'orn-ěx'ъ	wor'oněx	korlj'-ix'ъ	korol''ix	gord-ěx'ъ	gorod'ěx
k'orw-a	kor'ova	sux'-j-'a	s'uša	golw-'a	golov'a
k'orw-ǫ	kor'ovu	sux'-j-ǫ	s'ušu	golw-ǫ	g'olovu
l'ěz-ǫ	l'ězu	nos'-i-ǫ	noš'u	nes-ǫ	n'esu
lěz-e-t'ь	l'ězet'	nos'-i-i-t'ь	n'osit'	nes-e-t'ь	nes'et'
l'ěz-e-t'e	l'ězete	nos'-i-i-t'e	n'osite	nes-e-t'e	neset'e

The table illustrates salient points of principle on the basis of hypothetical underlying LCoS forms and approximations of early East Slavic words. The symbol (') stands before accented vowels.

In A, the masculine noun 'threshold' (Nsm, Gs, Lp), the feminine 'cow' (Ns, As; for pleophony see §26.51), and present tense forms of 'to clamber' (1s, 3s, 2p) illustrate that the stem-accent always generates phonetic stem-stress. The desinence of Lp was later replaced by the *-ax* of feminine stems.

In B, the masculine noun 'king' shows that in the same case-forms the stress is always post-stem (except that in Ns there is no post-stem vowel and the stress automatically must fall on the final stem-vowel. The femi-

---

[75] The analyses provided in traditional accounts (e.g. Meillet-Vaillant, 1934, Vaillant GC 1. 1950) have been fundamentally revised on the basis of the work of Christian Stang (1957), Paul Garde (1976), Vladimir Dybo (1981) and others. See particularly Morris Halle, in *Language* 1997: 275-313.

[76] *Tone* is not a distinctive feature in Slavic; it is phonetically important in SC and Slovenian, but not in underlying forms.

nine noun 'drought' shows a fixed stem-stress that is interpreted as a post-stem accent that has been retracted. The present of the verb *nosi+* 'carry' indicates that the post-accentuation yields stress on the desinence in 1s, but retraction back to the root in the other forms.

In C, the nouns 'city' and 'head' have stress on the first syllable of the stem unless the desinence is accented. If preceded by a preposition or other clitic that falls within the definition of phonological word (which varies by dialect), the initial stress moves as far left as possible. Theoretically, *z'a–gorod, n'e_za_gorod, 'i_ne_za_gorod*; *'i_ne_na_golovu*. Similarly, the 1s pres with prefix would be *'prinesu, n'e_prinesu, 'i_ne_prinesu*.

53 These fundamentals are still valid—with numerous provisos—in modern SC and East Slavic.[77] Slovene (with its many dialects) adds many complexities, among them a strong contrast between long and short vowels that results in phonetic changes or disappearance of short unstressed vowels. West Slavic (except for the Kashubian dialects) eliminated the lexical accents underlying types A and B, and Czech and Slovak have automatic initial stress, accompanied by lexical long vs. short vowels and morphophonemic alternations involving length. Polish and East Slovak now have automatic stress on the penult. Standard Macedonian has antepenultimate stress, although some dialects have fixed stress on the penult and others have more complex placement involving the final three syllables of words. Bulgarian has several systems that are modifications of the old LCoS situation.

On the Slavic lexicon.

54 The Late Common Slavic lexicon includes a solid framework of Indo-European words. Some are derived by specifically Slavic processes, but many—as we have seen—deviate in major or minor ways. There is no evidence of early borrowing from non-Indo-European groups, indeed nothing solidly datable before about 600, precisely when Byzantine and European observers are remarking on a Slavic presence.

55.1 Slavic and Baltic have particularly intertwined vocabularies. Intimate words like *head* and *hand* (**golwa,* OCS *glava* ~ Li *galvà*; *rǫka* ~ Li *rankà*) are unmatched elsewhere.[78] Germanic is lexically close to both

[77] Halle argues cogently that these fundamentals were valid for IE and for Lithuanian. Note that *tone* is a distinctive characteristic of underlying vowels in Baltic.

[78] Neither word has a clear outside etymology, but Li has a verb *riñkti* 'to collect' that furnishes motivation for **ronkā*. *OCS *rǫčka* 'jar, fig. womb [of the Theotokos]' implies **rǫk-j-ъk-a,* and the correlated verb.

Baltic and Slavic, although the phonology is often very different. Yet Slavic maintains its distinct individuality.

55.2 The OCS word for *man, human* is *člověkъ,* with an ESl variant, *čelověkъ.* A front vowel is needed to account for *č,* so unattested **čьl-* is proposed as a putative allegro-form; in any case, all modern forms except for ESl are explicable from *člověkъ.* Etymologists tend to see *čel-* as meaning 'kin' (cf. *čeljadь* f. coll. 'servants; members of household'). Sl *věkъ* 'age, eternity' does not fit. Perhaps a **woiko-* cognate to Li *vaĩkas* 'boy' is involved. *Man, husband* is *mǫžь,* presumably **man* (cf. Gmc **manw-,* E *man*) with a root-extension **-gj-* (or *-zj-*?).

55.3 The oldest form of the Slavic ethnonym is Np Словѣни (note desinential *-i,* not *-e*!),[79] almost certainly involving a soft twofold stem **slověnj-*. The root is surely *slow-* 'be known, renowned' < IE **k̑leu-* 'hear'; the suffix is possibly adjectival and perhaps ECoS **slow-ēn-as* 'characterized by, participating in fame' was used as a name. **Slověnji* would then be 'the band (soldiers, clan) led by Slověn'.

56.1 One requirement for a successful etymology is that differences in meaning be plausibly explicable. We know that meanings shift, but at the same time phonetic changes may cause formerly distinct words to fall together (e.g. E *rite, right, write, wright*). There is no question that OCS *ponosъ* 'reproach' (related to *ponosi+* 'revile') is historically "the same" as both R *ponós* 'diarrhea' (cf. *ponosit'* 'to revile') and SC *pónos* 'pride'. OCS *krasьnъ* means 'fine, beautiful' and *zivotъ* is 'life'. Mod. Cz *krásný život* means 'beautiful life'; R *krásnyj živót* is 'red belly' (in ordinary language). R dictionaries may distinguish *život¹* 'stomach' from *život²* '(archaic) life', but etymologists class them as descendants of a single older word. This is often difficult in seeking prehistoric etymologies.

56.2 Ukrainian шанець Gs шанця 'trench', P *szaniec, -ńca* 'trench (obsolete)', Slk *šiance* pl 'moat', SC *šanac, -nca,* Np *šanci* or *šančevi* 'trench (military), ditch', Mac *šanec,* and SC *ušančiti* P, *ušančivati ušančujem* I 'entrench', Mac *se ušanči* 'entrench self' would seem to indicate LCoS **šanьcь* and **u-šanьči+*. We have the evidence for another explanation: this is German *Schanze* and *verschanzen,* adapted long ago to the Slavic of the Hapsburg lands (and extended into Macedonia). The vowel-zero alternation and the automatic replacement of *c* by *č* when followed by a front-vowel morpheme are part of the rules of the individual dialects—they are "Pan-Slavic". Without the background information, this true etymology would be impossible to reach.

---

79 This philological fact needs to be taken into account in any etymological proposal. Forms like Словѣне, Словѧне do not appear until the mid-1300s. See Lunt, *IJSLP* 39–40 (1996): 281-2.

57 The *satem/kentum* distinction (see note to §27.2) is far from absolute. The *goose* must have been known to all Slavs as **gǫsь,* with a kentum-reflex for IE **ǵhans-*, like OHG *gans,* rather than a satem-reflex, like Li *žą̃sìs*. Perhaps the Slavs obtained a special, somehow preferable, variety from Gmc groups, along with the slightly changed name. The IE verb **melǵ-* that means 'rub, massage, caress' in Indo-Aryan was specialized in the west to mean 'to milk', ἀμέλγω, La *mulgēre,* OE *melcan,* Li *mélžti mélžiu*. *OCS **mlьzǫtъ* (with SC *mȕsti múzē*, Sln *molsti molze*) shows ECoS **mьlz-ti, *mьlz-ǫtъ,* while **melz-iw-o* 'colostrum, foremilk' is illustrated by Slk *mledzivo* (with secondary *dz*) and Uk dial *molozyvo*. Surely then ECoS had **melz/*milz*, with the satem *z*.[80] The universal word for *milk,* however, is ECoS **melko* (OCS *mlěko,* R *molokó*). The voiceless *k* can only come from a Gmc form. Why this basic item bears an imported name has not been explained.

58 It is tempting to speculate about differences that existed in the "homeland" as opposed to innovations that arose after the migration to new lands. It appears, however, that the Slavs who settled south and west of the Danube somehow kept in touch with their cousins to the north. Documentation is sparse and late for a large part of the everyday vocabulary. In theory, similarity of words in apparently related languages is to be explained by (1) genetic relationship, (2) borrowing, or (3) coincidence. In practice, borrowing from dialect to dialect obscures the difference between 1 and 2, and words can pass back and forth among various dialects. Items of commerce and warfare are particularly likely to employ this kind of word.

59 OCS *korabljь* 'boat' looks very like Gk καράβιον (with *o* for unstressed Gk *a,* and *a* for stressed *á*), but the stop *b* (rather than the spirant *v*) is improbable for a direct borrowing. Surely the Slavs learned this stem from an intermediary language.

60 The productive suffix *-arjь* (§24.522) is by origin La *-arius*, but surely came to Slavic from various sources. Thus Go *mōta* 'toll' and *mōtareis* 'taxgatherer' become OCS *myto* and **mytarjь* (the long *ō* was perceived as ECoS **ū*). Another adaptation takes Balkan Romance

---

[80] The verb is not recorded for North Slavic or, as far as I can discover, for Bulgaria; the sense is expressed by **doj-i+* 'nurse; suckle' < **dheh(i)* 'suck' (cf. Sa *dhāya-* 'nourishing'; La *fēmina* 'woman [<she who suckles]'. Compare also **doi-ten* > *dětę* 'child', **doi-w-ā* > *děva* 'girl, virgin'.

**pastōre* 'shepherd' to OCS **pastyrjь*, and then (by substituting a possibly affective suffix) to *pastuxъ* (§24.26).[81]

61 Gothic is recorded Germanic of a Balkan region (or more accurately of one individual writer, Wulfila, who died c383), so scholars try to derive Gmc words in Slavic from this language. Yet Slavs were interacting with Frankish military units and Saxons and Bavarians (including Catholic missionaries) with ever-increasing frequency after c750.[82] German peddlers and water-borne traders may well have introduced some words very early, and continued contacts may have resulted in slight modifications in the phonetics of words already borrowed. Latin-based terminology, with some Romance and Germanic (esp. Old Bavarian) details, was known to the Slavs who initiated the Cyrillo-Methodian mission that established OCS.

62 The stems of borrowed words are subject to KI and BdC for the early period, and borrowings from Germanic that have suffixal *-ing-* are assimilated to Sl *-ęʒ-ь* format. There is a short period when *velar + front vowel* in a stem conforms to KAI (§31), e.g. *ocьtъ* 'vinegar', from a Romance form based on La *acētum*. The wave of Greek stems taken into OCS illustrates a new set of rules: velar stops before front vowels remain in spelling, but very probably were pronounced as palatals (as were the Gk models, see §2.4121).

63.1 The word *church* and its Slavic equivalents are agreed to have something to do with the Gk adjective κυριακός 'the Lord's [temple; flock, people]', but just how the items are related is controversial. The stem [ḱiriak-] or [ḱirjak-] would not ordinarily lose the *a*. The shape actually spelled in Rusian mss, *cьrky* (G *cьrkъve, -vi*) fits some forms: OCS *crьky,* R *cerkov',* P *cerkiew,* SC, Mac *crkva*.[83] One sets up **kirkū* and its putative ancestor OBavarian **kirkō*. Yet the Kiev Folia have Gs *cirъkъve* and an adjective *cirkъnaě*, (generally interpreted as misspelled **cirъkъvьnaě*).[84]

---

[81] The Slavic and Latin roots *pas-* represent IE **pah₂s* 'protect, feed'.

[82] German *Grenze* 'frontier, boundary' is from Sl *granica*. Though it surely was borrowed during Carolingian times, before 800, it is first recorded in the 13th century in the Polish-German region.

[83] Regularization of feminines in *-y, -ъv-e* etc is easily achieved by combining the *v* with normal feminine a-stem desinences: roughly *-k-y -k-ov-ь* > *-kv-a -kv-u*. Bulgarian has dialectal *crъkva* (now being advocated as standard), but more usual is *čerkva,* apparently an older hypercorrect artificial form.

[84] Mod. Cz *církev* means 'body of believers, ecclesia'; the usual word for a Catholic church is *kostel,* < La *castellum* 'small fort, castle'.

The data of Old Czech, Slovene, and Croatian are complex; suffice it to say that scholars have posited "Arian Go **kirikō*", **cьrьky, *cirъky,* and other variants.

Surely competing missionaries spoke several languages and dialects and freely introduced new terms into the speech of their Slavic clients. It is highly possible that different (or at least variant) names were used for the houses of worship of different missions, as a village in Scotland might have both a *church* (Catholic) and a *kirk* (Protestant).

63.2 The near-universal Slavic *kupi+* and *kupova+* 'to buy' owe their root **kaup-* to Gmc sources, who learned it from La *caupō* 'shopkeeper'.[85] A rival verb, the anomalous *kriti *krьnjǫ* 'buy' is implied for 10th-c Bulgaria as well as early Rus' (§45.21), but there is no way to reconstruct possible dialect distribution. The *OCS noun **userędzь* 'earring' reflects **ausering-,* from a form similar to Go **ausihriggs,* but no evidence is available about the time and place of borrowing.[86] The variety of terms for 'profit, interest' offers a hint of dialect differences: the usual *lixva* is derived from a hypothetical Go deverbal noun from *leihvan* 'loan, lend'; *vъzvitь* and *vъzvitьje* belong presumably to *vъz+vьj-* 'go after, obtain' (n. 89, page 256); *namъ* is exclusive to early Novgorod, and is unexplained. Repayment is expressed (only in Su) by *žlěd-,* based on Gmc **geld-* (cf. Go *fragildan, usgildan* 'recompense'). Another loan where a velar was affected by KI is OCS **šlěmъ* 'helmet' (ESl *šelomъ*) < **xelmъ* < Gmc **helmaz*. OCS *mečь* m 'sword' requires older **mekj-,* with an alternate shape to account for Old SC *mьčь* (Gs *mča*). Scholars cite Go **mēkeis,* while readily admitting that the phonetic relationships are imprecise. One guess is that both Gmc and Sl inherited the term from a third group. *Sek-yr-a* 'axe' has a lax root vowel (though *sěk-* 'cut' is always tense) and a unique suffix *-yr-*; a synonym is *sěčivo,* with the expected root and a rare suffix. Latin *secūris* has the same meaning and gender. We may surmise that Slavs obtained the implement, with its name, through trade or plunder—from speakers of Romance or intermediaries—and regularized the declension.

63.3 The usual word for 'money, coin' is *pěnędzь* (Gmc *penning* [a silver denarius]). In Mt 22:19, for νόμισμα 'coin', Sav writes **скьлѧѕь** and Mar *sklęzъ* (I normalize **skьlędzь*). In the first, **penn-* yielded *pěn-*

---

[85] The source of La *caupō* is unknown. Sl could have borrowed from Go **kaupjan* or OHG *kouffen*. Note that OE *cēap* 'trade', in contexts implying "good price", shifted meaning: *cheap*.

[86] Contacts with Gmc peddlars may well have introduced some words very early; as Gmc shapes of words change, so might the Sl pronunciation. (A connection with later R серьги is possible, but the direct source appears to be Turkic.)

(§29.813) and *-ing* was equated with *-ęʒ-ь*. The second is Gmc **skilling-* (first coined c550); I interpret the first syllable as [śḱь] with automatic palatalization of *sk* before a front vowel—a dialect form corresponding to the normal *sc/st* spellings (§3.311, n). A puzzling word *cęta* means 'coin, money' and implies **kent-* or **kint-* but the source is elusive.

63.4 The name of the city of Rome, OCS *Rimъ* (Cz *Řím*) is presumably masculine because most Slavic town-names are. *Rōma* would be expected to yield **rym-*: the front vowel is explained from an Alpine Romance **ü*. The ethnonym *židove* 'Jews' (singular *židovinъ*) surely is based on La *judaeus,* from some dialect (not yet identified) with **žüd-,* perceived by Slavs as *žid-*.The fundamental symbol of Christianity, the cross, is called *krьstъ* in OCS, but western Catholics had **križь* (Cr. dial *kríž,* Gs *krīžȁ*; Cz *kříž*). The first is probably from OHG *krist*, while the second goes back to late La *crūce* [krūče], via a hypothetical Alpine dialect with a form **krōž*.

Latin *lactūca* 'lettuce' is known to Slavs as *loškíka* (Macedonian dialect), SC *loćika,* Sln *ločika,* Cz *locika*. It surely is a 7th-8th century borrowing from a word perceived as **loktyka,* and immediately adopted as **lotjyka*. It then developed in accord with local Slavic dialect phonology.

Dalmatian toponyms often begin with *sut-*, reflecting La *sanctus* 'saint' borrowed surely as **sęt-*. St. George occurs as *Sućuraj,* implying **sąt jurьjь* and the general name derived both from late La *Giorgius* [ǵorǵo-] and Gk Γεώργιος [yoryos], with the closed *o* Slavs perceived as *u* (cf. *Solunь* for *Thes**saloni**ki*). The *tj* developed according to local rules.

64.1 There are no titles that clearly indicate social ranking. Two terms are built on the root *wold* 'rule'; *vladyka* (common, with a unique formant *-yk-*) and *vlastelь* (rare, but with a productive formant, cf. §24.521); neither is used as a title. *Starějьšina* m. 'elder' (obviously built on the comparative of *starъ* 'old') translates a series of general names for leader. *Starosta* is only North Slavic; it apparently referred to a minor local dignitary, not necessarily elderly.

64.2 The supreme authority is *gospodь* 'lord, κύριος, δεσπότης, dominus [OHG trohtîn]', widely used to refer to divinity, and amply attested for earthly leaders. The word is a compound, IE **ghos(-ti)-* 'guest' and **poti-* 'master; power', reminiscent of La *hospes* (stem *hospit-*) 'host, guest, stranger' house-master'; Li *viẽšpats* 'lord', where *vieš-* is from IE **weiḱ-* 'house, home, community, clan', related to Gk ϝοῖκος 'house'). The voiced *d* (for voiceless *t*) is difficult.[87] A frequent substitute is

[87] Some scholars see IE **poti-* in the word spelled *potьpěžě* (Ls, Cloz), *podъpěg-,*

gospodinъ, with a singulative suffix, often in the phrase *gospodinъ domu* (*xraminy, xrama*) 'master of the house' (which may render οἰκοδεσπότης).[88] *OCS further attests *gosudarь*, and a collective, *gospoda*. *Gospoda* may also mean 'inn' (as in Sav; cf Cz *hospoda*, P *gospoda*). Two feminine derivatives, *gospožda* (< *-*pod-j-a*, possibly possessive?), and *gospodyni* occur.

64.21 In SW dialects, *gospoda* could be shortened to *gozda*, and Magyar borrowed it as *gazda*. SC took this form back with the meaning 'master, boss, chief, owner, landlord' and created a whole family of derivatives (e.g. *gazdarica* 'female boss, etc.; *gazdovati* 'to manage'). In Slovak, *gazda* is a farmer, *gazdiná* 'housewife', *gazdovstvo* 'agriculture'

64.3 Czech *pán* 'lord' and *paní* 'lady', are often linked by scholars with the *župan*ъ, the apparent ruler of a *župa*, known from Greek, Latin and Slavic texts as an administrative regional unit. In OCS, *župani* appear in one translated text as unspecified highly-placed functionaries. The feminine *paní* seems to be connected with πότνια 'mistress of the household, wife' (Sa *patnī*), although the long vowel in the initial syllable of hypothetical **pātinyā-* needs explanation. Masculine *pán* is seen by some as derived from this feminine. Others propose **geupānas* > *županъ* and zero-grade **gupānas* > **gъpanъ* > **hpán* > *pán*. A relationship to OHG **gawi*, G *Gau* 'region' has also been proposed. Another early medieval ruler, chiefly in Croatia, was *ban* (**banъ*?), perhaps from Avar **bojan* 'rich man', perhaps from Iranian *ban* 'keeper, guard'.

64.4 Another important personage is entitled *vojevoda* (m), made of *voj-* (*voji* mp 'soldiers, army', *vojьna* 'war') and *vod-* (*vodi+* 'to lead'), a compound that corresponds to OHG *herizogo* (*heri* 'army'; *ziohan* 'lead') and Gk στρατηγός (*stratos* 'army'; *agō* 'lead').[89] To judge from the range of terms it translates, OCS *vojevoda* designates not only a general, but a leader or chief in other spheres. As new societies emerge, the title acquires specific local meaning.

---

podъběg- '[wife] who has been put aside', conjecturing "wife who fled"; what is clear is only that the word was unfamiliar to the scribes.

88 *Domъ* 'house, household; members of household' reflects an IE u-stem (like La *domus*), and has survived into most modern dialects. MCoS **xormъ* and **xormina* are of unknown origin; puzzlingly, they share the same range of meaning in OCS. The modern sense 'temple' is a later specialization, still used in most of Slavdom.

89 The root *voj-* belongs to IE *wei-* 'to go after something', cf. Li *vejù výti* 'chase', Av *vayeiti* 'chases'; La *venāri* 'hunt'. The root *wed/wod* is from IE **wedh* 'lead, lead home; marry' (cf. Li vedù 'I lead'; Av *vādayeiti* 'leads'.

64.51 OCS gospel texts reproduced the Gk hierarchy, **kesarъ* 'emperor, Caesar, καῖσαρ' ~ *cěsarjь* 'king, rex, βασιλεύς' ~ *kъnęзь* 'prince, princeps, ἄρχων'. The first is strictly a book word, doubtless reproducing the Greek pronunciation [ḱésar], with a palatal *ḱ*. In the few passages where it is appropriate, it is modified within OCS to make it closer to and finally identical with *cěsarjь*.

64.52 *Kъnęзь* is clearly a general-purpose title denoting 'chief, head man'; it must reflect **kuning-*, corresponding nicely to Gmc **kuningaz,* OHG *kuning*. It must have been borrowed early in independent Slavic linguistic development, while the progressive palatalization (BdC, §29.2) was still operative, possibly in the 4th century.

64.53 OCS *cěsarjь* implies earlier **kaisārjas,* which predicts the shapes that in fact exist among Roman Catholic Slavs, viz. northern Croats and Slovenes (kajkavski, Sln *césar,* Gs *cesárja*), Czechs (Cz *císař*), Slovaks (*cisár*), and Poles (*cesarz*). The OCS noun is the same as the usual adjective *cěsarjь* 'belonging to the king'; an unambiguous possessive *cěsarjevъ* is also attested. The source seems to be a Latin adjectival form, *caesareus* [kaisārjus], or a later shape **kēsārju,* probably via Germanic. In OCS, the stem is usually abbreviated, **ц'рь, цр҃ь**, but it always has ѣ when written in full; this form surely was "correct" for OCS. The early Rus' scribes occasionally wrote **цьсарь**, providing the form that underlies царь.[90] This surely represents a second source, with a short vowel in the first syllable; the suggestions that *ě* was "shortened" or "reduced" to ь in an unstressed syllable, or else in an allegro form of a frequently-used title or term or address, are inapplicable.

64.54 The Frankish leaders facing 9th-century Slavs were "Karl's men" in the sense that they were deputies of Charlemagne (Karl the Great, 742?–814) and his descendants. The name **Karlъ* surely formed a possessive adjective **karljь* to refer to these petty rulers. This, I maintain, is the word that was adopted to refer to Slavic kings in Catholic regions: SC *krȃlj* Gs *králja,* Cz *král krále,* P *król króla,* R, Uk корóлъ королѝ. The possessive is **koroljevъ.*

---

90 Uk царѝця has hard *c* at the beginning, from *cs* < *cьs* but palatalized *c'* in the final syllable.

VERB INDEX

Roman alphabetical sequence: *a b c* **č** *d e* **ě** *f g h i* **ь** *j k l m n o p r s* **š** *t u* **ъ** *v x z* **ž** *ʒ ǯ*

SUBJECT INDEX

Bold-face numbers refer to paragraphs